Integrating Principles
of
Social Psychology

Integrating Principles of Social Psychology

by

JOSEPH B. COOPER

Professor of Psychology
San Jose State College

and

JAMES L. MCGAUGH

Associate Professor of Psychology
University of Oregon

SCHENKMAN PUBLISHING COMPANY, INC.
Cambridge, Massachusetts

TABLE OF CONTENTS

PREFACE

There are a number of problems in the field of social psychology that deserve re-examination in the light of contemporary facts and theories. The purpose of this book is so to re-examine certain of these problems in terms of what we choose to call *Integrating Principles*. These principles are imbedded in three perspectives which have shaped our approach to this task.

First, we are convinced that the psychological study of social behavior and experience must focus on the nature of the social individual. Second, we hold that the available facts of social behavior and experience provide strong support for a cognitive-theoretical position. Third, we believe that man's social behavior must be viewed as a constant process of adaptation; and, as a consequence, an adequate evaluation of man's place in nature requires a healthy respect for comparative psychological and ethological information.

In essence, then, we are hopeful that this book will acquaint students with some of the ways in which social psychologists have approached the problem of understanding the individual's social behavior. We emphasize the word *some:* we have reviewed the problems we believe to be especially relevant to the field. And with the help of our integrating principles, or concepts, we hope that we have suggested ways of making some psychological sense out of social confusion.

To the many students and colleagues who have helped us in thinking about and developing this book we express our thanks. Our special gratitude goes to Helen E. Amato, William N. McBain, James M. Cole, Beckie McGaugh, and Hazel Cooper.

I

Introduction to Social Psychology

Although all animals are at least to some extent social, man can easily be characterized as *the social animal*. The social complexity of insect colonies, of schools of fish, and of troops of apes is most impressive; but it is only at the human level that we encounter capacity for inventive imagination, language, religious belief, esthetics, and for culture itself. Thus, human social behavior incorporates an enormous and unique complexity found nowhere else in the animal kingdom.

SOCIETY AND CULTURE

Society is a loose term for an organization of individuals that lasts longer than the life span of any single member. We can refer to the entire human species as a society. We can also refer to the primitive bushmen of Australia as a society. Of course there are also many examples of societies among the lower animals.

The terms society and culture are not synonymous. Only some societies are cultures. Culture is a human phenomenon which implies the recording and transmission from one generation to the next of learned ways of behaving, believing, valuing, desiring. Culture is not only society at a purely biological level, but society with added processes. A comprehensive view of social man requires two related ways of studying social man. One is to view man in relief—set apart, but always against the thousands of other species which compose the animal kingdom. The other is to view man in his own right and at his own level, without regard to his biological relationship to and dependence upon any other species in the animal kingdom.

MAN AND SOCIETY

More than a century ago August Comte pointed out that man is both the cause and consequence of society (1852). Biologically, individual parents produce other individuals. At the same time, society largely determines the behavioral ways of new individuals. Individuals create society; society largely creates the behavioral pattern of individuals. This is not a paradox. It is a problem of immense proportion and one which invites thoughtful attention.

In a broad sense, an individual is a minute bridge, and society is both sides of many minute bridges. Biologically, but very gradually, these bridges may be modified. Mutations may arise, and the far side of the bridge may become a little different from the near side. This is what has continuously happened in the evolutionary history of every species.

At the human level cultural patterns are also sent across these bridges. Linguistic, script, gestural, evaluative, moral, religious, esthetic, emotionally expressive, appetitive, and other individually learned ways of behaving are transmitted to succeeding generations which, in turn, modify these patterns and transmit them to their progeny.

LEVELS OF ANALYSIS

It is obvious that the various classes of socio-cultural processes—political, religious, esthetic, criminal, familial, and so forth—can be studied at several levels. For example, an analysis of the structure and efficiency of our government at the federal level alone can at best provide only a limited understanding of it. The relation of the federal government to state, county, and city governments, as well as to other national governments, must be studied. A student of the federal government may draw together a great mass of data taken from these different levels and thus, by careful analysis and articulation, make certain political events at the federal level much more intelligible. He may be able to show, for example, that the federal income tax level is determined by certain military activities in eastern Europe and by certain domestic educational requirements. This is analysis at a given level, but it is limited. Even at the local government level, understanding is limited unless other levels are examined. There are pressure groups demanding more schools, parks, and hospitals. There are other pressure groups maneuvering for tax reductions on certain types of property and business operations. There are still other pressure groups working for increases in pay and shorter-working-hour legislation. Thus, a knowledge of these groups and their activities assists in understanding what local government does. And the whole business of the federal income tax structure becomes still more comprehensible.

Another level of analysis considers the total psychological individual. An understanding of any social organization is incomplete without an analysis of the psychological characteristics of the individuals in it. Certainly, the wishes and background of the individual have much to do with the nature of the pressures exerted on the society. These pressures, and society itself, cannot be understood without some psychological understanding of the individuals in the society. Of course, understanding at the individual level alone will not describe or explain the nature of any social organization. Just as the behavior of individuals is in large measure the result of their cultural situation, so the cultural situation is in large measure a function of the individuals who compose it.

There are, of course, levels of analysis "below" the individual psychological level. What and how a person thinks depend in part upon neurological events within his body. These neurological events depend, in turn, upon such complexes as metabolism, enzyme reactions, and so forth, which, in their turn, depend upon molecular and atomic events.

There is really no way in which these levels of analysis can be specifically isolated. Our conventional academic disciplines are cognitive-perceptual systems that make it possible for us to think and speak of one bit of information as isolated from another. We become so accustomed to thinking at perceptually isolated levels, however, that we often forget the real continuity from atomic events in the cells of the human body to international organization. Where we choose to focus our examination depends largely upon preconceived methods of perceptual organization.

In discussing the problem of level of analysis, Solomon Asch makes the point that psychology is to the study of man what physics is to the study of the physical, inanimate universe. He says, "All activities in society—economic, political, artistic—have their center in individuals, in their strivings, needs, and understanding. The individual is the point of intersection of nearly all that is of consequence in the social sphere." (1952, p. 4) We are in agreement with Asch that social psychology is properly the study of the individual in a social context, and that only by studying social *individuals* can we hope to understand social man.

Not all students of the social-psychological nature of man have agreed with this thesis. Some have looked to such social phenomena as family organization, economic institutions, myths, language, historical movements, and legal codes for basic principles to explain the social psychological individual. In early modern psychology probably the best example of this approach—the attempt to understand the individual by analysis at a different level—is found in the "group-mind" doctrine.

The group-mind doctrine proposes that any group of individuals generates a separate psychological entity, a collective consciousness, or supermind, and that the individual's social behavior is a function of this phenomenon. In its broadest conception it was an attempt to identify processes that could be used to explain both individual and social behavior. Many variations on this theme were developed. For example, LeBon wrote that the behavior of individuals in a crowd becomes qualitatively inferior, emotional, more influenced by suggestion, and reduced in rationality (1896). On the other hand, McDougall argued that group-mind-produced behavior is qualitatively superior (1920).

In the early 1920's the group-mind doctrine was seriously attacked. Thereafter most social psychologists rejected it, at least in its initial form. One of its principal foes was Floyd Allport (1924). Allport acknowledged that individuals frequently do things in group situations they would not do in relative isolation, but he insisted that the psychological nature of an individual must be studied in terms of empirically identifiable variables. An unusual act of bravery performed in the presence of a crowd can be understood more accurately as a function of the way the individual perceives the situation—his perceptual estimate of society's expectations, his anticipation of reprisal, and so forth—than as a function of a directing power lying outside the individual. According to Allport, then, the group is composed of individuals; and group behavior can best be understood in terms of the individuals who compose the group.

The Individual

In order to identify the basic unit of social analysis, it is necessary to inspect society from top to bottom. At the top is an international community—the total society of man. At the bottom are the neurophysiological systems that comprise every individual's body. Only when these abstracted levels of organization are related to the total human organism can they be observed in action and understood. Just as international events relate "down" to man, physiological events relate "up" to man.

The most meaningful point on this continuum, then, is the individual. The individual is the point of convergence to which all social events must be ordered. The individual invents, writes poems, composes music, draws up constitutions, loves, and hates. Since the group is composed of interacting individuals, in order to understand group action, some reference must always be made to the individuals who compose the group. To understand the unique nature of the individual in interaction with other individuals is the major task of social psychology.

STUDY OF THE SOCIAL INDIVIDUAL

Social psychology has developed a variety of methods to use in studying the individual as a determiner of social events and as a function of social events. These methods will be described in some detail in Chapter II. The subject matter of social psychology so closely relates to other areas of investigation that its proper designation often seems difficult. The problem concerning the proper subject matter of social psychology will be given specific attention in Chapter IV. However, a very brief preview of these two related problems—method and subject matter—will be helpful at this point.

Methods of Social Psychology

When it comes to making systematic inquiry into the social psychological nature of ourselves we encounter the seeming self-evidence of the very subject matter we propose to study. Thus, on the one hand, relatively few laymen seem convinced that there is really anything to study; and on the other hand, many of those who believe that man's social psychological nature should be studied, fail to be convinced that the scientific method is appropriate for such study. As Solomon Asch has put it, we are so close to our own behavior and experience that we may fail to recognize our own behavior and experience as proper subjects for scientific study (1952).

Social psychology uses the scientific method. This requires speculation, controlled observation, and statistical logic in drawing inferences and conclusions from measured observations. It also involves borrowing ideas, information, and conclusions from other scientific disciplines and from other specialized fields within psychology itself. Several of the social science disciplines make important contributions to social psychology. The most important of these are sociology and anthropology. The special fields within general psychology upon which social psychology is most dependent are comparative, developmental, learning, motivation, and perception. The central core of social psychology, however, is the attempt to achieve an understanding of man's psychological nature within a social context. It is the nexus between analysis at the social organization level and analysis at the individual behavior level.

Subject Matter of Social Psychology

We have already referred to behavior and experience. Behavior is what the person does—walking, talking, eating. Experience is the individual's awareness and appraisal of his walking, talking, eating, plus his approval or disapproval of these behavioral events.

While the individual's overt act is the observable social datum—the behavior by which he is socially judged—for the behaving individual there are concomitant experiential events. From the standpoint of social judgment, logical correspondence between social act and experience is not necessarily exact or even close. How the individual experiences his own behavior, and how he experiences the behavior of others, is in either case often very different from the ways in which the same behavioral events are perceived by others. For example, an individual may have a deep desire to be loved and admired by others; but if the behavior he uses in his attempt to achieve love and admiration is perceived by others as hostile and supercilious, he will fail in his bid. The dynamics of experience is not necessarily at a level of focal consciousness; in fact, it is probably seldom if ever completely available to the individual at a focally conscious level. At the same time, the assumption is that overt, socially significant behavior is a function of the individual's experiential dynamics.

The actual subject matter of social psychology, then, is composed of two psychologically important aspects of the individual. One is directly observable—overt behavior, what the individual *does*. The other is not directly observable, but it determines behavior—psychological dynamics, what the individual *experiences*. The first is referred to as the "phenotypic self," the second as the "genotypic self."

DEFINING SOCIAL PSYCHOLOGY

No two definitions of social psychology have ever been identical, but most current definitions are much alike. The only discernible distinctions are in emphasis—emphasis upon the group or emphasis upon the individual. Some contend that the basic unit of social psychological analysis is the individual *and* the social context. Others hold that the basic unit is the individual *within* the social context.

An example of the former (sociological) approach is represented by Newcomb (1950). His contention is that *interaction* constitutes the subject matter of social psychology. He says, for example, that no "merely psychological" treatment of the individual is adequate to account for the development of attitudes in the individual. Many social psychologists find this a healthy emphasis. The individual is not entirely neglected, but emphasis is placed upon the interacting group, and the inference is that the group itself is an object of psychological study.

The individual (psychological) approach is well expressed by Krech and Crutchfield. They maintain that: "Social psychology . . . is concerned with *every aspect of the individual's behavior in society*. Social psychology may therefore be broadly defined as the science of the behavior of the individual in society." (1948, p. 7) While their emphasis is obviously upon the individual, they take full cognizance of society, and groups within society, as determinants of individual behavior and as determined by the individual's behavior.

Many social psychologists regard preference for one over the other of these two different perspectives as an issue of little importance. The point of view of the authors of this book is compatible with the psychological approach. At the same time, we appreciate the importance of the sociological orientation and acknowledge the indispensible contributions of those behavioral scientists who choose to view the aggregate rather than the individual as the primary object of study.

The preference expressed here arises from many sources. One in particular is worth noting. Kurt Lewin propounded the view that there is a lawfulness that governs individual behavior and experience and that this same lawfulness governs every individual (1935). It is the task of the psychologist to describe this lawfulness. That which is bizarre and unique in behavior is not to be viewed as different in kind. It differs from the normal not in following a different natural "law" but in being the result of the operation of the same lawfulness in a unique situation. Social psychology is the behavioral science that attempts to understand the individual's social behavior and experience in terms of this lawfulness.

ORGANIZATION AND CONTENT OF THIS VOLUME

An examination of books appearing in the field of social psychology during the past few years reveals striking differences in both content and organization. Social psychology today is so broad and so concerned with virtually everything man does that such variation is not surprising. There is no truly adequate way to organize social psychological knowledge and theory, and no conceivable organization would be satisfactory to all or even to a majority of social psychologists. Thus, justification for one organization over another can amount to little more than an opinion that a given organization lends itself to exposition and development of understanding better than another. For instance, one way to deal with social psychological material is through the study of conforming and nonconforming behavior as defined by certain social institutions. This approach lends itself to an examination of such categories as criminal, familial, economic, and sexual behavior as functions of certain social institutions. Another organizational approach is through the study of social institutions themselves in a given cultural setting, or through the comparison of social institutions from culture to culture.

Our preference is to describe what may be called certain integrating or unifying principles which may be used profitably in the attempt to understand any psychologically significant social process. By integrating or unifying principles we refer to such psychological concepts as behavioral adaptation, learning, motivation, communication, and attitude. Our argument is that a psychological understanding of man's social behavior and experience can best be achieved by employing tools which have been designed for analysis at the psychological level. Understanding at the psychological level, whether the behavior to be studied is classified as criminal, familial, economic, or sexual, is possible only if we use psychological concepts as the tools of analysis.

Let us conclude this first chapter with a brief survey of each of the chapters to follow.

Methods of Social Psychology

The methods of a science are the basic tools a scientist uses in seeking understanding. Acquaintance with these tools familiarizes the student with the ways in which a scientist does his work. The student may develop maximum appreciation for the social psychological problems to be examined in the succeeding chapters if he learns about the ways such problems are systematically investigated. Any given problem can be investigated *best* by a given type of method.

Man and the Other Animals

The animal kingdom is composed of over a million species, of which man is but one. The underlying process common to all species is adaptation, and adaptation is accomplished in countless unique ways. In effecting adaptation, each species uses specialized processes and equipment, and the efficiency of its adaptation depends upon this interplay with the total environment. A truly comprehensive view of social man is possible only if we are willing to stand back and view him as part of this vast picture of adaptation struggle. While it is true that we cannot hope to understand man's social-psychological nature unless we study him in his own right and at his own level, it is also true that a healthy appreciation for the comparative perspective will assist immeasurably in this attempt. This may be spelled out in two principal ways. First, it helps in developing a comprehensive understanding of man's place in nature. Second, it assists in identifying those psychological characteristics which are of unique importance in man's continuing struggle to adapt. In view of these two benefits the third chapter focuses upon the infrahumans and their varied capacities for social adaptation. Also, in view of this emphasis, frequent comparative reference is made to infrahuman behavior throughout the remainder of the book.

A Psychological Approach to the Problem of Human Nature

The study of the ancient problem of human nature is more important today than ever before since psychologists are now better equipped than ever before to deal with it. In placing this chapter just after the infrahuman social behavior chapter we intend to accomplish the end of viewing man's unique nature in relief; in relief, that is, against a background of the other species. Three principal benefits should result from viewing the ancient and incredibly important problem of human nature in a modern context. First, we may learn to identify and to understand the types of errors which have so often been committed in the past by those who have sought to explain human nature. Second, we may recognize how crucial a theory of human nature actually is to all phases of social living. No person can live in society without some theory of human nature. Even the difference between war and peace rests upon the theories of human nature held by those in positions of consummate power. Third, we may grasp the significance of the fact that today we are much clearer than ever before about what we are looking for in our quest to understand man's nature. We believe that at last modern psychology is actually focusing upon man's psychological nature and that already some of the tools we must have to produce an accurate picture have been constructed.

Social Motivation

Closely related to the problem of human nature is social motivation, a subject that has sometimes been used by social psychologists as the "theoretical vehicle" for the study of human nature. The basic problem of social motivation is that of discovering and articulating the "springs of action" that are responsible for the individual's interactive behavior. This chapter is an attempt to clarify some fundamental concepts and to describe levels of motivational analysis. An accurate approach to the study of the social individual must begin with two primary assumptions concerning human motivation. First, all of the socially significant motivations which a human develops center around the protection of his ego. Second, the individual's social behavior and experience can be understood only in the light of an assessment of his contemporary pattern of motivation.

Learning and Socialization

Motivated animal organisms search their environments. The process of searching leaves its effect; the organism learns something. It learns means–ends relationships within its environment—what-leads-to-what. The human infant is born with an enormous behavior potential but by the time he has reached maturity he is using but an infinitesimal part of his endowed potential. The learning processes through which he passes in establishing these few and relatively stable ways of experiencing and behaving within the confines of his society are referred to as socialization. This chapter begins by examining learning as a psychological process. It concludes with a discussion of the significance of the socialization process and the difficulties encountered by psychologists who attempt to study it systematically and critically.

Communication and Language

In the broadest sense, all social animals communicate; that is, transmit sensory data from one to another. In those species where the individual's survival and adaptation are most dependent upon the group, communication takes on great importance and is usually highly specialized and intricate. At the human level communication is, of course, more complex than at any other. Man's principal tool for manipulating his social environment is language, the most complex of all communication systems. Language as a process is completely social; it plays a primary role in controlling the individual, and the individual uses language in controlling and interacting with other humans. This chapter is intended as an introduction to the social psychological nature of communication in general and to language, a specialized type of communication, in particular. Of specific concern in this chapter is the unique nature of language, its origin and the development of its use in children, and the relationship between language and thought.

Social Organization

Any social species is adaptively dependent upon some type of social organization and the individual member of any social species is, at least some time during its life, dependent upon the organization for survival. As with communication systems, there is great diversity in the nature of social organization from species to species; and again, the greatest complexity is found at the human level, where certain of man's unique psychological properties produce countless types of organization. In an attempt to understand the psychological nature of human social organization and its relationship to the behaving and experiencing individual, this chapter briefly examines some examples among the infrahumans, and then moves on and identifies certain of the unique properties of human social organization. As with communication, the nature of the organization bears an important relationship to the individual's behavior and the individual often has much to do with the nature of the organization. This chapter concludes with a brief review of some of the systematic psychological studies of social organization at the human level.

Leadership

One of the most important and interesting features of social organization is leadership; and, of course, leadership can be neither studied nor understood apart from social organization. In attempting to understand leadership at the psychological level of analysis, a distinction must be made between *leadership,* as an abstract phenomenon, and *the leader,* as a person behaving in a social situation. Since leadership has fascinated men for centuries, it is not surprising to find that many writers have attempted to explain it; psychologists are no exceptions. This chapter begins with a description of the two classical theories of leadership. It then shows how these two dominant theses have been channeled into the two major contemporary psychological approaches to the study of leadership. It concludes with a review and critique of present day psychological leadership theories.

Attitudes

The attitude construct is regarded by many psychologists as the unifying, central construct of social psychology. Its importance is attested to by the fact that we have long used such terms as *belief, judgment, opinion,* and *prejudice* to designate the "perceptual sets" which individuals have toward socially significant reference objects. *Attitude* is now used by social psychologists as a generic term which refers to all such psychological sets. If we know an individual's attitude toward a given stimulus (reference) object, we are in a favorable position to predict his future response when he is confronted by that object. In addition, we have some understanding as to why he responds as he does. This chapter begins by defining attitude in the light of certain historically important corollary concepts, and in the light of present-day psychological theory. The problem of attitude measurement is then considered. And, as an introduction to the book's final chapter, which deals with prejudice, the chapter concludes with a brief consideration of attitude change.

Prejudice

The concluding chapter is an amplification of one aspect of the attitude construct. Since prejudice is of such general and critical social significance in present-day society, it deserves special attention. Serious interest in the social and psychological significance of prejudice is very recent. Within the context of social psychology it is probably most appropriate to use the term "prejudicial attitude" since there seems little doubt that the attitude construct is generic and the prejudice construct is a specific type of attitude. This chapter is intended to acquaint the student with four important aspects of prejudice. First, prejudice as a psychological phenomenon is examined and the approaches to its study are described. Second, the principal modes of prejudicial expression, that is, the ways people behave prejudicially to one another, are outlined. Third, psychological research that has been directed to the problem of discovering the personality variables most conducive to the development of and use of prejudices is discussed. Fourth, brief attention is given to the avenues through which social psychology can most appropriately make a contribution to the practical problem of reducing prejudice.

II

Methods of Social Psychology

A knowledge of the tools the social psychologist uses will provide the framework for a better understanding of the aims of social psychology. The term "method" means a specific procedure or technique used in the solution of a problem. The methods of science are the various procedures that are used to procure, organize, and draw conclusions from empirical evidence.

It should be understood, however, that the methods themselves do not constitute science, and that laboratory equipment and statistical techniques alone are not science. Methods and equipment only enable the scientist to implement the scientific reasoning process.

THE BASIC MEANING OF SCIENCE

Science is a logic—a system of reasoning used in the search for truth. Such a system incorporates certain basic assumptions, advocates certain procedures, and specifies a set of rules to be followed. The logic of modern science is a union of two earlier logics, each of which played an important role in the intellectual history of western civilization: deduction and induction. Deduction is reasoning that begins with general premises and then proceeds to explain particular events. In its earliest form the premises were taken to be given, immutable absolutes; they were regarded as *a priori*. In later times deductive premises have been stated as theory based upon empirical evidence. In either case, the particular is deductively explained by the premise. Induction, at least superficially, is very different from deduction. It begins with particular events, and having assessed a set of particular events, it proceeds to generalize a law, principle, or theory. When used in conjunction, as they are in modern science, these two earlier distinct logic forms complement each other creatively. The great advances of science during the Nineteenth and Twentieth centuries are rooted in the skillful interplay of deductive and inductive logic.

Most important scientific investigations begin deductively; that is, the scientist already has a postulate, hypothesis, or theory which he believes may explain a given category of events. He then uses the inductive procedure to examine a representative sample of events within that category, thereby testing his postulate, hypothesis, or theory in order to discover whether or not it will in fact explain the particular events. In lieu of an initial theory, but with only a deep interest in and desire to discover lawfulness for a certain category of events, he may inductively observe instances of these events until he develops a tentative postulate. He is then ready to use deduction. The full circle of modern science depends upon both of these logic forms.

Basic Assumptions

The set of rules of any system of logic may be looked upon as assumptions or common agreements to which those who subscribe to the particular logic system must adhere. Only by such common adherence can any group of people seeking truth follow each other's reasoning, reach common understanding, and draw conclusions that are commonly acceptable. From a very broad perspective the logic of modern science incorporates four very broad, basic assumptions.

1. Nature is orderly. In view of this assumption the scientist seeks to discover instances of orderliness in nature. For such instances of orderliness the scientist develops theories and composes formal statements to describe such instances. A formula is the best example of such a formal statement.

2. Any given event is determined by other events. Phenomena have antecedents, and any phenomenon is to be understood as a function of a constellation of forces or variables which center upon that which is under observation.

3. Knowledge is acquired by experience. The *a priori* is viewed as invalid, the *a posteriori* as valid. Truth is sought by appeal to the empirical world, by direct, sense-tested observation. Empirical evidence is the final arbiter for scientific judgment and decision.

4. The human mind is capable of inquiring into the assumed regularity of the universe and of describing such regularity in lawful terms. Descriptions of lawfulness provide understanding and understanding permits the accurate prediction of future events and the systematic manipulation of variables in such ways that the control of nature becomes increasingly possible. Specific to this assumption is the psychological corollary that man is a part of nature, and since he is capable of understanding nature he is capable of understanding himself.

RESEARCH OBJECTIVES

One way to classify the research procedures used by psychologists is to identify what they are trying to discover. Edwards (1954) maintains that any research project is undertaken with the intention of accomplishing one of the four following objectives: ". . . to discover relevant variables, or to investigate a method of making observations, or to determine what action should be taken, or to test some hypothesis suggested by theoretical considerations." (p. 260) These four intentions can be designated according to the procedures used to satisfy them: survey, technique, applied, and critical.

Survey Research

Survey research begins in interrogation—the asking of questions. Essentially it is a formal, systematic way of observing behavior. Since the survey may be used for so many purposes and designed in so many ways, its essential nature is difficult to describe. Basically it is used when the researcher wants to know what a given sample's attitudes are toward some reference object or issue. Interviews and paper and pencil questionnaires are the standard devices used to collect such attitude information. The sample used must be comparable to the sample about which a later prediction is to be made. The prediction may involve the same or entirely different respondents. In either case, the attitudes recorded at the time of interrogation are assumed to bear some systematic relation to what they will be at a later time. This is assumed, however, only when the respondents are drawn from the same population.

While the construction and use of a survey involve intricate and technical details, there are certain major steps which must be followed no matter how simple or complex the design (Maccoby and Holt, 1947):

1. The objectives of the survey must be defined. In order to elicit the information desired, the problem being investigated must be stated explicitly.

2. The design of the survey must be carefully organized. This will be determined largely by the first step; that is, what is to be discovered? For example, if the purpose is to determine how stable people's attitudes are over a given period of time, a "repeat" design would be called for. In this case, the survey instrument would be administered twice to the same sample, or to comparable samples, and any shift in attitude would be calculated. The instrument might be used to compare two or more samples; or to estimate the effect of some intervening experience, such as an educational film, on attitude change.

3. The sample must be selected. Several basic procedures are involved here. For one thing, the "universe" must be decided upon; that is, the population about which predictions or descriptive statements are to be

made. The universe might be college seniors: in that case it would be necessary to interrogate only college seniors, not juniors, sophomores, or freshmen. In addition, the size of the sample must be predetermined. The larger the sample the greater the accuracy, but after a certain point increments in the sample size (i.e., percentage of the universe) add progressively less to accuracy. Also, stratification of the sample must be carefully detailed. Adequate stratification assures that the respondents are selected without bias. Again, if the universe is college seniors throughout the United States, the sample would be biased if the respondents were preponderantly male, or if they were drawn from only two or three colleges in one geographical area.

4. The interrogation device must be chosen. There are many such devices ranging from simple "yes" or "no" types to intensive interviewing procedures of the "open-end" and "funnel" varieties. The decision concerning the device to be used must rest upon the type of information to be elicited, the necessity of conducting personal interviews or not, and the amount of money available for the survey.

5. The interrogation device should be pretested by administering it to a small sample in order to eliminate weaknesses.

6. Procedures for administering the survey should be standard and uniform. It is extremely important that those who administer both written questionnaires and personal interviews are properly trained. In the case of the latter it is essential that they are honest in their work.

7. The data must be analyzed. This may involve nothing more than simple tabulations expressed in percentages, or it may require enormously complex statistical analysis that can be handled only by elaborate computational equipment. The statistical results are then expressed in terms of similarities and differences in central tendencies and variabilities, magnitudes of correlations, and so forth. Such measurement results are then all tested in terms of probability theory. That is, the researcher draws his inferences and conclusions upon the basis of significant and non-significant departure from chance expectancy of any statistical result.

The following study (Katz, 1950) illustrates the use of the survey research in identifying factors related to shipyard productivity during World War II:

Shipyards varied tremendously in their productivity—one yard might take three times as long to turn out the same type of ship as another yard. This was due in part to such technical factors as the flow of materials, the experience and technological know-how of the older yards, and the technical equipment of the company. But it was also due to the motivation or morale of the workers. In the design of the study, we were interested in the relative effect of two sets of independent variables upon the motivation of workers. One set of factors was the outplant conditions—housing, community living, transportation. During the war, workers who were attracted to the shipyards, as well as to other war industries, had to accept difficult, congested housing conditions often making family separation necessary, and a hostile community attitude against the interlopers as well as long hours of transportation to and from work. The other independent variable comprised the in-plant factors—the earnings and promotional possibilities on the job, the safety and working conditions within the plant, the treatment by management and supervision. Five yards were chosen for intensive study, an old South-coast yard with bad out-plant living conditions, a new Pacific-coast yard with similar undesirable out-plant factors, an old East-coast yard with fair community living conditions, and two yards in the same New England community under the same relatively bad out-plant conditions. Objective measures of performance were available in production and absenteeism figures. Fieldworkers themselves made observations of conditions within the plant and in the community. A cross section of workers was selected by taking every n^{th} name from the personnel records, and then every worker so selected was interviewed in his home.

This study showed that in-plant factors were the most important determiners of production and worker motivation. By measuring out-plant factors it would not have been possible to have predicted the differences in production, whereas in-plant measures were good predictors. In other words, while community conditions of living were minor contributing factors, the main cause centered in the job itself—whether the worker had satisfactory earnings and promotional opportunities, good conditions of work, good supervision, and psychological rewards from the job he was doing. When these criteria were met, the war worker could put up with considerable frustration outside the plant and still maintain a high degree of productivity. (pp. 74–76)

Survey research is of specific importance in contemporary psychology since so much information is needed with regard to the identification of relevant variables. The psychologist may profit from such exploratory work, since survey research may narrow the area of possible relationships by eliminating irrelevant variables. For example, in the study just cited, community living conditions were found to be largely unrelated to worker morale. The main determinants of worker morale were those related to job satisfaction.

Technique Research

Technique research is chiefly concerned with the problem of finding new and better ways to investigate particular problems. It is concerned with the development of procedures for obtaining and using psychological measures. It can concern the development of a new piece of laboratory equipment, a new statistical procedure, or an improved attitude scaling device. The ultimate purpose of technique research is that of furthering understanding, and it is an essential part of the scientific adventure.

Let us consider the problem of the measurement of prejudice as an illustration. Some years ago Bogardus became interested in measuring prejudicial attitudes (1925). He proceeded upon the assumption that an individual's degree of prejudice against a group could be measured by assessing the social distance that an individual wished to keep between himself and a given person or group. The simple scale designed by Bogardus to measure social distance consisted of seven statements, each indicative of a particular "social distance." The statements are as follows:

1. Would admit to close kinship by marriage
2. Would admit to my club as personal chums
3. Would admit to my street as neighbors
4. Would admit to employment in my occupation
5. Would admit to citizenship in my country
6. Would admit as visitors only in my country
7. Would exclude from my country

Subjects taking this scale were asked to check, for each ethnic group, the statement that best represented their feelings regarding the group.

The Bogardus scale of social distance has been used in many ways and its adequacy has been studied by many investigators. One of the questions raised concerning the Bogardus scale centered upon the psychological distances between the seven statements. Is the psychological distance between Statement 1 and Statement 2 the same as that between 2 and 3, and so on? Imagine the difficulty of measuring the lengths of various objects if the distances between the units of the scale varied so that the distance between one and two inches was not the same as the distance between two and three inches! Obviously, any summary statistic based on scores obtained with such a scale would be meaningless or—even worse—misleading.

In order to deal with this particular problem in the measurement of attitudes other techniques have been developed. Thurstone and Chave developed a new procedure for the measurement of attitudes, known as the "equal-appearing interval" technique (1929). The object was to develop a scale that would indicate the psychological distance between one statement and another. In physical measurement, the distance between two points may be determined by calculating the number of arbitrarily-agreed-upon units that lie between the two points. In psychological measurement, the distance between one feeling and another feeling, for example, cannot be calculated by an arbitrarily-agreed-upon measurement unit of objectively equal units. For one thing, the same responses made by two different individuals may have very different psychological meanings. Consider the following statement: Labor unions are responsible for the present economic condition of the United States. This statement might be made either by a labor union leader or an anti-labor union politician. The meaning of the statement would, however, be quite different for the two individuals. For another thing, the individual's responses, as measurable units, do not distribute themselves along a continuum at psychologically equidistant points. It is this latter fact that imposes such difficulty in psychological measurement of the type we are considering here. More explicitly, humans express themselves in ways that do not fit objectively equal intervals. The psychological difference between "I like you" and "I love you" is not necessarily the same as that between "I dislike you" and "I hate you."

The attempt by Thurstone and his colleagues to develop a technique by which the psychological distance between one indication of attitude could be equated with another involves several steps. First, many statements concerning the attitude object are composed by a variety of persons. These statements reflect all degrees of feeling, from most favorable to most unfavorable. Second, a large number of individuals independently judge the favorableness or unfavorableness of each statement on an eleven-point scale. Third, the statements that are finally retained are: those that judges can agree upon concerning their positions on the eleven-point continuum and those that are distributed fairly equally over the eleven-point continuum. Each statement is then given a numerical scale value, which is the median position assigned it by the judges. When the scale is administered to a subject, he is instructed to check those statements with which he agrees. The subject's score is the average of the median scale values of the items checked.

The Thurstone technique for measuring prejudicial attitudes is in some ways more valuable to the social psychologist than the Bogardus technique. The fact that psychological distances between points on a scale are estimated as a function of the combined judgment of many people is an improvement over a technique that uses verbal statements that a test constructor only assumes are psychologically equidistant from each other. The idea that Bogardus developed is not to be discounted, however, for it was basic to the later improvements.

The adequacy of the Thurstone equal-appearing interval type scale in turn has been studied by numerous investigators. Its validity is high, judged by two criteria. It has built-in validity as a function of its method of construction; if verbal statements upon which judges agree can be taken as an operational validity criterion, then it can be argued that invalid items are eliminated in the process of construction. In addition, correlations between scores on Thurstone scales and behavior are typically quite high. Although this type of scale is not a perfect attitude-measuring device, and although along with its strengths there are some weaknesses, its overall performance is quite good. It represents a significant technical advance in attitude measurement. There are, of course, many other attitude-measurement techniques besides the Bogardus and Thurstone methods. Some of these techniques, along with other problems of attitude measurement, will be discussed in Chapter X.

Applied Research

Applied research is the scientific procedure most readily understood and appreciated by the layman. It is the "practical" side of science—the use of scientific procedures to solve practical problems. The specific goal of applied research is always that of finding a better way of doing something; better, of course, from the standpoint of the person promoting the research. The quest for understanding the broad dynamics underlying the phenomenon being investigated is secondary to the desire to solve the immediate practical problem. It would be incorrect, however, to suppose that there is a necessary gulf between "pure" and "applied" research, for any research project may have implications of both kinds.

Applied research has made valuable contributions in many areas, such as education, industry, business, politics, and engineering. The following example is a study by Kurt Lewin (1958) that had its theoretical inception in the field of social psychology but was specifically designed for the purpose of answering an important social problem.

The problem stemmed from an interest in determining what factors are effective in bringing about changes in social habits. Specifically the question was, are lectures and group participation methods equally effective in modifying social attitudes? Lewin hypothesized that attitudes with reference to social habits would change more in group-participation situations, provided certain conditions obtain. Among these conditions are the following: individuals must become involved in the group situations but still retain the feeling of freedom of individual choice; individuals must be motivated with reference to the different avenues of choice to the extent that they will make decisions; individuals must realize that other members of the group are interested in whether or not they abide by their decisions—that is, something must be expected of them.

Lewin's study was conducted both with the intention of throwing light upon the general hypothesis and of obtaining information for a practical program for changing attitudes. The specific aim of the program was to increase housewives' use of beef hearts, sweetbreads, and kidneys. Six groups, each composed of from 13 to 17 housewives, volunteered for 45-minute instruction sessions centered around the advantages of incorporating these meats into their family diets. Three groups listened to well-organized, attractive lectures that emphasized the economic, nutritional, and war-effort value of these foods (this study was undertaken during World War II). The other three sessions were started by a leader who briefly explained the aims and then opened the sessions to group discussion. In concluding these participation sessions, the leader asked for a show of hands of those who were willing to use one of these meats during the following week.

At a later time these women were individually asked whether or not they had served one of the meats they had never served before. The results were as follows. Of those who had been in the lecture sessions, only three per cent served one of the meats. Of those who had been in the group participation sessions, 32 per cent served one of them. This finding suggests that active participation in group processes is more effective in bringing about attitude change than is passive perception of information.

The same result has come from other similar studies. When individuals feel enough a part of a group to participate with other members of the group, to share their views with others who are equally motivated to solve a problem, they will more frequently arrive at some decision and act upon the basis of that decision.

This simple study indicates quite clearly the practical applicability of research. It shows how changes in attitudes can be brought about in a relatively effective way. It may not be the best possible way, but it is more efficient than the traditional way.

There are obviously many needs for applied research. However, two cautions need to be emphasized. First, it is not the object of science to discover ways by which particular individuals can gain and exert control over other individuals for the advantage of the former. Second, the results of some applied research may not be derived from theory at all and may not provide tests of hypotheses that are relevant to other than the immediate, practical problems at hand. That is, some applied research may have virtually no theoretical significance. On the other hand, it is obvious that the end goal of the scientific enterprise is that of increasing understanding. Certainly one way to validate understanding is to put it to practical test.

Critical Research

Critical research is frequently called "pure" or "basic" research. It is research undertaken without regard for any *practical* value it *may* someday have. The aim of critical research is to obtain conclusive evidence to support or reject a particular hypothesis. In psychology, as in any field of science, there are many theories that purport to provide understanding for various classes of phenomena. Such theories are supported by a variety of assumptions. The scientist who proposes to test the validity of a theory selects one of the assumptions and states it as an hypothesis. He then tests this hypothesis by means he judges appropriate. He may follow this by testing other hypotheses that are in critical relation to the theory.

The critical test of an hypothesis introduces some problems. What evidence is to be used in appraising the outcome? What kinds of results are to be accepted as critical evidence? Does absence of positive results warrant rejection of the hypothesis? After a sufficiently large number of carefully controlled studies fails to confirm the hypothesis with positive evidence, it is usually judged as reasonable to reject the hypothesis on the basis of lack of supporting evidence.

An example of critical research will help to explain the significance of this aspect of the scientific approach to social psychological problems. Social psychologists have been interested in the phenomenon of prejudice for some time. One assumption of the general theory of prejudice is that prejudices are emotionally fortified. Until recently, support for this assumption came from the observation that persons expressing prejudice toward human groups behave emotionally and that emotionally-charged words and phrases used in prejudice-measurement scales are often selected by subjects as descriptive of their feelings toward particular human groups. It is well known that measurable physiological changes occur when an individual experiences strong emotion. If such changes are detected during the expression or defense of prejudices, and not when opinions or ordinary attitudes are being expressed or defended, it is reasonable to infer that relatively great affectivity is one of the psychological characteristics of prejudice.

Three studies were conducted with the intention of testing this assumption (Cooper, 1959). The physiological measurement obtained was the galvanic skin response—GSR. When an individual experiences strong emotion, one of the bodily changes that occurs is a lowering of skin resistance to a weak electrical current passed across a selected skin area. The change of resistance, as measured by a galvanometer, is used as an index of the GSR. Thus, if there is a relatively great GSR, the individual is in a relatively heightened emotional state.

In the first study (Cooper and Singer, 1956), twenty subjects who had previously expressed by rating and ranking scales both strong liking and disliking for two different groups were tested individually. After a short adaptation period, four brief statements were read to the subject. Two were complimentary and two were derogatory. The name of the group the subject liked was inserted into one of the derogatory statements and the name of the group the subject disliked was inserted into one of the complimentary statements. The names of two groups toward which the subject had expressed neutral feelings were inserted into the two remaining derogatory and complimentary statements. Subjects were instructed to think about the statements, not to verbalize their feelings to the experimenters. It was predicted that GSR's to liked groups and to disliked groups would be greater for the individual subject than responses to groups toward which relatively neutral attitudes had been expressed. Results of this first study strongly confirmed one part of the hypothesis and gave some slight confirmation of the other. GSR's to complimentary statements referring to disliked groups were greater than GSR's to statements containing the names of neutral groups in nineteen of the twenty cases. GSR's to derogatory statements referring to liked groups were greater than GSR's to statements containing the names of neutral groups in fourteen of the twenty cases. Statistical tests indicated that the first results would be obtained by chance less than one time in a thousand, while the second would be obtained by chance about six times out of a hundred.

According to accepted standards, a quantitatively expressed positive finding is regarded as in support of an hypothesis if it is shown statistically that it would be obtained less than five per cent of the time by chance alone. Thus, the first finding is supported strongly, while the second fails to reach the accepted criterion or level of significance.

The second study (Cooper and Siegel, 1956) followed the same basic design but attention was given only to negative attitudes. Subjects who indicated an unusually strong hostility toward some group by both rating and ranking attitude scales were selected for GSR measurement. Again, magnitudes of GSR's to the names of disliked groups were compared with magnitudes of GSR's to the names of neutral groups embedded in complimentary statements. GSR's of 20 of the 23 subjects were greater to statements incorporating the names of disliked groups than to statements incorporating the names of neutral groups. Once again, this finding would be attained less than one time in a thousand by chance and is thus considered statistically significant.

The third study (Cooper and Pollock, 1959) was done to discover whether a reversed design would reveal the same relationship. In this instance, GSR measurements were made first, and predictions of prejudice were then made on the basis of these measurements. The hypothesis was that relatively large GSR's of individuals in response to complimentary statements concerning particular ethnic and national groups would indicate prejudice against these groups. The results were as predicted and were statistically significant. That is, degree of emotionality under these conditions could be used to predict degree of prejudice as measured by rating and ranking scales.

These three studies are examples of critical research in social psychology. Had the results been equivocal, the hypothesis would not necessarily be rejected, since the possibility would remain that control, procedure, or inadequate equipment could account for failure to obtain the predicted results.

On the other hand, even though the results of the three studies all indicate that the expression of prejudice is emotionally supported, there remains the possibility that the results were functions of inadvertently introduced variables, such as equipment error, misread equipment indicators, or mistabulation of data. It is impossible to say how often critical researches must be repeated in order to insure definitive proof.

These four research approaches—survey, technique, applied, and critical—overlap considerably. Survey research is made increasingly adequate by technique research into the procedures used in survey research, and survey research is one of the chief adjuncts to applied research since it makes possible the accurate accumulation of data necessary for dealing with practical social problems. Technique research provides procedures that insure the adequacy of critical research. By use of adequate technical procedures, critical research tests hypotheses that purport to substantiate particular psychological theories. The basic purposes of research are usually clear enough to designate and define the most appropriate approach. Each of the four just described is essentially aimed at providing an understanding of human behavior, and in the attempt to understand human behavior these approaches are interdependent.

RESEARCH METHODS

Whereas a research objective concerns what we want to know, the research method defines how we go about discovering what we want to know. In this sense, method is technical. Methods used in social psychology can be classified conveniently into three categories: experimentation, controlled observation, and interdisciplinary information.

Experimental Method

The experimental method is frequently referred to as the ideal tool of science. It is not, however, a mechanical tool that works by merely pushing a button. Applied improperly, experimentation can easily lead to invalid inferences. With cautious use, it is the most rigorous, systematic, and exact scientific tool.

An experiment is the systematic arrangement and control of the conditions under which a phenomenon is to be observed. The assumption is that a particular condition is responsible for a particular phenomenon. Thus the conditions may be systematically varied, one at a time or in groups of two or more. If the phenomenon is observed to change concurrently with a controlled condition, then it is inferred that the phenomenon is a function of the condition. If A is suspected of being a function of B and not a function of C, controlled and systematic observation of A when B and C are separately introduced can provide the answer as to whether the suspicion is correct.

Standard terminology is used to designate the components of an experiment. The phenomenon to be observed is called the *dependent variable.* That is, what the experimenter is watching for is *dependent* upon some other condition (variable). Any condition that is systematically introduced because it is thought to be responsible for the observed phenomenon (dependent variable) is referred to as the *independent variable.* Other systematically introduced conditions that are found not to be responsible for the phenomenon are referred to as irrelevant variables. A dependent variable is roughly equivalent to "effect," and an independent variable is roughly equivalent to "cause."

Although psychological experiments are ordinarily conducted in laboratories, in social psychological research it is often impossible to use the careful control of a laboratory. Such control may distort the social behavior of some subjects. If the researcher brings a human subject into a laboratory, the subject may become so concerned with the surroundings that he ceases to behave as a normal social being. Strict use of the experiment in social psychology must be tempered by the fact that a social human is accustomed to a social environment. Unless the experiment provides an adequate social climate, the dependent variable may be the result of conditions other than the assumed independent variable.

Description of an experiment conducted by Rankin and Campbell (1955) will illustrate the nature of the experimental method used in social psychology. These researchers were interested in measuring possible differential emotional responses of white college men to contacts with a Negro and a white experimenter. Stated as an hypothesis, the relationship was: emotional response by whites to the presence of a Negro is greater than emotional response to the presence of a white.

Forty male white college student subjects were individually administered a word-association test in a laboratory setting. Galvanic skin response data (GSR measurements) were obtained from electrodes attached to the subject's right hand. On the subject's left hand a pair of dummy electrodes were attached. The experiment was conducted by two men—one Negro and one white. For half of the subjects, the experimenter was white and the Negro acted as the assistant. For the other half, the Negro was the experimenter and the white served as his assistant. During the word-association test period, (which the subjects were told was the "reason" for the experiment) the experimenter entered the room where the subject sat and adjusted the left-hand dummy electrodes once. Twice the assistant entered and made the same type of adjustment. In this way, the Negro and the white appearances were equalized and randomized. GSR's were recorded for every subject for each appearance. Each individual was given a GSR score, which was the difference between the sum of his responses on the two contacts by the white experimenter and the sum of his responses on the two contacts by the Negro experimenter. Of the 40 subjects, 36 scored positively, a result that would be obtained considerably less than one time in a thousand by chance. In other words, the white subjects responded with greater emotionality to the Negro experimenter than they did to the white experimenter. However, as has been pointed out, psychological experiments are seldom, if ever, definitive; and although Rankin and Campbell are of the opinion that the measured differences are primarily attributable to racial differences, they emphasize the fact that further experimentation would be required in order to draw this inference with certainty.

Let us examine this experiment briefly in order to identify its principal elements. The dependent variable was the GSR, and GSR was automatically recorded in such a way that it could be accurately quantified. The independent variable was the appearance of a person, either Negro or white. An increase in GSR followed the appearance of a person (independent variable). If the independent variable is differentiated into first and second and these are systematically and independently introduced, any consistent variation in the dependent variable that accompanies the first and doesn't accompany the second may be attributed to the first. This is what happened in the Rankin and Campbell experiment. When the first independent variable (Negro) was introduced, the dependent variable increased relatively. The inference may then be drawn that characteristics inherent in the response to the first independent variable are responsible for the relative change in the dependent variable.

Controlled Observation

Controlled observation is less precise than experimentation. It is an important and useful method, however, because it can be used in situations in which it is not possible or judicious to use the experimental method. In order to obtain reliable measures of the variables being investigated, uniform procedures of observation are maintained. Control of the situation is less precise with this method than with the experimental method since independent variables cannot be manipulated. The investigator is limited to making careful observations of the situation as it is, in his attempt to identify independent variables and to find possible relationships among variables.

Controlled observation is used in so many ways that any classification of its specific uses is to some extent overlapping. One general classification of the uses of controlled observation is the following: event observation, actuarial survey, and correlational survey.

Event Observation. This technique is essentially a field technique. Investigators study behavior as they see it. Dependent variables are identified before such studies are started, and it is the intention of an event observation study to discover the independent variable, or variables, responsible for the dependent variable. If the investigator is interested in discovering the reason some particular thing happens, and is unable to use the experimental method, he may decide upon the alternative of observing the thing very carefully and systematically with the hope of discovering what causes it. Of course, he may have some hypothesis about what the cause is. If he has, his work is obviously simpler and starts from a point beyond that of the investigator who has no hunches, postulates, or hypotheses.

The study of social behavior in animals has depended heavily upon the event observation technique and may serve as an example. Nissen, for instance, conducted extensive observational studies of laboratory chimpanzees (1951). One of his findings is that these primates differ greatly in the degree of their friendliness to human beings. Most of them display a high degree of friendliness, but some are actively hostile to humans. In some of the chimpanzees Nissen observed what he called a "strong fixation" on man. By careful observation of these particular individual animals he was able to discover an identifying social characteristic: these individuals consistently showed abnormal or inadequate relationships with their own species. Nissen has also observed that chimpanzees with a long history of human contact and little opportunity for association with other champanzees characteristically show extreme friendliness to humans.

Other examples of the event-observation technique may be found in the literature on such subjects as social behavior of children, small-group processes, and leadership. In research in which the experimental method is not feasible, the event-observation technique may operate well. It is essential that criteria for data collection be established and that there is strict adherence to them. In many instances, the independent variables associated with particular forms of behavior can be identified. This technique is frequently used as the forerunner of experimentation.

Actuarial Survey.   This technique is probably the most frequently used of the controlled-observation methods. Although the term "actuarial" literally refers to computing risks and rates upon the basis of previously recorded facts for insurance purposes, it has been borrowed for use here.

The actuarial-survey technique differs only in procedure—not in purpose—from the event-observation technique. Whereas the latter is an on-the-spot observation of behavior procedure, the actuarial method collects data that "reflect" behavior, ordinarily from a relatively large sample. Both techniques seek to identify possible independent variables, and both are limited by the fact that the variables suspected of being independent cannot be systematically introduced and controlled. The independent variables must be observed as, if and when they occur.

A good example of the actuarial-survey technique is to be found in the Kinsey, Pomeroy, and Martin studies of sexual behavior (1948). In these studies subjects were interviewed about their sexual experiences and habits.

Socio-economic, religious, educational, and other group-member classification data were also obtained. Among other things, these group-membership classifications were studied as possible independent variables. For example, it was discovered that significant differences exist in the sexual behavior of males in the different socio-economic groupings. A clue to the psychological importance of social-mobility anticipation as a possible independent variable was found in one of the relationships discovered: males who anticipated moving into a higher socio-economic grouping tended to adopt the sexual-behavior mores and patterns of that higher grouping before they had, in fact, moved into it. The significance of this finding is that a clue has been unearthed concerning the role of social aspiration as a possible determinant of behavior. This finding thus helps in the isolation of a possible independent variable.

Correlational Survey. A third example of the controlled-observation method may be found in the correlational-survey technique. Like the event-observation and the actuarial-survey techniques, it is designed to identify possible independent variables. It, too, is limited by the fact that variables postulated as being independent cannot be systematically controlled and introduced. The essence of the correlational-survey technique is that various specified *psychological characteristics* of individuals are measured, two or more at a time, and are studied for possible interrelationships. When significant correlations are found, one variable, by virtue of its correlation with another or with others, is identified as a likely independent variable. It is then feasible to design other studies to test the hypothesis that the variable postulated as independent is actually independent.

In correlational-survey research the first task is to "extract" certain psychological information from individuals. In this way it does not differ from actuarial-survey research. The distinguishing mark of the correlational-survey method is the measurement of particular psychological characteristics of an individual to indicate the degree to which he possesses such characteristics. For example, it might be postulated that for a given population, each member's amount of education will correlate with his social ideology, the hypothesis being that formal training influences ideology. One would hardly suppose that such a category (amount of education), which is a measurement involving relatively little information, would be of great psychological importance. And it is not. It can serve as a first approximation pointing to some possible relationship. However, what are we to do with those cases of seniors who are extremely conservative and of those seniors who are extremely liberal? It is at this point that the correlational-survey technique begins. The attempt is a step beyond the actuarial-survey technique.

The correlational-survey technique relates the measured amount of a psychological characteristic for a given individual with the measured amount of another of his psychological characteristics. The presence of such psychological characteristics is determined by measurement techniques more powerful than simple yes-no categories. Examples of such characteristics are authoritarianism, intrapunitiveness, feeling of security, anxiety, aggression, dependence, social attitudes, and social ideology.

Many social psychologists have supposed that social ideologies are in large measure functions of parental influence—like parent, like child. Probing this thesis, one correlational-survey study hypothesized that the child's evaluation of his parent is a principal determinant of the similarity of parent-child ideologies (Cooper and Blair, 1959). A parent-evaluation scale was constructed to measure subjects' feelings of rejection or acceptance of their parents. Subjects' social ideologies were also measured by a scale. The general finding of this study was that dislike of parent is closely associated with an ideology system markedly dissimilar to the parent's, and that love of parent and ideological similarity (between parent and child) are closely associated.

One specific finding from this study will help describe the correlational-survey technique. Those subjects who evaluated their mothers highest (top 11 per cent) were compared with those subjects who evaluated their mothers lowest (bottom 11 per cent) with reference to similarity of child-mother ideology. Those who awarded their mothers a high evaluation were, on the average, only 7 points away from their mothers on the ideology scale. Those who awarded their mothers a low evaluation were, on the average, 46 points away from their mothers on the ideology scale.

The chief difference between the correlational-survey technique and the actuarial-survey technique lies in the fact that the former deals with interrelations of psychological variables, whereas the latter deals with interrelations of psychological and sociological variables or with sociological variables alone. It is one thing to determine the percentage of five-year-olds who suck their thumbs and quite another to determine the percentage of overdependent five-year-olds who suck their thumbs. As with the other controlled-observation techniques, the correlational-survey technique rests upon control of the procedures of observation rather than upon control of variables.

Interdisciplinary Information

The third general method that social psychologists use is interdisciplinary. This method is dependent upon information provided not only by psychology but also by other disciplines, such as political science, history, economics, anthropology, and sociology. For example, the study of social motivation cannot avoid dependence upon physiological data, and the study of the distribution of social prejudice cannot be divorced from geographical information.

Some types of knowledge are more relevant than others to social psychology. The closer any item of information is to the individual, the more relevant it is to the basic concern of social psychology. Therefore, sociological and anthropological information are usually of greatest immediate value to social psychology. There are many instances in which social psychologists have directly used information from other disciplines to throw light upon psychological problems.

The writings of the social psychologist Otto Klineberg (1954) are good examples of the use of information from other disciplines in social psychology. In dealing with a comprehensive list of social psychological problems, Klineberg makes constant use of anthropological information by which he compares social behavior from culture to culture. His view is that the varieties of social behavior throw as much light upon human nature as do the constants.

There are many types of interdisciplinary information available to social psychology. Among the classic examples from anthropology are Ruth Benedict's *Patterns of Culture* (1934) and Margaret Mead's *Coming of Age in Samoa* (1928). These books lucidly describe certain socially-important value systems that have developed in conjunction with unique cultural patterns. Works of this type have had a profound influence upon the point of view of modern social psychology, which emphasizes the fact that interpersonal behavior and individual experience are in large part functions of the attitudes, beliefs and values that the given culture provides.

Another example of a significant anthropological contribution to social psychology is the book by Oscar Lewis, *Life in A Mexican Village* (1951). Although the approach is anthropological, experts in political science, sociology, historical economics, and psychology worked together in this study of social behavior in a relatively isolated village setting. Lewis' work illustrates the variety of perspectives that the interdisciplinary method affords.

There are numerous instances in which sociologists and anthropologists have brought comparative data to bear upon certain hypotheses in psychology. A very good example of this is to be found in a paper by Bateson (1941). He examined the "frustration-aggression hypothesis" of Dollard and his co-workers (1939) in the light of the varying ways the members of different culture groups meet frustrations. Specifically, he showed that data gathered from the Iatmul of New Guinea tended to confirm the hypothesis that frustration is the instigation to aggression. On the other hand, he found that the behavior of the Balinese tended to weaken the hypothesis.

An elaborate and highly significant example of the way in which anthropological information can be brought to bear upon psychological problems is to be found in the research and writing of Whiting and Child. In their book, *Child Training and Personality: A Cross-Culture Study* (1953) these investigators, an anthropologist and a psychologist, studied child-rearing practices in seventy-five primitive culture groups. Their intention was to discover particular practices of child-rearing that might determine adult personality structure. Their data source was the Human Relations Area File at Yale University. This file contains anthropological reports on the social habits and patterns of these seventy-five groups.

Five systems of behavior were analyzed: oral, anal, sexual, dependent, and aggressive. Since the statistical method of analysis was correlational, it was not possible, even when reliable correlations were found, to conclude with confidence which variables were dependent and which were independent. Thus the Whiting and Child findings were not definitive. Their correlational results are exploratory rather than conclusive. However, findings of importance did result. They found, for instance, that in personality development negative fixations (i.e., psychologically painful trauma "conditioned" to particular events) are more lasting than positive fixations. This discovery has long-range implications with reference to the age-old problem of punishment versus reward as effective reinforcements in learning. They also infer from their findings that oral, dependence, and aggressive behavior are unusually susceptible to early training. Certainly, the implication of the last item gives pause in our thinking about intergroup conflict. The overall conclusion of their study is that adult personality is largely shaped by the nature of child-training practices.

This study indicates how one discipline can take information from another and bring it to bear upon its own problems. (It should be added that sometimes, of course, information from psychology is similarly useful in anthropological theory.)

The interdisciplinary-information method is one that is being used more and more. Since social psychologists who use it employ data gathered by researchers in other disciplines, the use of the experiment is virtually impossible. In social psychology this method shows that the world of social behavior has many sides and may be viewed from many perspectives. A large view that draws as many perspectives as possible into a well-articulated composite will undoubtedly provide the most comprehensive understanding of social man.

III

Man and
the Other Animals

During recent years interest among social psychologists in the lower animals has lessened. This trend seems to have resulted from the fact that most of the psychologists who have continued to use lower animals in their studies have come more and more to regard them purely as convenient and readily available research material. Although early modern psychology had a very lively interest in certain aspects of the social nature of lower animals, there is today much less comprehensive information about infrahuman behavior than early experimental comparative psychology presaged. Two reasons for this trend are apparent. First, since the main stream of psychological study and theory has studiously bypassed infrahuman social behavior, comparative psychology and ethology have been forced to go it alone and have become less and less a working part of general psychology. Second, since psychologists have correctly veered away from the assumption that human behavior can be directly understood in terms of infrahuman behavior (Schneirla, 1946), the tendency has been for social psychologists to forget the lower animals altogether.

Despite this trend there is now a new and revitalized interest among some social psychologists in infrahuman behavior. Now that it is fully agreed among psychologists that appeal to infrahuman phenomena can not directly explain human phenomena, many psychologists feel free to take a fresh look at infrahuman behavior, fully aware of the fact that they are not trying to reduce explanations of the complexity of man to the relative simplicity of the lower animals.

Social psychologists who seriously pursue this renewed interest in infrahuman behavior assume that all species of the animal kingdom are in a constant process of adaptation. The warranted assumption is that the existence of every extant species, and of every living member of each extant species, depends upon adequacy of specialized adaptive behavior processes. The broad interest of these social psychologists is to view man's adaptive processes in the light of those of the thousands of other animal species.

Their specific interest is to identify the adaptive processes unique to man. If these unique adaptive processes could be seen in such a perspective, we should be better able to study and understand them.

REASONS FOR STUDYING INFRAHUMAN SOCIAL BEHAVIOR

While today most social psychologists are less impressed than they were some years ago by the facts and theories drawn from infrahuman studies, there are several reasons why a continuation and increase in the study of infrahuman behavior is of great importance to the general body of social psychology.

Understanding

Understanding is important for its own sake. Man is inquisitive. He likes to know how things work. As we asserted in the preceding chapter, the search for understanding is legitimate in its own right.

Little items of knowledge find their ways into more comprehensive systems of knowledge. The impatient person who argues that research should be undertaken only when the problem to be studied can contribute to the "practical" should be comforted to know that even the most abstruse bits of information often eventually throw light upon larger problems. There is, in the end, always the possibility of application. The study of the grasshopper's life cycle may be a theoretical end in itself to the entomologist, but such information is of unlimited value to the rancher whose crops lie prey to marauding bands of these insects.

These "practical" arguments are really aside from the point. Understanding is important and interesting to men in its own right. No apology is necessary.

Similarities and Differences

Man and the lower animals are both alike and unlike in many ways; and from the standpoint of the attempt to understand man's role in nature and the adaptive properties that have made his role possible, it is important to examine certain of these similarities and differences. Although every pattern of human social behavior has its infrahuman analogue, evidence does not support the theory that such analogous characteristics in the lower animals are the origins of their counterparts in man. Since it is now known that man did not develop from any other presently living species, we may only conclude that the prototypes of man's social behavior are not to be found in infrahuman analogies. Why, then, is it important to study these similarities and differences? The answer, which we will try to provide, is that it is impossible to identify adaptive behavioral propensities that are uniquely human unless we compare them with the adaptive behavioral propensities of other species. These unique properties of man can be identified only by scanning the animal kingdom. Once identified they can then be studied with a view to understanding the unique adaptive roles they play in man's place in nature.

Rats and humans go about the job of learning their ways through mazes perhaps somewhat similarly; but at more complex levels, the understanding of learning activities in the rat are of little help in understanding human learning since, among other things, rats speak no language and are comparatively limited in cognitive manipulation. Yet, even at the relatively simple level at which rats operate and the relatively complex level at which humans *usually* operate there is something in common: learning is indispensable to adaptation in both rats and humans. Human adaptation, however, requires a level of learning complexity enormously greater than, and in many respects different from, that of the rat.

One of the most interesting social human-infrahuman analogies is that between gibbon and human family organization (Carpenter, 1940). Like the human pattern, but unique among the apes, the typical gibbon family pattern is mother, father, and their young. This ends the analogy, however, since the variables which tie the two similarly patterned organizations together are quite different. Among the cohesive variables at the human level are: human affectional identifications, specialization of labor functions for the benefit of the group, and non-interrupted female sexual receptivity. The variables which seem to tie the gibbon family together into an analogous organizational pattern center around adult gibbons' intolerance for any other gibbons except their mates and their immature offspring. At, or shortly before, puberty young gibbons are driven from their family groups by their parents. The subsequent chance meeting of such a young, sexually receptive female and a newly isolated, sexually mature young male results in courtship and copulation. Presumably this mutual experience leads to a perpetuating consort relationship which involves high social tolerance for each other and low social tolerance for all other gibbons (except their own non-mature offspring). From the standpoint of biological adaptation this type of family organization serves very different requirements in the two species. On the basis of careful analysis it is clear that the adaptive functions of such superficially similar social organizations are substantially different in the two species. In the gibbon it is a geographical-social spacing mechanism which prevents the overpopulation of a single location and consequent food shortage. In the human it is a social mechanism which makes possible the mutual exchange of affectionally identifying intimacies and the specialization of labor for the benefit of the group, as well as the satisfaction of many other social and individual adaptive requirements.

Significance of Isolated Information

A third reason for studying infrahuman social behavior is that of determining the significance of seemingly isolated bits of behavior. Such bits of behavior often strike the layman as chance anomalies, or he may try to explain them anthropomorphically. Is it just coincidence that the sudden ascension of a few blackbirds at the edge of a flock is quickly followed by adjacent birds until the entire flock is in flight? Does the duckling follow its mother about because it loves her? Innumerable patterns of social behavior among the lower animals are neither fortuitous nor based on human-like motives. They are natively determined patterns of adaptive importance to the individual, to the species, or to both.

Some native patterns of social behavior are apparently no longer necessary either to the individual or to the species. For example, there seems no need in the modern lion for the male's sneeze-like grimace when sexually aroused, but it may very well be that at a much earlier time this response was critically important to the species as an assistance in olfactory detection of females in oestrus.

Understanding the significance of these bits of behavior that superficially appear to be either chance or "human in nature" reinforces the value of the adaptation concept. It strengthens the thesis that infrahuman social behavior is not random but highly organized. The means by which adaptation is achieved, more or less successfully, at different levels of animal life are enormously varied. But we assume that behavior is caused, and a knowledge of the causes of infrahuman behavior patterns provides a perspective that can assist us in understanding human as well as infrahuman social patterns.

Behavior Emergences

The study of infrahuman behavior contributes to our knowledge of the ways new patterns of behavior emerge. Scientists accept the concept of phylogenetic continuity as established by zoologists. That is, in the ascending scale of animal forms there are intimate linkages, some homological but most analogical, of lower forms to higher forms. In all, the animal kingdom represents a progressive gradation from one-celled animals to man. Almost every conceivable form is represented in the thousands of extant species. It is known that less complex species (now living) are not mere "stepping stones" over which new species walked, and, conversely, that present complex species are not mere outgrowths of less complex living species. The arrangement of all living species ordered by their degree of biological complexity, however, presents a convenient model to guide the construction of behavioral gradations from the simple to the complex.

Although comparative psychology takes its lead from comparative anatomy and physiology, psychologists have not been able to describe a behavioral phylogenetic scale similar to the zoologists'. From an evolutionary standpoint one species is not the descendent of the one just lower on the phylogenetic scale. But it is just a bit higher on the scale from a structural and physiological standpoint. In general, behavior complexity correlates with neurological complexity. The greater the ratio of nerve tissue to body tissue, the greater the learning capacity and conceptual facility of the species. One of the best examples in support of this generalization is that while the infrahumans have systems of communication, they do not have language. Language is clearly a *human behavioral emergence*. The presumption is that in man a structural-functional development has been reached that makes language possible. Anything less than man's nervous system is insufficient for language.

There are many identifiable behavioral emergences throughout the phyletic scale. For example, not until we reach the mammalian level do we find play behavior between parent and offspring. Perhaps this emergence results from the physiological dependence of offspring upon the parent for food and from the parent's need for the glandular relief that can be provided only by the offspring. Then, too, there is reason to believe that play constitutes a practice and a rehearsal of behavior patterns the young animal will need in adulthood in order to make adequate adaptation. Play becomes more and more complex and elaborate as we ascend the mammalian scale; in man its ramifications are widespread. The significance of the role of play at the human level is evidently more significant and more understandable when viewed from a comparative standpoint.

Reasoning is another emergence that has been studied by comparative psychologists for many years. Although the lowest phyletic level at which reasoning can be identified is still debatable, this behavioral phenomenon, upon which man's capacity to adapt rests so heavily, goes quite far down the animal scale. If reasoning is defined as the process of combining two or more past experiences in the solution of a novel problem, then many species below the human level are capable of reasoning, at least in minimal degrees.

Although our knowledge of behavior emergences is still limited, many psychologists find the concept significant for an understanding of human behavior. By viewing man's behavior as linked in many ways with that of the infrahumans, and in some ways as emergently different from that of the infrahumans, a clearer perspective of man's psychological role in nature is possible.

Nature-Nurture Debate

The "nature-nurture problem" is of particular importance to social psychology. Are patterns of social behavior the result of innate characteristics, or do they result from learning the ways of the older generation?

As we descend the phyletic scale behavior becomes more and more stereotyped. The lower animals display patterns of behavior that are, for a given species, relatively rigid and set, similar from individual to individual and from generation to generation. It seems evident that the dependence of adaptation upon learning is related to the complexity of the species. While the rat's sexual behavior is extremely stereotyped and affected relatively little by experience, the chimpanzee's sexual behavior is markedly affected by early social contacts. In much more striking contrast to the rat is the human whose sexual patterns may be highly influenced by early social experiences.

Many investigations of the lower animals have been conducted with the specific intention of throwing light on the nature-nurture problem. For example, sparrows reared with canaries typically develop song patterns somewhat similar to those of canaries (Scott, 1958). Shortly after hatching-out, goslings begin to follow most any nearby moving object. Lorenz and others have demonstrated that this specific behavior of following a moving object will, other factors held constant, persist into adult life for many species (Lorenz, 1937; Thorpe, 1956). The capacity to imprint is genetically determined, but what a given animal imprints on is experientially determined. (See Chapter VI.)

The value of these findings from the standpoint of social psychology is that certain patterns of behavior we commonly regard as instinctive in a given species can, under some conditions, be dramatically modified. If the sparrow sings a canary song it may properly be referred to as abnormal, for this behavior is strikingly different from the sparrow norm. The geese that follow a man rather than other geese are abnormal members of their species. An analysis of these social abnormalities is interesting and important from the standpoint of adaptation. For the individual, such patterns may be adequate; but from the standpoint of the species, they must be looked upon as inadequate. Were they to become typical for the species, the species could no longer adapt to its environmental requirements. The sparrow would be incapable of emitting the mating call that signals the beginning of courtship and copulation behavior. Greylag geese would soon extinguish themselves as a species if they persisted in following humans around and failed to attend to members of their own species.

The highly stereotyped social behavior of certain of the lower animals can be modified by novel environmental conditions. There is also reason to believe that social behavior at the human level is similarly not totally a function of man's genetic make-up but that it, too, can be modified by environmental conditions. For man, too, there must be certain very broad, genetically influenced categories of social behavior (Fuller and Thompson, 1960). But, of course, man's developed nervous system makes him obviously capable of much wider versatility in adaptation than any of the lower animals.

Undoubtedly, there are patterns of social behavior that are more beneficial to man than to the lower animals. This raises another question. The individual is capable of greater learning at the human level than at any other level, and at the same time he is dependent upon parental care for a relatively longer period of time than are members of any of the lower species. Insofar as is known, the most important learning that takes place during the human infantile and childhood periods is of a personality-depth type. That is, the human individual's learning during his very early life establishes a personality pattern that amounts to a way or system by which the individual appraises himself as he compares himself with other humans, and as he compares himself at one time with himself at another time. His mature personality characteristics have more than a little to do with the way he gets on with others, and with the ways in which others respond to him.

Study of the lower animals reveals that some patterns of social behavior are more adequate from the standpoint of adaptation than others. Many of these patterns are without doubt genetically determined. Although they may be modified in the case of individual animals, species survival depends upon adherence to them, and there is a tendency for the individual to "swing back into line" under appropriate conditions. The sparrow who learns the canary song pattern soon changes to the typical sparrow song pattern once it is exposed to other sparrows.

The nature-nurture problem has most frequently been put in terms of "how much nature, how much nurture?" For social psychology, at the present stage of development at least, how much one way or the other is neither the proper nor an answerable question. The essential question centers around the matter of adaptation adequacy. At the human level, although we may assume that there are particular patterns of interpersonal behavior that are more conducive to adaptation than others, it is difficult to determine what these patterns are. The criteria by which human adaptation adequacy is judged, however, are much more complex and obscure. To add to the difficulty of the problem, objective behavior itself must be interpreted in the light of subtle individual differences of impression and meaning. For example, we would agree that parental care is essential to the adequate development of the child, but overindulgence may produce personality inadequacies that will plague the child throughout his life, although such overindulgence may be viewed by the parent and the outside observer as completely adequate and proper behavior. The role that behavioral genetics plays in all this is obscure. While it is possible that certain human traits that are of great social adaptation importance are genetically determined, we can only wait for future research to discover the details.

Experiments and Controlled Observation

There are many cases in which experiments and controlled observations must be limited to infrahumans since the necessary manipulations and controls cannot be applied to humans. It would be impossible to isolate a human infant from all social contact and observe his development in order to compare it with that of a normally-reared child. It would likewise be impossible to produce brain lesions in humans in order to determine the neurological correlates of social behavior. And it would be out of the question to subject humans to various kinds of severe drug regimes in an attempt to further our knowledge of the biochemical correlates of behavior.

Thousands of studies directed toward these and similar problems have been conducted with the lower animals. Although it is often difficult to appraise the intrinsic worth of any individual study, the overall value of these studies is immense. From the standpoints of both individual and social behavior, there can be little doubt that early experiences have profound influences upon adult behavior. There is equally little doubt that the neurochemical condition of the organism is a significant determinant of behavior.

There have been many studies of the influences of early experiences upon later social behavior. For example, King and Gurney (1954) found that male mice that had been raised exclusively with other males were more aggressive in adulthood than males raised in isolation, but males raised with other males were no more aggressive as adults than males raised with females. In a study designed to throw light upon the beginnings of emotional behavior, Melzak raised puppies in a restricted environment (no visual contact with objects except other puppies), and others in a "normal" home-pet environment. When the experimental animals were tested for responses to emotion-provoking objects, they displayed diffuse emotional excitement in comparison with the control animals who typically avoided these objects. In adulthood, further tests indicated that the experimental animals were still diffuse in their emotional responses in contrast to the control animals which were much more aggressive. The experimenter concluded: "Well-organized experience in the environment in which emotion-provoking objects will appear is necessary for the emergence of adaptive emotional behavior such as avoidance and aggression." (1954, p. 168)

Another example of the importance of early experience upon adult behavior in lower animals is an experiment by Beach (1958). Male rats were isolated at fourteen days of age. At approximately ninety-five days of age, they were tested for sexual activity. Beach found that the isolated rats responded with adequacy comparable to animals that had been reared in groups. A similar study showed, however, that in guinea pigs early isolation had a retarding effect upon adult sexual activity (Valenstein, Riss, and

Young, 1955). Apparently certain early experiences may have profound and enduring effects upon adult life in one species and fail to affect adult behavior in another species in a similar way.

Careful observation of captive chimpanzees led Nissen to comment, "There is . . . a positive relation between the extremes of friendliness to man and a history of prolonged exposure to human contacts and little opportunity for chimpanzee company." (1951, p. 433) Köhler once wrote, ". . . a chimpanzee kept in solitude is not a real chimpanzee at all." (1925, p. 282) One chimpanzee that had been raised by a couple in their home for the first thirty months of its life was incapable of adjusting to other chimpanzees of the same age in a primate laboratory (Nissen, 1951). Observations of this type create the strong impression that social adaptation, even among the lower animals, depends heavily upon early social experiences, and lend support to the contention that early social experiences must be of even greater significance at the human level.

Another important line of investigation has dealt with the effects of brain extirpation on behavior. Loss of brain tissue in lower animals produces a loss in learning and problem-solving capacity roughly proportional to the amount of loss. It has also been shown that various aspects of social and emotional behavior in animals can be dramatically altered by removal of cerebral tissue.

Information obtained from studies of the lower animals may be used in a variety of profitable ways. One is the testing of hypotheses based upon observations of human behavior. In cases in which adequate controls can not be used, hypothesis testing at infrahuman levels is the only alternative. Literally thousands of such studies have been conducted. Experimental investigation of "critical periods" is a good illustration of this. It has long been suspected that during postnatal human development there are one or more times at which particular social experiences must occur in order for adequate personality development to follow. According to one theory (Huxley, 1961), unless the infant is given generous amounts of physically expressed affection, in maturity he will be deficient in the capacity for genuine affectional identification with others. Obviously this is not subject to direct experimentation at the human level. Next best is to experiment with the lower animals. Many such experiments have been conducted and several types of critical periods have been identified in different species. For example, experiments with dogs (Freedman, King, and Elliot, 1961) have shown the optimum time for socialization to be between 3 and 13 weeks of age. Through these studies it has also been discovered that unless puppies are handled by the age of 14 weeks they will never become docile with humans. Studies of this type so consistently point to the existence of critical periods of infrahumans that there remains little doubt about the existence of comparable socially significant mechanisms in man. The problem now is to identify them and to discover more about their requirements. In these ways, then, infrahuman studies are often of indispensable exploratory importance in the investigation of human psychological problems. (For further details concerning early experiences, see Chapter VI, pp. 126–130.)

A second and perhaps even more important contribution that infrahuman experimentation and controlled observation may make in furthering our understanding of human behavior and experience is that of furnishing detailed information concerning the many ways the lower species effect adaptation. The meaning of adaptation is, of course, far more complex at the human than at the infrahuman level. A biological criterion, which takes into account only efficiency in population stability and growth, is adequate for the lower species. At the human level, however, it is not. Although it is not the purpose here to describe a human utopia, we suggest that some such classification as Maslow's (1943b) five basic human needs—physiological, safety, love, esteem, self-actualization—points essentially to the human requirement. That is, a criterion, or set of criteria, by which human adaptation efficiency may be judged must take into account certain needs (e.g., love, esteem, self-actualization) which are, as viewed against the lower animals, subtle and most complex. At the human level we really do not know what these needs are; we still have neither identified nor described them. Until they are identified and adequately described, neither the meaning of "adequate human adaptation" nor the possibility of achieving it is feasible. By viewing the entire infrahuman animal kingdom from this perspective a base and a rationale are established for an adaptation appraisal of man. We are in no position to evaluate and understand ourselves unless we take as one of our fundamental perspectives the comparative view.

THE BIOLOGY OF SOCIAL BEHAVIOR

From the broadest standpoint man's social behavior is rooted in biology. For our purposes, there are three perspectives that help especially in viewing social behavior from a broad biological position: adaptation, genetics, and natural selection. Studies of infrahuman social behavior from these interrelated perspectives suggest some of the probable biological underpinnings of man's social behavior.

Adaptation

The history of the animal kingdom is one of anatomical, physiological, and behavioral adaptation to the physical and social requirements of the environment. Adaptive characteristics are easier to identify in infrahumans than in humans. For example, the howling monkey is anatomically well adapted to his treetop life. His tail, feet, and hands are beautifully designed for grasping—an ability essential to an arboreal life. This grasping propensity is so obvious and its use so characteristic to the species that the intimacy of the tie between anatomical fact and environmental limitation is striking. In man, on the other hand, the tie between specific environment and physical characteristics is seldom clear. Man is far more versatile and, though much less specific in his behavior, capable of adapting more or less adequately to a tremendous range of physical environments.

The behavioral traits of an infrahuman species are adaptive from the standpoint of species survival as judged by population stability and growth. For example, the honeybee may sacrifice herself when she stings the "enemy" but this act serves to protect the colony. On the other hand, certain genetically determined behavioral processes are of adaptation value in preserving the *individual member* of the species. Nursing behavior in mammals is of adaptive value to the young, to the mother, and to the species.

Since no two species are alike, there are innumerable examples of specific adaptively important behavioral characteristics and traits. Many of these are clearly social in the sense that the behavior of a given animal depends upon the behavior of other members of the species.

Starlings cluster together in flight when they are threatened by a falcon (Tinbergen, 1953). The falcon will strike only for a bird that is well on the periphery of the cluster. Were the falcon to swoop into the midst of the cluster, the great speed of his flight would result in injury to himself. Thus, the starlings' social-behavior trait of clustering is of adaptive importance for the species' survival, and the falcon's attack flight pattern is of individual survival importance. Were all falcons to dive into clusters of starling prey they would survive neither as individuals nor as a species. Starlings, as a species, would not survive were the group pattern not observed.

The "appeasement ceremony" of the night heron as a social-behavioral adaptation trait has been described by Lorenz (1952). When a night heron parent returns to the nest it raises its three thin, white plumes. After this ceremonial act, it steps down into the nest and proceeds with other brooding routines. In an experiment in which a parent's plumes were pasted down so that they could not be raised, the nestling young attacked the parent. The absence of the three raised plumes is a stimulus-signal releaser for attack, while their presence is a stimulus-signal releaser for parent acceptance. Such patterns of social behavior particular to a species have had, and many still have, survival and adaptation value.

Tinbergen (1953) has also experimented extensively with parent-infant feeding behavior. One of his most interesting descriptions is that of the feeding of the infant herring gull. The parent lowers its bill within range of the chick and the chick pecks at bits of food protruding from the bill. Tinbergen has discovered that the parent's bill must have a spot of orange-red in order to arouse maximum infant response. In one experiment, the chicks pecked only 25 per cent as frequently at a bill that had no orange-red spot as they did at a bill that had the orange-red spot. This behavior trait is obviously valuable to the individual species member and it may be supposed that this specific trait is necessary to species survival as well.

Grooming behavior in primates is another example of biologically-adaptive social behavior. It has definite biological utility; it frees them of skin parasites and is presumably the only means they have for keeping the skin clean. Grooming has been carefully studied in chimpanzees and has also been observed in such other primates as gorillas, gibbons, spider monkeys, macaques, baboons, and lemurs. Grooming behavior involves highly intricate hand-eye coordinations accompanied by lip-smacking. Grooming sessions often last for long periods, during which intense concentration is apparent. Some investigators have regarded grooming as the most truly social pattern found among the infrahumans and have been led to speculate about it as a phylogenetic forerunner of certain patterns of social cooperation in man. For our purpose, it serves as an excellent example of a behavioral trait that is both biologically and socially important.

Genetic Factors

Behavior traits that characterize a species seem to be just as much due to genetic make-up as are the characteristics of physical structure. Such behavior traits remain relatively stable under environmental change. Puppies can be house-broken and will observe the rules of their masters throughout their adult lives, but generation after generation of such training in the ancestors will not affect in the slightest the new puppy's inherited patterns of defecation and micturation. The environment may suppress or activate particular native behavior traits, but it neither creates nor stamps out native traits (Breland and Breland, 1961).

Species Survival. If a species possesses genetically-determined traits that permit it to adapt behaviorally to the conditions of the present environment, it will survive and propagate. If the genetic "storehouse" of that species does not contain the necessary behavior traits, adaptation will be impossible and it will not survive.

An interesting synoptic example of the importance of physical and behavior adaptation can be found in the lemurs. Fossil forms very much like modern lemurs have been found in North America and European Eocene deposits. Following the Eocene these representations disappear. Northern European and North American climates were chilling after the Eocene, and presumably these tropical animals were incapable of physiological adaptation to colder climates. Lemurs are found abundantly today on the island of Madagascar, a land area long separated from the African mainland. They are also found in tropical Asia and Africa, but are much scarcer in these areas than they are on Madagascar. Somehow, few flesh-eating animals were able to enter Madagascar. Since members of the civet family are said to be the lemur's only enemy on this cut-off land mass, the lemurs have adapted well. In Asia and Africa there is an abundance of predators with which the lemur is at a serious behavior disadvantage. Since the lemur is incapable of outrunning his enemies, organizing into social groups to overwhelm them by number, or hiding so effectively that predators cannot find him, his chances of survival are reduced. Even in a tropical climate, unless there is an absence of predators lemurs do not adapt well since the species does not possess those behavior traits that permit it to defend itself adequately (Romer, 1934).

The guinea pig has been described as an animal severely deficient in anatomical structures and behavior capacities equal to the environmental requirements of "modern animal living." (Scott, 1958) They are placid animals given to little but copulating and eating. They do not build nests, they dig no burrows, and care of their young amounts to little more than allowing the young to nurse. They are poorly equipped to fight, and their sexual behavior is extremely simple, almost devoid of courtship patterns. Man domesticated these animals to the point that they are common and the cultivated population is relatively large. The question has been raised as to how ancestral guinea pigs could possibly have survived in the animal kingdom. One hypothetical answer is that guinea pigs are well equipped to run and that they are most active at night. They were probably able to survive because enough of them were able to escape from predators by running efficiently in the dark. The behavior propensities for night activity and running have probably been the behavior traits that have permitted an adaptation at least adequate to species survival. It is interesting, too, that man has probably had a hand in the survival of guinea pigs as a species.

Although for ages man has done his best to destroy rats, the behavior versatility of these animals is so great that the world rat population is close to the world human population, and may even outnumber it. It is obvious that the genetically determined behavior traits of a species are of life-and-death importance to its existence.

Paleontology and Behavior Genetics. The ethologist and comparative psychologist are at a disadvantage when it comes to identifying the points in evolutionary history at which particular behavior traits appeared. The comparative anatomist can specify, with reasonable accuracy, the times at which particular structural features arose in the evolution of various animal forms. He can use paleontological evidence to trace lines of structural development and to identify with confidence the origins of newer structural features. But the ethologists and comparative psychologists have no such paleontological records. In the history of man there are, of course, records and artifacts which are of great importance in reconstructing the social patterns of man during the past few thousand years. But what of the lower animals? Very few of the traits that permitted survival and led to extinction can be reconstructed. Thus, most of our knowledge of the history of the behavior of the animal kingdom comes from secondary inference. The best sources of inference are paleontological information and behavior genetics.

Paleontology, the study of fossil plants and animals, has provided a storehouse of information concerning the structural characteristics of early animal forms and has greatly added to our knowledge of structural lines of descent in the animal kingdom. In many instances, prehistoric animals have been reconstructed so that fairly good "pictures" of body size, weight distribution, positions of muscles, characteristics of locomotion, dietary habits, brain size, body contour, and so forth are available. For instance, the LaBrea tar pits of California have provided many excellent specimens of flesh-eating animals. One of these is the now extinct saber-toothed cat, an animal about the size of a modern tiger or lion. This Pleistocene creature is best known for its great upper canine teeth, which have the appearance of sabers. It has been suggested that these canines represent an adaptation to the requirement of inflicting great slicing wounds into large, thick-skinned animals. When these large, thick-skinned animals (probably pro-boscidians) disappeared, the saber-tooth cat also disappeared. This prey was a necessary part of his environment, and without it, adaptation was impossible. It was not only the saber-toothed cat's structure but his behavior propensities as well, we may suppose, that led to his demise.

Paleontology provides us with many important and interesting facts, but at best they are fragmentary from the standpoint of behavior traits, especially social behavior traits. The intricate social clustering of the starlings under attack, the night heron's appeasement ceremony, parent-young feeding processes in the herring gull, and grooming behavior in the primates are all behavior traits that can be known and understood only by observing them. We cannot avoid the conclusion that comparable behavior traits were characteristic of primitive animal forms; we can only guess, however, about the behavior of these extinct animals. We are essentially dependent upon observations of living animals in order to understand the genetic nature of behavior traits and their adaptation values.

Behavior genetics provides us with important information concerning the stability of particular individual and social behavior traits. Together with the theory of organic evolution, the facts of behavior genetics clarify the mechanics underlying the distribution of behavior traits among the various species and within a particular species.

In an interesting as well as theoretically important series of experiments, for example, Tryon (1942) selectively bred rats upon the basis of their learning a 17-unit maze. After eight generations of breeding the "brightest" with the "brightest" and the "dullest" with the "dullest," there was virtually no overlapping between the groups in their error scores on the maze. This experiment shows that aptitude for a particular type of activity, in this example maze learning, is governed at least in part by genetic factors. Genetic factors have also been shown to influence traits of temperament and general activity. Such traits are often among the identifying characteristics of a strain or breed. Domesticated animals are the end products of selective breeding that has emphasized the particular traits desired by the breeders.

Recently many careful experiments have been conducted to test the effects that crossbreeding of pure breeds has upon various behavior traits. These crossbreeding experiments are the reverse of domestication; they represent "remixing" the genetic ingredients of a species. J. P. Scott has conducted experiments of this type on dogs. As he says, this species is ". . . a veritable gold mine of hereditary traits, having more variability in both form and behavior than any other domestic species, including man." (1958, pp. 117–118) In one series of experiments, Scott and his co-workers used cocker spaniels and African barkless dogs (basenji) as their pure-breed strains. Mendelian crosses were made in first-generation offspring. In turn, these were bred back to the parents in all possible combinations. Progeny were tested for behavior traits of many kinds and the behavior results were examined for degree of genetic determination. One of the temperament traits studied was that of timidity or wariness. The cockers were typically tame and lacking in wariness at age five weeks, whereas the basenjis were quite timid and fearful at the same age. The first-generation offspring were very much like their basenji parents with respect to timidity. Timidity at age five weeks is not only a genetic trait in the basenji but also a dominant one. Backcrosses of these hybrids to pure basenjis resulted in timid puppies again, but backcrosses of hybrids to pure cockers resulted in litters that were variable in timidity.

Natural Selection

One of the basic tenets of organic evolution theory is *natural selection.* In essence, this term abstracts the countless instances in which "nature" (the total environment) has "selected" particular physical-behavioral characteristics for survival and has "rejected" certain other characteristics. The many species of the animal kingdom are parts of the total environment. It seems reasonable to suppose that one of the principal reasons the proboscidians died out was that they became too easy a prey to the saber-tooth cats; and it can also be reasonably supposed that one of the principal reasons the saber-tooth cats died out was that there were no more proboscidians to eat. For the saber-tooth cats, no "lucky mutations" occurred to shorten their fangs. With shorter fangs, they might have been able to kill small animals and survive. "Nature" did not "select" saber-tooth cats for survival.

The environment in which a species develops and thrives does not remain stable. Many things may change—climate, vegetation, animal populations. One way a species may deal with environmental change is for particular members of the species to survive because they possess genetically determined traits necessary for survival in the new environment. It is to be supposed, for example, that in the early history of the basenji strain, those animals that were not wary were easy prey to predators, and hence were eliminated.

Although the environment does not directly produce specific species changes in either structure or behavior, it does contribute indirectly to such changes by producing genetic mutations. Mutations are direct changes in genes. Although much is still to be discovered about the causes of mutations, we do know that the rate of mutation production can be increased by temperature changes and by radiation. However, even man's control of those factors in the environment of a species will not produce predetermined mutations but only increase the number of random mutations in the species.

Mutations are mostly detrimental to adaptation. This is perfectly reasonable from the standpoint of probability theory. Since mutations are gene changes caused at least in part by chance environmental factors, the odds for a given mutation being the specific agent to assist in the adaptive relationship between a highly intricate organism and an equally intricate and specific environment are very slight. But once in a long while a mutation that is beneficial for adaptation does come along. Organisms endowed with such mutation-produced changes are thus more likely to survive.

Although artificial cross-breeding and natural selection are much alike, they are also very different in two respects. In artificial cross-breeding the breeder or geneticist takes the "gene bank" of a species and combines gene-determined traits in such ways as to produce animals with specific traits. This often can be accomplished in a relatively short time. Mutations are not involved in this process; the selective crosses are made between genetic traits that already exist. Thus, the trait variation is limited and the geneticist works within a set range of variability. In some species, such as the guinea pig, the variability is small; in others, such as the dog, it is great. Natural selection, on the other hand, is a long process—one that is going on constantly in nature but one that is so slow that it has seldom if ever been directly observed by man.

At the human level a new dimension enters the evolutionary process. Recently man has taken an active role in directing and controlling his own adaptation. Because man is capable of symbolic communication and has created a cultural legacy, he has been able to manipulate both the physical environment and the social environment in many ways. He has been able to adapt much of the environment to his own bio-psychological requirements. This is just the reverse of natural selection and it introduces problems which lie beyond the strict conception of behavior change as a function of organic evolution (Dobzhansky, 1962).

HUMAN AND INFRAHUMAN SOCIAL BEHAVIOR ANALOGIES

The tendency to anthropomorphize goes far back into man's history. Anthropomorphizing operates in either or both of two directions. Humans may perceive various of their own psychological propensities in lower animals, or they may perceive in themselves qualities which supposedly characterize certain of the lower animals. The "wise owl" exemplifies the former, and "Richard the Lion-hearted" the latter.

While no one can question the fact that many of the social behavior processes in man are analogous to those in various of the lower species, anthropomorphizing goes beyond the use of analogy. The anthropomorphic statement declares not only that the human and infrahuman processes in reference are in some respects similar, but that they are one and the same.

Comparative psychologists have borrowed the term *homology* from comparative anatomy where it is used to designate comparable structures in two or more species which can be traced back to a common ancestral form. For example, since the bat and the rat presumably arose from a common primitive mammal, their forelimbs are homologous. They are regarded as homologous even though they are very different in appearance, structure, and function in the two animals. On the other hand, since the bat and the mosquito arose independently, their wings are only *analogous* even though they permit both animals to fly.

The psychological use of the homology concept is more tenuous than its anatomical use because patterns of behavior are virtually impossible to trace back to common origins. In a few instances, however, behavioral homologies are evident. Infant nursing responses in bats, rats, and humans are homologous since the oral patterns in all three can confidently be assumed to have been derived from a common ancestral form. There are many instances of relatively restricted patterns of human behavior which are homologous with comparable patterns in other species.

C. Lloyd Morgan, the father of comparative psychology, was greatly concerned with the problem of homology, particularly as it relates to anthropomorphizing of the first type mentioned above—explaining the behavior of lower animals in terms of human psychological properties. He declared that, "In no case may we interpret an action as the outcome of the exercise of a higher psychical faculty, if it can be interpreted as the outcome of the exercise of one which stands lower in the psychological scale." (1894, p. 53) Although Morgan's Canon, as this statement has come to be known, has been used to support certain questionable views and interpretations, it represents a necessary caution for those who are interested in examining human behavior in the light of infrahuman behavior.

Morgan's Canon serves just as well to warn against the second type of anthropomorphizing—explaining the behavior of man in terms of the lower animals. If behavior patterns in lower animals are to be understood in terms of principals which are less complex than those required to explain analogous patterns at the human level, then it follows that an understanding of the variables which control patterns of behavior in infrahumans cannot necessarily be used to provide an understanding of analogous behavior at the human level. This conclusion is even more evident when we begin to examine complex patterns of socially significant behavior.

Among the many species of the animal kingdom man's social behavior is unique. This uniqueness rests upon a number of behavior emergences; that is, behavior and experience properties which appear at the human level only and for the first time. The presumption is, of course, that these emergent properties were the results of genetic mutations which were generally favorable to species adaptation.

Thus, complex categories or classifications of human social behavior must be studied in their own rights, and at their own levels, in order to be understood. At the same time, all such behavior classifications have their infrahuman analogues. Human social behavior may be better understood, we believe, by viewing it alongside and in contrast to infrahuman social behavior. Let us briefly examine a few of the more obvious and important analogies. If some are found to be homologies, not just analogies, we would be justified in looking to them at the infrahuman level as human prototypes which could assist us in understanding similar social processes at the human level. If we conclude that they are not homologies, we will still benefit by identifying some of the emergent properties in man which contribute to his unique nature.

Socialization and the Possibility of Culture

Socialization is defined as the process by which the young are trained by the parents or elders to behave in prescribed ways. The end result is that in maturity the young behave in ways that reflect such training. In most species parents give no indication of intending to train their young in particular ways; they do not plan, in the sense of conscious anticipation, the adult behavior patterns of their progeny. In man, however, there is very clear evidence that such planning is the rule, not the exception.

The fact that man does plan and consciously train his young in ways that are vastly different from family to family and from group to group demonstrates that *specific patterns* of training and adult behavior are not typical of the species. The ways in which subhuman primate mothers care for, nurse, and play with their offspring are stereotyped and set. A zoo-raised female gibbon cares for her infant in ways virtually identical with those of other gibbon mothers in other cages, in other zoos, and in the wild. This cannot be said for humans. Other things equal, if we know the infrahuman species we can accurately predict the mother-infant pattern. To know only that mother and infant are of the human species is of relatively little help in predicting the interaction pattern the mother will institute.

In Chapter I we drew a distinction between society and culture. Society, it was pointed out, implies a grouping of individuals that lasts longer than the life span of any single member. Culture implies something more. It is society, with the addition of transmitted ways of learned acting, believing, and valuing from one generation to the next.

If the transmission of learned ways of acting is used as one of the criteria for culture, then something analogous to this aspect of culture can be seen in certain of the infrahumans. Some of the best examples are to be found in certain species of birds. It is well known that the young of many species become imprinted by stimuli to which they are visually exposed. The longer the stimulus pattern is exposed to the young animal, the greater the imprinting effect. From this, it is not difficult to understand how the young of a flock come to follow their parents. When the parents take seasonal flight to another geographic area the young probably follow them because of their early imprinting. Along the way are land areas, bodies of water, and other signs that the parents have already learned to respond to as navigational aids. The young, it may be supposed, learn these too; and they probably learn to identify the area in which the flock settles for the season. Thus, learned patterns of migration and geographical habitation appear to be passed on from one generation to the next in some species.

Very tenuously, then, some might wish to support the thesis that certain of the lower species have cultures. Supporting evidence would be limited, however, to a few social-behavior systems such as territoriality and vocalization. That there is intention, in the human sense, would be next to impossible to demonstrate. But if the concept of intention can be forgotten, there do appear to be ". . . specific and restricted periods during which the stimuli which will thereafter evoke certain instinctive responses are permanently determined. After the critical period has passed, the environment cannot alter the nature of the effective stimulus." (Beach and Jaynes, 1954, p. 259) Upon these grounds, the unequivocal assertion that man has culture and the lower animals do not might be questioned by some. However, since there is no evidence at all to support the view that any of the infrahumans anticipate the future of the group with the intention of changing its future structure, the roots of culture do not seem to lie in any of the infrahumans.

At the human level there is clear intention to teach the young, as the history of civilization so amply attests. For thousands of years man has left written and pictorial records with the clear intention of providing patterns of continuity and transmitting knowledge to succeeding generations. Man alone has language, a communication capacity which is more than a mere signaling system; language transmits symbolic meanings and differs from group to group in structure and syntax. Thus, while it may be possible, with some imagination, to glimpse the simple rudiments of culture in a few of the infrahumans, only in man is there clear intention to organize group processes so as to increase the probability that what is anticipated will actually occur. Culture depends upon such an intention to mold the future as the individual, in consort with his fellows, would like it to be.

Socially-Important Motivation

There is an ancient theory that man develops and sustains culture only because he has "moral instincts"; that is, because he is motivated, at least at times, to do the right thing, to be altruistic to other humans. But there are similar views about the infrahumans. Folklore abounds with stories of the "noble beast." The "white dove of peace" is customarily looked upon by man as a "kindly" creature, motivated to demonstrate an altruistic way of life. One has only to observe its behavior to find that, on the contrary, it fully meets our human definition of viciousness and "immorality." Whenever we interpret infrahuman behavior in terms of human behavior, we are in trouble. We are, in effect, reading thoughts and values into the infrahumans that have meaning only at the human level.

Parent-infant relationships at the infrahuman level often seem to picture a version of human altruism. Provided there is no serious environmental or physiological disturbance, a mother cat performs the intricate parturition process without incident. Nest-making, delivery, umbilical-cord cutting, cleaning, nursing arrangement, retrieving, and all the attendant parturition patterns may be viewed as a most intimate and highly developed social process (Cooper, 1944). We have every reason to be profoundly impressed by such a complicated, socially-adaptive process without losing sight of the fact that its motivational origins are not identical with those at the human level. The feline motivation for these parturition and infant care patterns can be analyzed at an exclusively neurophysiological level. On the other hand, although neurophysiological involvements are by no means to be overlooked or under-rated at the human level, the motivational foundations of these behavior processes are clearly very different.

For several of the infrahumans, certain of the neurophysiological determinants of such complicated behavior processes have been identified. For example, Beach has demonstrated the roles of the hormones estrogen and progesterone in the control of sexual-behavior patterns in rats (1945). When a female rat that had displayed no sexual behavior patterns because she congenitally lacked ovarian tissue was treated with these hormones, her sexual behavior became normal. There is also some evidence to show that a variety of hormones can be used to induce maternal behavior in both female and male rats (Young, 1951). Another example is found in a description of a parturating cat whose lactation had not yet begun (Cooper, 1944). During the parturition this animal "cannibalized" the fetuses as they were delivered. The same animal displayed typical maternal behavior—nest-making, retrieving other adult cats and small, soft objects—once lactation had begun. Such evidence makes it reasonably clear that motivations for even these most intricate types of social behavior among the infrahumans are to be found in neurophysiological controls and probably very little in the cognitive controls that play such obvious roles at the human level.

In his analysis of social cooperation at the infrahuman level, Tinbergen (1953) has emphasized the importance of "releasers." A given animal displays a particular, innately-determined pattern ("releaser"), and another animal *of the same species* responds to it by another particular, innately determined pattern. This is reciprocal, interactive social behavior. Certainly, such specificity and stereotypy at infrahuman levels are striking in comparison with what is commonly observed at the human level. At the human level, the lines of control between neurophysiological events and behavioral events are by no means as clear. Maternal behavior cannot be turned on and off by glandular manipulation as it can in many of the lower animals. Humans perform vast numbers of social acts that the lower animals cannot. Humans teach each other in a great variety of ways. They have intention, agree, disagree, and kill each other over intention differences. Humans differentially develop complicated religious systems, esthetic practices, political institutions, courtship routines, and child-rearing techniques. We must include such cultural variables along with neurophysiological variables in our search for the sources of motivation at the human level.

We will have to look for most of the motivational origins of man's social behavior in his experiences. These experiences leave impressions that are brought into the present and projected into the future. Again, however, the study of infrahuman motivation is important from the standpoint of being able to see ourselves in relief, against a more diversified but less complex background. In this way we may be able to discover what is specifically human in human motivation and what is shared with the infrahumans.

Communication and Language

One of the most often discussed infrahuman-human analogies is communication. In the preface to his engaging book, *King Solomon's Ring,* Konrad Lorenz takes as his theme the biblical tale of King Solomon, who was supposed to have been able to talk with the lower animals. Lorenz says that he, too, can talk with animals, ". . . and without the aid of magic, black or otherwise." (1952, p. xiii) He points out that social animal species have signal codes and that these codes can be understood by men observant enough to learn them. Members of a species have a signalling vocabulary of sound and gesture that describes a present state, such as fright, or foretells a future act, such as courtship behavior. Lorenz goes on to say that the lower animals have nothing ". . . that could, even in a very wide sense, be compared with a language, for the very simple reason that they do not have anything to say. For the same reason, it is impossible to say anything to them . . ." (p. xiv) In these few words he summarizes the view of scientists who have carefully studied the problem that the communication and language analogy poses.

Vocalization is a commonplace among the lower animals. We might expect vocalization to become increasingly complex as we ascend the phyletic scale, but this is not entirely the case. Many birds and lower mammals have vocal patterns that are at least as complex as those of the highest nonhuman primates. Vocalization patterns of African lions, for example, have been classified into several types (Cooper, 1942); and we all know how spectacular, modifiable, and "imitative" the vocalizations of some birds are. Alarm cries, food discovery sounds, courtship calls, and so forth, have been identified in many species.

Several scientists have attempted to teach chimpanzees to talk. Chimpanzees are not limited by an inadequate vocal apparatus. Their ordinary vocalization is rich in phonetic elements, and observations of laboratory chimpanzees reveal that cage-mates carry on a great amount of vocal communication. Keith and Catherine Hayes (1952) have described many interesting instances of imitative behavior in a chimpanzee they reared in their home for four years. They report that it is possible to teach chimpanzees a few words. Such words have meanings and can be elicited by appropriate stimuli. Hebb and Thompson (1954) stress the point, however, that language is syntactic behavior. They take the position that true language employs not only intercommunication of representational symbols, but that it requires "the capacity to combine and *readily recombine* representative or symbolic noises (words), movements (gestures), or modifications of inert things (writing, carving)." (p. 538) Therefore, they conclude that language differs from simple, purposive communication in two respects. First, it "combines *two or more* representative gestures or noises purposefully, for a single effect; and secondly, it uses the *same* gestures in different combinations for different effects, changing readily with circumstances." (p. 539) They have gone on to theorize that although language is unique to the human species, there is probably a continuity between man and the lower animals insofar as the behavior capacities that make language possible are concerned.

It seems probable that language became possible when man had evolved to the point that his conceptualization was "liberated" from the immediate sensory environment. When it became possible for man to entertain memories of past events and objects, to anticipate, to imagine, to abstract essence, he was then ready to respond to conceptual events. Communication, as language, must have begun when two or more primitive men interchanged behavior (sounds and gestures) that referred to conceptual, classified events—events removed from the immediate stimulus world. Detour and delayed-response behavior, which evidence planning, as may be observed in chimpanzees, approaches a level that needs little more to become language.

Language is syntactic behavior that takes the form of vocalization and gesture. It necessitates the use of symbols and it is social in requiring another creature capable of like experience and behavior in order to be functional. Language is exclusively human. Communication in lower species is in many respects analogous to language in man. Since, however, it is only analogous, and not the same psychological phenomenon, the nature of language can be directly studied only in man. And since man's social behavior is so completely dependent upon language, the study of language is indispensable to the study of social man.

Leadership

Leadership has been defined in many ways. We are all so familiar with leadership that most anyone is ready with a "Leadership is when . . ." definition. But the fact is that there is great variability among the definitions offered by laymen. The psychological dynamics of leadership is highly complex and varies from one situation to another. Even though two instances of leadership may appear to be the same, the psychological variables responsible for them may be quite different.

Leadership is a social phenomenon. Two or more individuals are always involved. Leadership power may emanate from a single individual, from several equally potent individuals, or from several individuals who share unequal degrees of power. Individuals may be followers of the same leader in a given situation for widely different reasons.

Some fascinating examples of leadership are to be found among the infrahuman species. The most obvious are those in which one animal moves ahead and others follow. Naturalists and ichthyologists have described some symbiotic interspecies relationships that have at least the outward characteristics of leadership. The relationship reported between sharks and pilot fish is an interesting example. The small pilot fish stay close to sharks and guide them to their prey. It is interesting to speculate what evolutionary and learning processes may be involved in this relationship. It is quite possible that food reward was originally the factor that created this relationship and that genetic selection within the operation of natural selection brought about this interdependence.

Leader-follower patterns have been identified in many species. In flocks of sheep, older females are typically the leaders. Scott has described the basis for the leadership pattern in sheep as *allelomimetic,* which means "mutual" and "mimicking." (1958, pp. 170–171) The mother consistently calls the lamb and permits it to nurse. This mutualism is probably rewarding to both, and establishes tendencies for the mother to wait and call to the lamb and for the lamb to move toward the mother. When the lamb is frightened, it runs to the mother's side. The pattern is that of the mother moving away in her grazing, but attending frequently to the lamb. The lamb thus develops strong approach responses to the mother. Scott describes the development of an intra-flock leadership pattern as follows: A female gives birth to twins, a male and a female. In line, the female follows the mother and the male follows its sister. The following year both mother and daughter give birth to one lamb each. Now the older mother is followed by her new lamb; the new mother comes next, her lamb following her, and the old mother's son brings up the rear. Such patterns are said to be characteristic of the species, and wild herds of red deer in Scotland seem to be organized along the same lines, the older females leading the others (Darling, 1937).

Information on leadership among the infrahumans in their native habitats is sketchy. We are accustomed, of course, to flights of birds that maintain great precision in formation; but the lead bird's characteristics and its dependence upon the followers is not understood. It is probable that imprinting plays an important role in such social behavior.

Karl von Frisch (1950) has provided much information concerning the methods by which bees communicate the sources of food. Part of this social behavior might be interpreted as leadership. The essentials involved include the release of an odor that attracts and excites others, and then a "dance," the characteristics of which provide other bees with "data" that will lead them to the food sources. In the sense that these responses instigate particular responses in other bees, the entire process may be thought of as leadership. Notice, however, that in this instance the other animals are responding to cues that were provided by a "leader"; in flight they have no leader to follow as a present stimulus.

In the human species, males are much more frequently in leadership positions than are females. However, the complexity is so great and cultural variation so vast that any attempt to specify a typical leadership pattern or hierarchy would be not only inaccurate, but worthless. At the human level, leaders are not always followed voluntarily. Some leadership patterns depend on dominance; the stronger push the weaker around. Particularly in small groups, the physical placement of the participants is no indication of the reasons one leads and others follow. Fear of reprisal can be as potent as actual physical force in maintaining a leader-follower relationship. Only if the interpersonal dynamics of such a relationship is known can it be stated whether the relationship is "pull" or "push" leadership. Since the lower species are almost all totally limited to response to the immediate environment, the "push" dynamics would be expected to follow a different pattern at the infrahuman level.

The "push" dynamics in social relationships in lower species has been studied considerably. It is referred to as dominance. The dominant animal, in some way, determines the behavior of another. In this sense, the dominant animals play the role of leader and the dominated animal plays the role of follower.

The development and interaction of dominance hierarchies in flocks of birds have been investigated quite carefully and from several standpoints. Lorenz has described the interesting "rank-order disputes" in jackdaw colonies (1952). In contrast to domestic hen flocks, in which the top dominator pecks at any and all below her and the lowest is set on by virtually all above, jackdaws respond principally to those just above and just below. In a hierarchy of ten, for example, the bird in position number five will dominate number six and be dominated by number four. According to Lorenz, birds in positions five and ten would show neither significant dominance nor submission toward each other. However, the highest-ranking bird will often interfere in a "heated argument" between two birds of lower status, and his aggression is greatest toward the higher ranking of the two combatants.

The dominance hierarchy of a flock of five white leghorn hens has been described by Collias (1951). The despot of the flock had "free pecking rights" with the other four. The hen next to the top had such rights with the other three, and so on down to the most subordinate animal, which was observed to peck another only once. This behavior is most frequent at feeding time and is an obvious factor in the distribution and availability of food. In the sense that the behavior of certain animals in such a hierarchy seems to be prescribed by their positions in the order, these relationships have some qualities of leader-follower relationships.

Interesting dominance-subordination relationships have been observed in captive African lions (Cooper, 1942). One example is found in sex behavior. In copulatory sessions, the female is the aggressor. The male's behavior is always at the invitation of the female. Between copulations the male stays on his guard and avoids the female. The female's activities give the impression of unpredictability, and her attacks upon the male are frequent. The entire pattern is one of dominance-submission. And although the male's behavior is vigorous and highly patterned, it gives the striking appearance of response to leadership stimuli.

Animal handlers sometimes form lion cub groups of ten to twenty animals, including both sexes, at about five months of age. Very soon thereafter dominance-subordination relationships appear. The dominant cubs are usually larger and male. Dominance sometimes takes the form of feigned coitus which is directed toward both sexes. Dominance is also shown at feeding time, when animals are separated into individual cages. The dominant animals push through the runway gate first; the subordinates take later turns. Tail-chewing and sucking behavior is another dominance outlet. Specific relationships have been observed in this behavior. In some instances a given animal "permits" only a certain other animal to chew his tail. He, in turn, may simultaneously be chewing on a third animal's tail, who, in turn, is chewing on still a fourth. Instances of physical restraint in tail-chewing have been reported. A smaller animal may be cuffed and pulled into position if it tries to free itself from the tail-chewing ceremony.

Social behavior in chimpanzees has been studied from many perspectives. One of the most interesting and important is that which views relationships between individuals in an attempt to discover the factors that determine dominance. One of the best-known students of chimpanzee behavior, Yerkes, has described many social situations in which leadership is a function of the dominance, one way or another, of one animal over another (1941). By contrast with species lower on the phyletic scale, chimpanzees' establishment of dominance is much more variable. This might be expected since chimpanzees are highly developed in comparison with lower primates and in many respects begin to approach the human behavior level.

In commenting on a series of observations that he made of chimpanzees in pairs, Yerkes concluded that sex status is not the determiner of dominance, since ". . . individuality seems more influential than traits of masculinity or femininity in shaping expressions of natural dominance." For example, when the female of a pair is sexually receptive, she may become dominant, though she is ordinarily subordinate at other times. During her sexual receptivity period the female chimpanzee literally employs prostitution for purposes of gaining dominance status. As Yerkes said, ". . . prostitution is a natural development among such highly adaptive and intelligent animals as the primates." (1941, p. 196)

In summing up the factors that are of greatest importance in the establishment of dominance-submission relationships in lower species, Collias specifies ". . . fighting, bluffing, or passive submission at the initial encounter between individuals or during an early series of such encounters." (1951, p. 392) He also lists a series of specific characteristics that can effect an individual's establishment of dominance in the initial encounter: greater maturity, maleness, familiarity with the territory, assistance from other animals, high rank in the home group, inexperience with other dominant animals, experience in winning fights, evidence of fear or lack of aggressiveness in the opponent, size, endurance, skill, good health, and endocrine balance.

Among insects, dominance-subordination relationships within a social organization seem to be mainly determined by native, relatively unmodifiable characteristics that determine the roles the members of an organization are to play. Higher on the animal scale, especially among the birds and mammals, these roles seem to be determined much more by social-learning factors. This introduces another interesting and important factor; namely, individuals within a colony must learn to recognize each other. Tinbergen has studied and reported on many instances of the amazing capacity for recognizing individuals within various infrahuman organizations. He comments that ". . . this power of discrimination is often amazingly acute; many birds, for instance, recognize their mates, or their chicks, or their social companions, at a glance, when the ablest human observer fails. . . . It may be that each species shows the best achievement when distinguishing between individuals of its own species." (1953, pp. 108–109)

The establishment of dominance-submission roles seems to be more and more dependent upon learning as we ascend the phyletic scale. In accordance with the information provided by Collias, it seems justifiable to conclude that certain types of exchanges among individuals are particularly potent learning situations for the establishment of dominance-submission behavior patterns. It is not difficult to translate this construct to the human level if the additional degrees of complexity are not neglected. This seems to be one good example of a human-infrahuman analogy that is more than a surface similarity. This is not to say, however, that we have found a true homologue.

It is conceivable that the roles humans play in their complex social organizations may be better understood in the light of information gathered from various of the infrahuman species. The techniques by which roles are set within lower species' societies may be a clue to an approach that might help us at the human level. Whether a leader-follower relationship is the result of "push" or "pull" tactics, the end result is a social process of practical consequence. At the human level we have strong admiration for certain types of leadership and we condemn other types. To understand the dynamics of all types is the concern of the behavioral scientist. Much of the mystic aura that seems to cloak leadership phenomena can be removed by examining leadership from the standpoint of interpersonal learning experiences.

Infrahuman Attitudes

Another human-infrahuman analogy is that of attitudes. It is a commonplace that a given species is friendly while another is characteristically vicious toward humans. Some dogs are friendly toward certain people and quite withdrawn or bellicose toward most others. Thus, within a species, there may be striking differences among individuals with reference to their behavior toward other living creatures. For example, an adult female Siamese cat, used by one of the writers in an observational study, was notorious for her belligerence toward dogs and all other cats and for her extreme fondness for all humans. She would attack on sight the largest dogs and rub against and purr for any human, stranger or not.

Attitudes are to be thought of as *sets,* readiness for action toward particular classes of stimuli. Some of these sets are native, and no amount of training will change them. Some are built into the individual species member by the learning process. At the human level, of course, we operate on the assumption that all social attitudes are learned. Although it is possible that some human social attitudes are natively determined, there is no substantial evidence to support the possibility and the learning assumption is generally accepted.

Attitudes of infrahumans are inferred by humans and infrahumans from human and infrahuman experience. In commenting on chimpanzees' behavior as described by the caretakers, Hebb and Thompson say, "The behavior is often very puzzling to the caretaker, but when he names an attitude or motivation with confidence it is generally a dependable guide to the animal's future behavior." (1954, p. 545) The discernment of the caretaker has been toward two sets of variables—behavior samples and stimulus situations. When these consistently correlate, the caretaker makes a prediction that they will correlate in the future. He infers that the animal has a set to respond to a particular class of stimuli in a particular way. As they point out, in chimpanzees ". . . history seems crucial always." What the chimpanzee *is prepared to do* when confronted by particular stimuli is his attitude toward those stimuli. Past conditions of learning have made the chimpanzee ready to respond at the moment of stimulation. For better or worse, he needs not reexamine and retest the stimulus situation. He is set, ready to go.

Social psychologists have spent great effort in the attempt to specify the meaning of and to measure social attitudes. This effort has been almost entirely at the human level, and little use of the infrahumans has been made even in developing the concept of social attitude. Social psychological interest in the social-attitude concept stems from the desire to predict behavior and to understand the development of the individual's unique psychological nature. If the individual's attitudes toward certain classes of stimuli are known, the accuracy of prediction of future behavior will be increased. If the experiences that lie behind attitude formation are known, the individual may be understood more adequately as a psychological unity. Although from the standpoint of prediction, knowledge of an individual's attitudes is of great value and is probably the best guide we have, it cannot be used blindly. There are many instances in which behavior does not follow attitude. Though an individual may possess a particular attitude, his behavior may often be out of line with it. Attitude and behavior need not coincide. This is particularly true at the human level.

Many times both negative and positive attitudes are inhibited from conversion into action for long periods; but once the proper situation develops, the overt aspect of the attitude comes out. This is amply documented at the human level; it may also be found, though less often, among the lower animals. To illustrate, a lion trainer had worked with a group of lions for three years, starting their training when they were about six months old. Using whip and pole as threat props, he maneuvered the lions into various formations and stunts. Always he faced them and observed their individual activities with calm studiousness. One day during training he stepped backwards and tripped over a stool. Before he had fallen to the ground all the lions were attacking him. The configuration of the situation had been sufficiently changed to remove the inhibitions that had up to then prevented the "attitudes" of these animals toward their trainer to issue into overt behavior.

As we descend the animal scale, the possibility of keeping attitude and overt behavior separate becomes smaller and smaller. For example, a given species of snake is natively equipped to strike at specific targets. This is a native "attitude" and it issues into overt behavior invariably. The correlation, in this case, between "attitude" and overt behavior is positive and perfect.

The converse is encountered as we ascend the animal scale. Leaving the lower forms, in which "attitude" and overt behavior are dependent upon particular native behavior patterns and virtually independent of learning, we encounter more and more behavior and attitude divergence. As with language, man can remove himself from the immediate stimulus situation by way of thought, and communicate his impressions of the past and the future while responding adequately to the present stimulus situation. Although no other species can attain this level of disassociated psychological association, some of the higher primates give indication of approaching it—only the syntactic use of words is missing. A very close psychological relation between man and a few of the higher infrahumans is represented by attitude formation and attitude-determined behavior.

Among the higher infrahumans, attitudes toward other species members and toward humans are readily developed through learning. These attitudes issue into overt behavior at certain times and not at other times, depending upon the total social-physical configuration. The cowering dog is inhibiting his threatening gesture toward the cornered cat when his master is standing close by with a club. His "attitude" toward the cat has not changed, but his behavior is a function of a greater stimulus configuration than just a cat; there is also a severe threat stimulus present.

In summary, attitudes are to be conceived of as sets for action toward various classes of stimuli. At lower levels on the animal scale, little learning is involved. At the human level, it appears that all social attitudes are learned. And in addition, as will be described in Chapter XI, prejudicial attitudes seem clearly to be endemic to the human species. This virulent type of attitude is so complex that only man with his enormous nervous system is able to develop and use it. Prejudicial attitudes, the most complex and highly developed type of attitude, can tell us much about the capabilities of man as distinct from those of even the highest nonhuman primates.

Social Behavior Disorganization

The history of human society is replete with instances of behavior disorganization. The term "behavior disorganization" may be defined as a breakdown in social organization in such ways that certain individuals or large groupings suffer because of the predacity, ignorance, or psychopathy of other individuals or groups.

If we return to our earlier discussion of the evolutionary perspective of the animal kingdom, we are reminded that every species exists as a function of its capacity to adapt. So far as is known, all extant species depended, in part, upon stealth for development and survival. If we look at man and his relationships with lower species this picture still holds.

Man domesticates lower animals for a variety of reasons—food, pleasure, transportation, worship, protection. He sometimes hunts lower animals, again for a variety of reasons—food, sport, and so forth. He also expends great effort toward the extermination of various of the lower species since certain of them constitute dangers and annoyances. It is obvious that man, as a species, interacts intimately with many other species. Much of this interaction amounts to interspecies warfare, and in this sense, social disorganization is frequently introduced into various lower animal groups.

The early popular interpretation of the evolutionary concepts of *survival of the fittest* and *struggle-for-existence* which pictured the various species, as well as the individuals within each species, as constantly pitted against each other in deadly combat was greatly overdrawn. Allee makes the point that while these principles may be interpreted as having survival and adaptation value, taken together they represent the counterpart of another survival and adaptation principle—*cooperation*. Both the struggle to survive and the necessity to cooperate are fundamental biological principles that ". . . penetrate all nature" and ". . . have acted together to shape the course of evolution. . . ." (1951, p. 177) It should be pointed out that cooperation in this sense is not to be equated with cooperation at the human level, since at the human level cooperation involves several psychological variables not found in the infrahumans.

Within a given species, the interplay of these two factors, struggle and cooperation, is frequently in clear evidence. Lorenz has described certain of the signal and response mechanisms that are used to preserve cooperation and prevent struggle from erupting into wholesale slaughter of the species. For example, he describes the sparring, prefighting behavior of dominant and subordinate timber wolves. Eventually, when the subordinate has been maneuvered into a corner, both animals become rigid, ". . . the older wolf has his muzzle close, very close against the neck of the younger, and the latter holds away his head, offering unprotected to his enemy the bend of his neck, the most vulnerable part of his whole body!" (1952, p. 186) The two animals may stand in this position for some minutes, but so long as the subordinate presents his neck in this submissive position, the dominant animal responds to this signal by inhibition; he does not bite into this vital point. One is "top dog" and the other is "under dog." Here is a social mechanism that has survival value not only for the individual but also for the species. In such instinctive social behavior patterns struggle may also be viewed as cooperation.

It is surprising to some to learn of the small amount of fighting that goes on within certain species known for their ferocity. Among captive lions there is much less fighting than is ordinarily supposed. Although the introduction of a new adult to an established group is ordinarily followed by a group attack upon the new animal, it is usually able to break away and run to the other side of the enclosure, at which point the fight is broken off. It is also interesting to note that serious fighting almost never occurs in close quarters. If two strangers are housed in one small cage, they growl and show patterns of hostility, but they seldom break into destructive fighting. If these two strangers are released into a large enclosure, actual though probably nonlethal fighting may follow. Running room makes escape and the consequent establishment of dominance possible. Such a social mechanism is obviously important for both individual and species survival.

The balances within and between species that make individual and species survival possible are varied and intricate. Such balances are often, if not always, dependent upon relatively unchanging patterns of social organization. These patterns no doubt are genetically determined, having been produced through evolution and at every step of the way having played an important adaptation role. While probably many species have become extinct as a result of inadequate social organization patterns, there seems to be no evidence which points to the extinction of a species as a result of intraspecies *breakdown* of social organization.

An example which superficially approximates intraspecies social organization breakdown is found in lemmings. Every few years these rodents leave their home territory in great droves and migrate. There seems to be no particular pattern to these panic-like mass migrations, except that the lemmings stay close together and travel forward without regard either to water or to land obstacles. The result is that the animals die in vast numbers. The most plausible hypothesis for these migrations is that when population density within the confines of their burrows becomes excessive, animals come under severe stress since they are constantly forced to come in contact with so many other unknown animals. Such stress leads to certain severe physiological changes, such as enlargement of the adrenal glands. When these physiological imbalances reach a given point the mass migration begins and the home burrows are virtually deserted. Apparently a few of the older lemmings remain, and again begins the process of rebuilding a new population which eventually will grow to overcrowding and another mass migration. Thus, while lemming social organization breaks down at a given point and disorganization in the behavior of most of the colony members results, this very process of social disorganization may be interpreted as a built-in social mechanism which actually permits species survival (Scott, 1958, Deevey, 1960).

In other cases interspecies imbalances may lead to breakdown in social organization to the point that members of a given species occupying a given territory are reduced to virtual extinction. In areas where deer hunting has been prohibited and hunting of such predators as mountain lions has been encouraged, severe imbalances have sometimes occurred. With such protection from predators deer increase to the point that the food supply will not support the population and starvation results. In addition, reproduction decreases since semi-starved animals are reduced in sexual behavior. With the population so severely limited, the few that survive must eke out an existence until vegetation has replaced itself. After this, a limited and slow social process of rebuilding the herd begins. Other things equal, the size of the herd will eventually reach and remain at a level which the food supply will support. What seems to be social disorganization is, from a long range standpoint, an important means of adaptation.

At the human level the meaning of social organization and disorganization is dynamically different. Man develops culture, and individuals who are reared in a particular culture ordinarily use the values and practices of that culture as constant frames of reference. The learned patterns of a human come to be as fundamental in his living as the natively determined patterns of any of the infrahumans. In this sense, learning is the most significant determination of response in man. Any normal human is so docile, so subject to modification as a result of his social experiences, that he may even become a virtual isolate in the midst of others. A social group may, by way of common learning, come to be distinctly out of line with surrounding social groups. For example, in the United States there have been instances in which small, tightly-knit groups of people have organized themselves polygamously. Majority groups have always created difficult problems for these small polygamous groups and the small polygamous groups have usually moved on into new territories in order to escape persecution. But their migrations have never been totally successful. The body politic has followed and forced them to abide by the rules of the monogamous majority. From the majority standpoint, not only is monogamy adopted as moral and right, but polygamy is regarded as immoral social disorganization. Thus, human social disorganization, real or imagined, is seldom tolerated, even if it exists in faraway places.

Within a human family, one person may become so deviate in his behavior that he brings suffering to the others. Within another family learning opportunities may be so limited that constant physical and psychological conflicts result and are perpetuated. In still another family, interpersonal patterns may be such that a member "escapes" into the larger society and brings trouble and suffering to strangers. These are examples of social disorganization which is a function largely of the individual's behavior.

One nation bent on subjugating a weaker nation attempts to create and perpetuate social disorganization in the weaker; but inadvertently it does the same to itself as well. International warfare is the ultimate in social disorganization. In war, man uses his most creative talents in a highly social way to foment social disorganization by means that include human destruction. Social disorganization is the goal in war (Cooper, 1955a).

At the human level there is much cognitively directed interest in others. When there is behavioral or ideological deviation within the group such interpersonal interest is often converted into attempts to bring the deviator into line to require him to conform. The tendency to impose conformity on others is so strong in man that conflict often results. Many in our culture are convinced that some form of egalitarianism is the best basic pattern of human social organization. On the other hand, there are those who regard some form of totalitarian organization as best. Those who support one of these positions look upon those who embrace the other as advocates of social disorganization. The potent human tendency to bring others into line often leads to violent overt conflict over the issue of social organization patterns themselves, and this represents overt social disorganization.

The dynamic controls of human social organizations are very different from the essentially genetic controls that determine the social organizations in any of the infrahuman species. This unique type of social organization conflict, so evident at the human level but so clearly absent in the lower species, is possible only through culture and learned adherence to cultural patterns.

The criteria by which the adaptation efficiency of a human social organization is correctly judged are very different from those we use in correctly judging the adaptation efficiency of infrahuman social organizations. The basic reason for this difference is that man alone among all the animal species is capable of planning his social future. As Dobzhansky (1960) has put it, ". . . man is the only product of biological evolution who knows that he has evolved and is evolving further." (p. 7) Adaptation efficiency must always be judged in light of the behavioral capacity of the species. In an attempt to make any comparison between humans and infrahumans with reference to social disorganization, we must keep in mind the fact that overt acts of aggression, dominance, and destruction, which are indexes of social disorganization in human society, are native adaptation patterns in many of the lower species. No prototype of human social disorganization is to be found at the lower animal levels.

Higher Order Phenomena

Finally, what are the possibilities of discovering higher-order phenomena among the lower species? By higher-order phenomena are meant such psychological processes as esthetics, humor, religious experiences, and the quest for understanding. At the human level, quite obviously, they are of limitless social importance.

Gardner Murphy poses this question: "Is it not possible that because we are complex creatures we have drives which result from our complexity?" (1954, p. 616) Higher-order phenomena must be thought of not only as the results of complex neurophysiological systems but also as the results of socially-determined motivation. Man alone seems motivated to be esthetic, to create wit and perceive humor, to worship, to seek understanding.

Esthetics refers to those processes that result in the creation of stimulus patterns that may produce affective, intellectual, and imaginative experiences in the creator and in at least some of those who perceive the created stimulus pattern. The best known esthetic areas are poetry, the graphic arts, and music. Folklore abounds with tales of the literary, artistic, and musical talents of many of the lower animals. We have all heard anecdotes about dogs, monkeys, and other animals that responded to music in interesting and curious ways, but we have yet to be furnished with any scientific evidence that identifies either the creation of or response to tonal patterns in any of the infrahumans as meeting the criterion of esthetics. The singing of birds is principally set by genetic factors and does not incorporate the characteristic of creativity that is so common at the human level. Certainly, no lower animal has created anything literary. The spider's web may provide the stimulus for esthetic experience in humans, but it does not indicate creativity or esthetic receptivity in spiders. The argument that we do not know that lower animals do not create or experience esthetically because we cannot talk with them does not stand up. Since there is no evidence in support of the thesis that any of the infrahumans either create or experience esthetically, we are bound to conclude that esthetic processes are emergent at the human level and unique in man.

Play behavior in various of the infrahuman species is quite suggestive of humor and wit at the human level. However, it is only suggestive. The complex psychological involvements of humor and wit are yet to be comprehended by an adequate theory. When a dog is startled by another animal in play he may crouch, wag his tail, bark, run in circles, threaten by a nip, and carry on a variety of patterns that are socially reciprocal. It is possible to view these response patterns as socially intentional in the sense that they produce erratic behavior in another animal. At the human level the "banana-peel fall" usually produces laughter in others, whether intentional or inadvertent. Slapstick is often said to be "a natural" since it so characteristically produces laughter in others. The unexpected startles both human and infrahuman. If the startle is in a nonthreatening motivational context, the response may be emotionally pleasant. It is tonic and pleasantly experienced. The playful antics of the dog may possibly fit this description. It is, at least, a possibility. If there is any validity in this possibility, then perhaps the prototype of wit and humor may be glimpsed at the infrahuman level. Some are of the opinion that one of the characteristics of mammals is that they all play with their young. This does not mean that human wit and humor developed out of such possible infrahuman processes. It means only that the basic wit-humor process may be more pervasive than we commonly believe. Most germane to the human level of wit and humor is that which involves symbolic communication and recording. Here man definitely departs from the lower species. The symbolic character of wit and humor at the human level merges so intimately with esthetic experience and creation that we are on safe ground when we deny the existence of symbolic wit and humor to all species except man.

Religious experience and behavior seem most definitely to be purely human phenomena. Religious processes differ vastly from human community to human community, though there is a common core of meaning. Religiosity involves several psychological variables including time perspective, faith in intangible power, and a feeling of need to perform ritualistic acts. Among the infrahuman species nothing resembling these behavior variables has been identified.

A final higher-order phenomenon, which has all the appearances of being characteristic only of humans, is the quest to understand. Interesting examples of inquisitiveness in lower animals immediately come to mind. Rats often investigate alternative maze pathways even though they are thoroughly familiar with the shortest route to the food box. Monkeys frequently sit and observe objects and moving stimuli for long periods of time. Butler and Harlow (1954) have shown that monkeys can be taught to perform visual discriminations when ". . . the only reward was that provided by visual exploration of the surrounding environment." This is only to say that the drive to explore the environment is what we commonly refer to as curiosity. Lower animals, as well as man, explore their environments and become familiar with their surroundings. In the broadest sense, the drive to investigate seems universal, but to organize information systematically is a unique phenomenon.

While there is no way categorically to know whether or not investigatory behavior was preliminary to what we call the quest to understand at the human level, man's psychological evolution undoubtedly passed through such a stage, and man did not give it up when he moved on to a more complex level. Ontogeny at the human level reveals an early stage in which the child seems to be motivated to explore, to learn everything possible about his environment. He does not, at this stage of development, demonstrate what we think of as a desire to understand. It is worth noting that a desire to understand seems never to develop in some humans. This arrest in development seems confined mostly to the feeble-minded, though there are normally intelligent persons who demonstrate the desire to understand so little and so infrequently that it is tantamount to absence.

The quest to understand, like language, brings us to the highest level of psychological organization. It involves generalization, symbolic manipulation of traces in the absence of direct stimulation, and motivation to know that which lies back of stimulus phenomena. Certainly, only man at a post-childhood level of psychological maturity is capable of this sophistication.

A Psychological Approach
to the Problem
of Human Nature

Most great writers and students of human affairs have paid considerable attention to the problem of the nature of man. Although their points of view have differed greatly, there has been agreement on one point: what man is like is a most important problem.

Theories of human nature are more than recondite fancies. They are of concrete importance in influencing the affairs of men. There is the vague but active theory, for example, that all humans fall conveniently into two great categories, the good and the bad. Those who subscribe to this theory treat other humans in ways that reflect it. Taken together, the many theories of human nature reduce man to a "psychobiological inkblot." Since each human being tends to picture all of humankind in the light of his own experiences and expectations, human nature is all things to all people.

Were we called upon to describe canine nature we would find it difficult to agree upon a common set of characteristics. One person might insist that dogs are clean, intelligent, loyal, and brave. Another might claim that they are dirty, stupid, treacherous, and cowardly. Such discrepancies could lead an observer to conclude that two different species were being described. By turning the tables, it is a common observation that dogs respond to humans as though the nature of man were not a unitary, stable composite. Man is obviously many things to many dogs. To some dogs all men are objects of fright or rage; to others some men are to be feared and others to be approached with affection; to still others man has no nature.

The fact is that theories of the nature of man are constructed by men of diverse experience. At the same time, it is reasonable to suppose that some theories are more valid than others. A theory which accounts for the greatest number of dependent variables is, from the standpoint of science, the best theory.

CLASSICAL THEORIES OF HUMAN NATURE

Until very recently most theories of human nature have generally adhered to the principle that man's social behavior is to be understood solely as a function of his membership in the human species. A brief review of four classical theories of human nature will help in appraising the efficiency of this approach.

The Judaic Theory

In the Book of Genesis we find a description of man's origin and the basic characteristics of his nature. According to this account, man was created in the image of God. He is essentially different from even the highest beasts, since he alone has a religious nature and an affinity with God. He is spirit, soul, and body.

Spirit is the part of man that permits him to have knowledge, ties him to his spiritual creation, and gives him his consciousness of God—his religious nature. Soul is the part that gives him his self-conscious life and his emotions and desires. The term "heart" is often used synonymously with soul, and in this sense conveys the meaning of "the psyche" or "the individual." Body is the physical part, and makes possible soul and spirit consciousness of the outside world by way of the sense organs.

God endowed man with a variety of privileges and duties. He was directed to "multiply and replenish the earth" and to exert power over all other living things. When man disobeyed God's injunction not to eat from the tree of knowledge of good and evil, he learned about good and evil. This introduced the problem of ethics by burdening man with the responsibility for choosing between good and evil.

In the Biblical account of original human nature there is, of course, great detail and symbolism. Although theologians are in dispute on many points, the essence of the account is to be found in the following items: Man was formed in the image of God, the essence of good. Man disobeyed God and permitted Satan's (evil) tool (serpent) to teach him about good and evil. Man was forced constantly thereafter to struggle between good and evil. Still, by atonement and labor he may forsake evil and choose good. His soul may thus be saved, even though his body is condemned to return to the dust from which it was made. This relatively precise account of man's origin, limitations, duties, and possibilities has exerted an omnipresent influence on Western values and conduct.

The Platonic View

In his dialogue the *Republic,* Plato described the "perfect" state. The kinds of men found in society are determined in large part by the nature of government. For example, in a democracy we should expect to find greatest variability since a democracy affords maximum freedom.

Plato inferred that what an individual customarily does constitutes his nature. He did not, however, accept the thesis that whatever the individual's present behavior disposition is like is either good or in line with the basic nature of man, since a good man is the image of the perfect man. Governments are the images of individuals; but governments are evil when the images from which they are made are distorted and out of key with the true nature of human nature. Were it possible to discover the true nature of man, then a state could be created that would be in man's likeness, and such a state would be good.

According to Plato, human nature has three basic components: appetite, courage, and reason. Every human is composed psychologically of these three elements, but they appear in different proportions and degrees in different individuals. Appetite is the trait characterized by desire for goods, food, material possessions. Courage is a spirited, emotional, power-in-self trait. Reason describes those desires that seek truth, knowledge, and understanding.

Since these are basic components of human nature, a society can develop one or another and neglect or deflate the others. Usually the appetitive or the courageous have been developed. Since the most animal-like characteristic is the appetitive, this has tended to overpower the others. But the appetitive can function effectively only if the courageous is brought into play in order to obtain and make secure the objects of man's appetite. With this, the spirited has often taken over so as not only to combine the appetitive with the spirited but to become an objective in itself.

The perfect society, according to Plato, is a republic in which an aristocracy of intellectuals rules and directs the activities of the appetitive and courageous classes of men. The perfect society is the perfect expansion of the perfect man.

Plato's theory of human nature has probably influenced our civilization more than any other insofar as the design of government is concerned. It is explicitly clear. This is not to say that it is an adequate theory, but it is one that has had great influence on modern political thinking.

Hobbes' Utopia

Another well-developed classical theory of human nature is that of Thomas Hobbes, the British philosopher. Hobbes was a political philosopher, and in his description of the good state he felt obliged to say something about the units that compose the state.

According to Hobbes, man is a self-seeking, power-hungry creature who, in the "natural state," destroys himself because he continually wars with others over material things. Man can survive only if he establishes a compact with others whereby there is general agreement to respect each other's rights. This compact can be enforced only by a sovereign.

The essential point for our purpose is that Hobbes developed a theory that described man's nature as evil. Since men live in groups and almost never in isolation, the "state of nature" must be altered for the sake of survival. According to Hobbes, human nature is not only imperfect, it is socially bad. There is much more to Hobbes' psychological theorizing, though the need for a strong state—personified in a monarch with the divine right to govern—essentially explains the view he took of the original nature of man.

Rousseau's Theory

Still another classical theory is that of Jean Jacques Rousseau, who lived about a century after Hobbes, but who had philosophical interests that were in many respects similar to those of Hobbes. However, Rousseau's view of human nature was almost the diametrical opposite of Hobbes'.

Rousseau's thesis was that man is by nature "good." It is society, the state, that is corrupt; and the state corrupts man. Man's natural qualities of virtue become distorted, overlaid, and subjugated. Whereas Hobbes began with the thesis that man is so driven to seek power that only by way of a social compact with a strong sovereign can he survive, Rousseau began with the assumption that man is by nature good and were it possible for him to throw off the chains of society and "return to nature" he would live happily. It was Rousseau's contention that the true determinant of ethical behavior is emotion, not reason. Thus, for Rousseau, man is best suited to relative social isolation.

MODERN PSYCHOLOGICAL APPROACHES TO THE STUDY OF HUMAN NATURE

The Need for an Adequate Modern Approach

These four theories demonstrate the point that man's nature, what he is really like, is at least in part phenomenal. That is, the same object is perceived and interpreted by different people in different ways.

One reason for the wide discrepancies in these classical theories is to be found in the personal views these scholars took of society. Each pictured for himself a society to his own liking. For example, Hobbes was an apologist for royalty and closely associated with British aristocracy. A strong monarch could provide him with the ways of living he had learned to enjoy. It is not difficult to see his theory of human nature as a support for the type of society he wanted. On the other hand, Rousseau was an impetuous man, resentful of societal curbs and restrictions. His plea for emotional rather than rational control, and his disdain for the organized state, described his view of the good life. He, too, seems to have pictured human nature as it best fit the type of society he wanted. It cannot be denied that the modern scientist who examines human nature and then attempts to develop a theory of human nature is also biased. However, those aspects of the problem of human nature which the scientist chooses to investigate and the interpretations he gives to his findings are determined more by the rules of empirical evidence than is the case with any other approach.

Again, the practical side of the problem lies in the fact that such socially important phenomena as opposing political and economic doctrines are frequently supported by *ad hoc,* loose, nonempirical theories of human nature. There is little reason to believe that one such theory is more valid than another. But once some theory of human nature is accepted it has much to do with the program a politician pursues, the ways a business executive treats his employees, the attitudes of a teacher toward his students.

For purposes of historical perspective and present social orientation these classical theories are of immense importance. However, as far as providing comprehensive and valid understanding of the nature of human nature, they are virtually useless. Unfortunately modern psychology has not as yet replaced these classical theories with a completely adequate modern theory. Of course, there are those who take the indefensible position that a theory should never be exposed as inadequate or invalid unless the critic has a better theory with which to replace it. On the contrary, it is perfectly reasonable and valuable to recognize and point to the flaws in a theory without being able to offer an adequate substitute for it.

Modern social psychology actually had its inception in the quest for an adequate theory of human nature. And today much of what is new in psychology can be found in its unique approach to the study of human nature. Anyone can construct a neat theory of human nature if he bases it upon a small, homogeneous sample. But, as we have seen, such limited theories fall short when they are called upon to account for behavior and experience which lie outside the homogeneous samples upon which they are based. The "new look" at human nature which modern psychology has provided is essentially a scientific examination of the obvious; obvious, that is, to the layman. For example, the layman may accept it as obvious that all humans are equally motivated by an acquisitive instinct and, indeed, many economists and industrialists use this "obvious fact" as the supporting psychological basis for a given political-economic system. The given political-economic system may be a good one—but not because man is instinctively acquisitive, because there is now evidence that he is not. Rather than being determined by species-specific variables, behavioral science has shown that the motivation to acquire is learned under certain conditions of social reinforcement. A proper, information-producing question about human nature is not, "Is man acquisitive?" The answer to this is both "yes" and "no." Rather, the question needs to be, "What produces acquisitive behavior in an individual?" This is a question that will elicit information about the social behavior of any individual. It is the type of question the scientist must use in addressing himself to any problem since the information it seeks provides understanding of the dynamics which lie beneath and are responsible for observable events.

The greatest difficulty in attempting to develop an adequate theory of human nature is that man must do it himself. Things human seem so obvious to most of us. As Asch has said:

The fact that we belong to the subject matter we are investigating may, although helpful, hamper the perception of problems and blunt our sensibilities for the scientific task. The danger is precisely that facts of human action and experience have a self-evident character before inquiry has begun. (1952, p. 7)

Unique among the many approaches that have been used in seeking an understanding of human nature is the modern psychological approach. It amounts to two things: First, new kinds of questions about "the obvious" have been posed. Second, answers to these questions have been and are being sought through the logic and methods of science.

As we will see, modern psychological excursions into the problem of human nature have not all fared well in providing answers as to what human nature is. On the other hand, they have at least all provided us with useful information with reference to what human nature is *not*. This may be taken to mean that modern psychologists did not all at once begin asking the proper questions. Their questions have been significantly better than the classical question, however, and the questions asked have continued to improve. While it is true that the end of the psychological search for the true nature of human nature is still not in sight, there is ample reason to believe that we are today standing in a better position than ever before to examine the problem.

Twentieth Century psychological approaches to the study of human nature have not all adhered to a common program. As we have said, however, the questions have become more comprehensive and more answerable. Today, instead of trying to define human nature, psychological interest has turned to developing a new perspective of human behavior and experience. This new perspective also comes from asking a question. Figuratively, the question is: Where must we stand in order to identify the variables responsible for an individual's behavior and experience? As Asch has suggested, familiarity with ourselves and those close about us tends to blunt our perceptions and render those things that are actually most complex and obscure seemingly obvious. In view of this, a vantage point which lies outside self and away from pedestrian intimacy with others needs to be sought. From such a vantage point this new perspective is possible. What we begin to perceive is a human organism whose behavior and experience are functions not alone of the nature of his species classification, but also of unique genetic characteristics and variable outside stimulus agents.

The remainder of this chapter will briefly examine a small sample of modern psychological approaches to the problem of human nature, and will conclude with a somewhat more comprehensive examination of a contemporary research perspective which, as we have suggested, seems to be the most fruitful for the present stage of psychology as a science.

Instinct Theory

One of the best-known and most influential modern psychological theories of human nature is the elaborate system known as "hormic psychology," developed by William McDougall (1931). McDougall emphasized the conative, striving, goal-seeking nature of man. Since man's striving is mediated by certain instincts, human nature can be understood as a "functional mosaic" of instincts.

McDougall described instincts as native, pattern-like behavior processes that display three attributes—cognitive, affective, and conative. From time to time he changed his listing of the major and minor instincts; for instance, at one time he listed twelve in all and at another time as many as twenty. One of his lists of the major instincts or propensities, as he later termed them, included: flight, repulsion, curiosity, pugnacity, self-abasement, self-assertion, parental, reproduction, gregarious, aquisition, and construction. Instincts are not simple reflexes, nor are they inborn mechanisms of a "pushbutton" design. They are defined and described by the goals toward which they impel the individual. Certain fundamental human goals are to be reached—one way or another. These goals are determined not by the individual, but by the nature of human nature. It is thus a teleological endowment; that is, man's behavior is determined by a universal purpose. It might be said that McDougall's view was that man's destiny is born within him and that his instinctive properties make its fulfillment possible.

McDougall's instinct doctrine is untenable today because, among other things, it overemployed deductive procedures. He envisaged a wanting, striving human creature supported and sustained by a universal purpose. He presupposed certain goals, and then sought to describe the instincts that would permit man to achieve them. Since any universal teleology such as this represents speculation that cannot be tested by the methods of science, it has no place in science.

For another thing, the instincts really amount only to words used to explain behavior. Holt commented on this point as follows:

. . . man is impelled to action, it is said, by his instincts. If he goes with his fellows, it is the "herd instinct" which actuates him; if he walks alone, it is the "anti-social" instinct; if he fights, it is the instinct of "pugnacity"; if he defers to another it is the instinct of "self-abasement"; if he twiddles his thumbs, it is the "thumb-twiddling" instinct. Thus everything is explained with the facility of magic-word magic. (1931, p. 4)

Still another reason for rejecting instinct doctrine was that the various instincts were thought of essentially as unrelated systems, as relatively isolated "motors." This interpretation is supported by McDougall:

. . . an instinct, no matter how profoundly modified it may be in the developed human mind as regards the conditions of its excitement and the actions in which it manifests itself, always retains unchanged its essential and permanent nucleus; this nucleus is the central part of the innate disposition, the excitement of which determines an affective state or emotion or specific quality and a native impulse towards some specific end. (p. 77)

Thus, the individual's behavior was thought to be controlled and directed by a mosaic of discrete, innately determined response tendencies.

In spite of these criticisms, McDougall's theory is not to be dismissed lightly. His influence upon psychology during the second and third decades of this century was compelling and great. He opened up and exhausted a particular approach to the problem of human nature and we have learned much from his bold and exhaustive excursion.

Without doubt, McDougall's insistence upon the importance of motivation will be of lasting value to the main body of psychological theory. And it is this feature that was really most basic in his system. This emphasis upon the importance of motivation in human life may be extracted from his system without accepting the restrictions of his instinct doctrine. He stressed the idea that human organisms are natively endowed with motivational resources and that human behavior is a function of these resources. The essential difference between McDougall's view and the view that seems more in line with present knowledge is that whereas McDougall found the sources of man's motivation in a set of teleologically determined instincts, the current view is that man's motives are essentially determined by socially reinforced learning.

Feral Man Approach

Another modern approach to the problem of human nature has been through the study of *feral man*. The term *feral* means "wild" or "untamed." Interest in collecting information about feral men centers around the ancient and still widely held belief that underneath it all there is a real human nature, which can be discovered by examining man in the raw.

Throughout the years there has been a growing body of stories about children who have supposedly been abandoned at an early age and nurtured into adolescence by wild animals, or who have somehow managed to survive on their own. Since these children have not been distorted by human social learning, so the argument goes, they represent the best examples of "true" human nature. Of course, humans learn whether they abide with beasts or humans. Thus, these stories represent neither true social isolation nor absence of learning.

A collection of such tales by travelers, missionaries, and primitive historians, was compiled by R. M. Zingg (1940). From these descriptions he identified the most common behavior characteristics. The suggestion is that these characterize the basic nature of man. Principle among these were mutism, quadrupedal locomotion, keen specialized senses, modified food preferences, no desire to clothe the body, emotional modifications, and lack of gregariousness.

The value of this approach to the problem of human nature is to be questioned on two grounds. First, the conditions under which the data were collected were not controlled. Second, these reports are presumably descriptive of individuals in isolation. They would, even if accurate, be distortions of the nature of man since humans are social creatures.

Further, in a critical evaluation of the Zingg report, Wayne Dennis (1941) has pointed out that these feral children may have been abandoned by their parents and, by chance, survived for brief periods until found. Since the reasons for abandonment may have been physical defect or feeble-mindedness, there is reason to question the proposition that these cases represent normal creatures even from the physiological-anatomical standpoint.

Denial Approach

Still another contemporary psychological approach is to deny the existence of human nature in the traditional sense. This, of course, contrasts sharply with both the instinct and the feral man approaches. The best representative of this approach is J. F. Brown, who suggests that there is no such thing as *original* human nature.

Brown's argument runs as follows:

> One may well say that there is no such thing as original human nature, that
> the age-old quest for a definitive list of traits common to humans as humans
> is a hopeless quest for constants which do not exist. If by human nature one
> means . . . *the necessary forms of human reaction for each concrete and mo-*
> *mentary field structure,* the concept may be saved. It is, I believe, not worth
> saving because historically it has always been used to refer to certain constants
> in human behavior. (1936, p. 273)

His contention stems from the historical fact that almost all those who
have tried to describe human nature have classified certain socially significant behavior processes and called such classifications "human nature."
Brown's argument is that such listings are nothing more than descriptions
of behavior under particular social conditions. If these conditions are
changed, the same social acts do not necessarily occur. Also, observed
behavior is not a specification of human nature; any behavior process is
only an instance of the limitless resources of human capacity. Queener
makes the same point with a slightly different emphasis when he asserts,
"It will not be difficult to show innate responses in man, but it will be
exceedingly difficult to show *socially relevant* innate responses." (1951,
p. 45)

In other words, the universal human responses—e.g., pupillary reflex,
sneeze, planter reflex, emotional startle pattern—are not socially relevant
responses. Those response patterns that are socially relevant are so variable
from human to human that they are not to be mistaken as indexes of a
set and rigid human nature. It seems much more reasonable to view
socially relevant behavior as a function of past experience operating in a
presently unique field situation, than to view socially relevant behavior as
the function of a precisely set, predetermined, universally stereotyped
human nature.

Though Brown prefers to throw out the age-old human nature quest,
he is still faced with the problem. In reality, he is arguing only against the
questions and methods that traditionally have been asked and used. Elsewhere Brown agrees that man does have unique and identifying characteristics. He is a unique psychobiological creature. But he is not to be
characterized by some *a priori* list of behavior traits that are familiar only
to the experience of one or another theorist.

Brown's argument has had an important impact upon more recent
attempts to deal with the nature of human nature. Lists of things humans
do most frequently under a given set of circumstances do not describe the
basic nature of man. Such lists only give us the probabilities for the occurrence of these acts under similar circumstances. Actually, as Brown has
pointed out, the behavior possibilities of man are almost limitless.

Cultural Relativism

From the standpoint of trying to answer the question, "What is the nature of human nature?" *cultural relativism* has had an important influence on the current thinking of social psychologists. The main thesis of cultural relativism is that human behavior is to be understood and evaluated in terms of the culture of which the individual is a part. Cultural relativism tends to reflect, if not completely to accept, the doctrine of social determinism which holds that the individual's socially significant behavior is determined completely by cultural variables. This was a reaction to early individualistic doctrine which held that social as well as nonsocial behavior can be understood by studying the individual under carefully controlled, socially uncontaminated, individual isolation conditions. Once the characteristics of the organism in isolation are understood, so the argument ran, then these principles can be used to explain man's social behavior as well as his native reflexes. The reaction to this was a cultural relativism psychology, a "social psychological revolution" which used the new-found wealth of anthropological information as its ammunition.

Careful examination of individualistic human nature theories, such as instinct theory and feral-man theory, led to the sound conclusion that man's psychological nature is not simply a function of his membership in the human species. This being the case, where should the psychologist look for the independent variables? The "logical" place to look, in keeping with the ancient nature-nurture dichotomy, was in society itself. This source of information, mainly cultural anthropology, indicated that man's behavioral and experiential variability is so immense that he can believe anything and do almost anything. Eating habits, child care procedures, sex practices, work habits, aggression techniques, virtually all patterns of human social behavior differ in innumerable ways from culture to culture. Although anthropological evidence does not tell us what human nature is, it does emphasize the fact of human social behavior diversity. It indicates clearly that there are no set, restricted patterns of behavior that spell out what human nature is, and that socially significant experience and behavior are functions of an amazingly resilient biological creature who is significantly shaped and modified by the culture of which he is a part.

Any current appraisal of cultural relativism as sound psychological theory must admit that its influence upon contemporary social psychology has been conceptually healthy. One of its significant contributions is that it has forced social psychologists to recognize the fact that an ethnocentric psychology violates one of the cardinal rules of scientific method, which is that the study sample upon which understanding is claimed and predictions are based must be representative of the referent universe. On the other hand, the psychological use of relativism has given disproportionate attention to content; that is, too much attention to what people do and too little attention to the variables responsible for how such things are done. The relativism emphasis has really tended to wash out the very problem the science of psychology has "commissioned" itself to study. As Littman has said,

> For a while, indeed, we were so impressed by the enormous differences among societies that a complete psychological relativism seemed to own the field. Now, however, balance has been restored, and we can see that relativism was with respect to cultural contents: we have salvaged for our study the rather abstract, general, psychological properties that characterize all humans, just as we have begun to find those which are characteristic of mammals and of vertebrates. (1961, p. 233)

The proper position from which to study the psychological nature of man lies on a continuum between two poles (Asch, 1952). At one end is individualistic doctrine; at the other is extreme cultural relativism. Individualistic doctrine rests upon the assumption that behavior emanates from an essentially autonomous individual who may be understood by studying his psychological properties in and of themselves, without reference to changing outside stimulus conditions. The instinct theory of human nature is based upon this position. The doctrine of extreme cultural relativism rests upon the assumption that the variables responsible for individual behavior are to be found in society, and that the individual's behavior is to be understood as a reflection of society. The denial approach is an example of the relativism position.

Direct Psychological Approach

The rigorous and truly psychological approach to the study of human nature, lying as it does between these extremes, follows a more difficult program since it is based upon the assumption that an individual's behavior and experience are functions of variables from all along the continuum. For want of an adequate label we will term this the *direct psychological approach*.

This approach begins with the thesis that man is biologically unique, and by virtue of this is capable of experiencing and behaving in ways that are unique in the animal kingdom. Man's unique nature incorporates three characteristics that are of special psychological importance. First, man is more structurally-functionally complex than any other animal organism. Second, man is unique since at the human level we encounter certain behavioral and experiential emergences not found in any of the infrahumans. Third, man's behavioral and experiential variability, both individually and species-wide, is vastly greater than at any other phylogenetic level.

In light of these three characteristics—complexity, certain emergences, variability—the direct psychological approach is a theoretical formulation that represents a stage in the development of social psychology as a science. It represents an organization and theoretical integration of relevant psychological knowledge. In this sense, then, it can be thought of as a consolidation of the past and a program for the future. The question for social psychology now becomes: In order to further our understanding of human nature, upon what problems should social psychology focus?

A CONTEMPORARY PSYCHOLOGICAL FOCUS ON HUMAN NATURE

From the standpoint of a direct psychological approach, social psychology is in a position to examine the experiential and behavioral nature of man with a new focus. In other words, today we have a clearer conception of what we are searching for.

With reference to any dimension of socially significant behavior—such as susceptibility to rumor, competitive behavior, sexual outlets, need for identification and affiliation, social ideology, social attitudes—humans are in many ways alike and in many ways different. As we have seen, any restrictive theoretical approach that purports to provide an understanding of human nature in terms of set, species-specific behavior variables common to all members of the species is inadequate.

The principal reason for the inadequacy of such an approach is that it misinterprets the significance of the data upon which it focuses. This misinterpretation results from the fact that the focus itself is inadequate. For instance, it is a common observation that most of us spend much of our time in groups and that most of us seek the companionship of others. McDougall referred to this as "gregariousness" and then posited an instinct to account for it. What was the inadequacy in his focus? Essentially, his focus should have been broadened to include the full range of gregarious behavior. Had this been done he would have observed great variability from individual to individual and from situation to situation. Such an independent variable (instinct of gregariousness) could not account for the vast fluctuation in the dependent variable (differing manifestations and amounts of gregariousness). From the standpoint of setting a new focus, the important point to observe here is that this type of theorizing disregards the atypical; it looks to the central tendency of any behavior system or pattern as "that which man is supposed to do." Often laymen and even professional psychologists have exalted central tendencies in behavior and sanctioned them for emulation. This traditional approach has tended to follow a circular pattern: (a) focus upon behavior outcomes that appear to be most typical in a given population, (b) claim understanding by positing a species-specific agent (such as instinct) as responsible for such a typical pattern, and (c) base predictions of future behavior upon such an imaginary independent variable (actuarial prediction).

Kurt Lewin went to the heart of the problem by showing that this traditional approach not only had focused upon the available data inaccurately but had misclassified relevant variables as well. To use the last illustration: we may call close human association gregariousness, if we like. This only names a behavioral central tendency, however, and does even this only in the sense that superficially there is a similarity from one to another instance of "togetherness." As Lewin puts it, this is an instance of classifying behavior ". . . on the basis not of purely psychological characteristics but of more or less extrinsic ones . . . so that particular cases having quite different or even opposed psychological structure may be included in the same group." (1935, p. 68) Thus, two or more instances of observed behavior may be conveniently classified into a single category because they have the external appearance of similarity, though psychologically they may be very dissimilar.

Lewin used the biological terms *genotype* and *phenotype* analogically in an attempt to clarify this important psychological distinction (1935). By phenotypic data he meant directly observable behavioral events, such as rats running in mazes, chimpanzees stacking boxes, and humans making speeches. By genotypic data he meant the underlying psychological determinants of observable behavior. Anderson describes the psychological distinction as follows:

A genotype is a homogeneous context of factors, either simple or complex, that produces effects which may differ widely; a phenotype is a classification in terms of the homogeneity of end results, which may have arisen from very different origins. (1946, p. 10)

This distinction serves as a caution for those who seek to equate psychological objectivity with inanimate-physical objectivity. As Lewin has said, *"Objectivity* in psychology demands representing the field correctly as it exists for the individual in question at that particular time." (1946, p. 793) Failure to draw this distinction will invariably result in an inaccurate focus on the psychological problem. In effect, then, this means that there has often been some confusion concerning the proper subject matter of social psychology. Again, as Littman says, "And the reason for all this is that the main areas of social activity are only the *place* where psychologists study interesting sorts of things, rather than being the *focus of inquiry.*" (1961, p. 236)

The genotypic-phenotypic distinction is by no means easy to maintain. But, if behavior is always determined by a "field of forces," then for purposes of psychological investigation it is necessary to represent the "field of forces" as it exists for the individual. From the standpoint of social psychology this is only recognition of the fact that the motivational-perceptual field of any individual is unique. If we are interested in understanding the individual's socially significant behavior from a psychological standpoint, we are obliged to study not just the simple end result of an involved psychological process but the earlier phases of the total process as well.

For the sake of convenience and in consonance with the logic of science, it is essential that the independent-dependent variable distinction be maintained. In the study of experience and behavior this is at best difficult and always arbitrary, since any designated behavior is but an arbitrarily isolated "slice" taken from a "life space" continuum (Lewin, 1935). If A and B are running down the street, one after the other, observers may disagree with reference to both the independent and dependent variables involved. Some of the more obvious possibilities are: A is afraid of B, and B is angry with A; B is imitating A; A and B are independently trying to break a foot race record, and so on. In order to understand the behavior of B it would be necessary to know the true nature of the independent variable (actually, a variable complex) involved. The easily observed dependent variable is "running"; but how is it possible to determine what we have called the independent variable? Any simple descriptive statement about the independent variable, such as one of those suggested above, would, of course, be incomplete. That is, it would not contain all of the elements of the total independent variable complex. However, provided the statement is correct, as far as it goes, it designates part, and perhaps an important part, of the total independent variable complex. Whatever the case, the independent variable—perhaps B's desire to imitate A—is genotypic; and, as Lewin has said, an accurate representation of the individual's psychological field at the particular time is essential if we are concerned with psychological objectivity. The direct psychological approach to the study of social behavior is properly that of examining behavioral sequences in depth—studying what cause leads to what effect. Viewed this way, the "cause" is the independent variable, and "effect" is the dependent variable.

One of the most important parts of the independent variable complex (to follow our illustration, the genotype) is the individual's "phenomenal world." This refers to the individual's perception of his total situation at a given time. Emphasis upon the importance of the individual's world as perceived by the individual himself has been stressed by many contemporary social psychologists. It has become clear that the way an individual perceives a pattern of social stimuli will not necessarily be determined by the objective nature of the stimuli themselves as measured by physical instruments. Of course, there are genotypic factors other than the individual's phenomenal world which enter into the independent variable complex in the determination of behavior. However, the components of the individual's phenomenal world are of such specific social importance that social psychologists are giving increasing attention to procedures and techniques for their assessment.

The phenomenological approach begins by the psychologist asking himself a very simple, direct question: What does the individual perceive? MacLeod describes it well in the following statement:

> By the phenomenological method, as applied to psychology, is meant the systematic attempt to observe and describe in all its essential characteristics the world of phenomena as it is presented to us. It involves the adoption of what might be called an attitude of disciplined naïvete. It requires the deliberate suspension of all implicit and explicit assumptions, e.g., as to eliciting stimulus or underlying mechanism, which might bias our observation. The phenomenological question is simply, "What is there?", without regard to why, whence or wherefore. (1947, pp. 193–194)

Phenomenological descriptions involve two types of information: content and structure. Content refers to what is perceived. Structure refers to the way in which the content is organized. Content and structure are, of course, psychologically interactive, and cannot be studied independently. To return to the example of A and B running down the street, one after the other: two observers may have very different perceptions of this event —their phenomenological fields may differ significantly. For instance, one may perceive B as imitative while the other may perceive him as angry. In this case, although the two observers' phenomenal contents are quite similar, the structures of the content are very different.

To date no technique has been devised which will provide completely adequate phenomenological descriptions. There are, however, certain techniques that have been used with some success. Techniques range in complexity from the extremely simple that provide impressionistic descriptions to the extremely sophisticated that provide quantitative indexes. Obviously the goal of any technique designed to provide phenomenological information is to provide understanding. Classified according to the purposes for which phenomenological information is sought, there are two categories: *reconstruction* and *prediction*. In general, the simple, impressionistic techniques are used in attempting to *reconstruct* the subject's phenomenal world so as to picture the psychological forces responsible for some phase of past behavior. On the other hand, quantitative techniques are more useful when the aim is to *predict* future behavior. It is important here to note that such prediction is not actuarial in nature; it is based upon genotypic rather than phenotypic data.

In the following brief descriptions of some of the techniques used in procuring phenomenological information, no attempt will be made to classify techniques according to the two categories: reconstruction and prediction. It will readily be observed, however, that the choice of one technique over another will depend in part upon the use to be made of the data. For instance, "verbal reports" are often quite helpful when the purpose is that of simple reconstruction of the subject's phenomenal field at a given time in the past. On the other hand, if the purpose is to predict how an individual will behave in a given situation at a later time, then a more comprehensive, quantitative technique, such as a measure of "level of aspiration," might be indicated.

Verbal Reports and Observed Behavior

The ideal approach to assessing the phenomenal fields of individuals might be that of asking subjects to describe their motives and perceptions. However, there are many reasons for regarding verbal reports with suspicion. Subjects may lie; or they may not be able to report what they perceive, what they want, or how they feel. In spite of these obvious and severe limitations, descriptions individuals make of their phenomenal worlds may frequently be of considerable value. Woodworth cites the following example:

If we ask a person why he is going out he may report, "because I feel thirsty and I know where I can get a drink." He is reporting a motive for his "instrumental act" of going to a certain place. There is certainly no reason for rejecting this introspective report as untrustworthy. (1958, p. 9)

Verbal reports are sometimes considerably more useful than other types of data in understanding and predicting behavior. Smith, Bruner, and White have illustrated this point with the following example:

There is a possibly apocryphal story about the selection of officers for duty in the tropics and in the arctics in which the whole gamut of projective psychological tests and physiological measures was employed, along with a brief questionnaire that included an item on the candidate's preference for one or the other climate. According to the story, the only item that correlated with the later performance was the preference item. One can infer much about a person by letting him tell what he likes, what moves him to action, what he is like. (1956, p. 281)

In addition to, or in place of, using verbal reports, the psychologist may attempt to construct or approximate an individual's phenomenal field by making inferences on the basis of observed sequences of behavior. In attempting to achieve understanding by way of sequential observation the psychologist attempts to reconstruct the individual's phenomenal world; that is, as the individual perceives his world. Ideally, this phenomenological view would consist of a detailed description similar to that actually experienced by the subject. This, of course, is never completely possible, since no one can actually "get into" another person's psychological world. Hence, the observer can only approximate the individual's view by making inferences on the basis of observed sequences of behavior.

There are many classical examples of social psychological studies of behavior sequences that have led to inaccurate conclusions because they have failed to consider the importance of phenomenological data. Asch (1952) has written convincingly on this point in his evaluation of the famous 1928 Hartshorne and May study of honesty. These investigators observed and tested children in a variety of situations in an attempt to determine whether or not honesty is a general personality trait. They found that correlations between honesty scores on their various tests were uniformly low. From this they concluded that honesty is not a general trait; that in order to rear an honest child it is necessary to provide honesty training in each type of situation he will encounter during his life. Asch pointed out, however, that two children may behave in the same manner for very different reasons. One child may be honest because he is afraid of being caught, and another may behave honestly simply because he isn't sufficiently interested or involved in the outcome to cheat. Obviously, from a psychological point of view the situation is quite different for these two children, and the common behavior (honesty) is based on quite different determinants. Asch has made the following comments:

> What is the central difficulty? In the interest of objectivity and exactness the investigators have selected a particular (because easily measurable) act which is the end result of a psychological process. Without regard to the source of the act in each individual's thinking and motives they have proceeded to identify all acts that are externally alike. They have short-circuited the questions of major psychological interest, namely, what did this situation mean to the given child and what forces determined his final action? It would have been permissible to proceed in this same manner if prior investigation had established that the act investigated has the same psychological meaning for all. Although the quantitative procedure had the appearance of exactitude, it missed what was of significance. (1952, p. 63)

The Predictive Importance of Phenomenological Information

Many studies have illustrated the predictive importance of phenomenological information. In one such study (Cooper, 1955b) college students were asked to describe in writing a controversial political event as objectively as possible; they were instructed to conceal their own biases in order to prevent coloring their descriptions of the event. Following this they were asked to indicate their political preferences. At a later time other subjects were asked to read these descriptions, identify the political preference of each author, indicate their own political preferences, and evaluate each description in terms of its objectivity. It was found that each description was evaluated as objective by about half of the judging subjects and biased by the other half. There was, in other words, no general agreement concerning the objectivity of the descriptions. However, when each subject's guesses as to the political preference of the writers and the subject's own political preference were considered, a different picture emerged. It appeared that once a judging subject had decided upon the political preference identity of a writer, he considered the description to be objective only if he believed the writer shared his own political preference. In other words, if a Republican subject judged a given writer to be Republican, he considered the description objective. It was also found that even though the writers were asked to make their descriptions objective, they were unable to do so; the judging subjects were able to identify at a significantly better-than-chance level the political preferences of the writers. This study indicates quite clearly that even a little knowledge about an individual's social perceptions can be of considerable help in understanding the psychological nature of observable behavior.

Phenomenological data may, of course, be of little or no importance in understanding simple, reflexive behavior. A beam of light directed into the eye is followed by a reduction in the size of the pupil. This does not vary for people with normal vision, and the sequence may be predicted without error. The stimulus activates a central neurological circuit that, in turn, directs efferent impulses to the iris muscle. The iris muscle is then stimulated to contract. In this case the neurological circuit's function is analogous to the genotype. It is "that which is inside" directing the neural impulses initiated by the beam of light to the proper effectors.

This simple, reflexive paradigm is similar to but not the same as that involved in complex behavior situations. Whereas the neurological circuit is set from individual to individual, its counterpart in complex, socially significant behavior is not. In the simple reflexive situation we can predict the result solely on the basis of the stimulus. In the complex behavior situation, phenomenological as well as stimulus information is necessary for prediction. In understanding the individual's behavior and experience it is necessary to acquire a considerable amount of information about the individual's "internal world," since it varies so much from individual to individual and for the same individual from time to time.

Recently psychologists have spent much time and effort in attempting to develop specialized techniques which will provide information about the individual's socially significant "inner world." One thing these techniques have in common is that they express the information they elicit quantitatively. That is, measurements or scores are used to summarize the data the techniques provide. The scores are then used as a basis for inference concerning the individual's phenomenal field. In concluding this chapter we will describe briefly three such specialized investigations: (1) Authoritarian personality measurement, (2) Level of aspiration and decision making, and (3) Connotative meaning.

Authoritarian Personality Measurement as an Aid in Obtaining Phenomenological Information

In the past few years many social psychologists have shown an increasing interest in the relationship between personality characteristics and social behavior. Much of this interest was stimulated by research into the authoritarian syndrome. Scales were developed to measure the personality traits which characterize the authoritarian. By the use of intensive interviews, projective tests, and other devices, it was found that individuals who were high in authoritarianism, as measured by their scale, were characterized by unquestioning respect for authority, fear of outsiders, exaltation of the ingroup, belief in imperious practices in dealing with subordinates, disdain for "below status" individuals, great respect (by way of fear and identification) for "above status" individuals and groups, and well-founded beliefs in and acceptance of social status rigidity within a society of classes (Adorno *et al.,* 1950). Although there has been a considerable amount of critical evaluation of certain aspects of the authoritarian construct, the authoritarian scales have been extremely useful in providing phenomenological information for use in social psychological research. (For a detailed discussion of this problem, see Chapter XI.)

The importance of personality measures for purposes of providing phenomenological information is illustrated in the following study (Cooper, 1956). College student subjects were measured for authoritarianism and various aspects of their attitudes toward artists, bankers, doctors, engineers, Jews, Mexicans, Negroes, Filipinos, scientists, and socialists. The results indicated that, in comparison with subjects low in authoritarianism, highly authoritarian subjects tended to think of those groups they liked as belonging to an extremely high social class and those groups they disliked as belonging to an extremely low social class, expressed more negative attitudes toward disliked groups, evidenced significantly more concern about social mobility when they were asked what they thought would happen to them socially if they were to associate with certain of these social groups, and agreed substantially with each other in their evaluations of the social groups. Highly authoritarian individuals appear to be quite aware of and concerned with problems of social status; they identify with socially respected groups and evidence considerable disdain for groups they consider to have low social status. Such a study illustrates that a personality measure which provides phenomenological information may be of importance in understanding an individual's behavior. In this example, knowledge of the authoritarianism of different individuals helped to "make sense" out of their differences concerning social status.

Level of Aspiration and Decision as Phenomenological Information

Still another means by which phenomenological information can be obtained is through the use of *level of aspiration* and *decision theory* measuring techniques (Siegel, 1957). These theoretical approaches, though differing in name, represent a common attack upon the problem of obtaining phenomenological information. The level of aspiration concept will be discussed in greater detail in Chapter V.

Level of aspiration refers to the relative level at which the individual sets his goal. *Decision-making* also refers to goal setting, in this case described as a point on a scale of value for which the individual has made a decision to strive. An individual's level of aspiration at any particular time depends upon the positive valence-strength or importance of success, the negative valence-strength or importance of failure, and his estimate of his chances for success or failure (probability judgment) (Lewin, Dembo, Festinger, Sears, 1944). That is, Mr. Smith will not aspire to shoot in the 70's unless it is of some importance to him, failure will not be too painful to tolerate, and his chances for success are at least reasonably good. In decision-making terms, the positive valence-strength of a particular point on some scale of values has a certain utility for the individual. It is subjective utility as contrasted with objective utility; it is the individual's own personal evaluation—the value he ascribes to that point on the scale. He anticipates that reaching that particular goal will constitute a feeling of success, whereas anything less will constitute a feeling of failure. The individual's estimate as to whether or not he can reach that goal represents his subjective probability judgment. As Siegel puts it:

The decisions are a function of these two variables (utility and subjective probability) in which the individual seeks, by his choices, to maximize the sum of the products of probability and utility. (1957, pp. 259–260)

The individual makes a decision about "what to shoot for," and this decision is the result of a compromise between how valuable a particular goal is to him and the amount of effort he is willing to expend in achieving it. The final decision, then, designates his *level of aspiration*.

Following is a description of a study in which an ordered metric scale was used to determine the level of aspiration for academic grades. On the basis of this information (genotypic), predictions were then made and verified by behavior tests. An ordered metric scale is one that ranks the different distances lying between an individual's preferences. Figure 1 depicts such a scale. If the letters on the horizontal line represent the possible

A   B   C   D   F

FIGURE 1

grades a subject may make in a college course, the linear distances between the grades indicate the subject's relative preferences for the possible grades. For example, the subject whose preferences are described by Figure 1 obviously prefers an A to a B. However, an A is evaluated by the subject as only slightly better than a B, though a B is evaluated as vastly better than a C. C and D are evaluated as being about the same, though a D is greatly preferred to an F. Such a scale is devised for a given subject by offering the subject all possible choices of grades and allowing him in each instance to indicate his preferences.

Becker and Siegel have conducted a study wherein they tested the hypothesis that the ordered metric utility function would yield information on the individual's level of aspiration.

The subjects were twenty students enrolled in an elementary course in statistics. These were students who volunteered to gamble with the instructor for their midterm grade, with the understanding that the grade they obtained in the gambling session would be entered in the course records in lieu of their score on the regularly scheduled midterm examination. An ordered metric scale of the grades A, B, C, D, and F was derived for each subject by the method described elsewhere. This method derives the subject's scale from his choices among alternatives like those listed above.

The subjects were required to make choices between alternatives in a number of offers. Each of the offers was numbered, and the subjects understood in advance that the offer on which the pay-off (midterm grade) would be based would be selected at random from all of the offers given. Therefore, each decision they made had an equal likelihood of being the crucial one on which their midterm grade depended.

After the subjects had made all the required choices, two ruses were introduced. First, the allegedly random device by which each student's grade would be determined was actually controlled so that each subject "won" a C for his grade. Some subjects responded to this pay-off with considerable dismay and disappointment. In response to this, the experimenters perpetrated the second ruse. The group of subjects was told that if they were dissatisfied with the grade they had won, they could obtain an interview with the instructor and the other experimenter, in which, perhaps, some way of raising their grade could be worked out. The implication contained in this announcement was that performance of extra work would be the mode of raising the grade. The subjects were told that anyone who desired such an interview would have to wait until the instructor placed an urgent long-distance telephone call, after which he and the other experimenter would return to conduct individual interviews with those students who desired them. The instructor said he would return in about five minutes, but actually his absence was unexplainedly extended to an hour's time before he returned for individual interviews. As will become clear, this ruse permitted a test of one of the hypotheses of the study.

The interviews were structured to obtain a careful independent measure of each subject's level of aspiration for his midterm grade. Both experimenters were present, and their independent judgments of each subject's level of aspiration were in very close agreement ($r_s = .99$). The interviews were conducted before either experimenter had any information concerning any subject's ordered metric scale of utility for grades.

The experiment was designed to test two hypotheses. For this summary it may suffice to state these briefly and to report the outcome of each hypothesis test.

Hypothesis 1 was that those subjects who would not wait for an interview with the instructor would be persons on whose ordered metric scales the largest distance was between D and F—persons whose ordered metric scales would reveal that their level of aspiration was below the C which they had won. This hypothesis was supported by the data. Four subjects left the room before the experimenters returned from their hour-long errand. All had ordered metric scales with the largest distance between D and F. Seemingly they were satisfied with the C grade they had been assured and therefore saw no reason to seek an interview.

Hypothesis 2 was that subjects' levels of aspiration, as determined from their ordered metric scales of utility, would be positively correlated with their levels of aspiration as judged from the interview material. This hypothesis was confirmed: the correlation between the two independent indices of level of aspiration was $r_s = .83$. (Siegel, 1957, pp. 259–260)

Connotative Meaning as Genotypic Information

The *semantic differential,* a technique developed by Osgood, Succi, and Tannenbaum (1957), has provided another promising approach to the problem of obtaining genotypic information. This technique attempts to measure the connotative meaning that particular concepts and events have for individuals. To do this, subjects are requested to rate each of the concepts being investigated on several seven-point scales. In the study to be described the concepts shown in Table I were used.

Person concepts	Issue concepts
Robert Taft	Universal military training
Adlai Stevenson	U. S. policy in China
Winston Churchill	Federal spending
General MacArthur	Socialism
Estes Kefauver	Government employees
Josef Stalin	Government price controls
Harry S. Truman	European aid
General Eisenhower	Labor unionism
Franklin D. Roosevelt	Use of atomic bomb
Senator McCarthy	United Nations

TABLE I

Each of the concepts was rated on a number of scales or differentials, including the following: fair-unfair, weak-strong, active-passive. The scales were set up as shown in Table II.

Labor unionism

fair __:	__:	_X_:	__:	__:	__:	__ unfair
weak __:	__:	__:	__:	_X_:	__:	__ strong
active __:	__:	_X_:	__:	__:	__:	__ passive

TABLE II

Subjects were instructed to mark the space that best represented the meaning of the concept. The example in Table II illustrates responses of an individual who feels that labor unions tend to be fair, strong and active. A mark in the center space would indicate either neutrality or that the scale is irrelevant to the concept.

These scales and concepts were administered to 49 subjects 14 weeks before election day in 1952. At that time 12 subjects indicated that they were very certain that they would vote for Stevenson, 25 subjects indicated that they were very certain that they would vote for Eisenhower, and 18 subjects placed themselves in the category "don't know." It was reasoned that if voting behavior depends upon attitudes and meanings, then it should be possible to predict the vote of each "don't know" subject by measuring the similarity or correspondence of his concept-meanings, as measured by the ratings on the scales, with those of the typical Stevenson voter and the typical Eisenhower voter. Thus, if a "don't know" subject's ratings of the concepts were similar to those of the typical Eisenhower voters, it was predicted that he would vote for Eisenhower, while if the ratings were similar to those of the typical Stevenson voter's ratings, a Stevenson vote was predicted.

After the election the subjects reported their actual votes. The results, based on the fair-unfair scale as a predictor of voting, were striking. Of the 18 "don't know" subjects, 14 voted as predicted according to the criterion. When the results of the weak-strong scale were combined with those of the fair-unfair scale, the successful prediction rose to 17 out of 18. The third scale (active-passive) failed, however, to predict at a better-than-chance level. In spite of the failure of the third scale, this study suggests that the measurement of meaning can provide highly useful genotypic data.

Since we have stressed the importance of assessing phenomenological data in attempting to understand social behavior and experience, it should not be inferred that past experience, genetic factors, physiological states, and other similar independent variable conditions are of less genotypic importance. On the contrary, present behavior and experience are significantly determined by such variables since they constitute important parts of the individual's present genotypic condition. The individual's behavior is not, however, to be understood in terms of any of these raw variables alone, but rather in terms of the phenomenological field the individual superimposes upon them.

Although genotypic information is difficult to obtain, most social psychologists are now aware of its indispensability, and are exerting increased effort toward the development of techniques that can be used to assess human perception and motivation. Although, as we have seen, the present techniques for obtaining such information are essentially exploratory, on the basis of present information two inferences are warranted. First, the reasons that lie behind particular patterns of human behavior must be known before behavior itself can be understood. Without knowledge of the underlying determinants, directly observable behavior is psychologically meaningless. The fact that half of a sample declares an object to be "good" and the other half declares the same object to be "bad" gives us actuarial information; but it is only that, and cannot be used for purposes of understanding and predicting *individual* behavior, since such actuarial information refers only to groups and psychology is concerned with individuals. Second, a corollary, is that genotypic information is indispensable for purposes of social psychological investigation. This cautions against the lazy hope of short-circuiting genotypic data because they are difficult to obtain, and of assuming that a great mass of phenotypic data will somehow compensate for a dearth of genotypic data. If nothing more, we are obliged to recognize that an adequate psychological understanding of human nature depends upon a focus which is sufficiently comprehensive to discern the articulation of the genotype with the phenotype.

Social Motivation

Man has always been interested in why he behaves the way he does. Understanding the motivational determinants of behavior is one of the dominant concerns of modern psychology. Although psychologists are primarily interested in this problem for purely scientific reasons, the problem of motivation is also of great practical importance. This is because a large part of our environment—perhaps the most important part from the point of view of adaptation—consists of behaving animals.

GOAL DIRECTION

Tolman once wrote that behavior reeks of purpose. The problem of motivation would be much simpler than it is if Professor Tolman's statement were not true. If the behavior of organisms consisted merely of discrete responses to particular stimuli, then it could be understood by a careful analysis of the stimulus conditions which elicit the discrete responses. Unfortunately, from the point of view of simplicity, carpenters do not merely move their arms; they drive nails, saw boards, and, more important, build houses. Similarly, as you read this page you are not just moving your eyes back and forth in a jerky fashion; you are studying. This complex behavior called *studying* is part of a larger behavior of going to college or earning a college degree. Even the rat in a maze is doing something a great deal more complicated than contracting and relaxing his muscles, moving his legs or running; he is going to the goal box where he has previously found food. Studies have shown that hungry rats will continue to choose the correct path to the goal box of a maze even if they are able to walk only in circles because of cerebellar injury (Lashley and McCarthy, 1926) and that they will swim through the maze after it is flooded with water (MacFarlane, 1930). These studies are important because they show quite clearly that even though the patterns of movements required to reach the goal are drastically modified, the essential feature of behavior, *goal direction,* remains unaltered. Hence, any attempt to understand behavior must include reference to the goal toward which the behavior is directed. It is just this fact of behavior—goal direction— that makes the problem of motivation so difficult and challenging.

Although the point of view taken by Bindra (1959) is quite different from that expressed in this book we agree with his comments regarding the importance of goal direction:

If one observes the behavior of an animal in its familiar surroundings, one is likely to be struck by the effectiveness with which it manipulates and adapts to its environment. It feeds, protects, and amuses itself in what appears to be a fairly efficient way. Each response systematically follows, or is accompanied by, others in such a way that the animal usually manages to effect an adaptation in relation to changing objects, events, and other classes of sensory stimulation. The activities of animals seem almost always to be aimed at some particular consequences, directed toward some "goals." In common-sense language we say that behavior tends to be "purposive" or that animals "have purpose." It is this "purposive" or "moving-in-the-direction-of-goals" aspect of behavior that is the dominant feature of the phenomena that are termed motivational, and that has been generally considered to present the core of the psychological problem of motivation. (p. 17)

We do not merely respond; we respond with reference to particular goals. Further, we continue to respond until we reach a particular goal (or change our goal) and, most important, many different responses or behavior techniques may be used in attaining the goal. As every student knows, the goal of achieving a particular grade average may be reached by many different techniques, such as studying consistently in all subjects, studying very diligently in a few subjects while letting others slip, or when worst comes to worst, perhaps even cheating. Any specific goal may also be viewed as a sub-goal embedded within a more general goal of the individual. The goal of achieving a particular grade average, for example, is undoubtedly related to a more general goal of maintaining self-esteem (protecting one's ego) by achieving a certain degree of success and avoiding failure. In fact it is likely that all of our socially significant goals and the techniques we use in attempting to attain them are regulated by our anticipations of the esteem they will provide. Whether we like it or not, we choose our social activities, friends, houses, hobbies, pets, cars, clothes, and even food because of the esteem or ego-protection they provide.

Reflexes and Tropisms

Some responses seems to be completely regulated by stimulus changes. For example, as the intensity of illumination increases the pupil of the eye contracts, and as illumination decreases the pupil enlarges. This pupillary reflex, which is regulated by a built-in sensory-neural mechanism, is found in all who have normal vision. In fact it is such a reliable response that it is difficult if not impossible to modify it by elaborate training procedures. The pupillary reflex is but one of many human reflexes (e.g., startle reflex, Babinsky reflex) that could be mentioned to illustrate the fact that some parts of human behavior are under the direct control of stimulating conditions. We do not have to study the goals of the individual in order to understand why he contracts his pupils when we shine a bright light in his eyes.

Moths fly into bright light. Fish in a tank of water charged with a direct electrical current align themselves in the direction of current flow. Such complex orienting responses are called *tropisms* and are found in many infrahuman species. Tropisms, like reflexes, are examples of responses that are under stimulus control. In a series of experiments, Hirsch and Boudreau (1958, 1959) have studied the phototropic (light orienting) and geotropic (gravity orienting) behavior of the fruit fly (*Drosophila melanogaster*). By selective breeding they have been able to increase and decrease the phototropic tendencies of successive generations of fruit flies. Further, they have shown that different populations of flies differ in incidence of geotropic responses. From these studies it seems clear that the existence of any such orienting response is determined largely by genetic factors. In these simple experimental situations one needs to know only the stimulus conditions and the strain of *Drosophila* being tested in order to predict orienting behavior with considerable accuracy. We may wish to know why the flies orient toward light or why fish orient in the direction of electrical current flow, but such information is not necessary if we are interested only in predicting behavior solely from a knowledge of stimulus conditions and genetic strain.

Even some very complex infrahuman behavior patterns such as mating, communicating, and nest-building are regulated by particular internal and external stimulus conditions. The mother rat will ordinarily take quite adequate care of even her first litter of newly-born pups. Behavior patterns such as nursing, cleaning, and retrieving seem to be regulated at least to some degree by innate tendencies to respond in particular ways in the presence of particular stimulus conditions. In fact, the maternal behavior of experienced mother rats seems to be no different from that of rats with their first litters. Wiesner and Sheard (1933) have shown that one aspect of maternal behavior, retrieving, is regulated or elicited by the appearance of the pups. Ordinarily a mother rat will retrieve her young for only a few days following parturition. However, when the older pups are removed and replaced by newly-born pups every few days, the retrieving behavior can be maintained for months. Maternal behavior in rats is also regulated by hormonal conditions. Components of maternal behavior can be elicited in virgin females or even male rats by injecting them with sex hormones.

Fisher (1956) reports that when certain hormones are injected directly into a male rat's hypothalamus it retrieves anything available, even another mature rat or his own tail.

These examples point to the conclusion that in the infrahumans many complex, seemingly goal-directed behavior patterns emerge without the benefit of specific training. It is not necessary to infer "goals" or "anticipations" in order to account for such behavior. It is behavior which is regulated by specific sensory-hormonal conditions but which fits into the adaptation requirement of the species.

Problems of Goal Direction

Reflexes and tropisms, interesting as they may be, are simple when compared with activities such as retrieving that require the integration of many responses into larger behavior patterns that have the appearance of goal direction. Goal-directedness that emerges without specific training raises several difficult and important questions. First, is all infrahuman behavior controlled by unlearned tendencies to respond in particular ways in the presence of particular stimuli? Although much infrahuman behavior does appear to be unlearned, most if not all animals can learn. As we pointed out earlier, the fact that lower animals can learn is one of the major reasons they are studied by psychologists. As a matter of fact, relatively few psychologists have ever studied the nonlaboratory behavior of any of the various species of animals commonly used in psychological research. We know a great deal more about what rats are capable of learning and the factors affecting their learning processes than we do about how rats as a species ordinarily behave (Beach, 1950).

Second, is human behavior regulated by unlearned response tendencies? McDougall once wrote, "The human mind has certain innate or inherited tendencies which are the essential springs or motive powers of all thought and action. . . ." (1931, p. 2) This view is rejected by contemporary psychology. It is highly unlikely that any complex human behavior pattern of social significance is innate. Indeed, it is difficult to point to any *specific goals* that are sought by all humans or any *behavior patterns* that are the same throughout the world. As far as human goals and behavior patterns are concerned, variability seems to be the very nature of human nature.

Third, how does human behavior become goal-directed? What are our goals, how did they develop, and why do we do the things we do in order to obtain them? These questions form the central problem in the study of human motivation. The rest of this chapter will be concerned with these issues. Since this is perhaps the most difficult and important question in psychology and since this area of psychology is presently "short" on data, it should not be surprising that there are currently several different theories of motivation. The point of view presented here is in general agreement with the views of McClelland *et al.* (1953), Young (1955, 1959), Tolman (1932), and Lewin (1935).

HOMEOSTASIS AND THE AROUSAL OF MOTIVES

Although many theoretical attempts to explain human behavior in terms of unlearned response tendencies have been made, it is clear that socially significant human motivation is much too variable to be accounted for so simply. Man's motives are not innate.

Needs

There are many activities in which all humans engage. We all eat, drink, breathe, eliminate waste products, exercise, and sleep. Such activities are obviously necessary for the maintenance of life. But with the exception of eating and drinking, these activities are ultimately involuntary; we cannot prevent ourselves from breathing, urinating, defecating, moving our muscles, and sleeping. Eventually the bodily requirements fulfilled by these activities will be satisfied whether we like it or not, even if they result in other forms of discomfort, such as embarrassment. Further, through very complex processes collectively called "homeostasis" (Cannon, 1939), the physiological systems of our bodies automatically maintain a relative equilibrium of conditions that are necessary for life. Body temperature, pH, oxygen and CO_2 levels, blood sugar level, and many other conditions are all maintained without any effort or awareness. When we accumulate CO_2 we breathe; when our body temperatures increase we perspire.

There is, however, a limit to the abilities of these automatic processes. As long as there is plenty of readily metabolized food in our bodies the energy requirements of the cells of our bodies are maintained automatically. But when our stomachs become empty and stored food supplies are used up, this process cannot continue; food must be brought into the body if the cells are to continue to live. Similarly, oxygen balance cannot be maintained without ingestion of oxygen through breathing. A continuous supply of water is necessary for proper cellular osmotic pressure. In other words, homeostatic processes are able to maintain quasi-constant states within our bodies only when the materials necessary for maintaining the states are readily available, or are readily eliminated as in the case of waste products.

Drives

Extreme imbalances in any of these conditions give rise to readily identifiable sensations. Such sensations we will refer to as *drives*. Drives are not in all cases absolutely necessary, because certain physiological needs can be reflexly satisfied under ordinary conditions. Since, however, we are not surrounded by food and water there is no way the body can automatically obtain these needed substances. It is fortunate, therefore, that these bodily needs, like many other needs, give rise to drives—sensory experiences of hunger and thirst. When our bodies have become depleted of nutrients necessary for maintenance of internal balance we do not die; we become plagued by sensations we call "hunger." Similarly, as we become dehydrated either through loss of water or ingestion of salt we do not just dry up; we become "thirsty." Unfortunately, from the point of view of health and survival, many bodily needs do not give rise to particular discriminable drives. For example, no peculiar sensations result from a vitamin B-12 deficiency, although if the deficiency is not detected death will eventually result. As a species, we are able to survive because the foods we ordinarily eat contain the bodily requirements, even though they are not signaled by drives.

To summarize, some bodily needs produce particular sensations we call drives and some do not. Drives serve as signaling devices similar to automobile dashboard gauges that indicate gas level, oil pressure, and engine temperature. As long as gasoline, oil, and water levels are high the engine will automatically maintain the balances necessary for relatively efficient running. Deficiencies in these substances are signaled by the gauges. Obviously, automobiles as a "species" would soon become extinct if they did not have both homeostatic devices (thermostats, and so forth) and drives (gauges). But just as it is true that most automobile breakdowns are caused by deficiencies such as lack of wheel bearing grease for which there are no signaling mechanisms, there are also certain human bodily needs that are not signaled by drives.

We have defined drives as the particular sensory experiences produced by particular bodily needs. Such sensations have two effects. First, they arouse the organism. Anyone who has tried to fall asleep while hungry is well aware of this. Second, drives initiate goal-directed behavior. When we feel hungry, we are not only aroused, but we seek food. How do drives initiate goal-directed behavior? This is part of the central problem of motivation we discussed earlier. Why do we want food when we are stimulated by a hunger drive? In many infrahumans, as was pointed out earlier, drives may innately elicit appropriate behavior. But at the human level goals must be learned. The human infant has no way of knowing what it needs to do in order to eliminate the uncomfortable sensation a child or an adult would call hunger. It is only through learning that the hunger drive as a stimulus comes to elicit a wanting of food and the consequent goal-directed activity of seeking for food. Similarly, the thirst drive is a sensation and only a sensation until, through learning, it arouses an anticipation of some liquid that has been found to quench the thirst. We will use the term "motive" to refer to the anticipation of such incentives (particular goals). As a result of learning, motives may be aroused by an almost un-limited number of internal and external stimulus conditions.

A schematic representation of the way needs and drives activate moti-vated behavior is shown in Figure 1. Parts 1 and 2 indicate the unlearned portion of the sequence; some needs innately arouse drives. Drives, in addition to being distinctive sensations, are also unpleasant when they become intense. The new-born infant's response to hunger consists simply of general activity and crying. The infant is not motivated; it is only re-sponding to the unpleasant sensation of hunger. From numerous and frequent feedings it learns many things: warm milk is pleasant-tasting; contact with the mother is pleasant; milk eliminates the unpleasant hunger sensations. For the present discussion let us consider only the removal of the unpleasant sensations; we will return to the role of pleasant stimulation shortly. As the infant learns the association between milk and reduction of hunger the hunger drive begins to arouse a hunger motive; this is part 3 of the sequence. Thus, when a baby has learned that milk eliminates hunger, the hunger drive will elicit (in addition to crying and activity) an anticipa-tion of milk. As the baby matures it learns that some behavior (part 4), such as a particular type of crying or certain noises, is followed by the mother providing food. At the same time the mother learns to infer the child's motives and drives on the basis of his behavior. This is the begin-ning of the socialization process, since the child learns that some behavior is effective in obtaining goals while other behavior is not. As we have indi-cated, the important characteristic of a goal is that attainment of the goal (part 5) results either in a reduction of unpleasant states or an increase in pleasant ones (part 6). We will consider the importance of the affective (pleasant-unpleasant) consequences of goals in greater detail shortly. First, however, let us return to the problem posed by our definition of a motive as an anticipation of incentives.

The Motivational Sequence

Unlearned portion		Learning	Learned portion			
Need	Drive		Motive	Behavior	Incentive (Goal)	Consequence
(1)	(2)		(3)	(4)	(5)	(6)
food	hunger: dis-criminable sen-sations—un-pleasant when intense	———	anticipation of food	asking for food	milk	removal of hun-ger drive (and pleasant taste)

FIGURE 1

Motives as Anticipatory

As Tolman (1925) long emphasized, all behavior is characterized by "goal-seeking." But by this he did not mean that behavior is regulated by a universal purpose, as did McDougall (1931). McDougall described behavior as striving always toward "natural ends." This was, of course, a direct espousal of a universal teleology, an assumption which must be rejected by contemporary psychology.

Our emphasis upon the goal-directed nature of behavior does not commit us to a universal teleology. Behavior is not guided by the goal; it is guided by *present expectations* of a goal. For example, the teen-age girl who wants to marry may be guided by her expectancy concept of the state of marriage that may very well include a vine-covered cottage. This is true even though her present expectation of the marital state is in all probability somewhat different from the state of marriage she will later actually experience.

Contemporary psychologists agree that motives are learned—not part of an organism's native equipment. Behavior is guided by learned anticipations of end results; it is not drawn by end results *per se*. In maze-learning experiments with rats, putting food in the goal box will in no way affect the rat's behavior on his first trial through the maze unless, of course, he can smell the food. The rat has to learn that the maze has a goal box. After the rat finds food in the goal box his subsequent behavior in the maze is governed by his anticipation of finding food again in the same place. If the food is removed from the goal box the rat's behavior will not be affected on the first trial since he still "expects" to find the food. When he fails to find the expected food his behavior is quite different on subsequent trials.

Affective Basis of Motives

Motives are to be thought of as learned anticipations of goals. Thirst, as a drive, does not arouse a "water motive" until water has quenched the unpleasant thirst sensation. In addition, the thirst drive is only one of many conditions that can arouse a water motive. There are many stimuli than can, as a consequence of learning, regulate goal-directed behavior. As advertisers well know, eating and drinking as well as most all of the other activities in which we engage can be initiated by numerous "external stimuli." Indeed, it is fortunate that we do not have to depend upon drive for the arousal of motives since, as Harlow (1953) has pointed out, many people in the United States go for days or even years without actually experiencing hunger or thirst drives. If it is true that we are typically motivated to eat even when we have no hunger drive, then what is the function of eating? Obviously, if the hunger drive is not intense then eating cannot reduce the unpleasant hunger drives. Eating can, however, provide pleasant sensory stimulation in the form of tastes and smells. In the same way that the hunger drive can arouse the anticipation of food that will reduce the unpleasant sensations, any stimulus that is associated with the occurrence of pleasant sensations can come to arouse anticipations of stimuli that produced the pleasant sensations. All motives, we suggest, are based upon *affective* experiences. In common-sense terms, we want things that we anticipate will either eliminate unpleasant experiences or provide pleasant experiences. Fortunately, many of our activities have pleasant consequences and, in addition, eliminate or postpone unpleasant ones.

From this point of view, the motivational sequence shown in Figure 1 is obviously incomplete. Motives are aroused by drives, but they may be aroused by other stimuli as well. Part A of Figure 2 shows the sequence initiated by a water need. Part B shows the motivational sequence modified to illustrate the arousal of motives by stimuli other than drives. In the example shown, a "Coke" motive is initiated by a picture of a Coke advertisement. The arousal of a motive, in other words, may require neither a bodily need nor a drive. The Coke may be an incentive just because of its pleasant taste. The importance of pleasant stimulation in hunger and thirst motivation has been stressed by Cannon as follows:

The ways in which appetites for food and drink and sensations of hunger and thirst act to maintain the bodily supplies of nutriment and water may be regarded as typical of other arrangements in the organism which operate for the welfare of the individual or the race. Behavior may be directed either to get rid of disturbing, annoying stimulation, or be movements to prolong or renew agreeable stimulation. Hunger and thirst belong to the first category. Each of these states is associated with a natural impulse: each one more or less vigorously spurs or drives to action; each may be so disturbing as to force the person who is afflicted to seek relief from intolerable annoyances of distress. On the other hand, experience may condition behavior by revealing that a certain food or drink is the cause of unanticipated delight. An appetite for the repetition of this experience is thus established; the person beset by an appetite is *tempted,* not driven, to action—he seeks satisfaction, not relief. It is not to be supposed that the two motivating agencies—the pang and the pleasure—are as separate as we have been regarding them for purposes of analysis in the present discussion. They may be closely intermingled; when relief from hunger or thirst is found, the appetite may simultaneously be satiated. Insofar as an assurance of supplies of food and water is concerned, appetite, or the habitual taking of these substances is the prime effective agency. If the requirements of the body are not met, however, in this mild and incidental manner, hunger pangs and thirst arise as powerful, persistent and tormenting stimuli which imperiously demand the ingestion of food and water before they will cease their goading. By these automatic mechanisms the necessary supplies for storage of food and water are made certain. (1939, pp. 75–76)

Revised Motivational Sequence

A

Need (1)	Drive (2)	Learning Motive (3) anticipation of:	Behavior (4)	Goal (5) (specific incentive)	Consequence (6)
water	thirst	"Coke"	obtaining and drinking "Coke"	"Coke"	reduction of unpleasant thirst drive

B

Need (1)	Stimulus arousing Motive (2)	Learning Motive (3) anticipation of:	Behavior (4)	Incentive (Goal) (5)	Consequence (6)
none	any stimuli previously associated with incentive (goal)	"Coke"	obtaining and drinking "Coke"	"Coke"	pleasant stimulation

FIGURE 2

Food Preferences. The importance of the affective consequences of incentives has been emphasized by several recent investigators (McClelland *et. al.,* 1953; Young, 1955, 1959; Pfaffman, 1960). In Young's 1955 studies, for example, it has been shown that even rats have food preferences that are based upon something other than nutritive value. Despite the fact that saccharine has no known nutritive value, rats prefer water flavored with it to tap-water. Humans, as we know, also have strong food preferences that depend upon the "pleasantness" of food tastes. Beef liver, nutritive though it is, is rarely chosen by children in preference to candy or ice cream. Though a child might agree that beef liver is good for him, his cognitive agreement is unlikely to have much effect upon his real preference.

Obviously, human food preferences are not determined solely by palatability. An individual may be very fond of filet mignon, but he doesn't want to eat only filet mignon. Men, as well as rats, satiate on even the most desirable incentives.

Food preferences may also be affected by bodily needs. Animals deprived of protein, for example, develop a preference for foods containing protein, providing they have not established a preference for some other substance in the same testing situation. Rats preferring sucrose in a testing situation will continue to choose sucrose even when they are nearing starvation from protein deficiency. Animals deficient in vitamin B complex are unable to select food containing small but adequate amounts of vitamin B complex. If they are isolated and fed a vitamin B-adequate food with a distinctive flavor, they will later associate the flavor with the relief of avitaminosis symptoms and will continue to prefer the flavored food to other foods, even after the vitamin is withdrawn and the diet is once again inadequate.

These studies point to two basic facts. First, although food preferences are ordinarily determined by native palatability they can be altered by association of the taste of a particular substance with relief from discomfort. Second, once particular food-taking habits are formed in particular situations such habits regulate food selection independently of palatability and bodily needs. Apparently the stimulus situation continues to arouse motives for incentives that have been previously obtained in the situation even though other incentives would provide greater affective consequences. Motives are based upon the affective stimulation provided by incentives. However, once we become habituated or accustomed to a particular incentive we may continue to choose that incentive over others that potentially could provide even greater satisfaction.

Contact Comfort. According to one view of motivation, hunger, thirst, elimination, pain, and sex are the basic drives of rats and men. Any stimulus, according to this view, can become an incentive if it reduces one of the basic drives or is associated through learning with incentives that reduce basic drives. A baby's love for its mother is assumed to develop from the association of the mother with the reduction of primary drives, particularly hunger. In other words, nursing is presumed to serve as a basis for the development of love for one's mother.

An alternative hypothesis, one consistent with the point of view proposed in this book, is that the important factor in the development of affection for one's mother is the pleasant stimulation provided by contact with the mother, a factor called "contact comfort" by Harlow and Zimmerman (1959). In a series of studies these investigators have attempted to assess the roles of nursing and "contact comfort" in the development of affectional responses in the infant macaque monkey. In an initial study, eight newborn monkeys (6 to 12 hours old) were taken from their mothers and placed into individual cages that contained two artificial mothers. One of the artificial mothers was constructed of wire (hardware cloth) while the other mother was constructed of a cylinder of wood covered with terrycloth. Bottle holders were installed in the upper middle part of the dummies' bodies to permit nursing. For four of the monkeys, milk could be obtained only by nursing the cloth dummy. For the other four monkeys, milk could be obtained only by nursing the wire dummy. The infants were kept in these experimental cages for a minimum of 165 days. During this period they were given a number of tests designed to measure the development of affectional behavior. One measure that indicated the development of affection was the average number of hours during the day the infants spent on each dummy. The cloth "mother" was preferred to the wire "mother" by all of the infants, even though for four of the infants milk was provided only by the wire "mother." This initial test suggests quite strongly that primary reduction provided by nursing does not lead to the development of affection when the contact made during the nursing is, judging from the appearance of the wire "mother," relatively uncomfortable. In other tests, Harlow and Zimmerman demonstrated that the cloth "mother" is not just a more convenient resting place than the wire "mother." When various fear-producing stimuli (e.g., a toy mechanical bear playing a drum) were introduced into the infants' cages, the terrified infants retreated almost without exception to the cloth "mother" and then seemed rapidly to lose their fear of the stimuli, even to the point of investigating the object that initially elicited the fear.

In still further tests the infant monkeys were placed individually in a small room containing several strange objects. When the cloth "mother" was present the infants immediately ran to it and, as their fear subsided, began to explore the room while using the "mother" as a base of operations. Some of the monkeys even brought objects back to the "mother." When the monkeys were introduced into the room where the cloth "mother" was absent they typically either froze in a crouching position or ran around the room clutching themselves with their arms. In either case, they did not play with the objects as they did when the "mother" was present. Infants raised with only wire "mothers" were not comforted by the presence of the wire "mother" in the testing room. In fact, their behavior in the presence of the wire "mother" was similar to the behavior of the other monkeys when the cloth "mother" was not present.

Although these studies should be regarded as exploratory rather than definitive, the following conclusions seem to be warranted by the data:

. . . the experimental analysis of the development of the infant monkey's attachment to an inanimate mother surrogate demonstrates the overwhelming importance of the variable of soft body contact that characerized the cloth mother. . . . The results also indicate that, without the factor of contact comfort, only a weak attachment, if any, is formed. Finally, probably the most surprising finding is that nursing or feeding played either no role or a subordinate role in the development of affection. . . . No evidence was found indicating that nursing mediated any of . . . the responses studied. . . . Certainly, feeding, in contrast to contact comfort, is neither a necessary nor a sufficient condition for affectional development. (p. 428)

The question as to whether these conclusions may be related to other species, including man, will, of course, depend upon much additional research. It may well be that the dynamics of the process of affectional development in humans is not greatly unlike that in monkeys. This exciting and important research by Harlow and his associates will undoubtedly stimulate much future research designed to answer this question.

Variety of Motives

The incentives that can provide affective satisfaction are limitless in number. For present purposes, two examples will suffice.

Stimulus Change. One of the most powerful human (as well as infrahuman) motives is curiosity—the anticipation of slight novelty. Even the most hard-headed drive-reduction theorist recognizes that stubborn children can sometimes be urged to eat certain nutritious foods by being bribed with novel toys. In fact the toy industry is, to a large extent, based upon general curiosity motivation. And, as we have just said, many infrahumans are amazingly curious. The story is told of the psychologist who, curious to find out what laboratory monkeys do when they are not being watched by psychologists, peeked through the laboratory door's keyhole only to find a monkey staring back at him. Butler (1954) has shown that monkeys will continue to press a lever for hours just for the opportunity to peek through a window at an electric train, the experimental room, or the experimenter. Harlow and McClearn (1954) demonstrated that monkeys will solve complicated problems when the only reward is the manipulation of the materials used in the problems. Even rats seek stimulus change. Experiments have shown that rats will press levers to turn lights on and off and will run mazes for the opportunity of exploring a novel stimulus situation. While it seems clear that only humans are systematically curious, many of the infrahumans are certainly motivated by the anticipations of stimulus change.

Sex. Another obviously important motive is sex. Although sex has sometimes been classified as a homeostatic drive, satisfaction of the sex motive is not necessary for the maintenance of life; and, as far as is known, no physiological equilibrium is restored by sexual activity. There is much evidence, however, that sex motivation is based on the pleasure derived from sexual activities (Sheffield, Wulff, and Backer, 1951). It has been shown, for example, that male rats will continue to run a maze where the only reward is interrupted copulation. Obviously, this was a situation in which the hypothetical sex drive could not be reduced. In humans, the affective consequences of sexual activity are well-known. Human sex motivation, in contrast to that of lower animals, seems to depend little upon internal hormonal conditions. Humans learn to anticipate the affective consequences of sexual activity.

EGO MOTIVATION

All of our motives are not, as the previous sections might seem to imply, concerned solely with sensory comforts. It is of course true that the food-starved man wants food, the sex-starved man wants sex, and the tortured man wants relief from pain. More important, however, as far as social behavior is concerned, humans want to achieve feelings of worth and success, and to avoid feelings of failure, guilt, and embarrassment. In other words, human *social* motives are concerned with the maintenance of self-esteem. We have sharply emphasized that it is man's nature to engage in behavior that he anticipates will provide self-esteem or ego protection.

The hypothesis that self-appraisal is an important regulator of human behavior is not new. Many years ago McDougall wrote the following:

. . . the study of the development of self consciousness and of the self-regarding sentiment is an important part of the preparation for the understanding of social phenomena. And these two things, the idea of the self and the self-regarding sentiment, develop in such intimate relations with each other that they must be studied together. This development is . . . essentially a social process, one which is dependent throughout upon the complex interactions between the individual and the organized society to which he belongs. (1931, pp. 150–151)

Unfortunately, insufficient research has been directed toward understanding the factors responsible for the development of ego-protection as a motivational process. Undoubtedly, as McDougall and many others have argued, ego-awareness and ego-protection are products of social interaction. Lewin (1935) has emphasized that the world of the young child is quite undifferentiated. As the child develops he becomes increasingly aware of his own body as distinct from other objects in his perceptual world. This discrimination is accomplished with the aid of family members who urge the child to "show us your nose" and by the fact that bodily sensations and visible parts of his body are relatively stable portions of his total environment. At the same time that the perceptual differentiation of self and nonself is occurring, that part of the environment that is perceived as "self" begins to acquire value; it becomes important and "good." Presumably this positive attitude toward self results, at least in part, from the attention provided by those around him. As his language skill develops, these affective responses are reinforced by the things the family members say to him and about him. The child learns that he is comforted and loved when he is a "good boy" and punished when he is bad. Soon he learns to avoid, if possible, being appraised as bad, that is, at least when other motives do not interfere too severely. As emotional responses develop and become increasingly differentiated the child experiences feelings of guilt, remorse, and embarrassment when he feels that he has been bad. Embarrassment results not from objectively bad behavior but from behavior that is not in keeping with a "good" self-concept. The very young child is not embarrassed when he soils his diaper. The same behavior may become quite embarrassing to the older child when he learns that this is typically judged by others to be "bad" behavior. As Sherif and Sherif (1956) have pointed out, painful, unpleasant experiences of anxiety, insecurity, personal inadequacy, aloneness, shame, and guilt can be accounted for only by reference to damage to one's self-esteem. Further, these emotional responses are based upon the fact that they are associated with social disapproval, not physical punishment. It may be, as many authors have pointed out, that social isolation is the severest form of punishment. A safe assumption is that social disapproval, and its anticipation, are the severest forms of punishment used in the regulation of human social behavior.

Level of Aspiration

In a culture as complicated as ours it is impossible, of course, for anyone to obtain social approval in every single task or activity. Since we are "objectively" successful in relatively few areas how do we avoid continuous feelings of failure? William James commented on this problem in the following way:

Not that I would not, if I could, be both handsome and fat and well dressed, and a great athlete, and make a million a year, be a wit, a *bon-vivant,* and a lady-killer, as well as a philosopher; a philanthropist, statesman, warrior, and an African explorer, as well as a "tone-poet" and saint. But the thing is simply impossible. The millionaire's work would run counter to the saint's; the *bon-vivant* and the philanthropist would trip each other up; the philosopher and the lady-killer could not well keep house in the same tenement of clay. Such different characters may conceivably at the outset of life be alike possible to man. But to make any one of them actual, the rest must more or less be suppressed. (1890, p. 309)

It is not necessarily our abilities that keep us from excelling in all areas; equally or perhaps more important is the fact that achievement in different areas may require different and incompatible patterns of behavior. Fortunately, however, objective failure does not necessarily produce feelings of failure. This is true because feelings of failure result from failure to obtain goals for which we strive; goals which we anticipate will provide esteem. Self-esteem, as James expressed it, is equal to success divided by "pretensions." According to this formula, it can be increased either by increasing objective success or by decreasing one's pretensions. To a large extent, we maintain self-esteem by minimizing our pretensions. Most of us are not the least concerned that we are among the world's worst harpsichord players, tightrope walkers, and fire-eaters. We become anxious or psychologically dejected only when we are unsuccessful in activities in which we attempt to achieve some measure of success. Again, James expressed this in the following way:

I, who for the time have staked my all on being a psychologist, am mortified if others know much more psychology than I. But I am content to wallow in the grossest ignorance of Greek. My deficiencies there give me no sense of humiliation at all. Had I "pretensions" to be a linguist, it would have been just the reverse. (1890, p. 310)

The effect of achieved success upon pretensions, or level of aspiration, has been investigated in many contemporary experiments. The term "level of aspiration" was introduced into psychology by Kurt Lewin and his students in the early 1930's. Originally the term was used to refer to subjects' momentary goals as revealed by their remarks about successes and failures, and their modes of attack on the problems assigned them.

As we pointed out in Chapter IV, an individual's behavior does not necessarily reveal his subjective aims or aspirations. In an experimental situation where a subject must reveal his aspirations in the presence of another person—the experimenter—secretly cherished goals may well be "edited" before they are reported. We do not have reliable access to individuals' momentary goals. We can, however, study the stated goals of individuals. In view of this, Frank has proposed the following definition of level of aspiration:

. . . level of aspiration represents the level of future performance in a familiar task which an individual . . . explicitly undertakes to reach. (1941, p. 218)

Many factors, all of which operate in a way that produces the greatest amount of self-esteem that is possible in the particular situation, affect an individual's level of aspiration in a task. Hoppe (1930) showed that feelings of success or failure resulting from performance on a task depend upon the objective difficulty of the task. Most of us do not feel that we are failures if we cannot run the hundred-yard dash in 9.2 seconds. Similarly, the thrill of success is not usually experienced by college students successfully adding columns of two-place numbers. That is, we do not feel that we have failed when we perform poorly on obviously difficult tasks, nor do we feel successful when we succeed at obviously easy tasks. Consequently, we tend to set our goals just high enough so that, in view of the objective difficulty of the task, we have a possibility of achieving a "respectable" goal (psychological success); but not so high that we are almost certain to fail to achieve the stated goal (psychological failure). As Figure 3 shows, we do not become ego-involved in tasks that are either very difficult or very easy for us. Under such circumstances, the likelihood of obtaining additional self-esteem is too small. Obviously, the level of difficulty of a task depends upon the ability of the subject performing the task. In fact, level of aspira-

Task Difficulty and Ego-Involvement*

Task Level	Subject's Perception of Task		
	▬		
extremely difficult ▬	much too		
▬	difficult		
very difficult ▬▬▬▬▬▬▬▬▬▬▬			
difficult ▬		Zone of "ego"	(i.e., zone within
medium ▬		Involvement	which experiences
easy ▬			of success and
very easy ▬▬▬▬▬▬▬▬▬▬▬			failure occur)
extremely easy ▬			
▬	much too		
▬	easy		

FIGURE 3

* Modified from Hoppe as presented in Lewin, 1935

tion does not depend upon the objective level of difficulty per se but upon the level of objective difficulty relative to the individual's perception of his own ability. This, in turn, affects one's estimated or subjective probability of reaching a particular goal. No doubt most of us would consider twelve or even fourteen seconds an extremely short time in which to run 100 yards, while an able sprinter would find even ten seconds well below his level of highly ego-involved aspiration.

Lewin (1943) assumed that the attractiveness of a goal depends largely upon the likelihood of attaining it. The less the likelihood, within limits, the greater the attractiveness. Very difficult goals, if reached, provide considerable self-esteem. An anticipated probability of failure will usually keep one from seeking a very difficult goal; or, at least, it will keep him from telling other people that he considers the goal attractive. This is the difference between subjective levels of aspiration and level of aspiration as defined by Frank. Feather (1959) has suggested that if Lewin's assumption is correct, then the stated attractiveness of a goal should continue to increase as the likelihood of attainment decreases only when subjects are ego-involved and not committed to attempt to attain goals considered to be very attractive. That is, when the choice of a goal does not entail the possibility of failure, subjects are more likely to reveal their attractiveness.

To test these assumptions Feather offered 24 boys choices of incentives that varied in probability of attainment. For half of the boys ego-involvement and probability of goal attainment were controlled by telling them that if they performed well on a task (previously practiced) they would receive one of two candies and if they performed poorly they would be given the other candy. The candies used had been previously found to be similar in attractiveness to other boys. The other half of the boys were told that the candies would be given to them on the basis of chance and that one of the candies had a much greater probability of being obtained. Half of the boys were asked, "Which one do you *wish* you could get the most?" while the others were asked, "Which one would you actually choose to get?"

The results of this study were clear-cut. Under the wish instructions, where no commitment and possible failure could affect the choice, 87 per cent of the choices of the boys given ego orienting instructions were for the candy which was more difficult to obtain, while only 56 per cent of the choices of the boys given the "chance" instructions were for the less probable incentive. Under the actual-choice instructions the ego oriented boys chose the more difficult incentive on only 65 per cent of the choices while the boys given "chance" instructions chose the less probable incentive on only 19 per cent of the choices.

These results provide strong support for Lewin's assumption that goal-attractiveness depends upon the difficulty of goal-attainment under conditions where self-esteem is at stake. When subjects commit themselves to trying for a goal, however, they are somewhat less likely to strive for a goal that is not likely to be reached. Hoppe's region of ego-involvement (Figure 3) is meant to illustrate situations similar to the actual-choice conditions in Feather's experiment, since the choice of a difficult goal entails a substantial possibility of failure.

Levels of aspiration are not stable. If an anticipated goal is successfully achieved the individual then tends to raise his level of aspiration. Goals must be continually raised, since success does not result from continually reaching the same readily obtainable goal. Failure, on the other hand, generally results in lowering the stated goal. Failure indicates difficulty, so a lower, less difficult goal will lessen the probability of failure. Feelings of success and failure that result from attempts to reach goals operate to modify subsequent goals that are sought.

Sears (1940) has demonstrated that the setting of a level of aspiration is affected by individual differences in past experiences of success and failure on the particular task. Three groups of fourth, fifth, and sixth graders were matched on the basis of variables including sex, mental age, and chronological age. One of the groups had had a history of success in both arithmetic and reading. Another had had success in reading and failure in arithmetic. A third group had had success in arithmetic and failure in reading. In the laboratory, all children were given reading and arithmetic tasks to perform. After a child finished one page of exercises he was given a fictitious score of the time taken to complete the page and was asked to estimate the time it would take him to complete the next page. This estimate was taken as his level of aspiration. Fictitious scores were used so that each child could be made to experience both success and failure in the experimental situation. The results indicated that on tasks in which children had previously experienced success in school, goal setting tended to vary realistically with experimentally induced experiences of success and failure. That is, they tended to set their levels of aspiration very close to their reported levels of performance in the laboratory. However, when they were tested on tasks in which they had experienced failure in school, they tended to set either very high or very low levels of aspiration. Presumably, this type of goal setting provides ego-protection for the child. Low goals provided protection from objective failure since low scores could readily be obtained; thus success was guaranteed. This is comparable to the C level of aspiration that is set by many college students at the beginning of each semester. On the other hand, high goal setting could be interpreted as indicating that the child had learned that he would be rewarded for effort, even if unsuccessful. In these cases it seems probable that the stated estimates do not represent the child's subjective level of aspiration; the unsuccessful child may "edit" his level of aspiration in order either to avoid failure or to receive approval for trying.

In a study by Gruen (1945) it was found that maladjusted and well-adjusted (as measured by a personality test) high school students differed in their responses to success and failure in a level of aspiration task. Following success, 100 per cent of the well-adjusted students raised their levels of aspiration, while only 78 per cent of the maladjusted students raised their levels of aspiration. In fact, 7 per cent of the maladjusted lowered their estimates following success. Following failure 7 per cent of the well-adjusted students raised their estimates, 65 per cent did not change their estimates, and 28 per cent lowered them. Twenty per cent of the maladjusted students increased their estimates following failure, 23 per cent did not change their estimates, while 57 per cent lowered them. In other words, the well-adjusted students tended to increase their levels of aspiration following success, and either to keep them at the same level or to lower them following failure. On the other hand, the maladjusted students were less inclined to raise their levels of aspiration following success, and tended to respond to failure by making significant shifts in their estimates. These findings suggest that the maladjusted students were more sensitive to failure and attempted to protect themselves after a failure by aspiring for readily obtainable low scores or effort-rewarded excessively high scores.

These and many other studies point to the fact that our levels of aspiration are regulated by our experiences of success and failure. We set our goals in ways we anticipate will produce the greatest amount of ego-protection; we choose goals we believe will result in greatest gains and/or smallest losses in self-esteem.

Ego-protection as a motivational process does not require any special principles of motivation; fundamentally, ego-protection differs in no way from other motivational processes we have considered. In fact, ego-protection as a process is perfectly analogous to that of homeostatic drives. For example, as we pointed out previously, we learn to seek food either when the hunger drive increases or when stimuli arouse anticipations of highly palatable foods. The goal produces net pleasant consequences either by reducing the unpleasant hunger drive or by providing pleasant tastes and smells. Similarly we seek ego-protecting goals either when self-esteem is threatened or when we anticipate obtaining the pleasant experiences of success. Further, in the same way that highly pleasant foods may be non-nutritive and hence are in the long run maladaptive choices, some successfully obtained goals provide little ego-protection. The world's best dart thrower is accorded little esteem by the majority in our culture; many other activities are more rewarding from an ego-protection point of view.

Another important psychological fact is that yesterday's success, like yesterday's food, does not necessarily satisfy today's need. Adequate ego-protection requires a motto of "Excelsior." It is provided only by constantly seeking and reaching new, more difficult goals. As soon as a goal is reached the ego-protection provided by that success begins to "evaporate or decay" and new goals must be reached if the feeling of protection is to be kept at the same level. As strange as it may seem, some straight A students are unhappier than straight C students. Since the straight A student has reached the highest obtainable goal as far as grades are concerned he is in a very vulnerable position. Lower grades will produce feelings of failure, while additional A's will not provide the amount of self-esteem they provided when they were first obtained. Once again, the attractiveness of ego-related goals depends upon the subjective probability of attainment; as objective attainment increases, attractiveness decreases.

Motives in Conflict

As Lewin (1935) stressed, motives do not appear in a vacuum; they always appear in combinations, and they are always in conflict with other motives. The "simple" planning a young man may engage in before taking a girl out for dinner may involve simultaneous anticipations of relief from hunger, pleasant tastes of novel and familiar food, the esteem provided by the reputation of the restaurant chosen, and, perhaps, some amount of sexual conquest. Ordinarily, we choose our goals from among many alternatives; and choices always involve conflict. Conflict may arise from different motives, different incentives, or different means of obtaining incentives. For example, the young man may have had to choose from among the following alternatives: going to a football game with his friends or taking the girl to dinner (different motives), several possible girls (different incentives), and several restaurants (different means of obtaining incentives).

Approach-Approach. Lewin classified conflict situations into three basic types: approach-approach, avoidance-avoidance, and approach-avoidance. In approach-approach conflict, the individual must choose one of two attractive goals. Buridan's Ass starving between two stacks of hay illustrates this conflict. The young man in our example, taking the girl out for dinner, was in the midst of several approach-approach conflicts. We are constantly required to choose one of perhaps several attractive goals. Although the choice may be difficult when the incentives are nearly equal in attractiveness, this type of conflict is usually solved without much difficulty. Barker (1942) found, for example, that the more similar the attractiveness of incentives, the longer the time required to make a choice and the greater the amount of vacillation. All choices were made, however, within a few seconds. Studies with rats have shown that there is much vacillation even when it is simply a matter of choosing between two alleys leading to the same attractive incentive (Thiessen and McGaugh, 1958).

Avoidance-Avoidance. In the second type of conflict, avoidance-avoidance, the individual is forced to choose one of two equally undesirable alternatives; he is placed "between the devil and the deep blue sea." For a student taking a required course that he dislikes intensely, the choice between attending classes and studying for examinations on the one hand and flunking the course on the other represents an avoidance-avoidance conflict; there is no pleasant way out. This type of conflict frequently results in the individual's trying to escape from the situation. Our unhappy student may decide to go to bed early on the night before the final examination. Sleep, like drugs, offers temporary reprieve from conflicts. Avoidance-avoidance conflicts are not easily resolved.

Approach-Avoidance. In the third type of conflict, approach-avoidance, the goal has both attractive and unattractive features. A child may simultaneously want and fear dogs, waves on the beach, and perhaps even his mother. The young man must spend money to impress his girl friend; a student must study hard in order to achieve his level of aspiration; the drug addict must undergo exceedingly painful withdrawal symptoms in order to break the drug addiction. Sawrey and his associates (1956) have shown that rats develop ulcers when they are forced to cross an electric grid in order to obtain food. Animals left in this conflict situation typically die from stomach ulceration. In more ways than one, approach-avoidance conflict is the most irritating type of conflict.

More complex types of conflict, not discussed explicitly by Lewin but implicit in his theoretical analysis, are multiple approach-approach and multiple approach-avoidance conflicts. We typically try to achieve many goals at the same time, and the choice of any one incentive may mean that others cannot be obtained. A person choosing from among several attractive jobs must choose only one. This simple fact means that the individual is forced to exclude many potentially attractive goals. Since humans can anticipate losses of potentially attractive goals as well as the attractiveness of the chosen goal, most choices involve both approach and avoidance conflicts. Further, since obtainable goals are less attractive, once a goal is chosen another previously less attractive goal may become relatively more attractive. A considerable amount of remorse may result from this phenomenon. Conflicts are never simply resolved.

Frustration of Motives

As we emphasized in our discussion of levels of aspiration, humans are not always successful in attaining the goals they seek. Krech and Crutchfield (1948) have pointed out that in view of man's physical environment, his biological limitations, the complexity of his psychological make-up, and the nature of his social environment, frustration is inevitable. Man is faced with continual frustrations, ranging from such insignificant daily events as the inability of a driver to find a convenient parking place to such immensely important obstacles as the inability of a father to find a job to support his family or the failure of law students to pass the bar examination. Just as there are many sources of frustration, there are also many effects of frustration. The effects that a frustrating event will have on the individual depend upon many factors—the type of block, the amount of ego-protection damage, the intensity of the blocked motive, as well as the individual's learned modes of response to frustration. Responses to frustration, like those to conflict, are never simple.

Emotional Response.   Emotional response is one consequence of frustration. If the individual perceives the block as originating from some external source he may become angry—particularly if the frustrating block is perceived as hostile and/or aggressive. McClelland and Apicella (1945) found that when the experimenters in a frustration experiment increased their hostility the subjects responded with increased anger. Subjects' anger did not increase, however, simply as a function of an increased number of successive frustrations. If, as in a typical ego-involved level of aspiration study, the individual perceives his own ability or personal characteristics to be the source of the block, frustration is more likely to produce feelings of failure and anxiety resulting from loss in self-esteem.

Goal-Oriented Response.   The frustrated subject may respond to the block in ways he believes will result in goal attainment. He may, as Krech and Crutchfield (1958) have pointed out, intensify his effort, change his means of attempting to reach the goal, or substitute another similar goal. For example, a student failing to attain an aspired-for B average in college might study harder, change his study habits, or lower his level of aspiration. Goals are not easily changed, and when they are changed, loss in self-esteem may force a person to "justify" his alternate goal by a process of rationalization. The student may say, for example, that grades are really unimportant, and besides, people who study and get good grades are "squares."

Defensive Reaction.   Defensive reactions to frustrations occur when the individual's self-esteem is at stake and he either has failed to surmount the block by goal-oriented responses, or is afraid to risk further goal striving because of the risk of greater ego-protection damage. The student's rationalization of his poor grades is an example of a defensive reaction. In fact, goal substitution may be a defensive reaction if it occurs without a prior intensification of effort or modified attack on the block. The greater the degree of ego-involvement, the greater the likelihood a defensive reaction to frustration will be used. The type of reaction to frustration also depends, however, on the success the individual has had with various goal attainment techniques. An individual who has experienced success in the past by intensification of effort may continue to respond in this same way even though he is highly ego-involved. A "successful" student does not give up trying if he receives a low grade on a midterm examination; he has learned how to respond appropriately to such a frustration.

Aggressive Reaction. Frequently, the emotional manifestation of frustration is physical attack upon the apparent source of the frustration. It may have been that in the early history of man this was an effective way of eliminating frustrating objects. That is, if the barrier to goal attainment is obvious, aggressive attack may be adaptive. Usually, however, we are unable to strike back directly at sources of frustration—parents, bullies, institutions, policemen, professors—so the aggression is frequently displaced to some substitute object that is either more available or less potentially dangerous. The office worker who is reprimanded by his boss the same day he fails in his bid for a coveted raise may vent his aggression upon his wife who in turn scolds the children who in turn yell at the dog who in turn chases the cat.

The anxiety and aggression produced by frustrations are important factors in the development, maintenance, and modification of prejudice. For example (Miller and Bugelski, 1948), boys in a summer camp were frustrated by being prevented from going to a much anticipated movie. Before the frustrating experience they rated their attitudes toward Mexicans and Japanese. After the frustration they rated their attitudes again toward the same groups. The results were that after the frustration the attitudes were considerably less favorable than they had been before the frustration. Presumably, aggression generated by frustration was displaced to these convenient, defenseless, nonthreatening groups. Socially recognized and condoned scapegoats are convenient targets for aggression.

MOTIVES AND BEHAVIOR TECHNIQUES

Motives are not to be equated with behavior. The attempt to reach a goal may be made in many different ways and any given behavior pattern may result from any of many different motives. Both the motives and behavior techniques of men vary; in the same individuals from time to time, from group to group, and from culture to culture. Modern Americans, Kwakiutl Indians, and Zuni Indians all seek self-esteem. The techniques they have used to obtain esteem, however, are quite different. Social status for a Kwakiutl Indian tribe was determined by the amount of personal property that could be destroyed in a public burning ceremony called a *potlatch.* Prestigeful status, or ego-protection, was obtained by ostentatious waste. The Zuni Indians, on the other hand, seemed to gain self-esteem by avoiding competition and self-assertion. For instance, anthropologists have reported that these people deliberately avoided winning foot-races.

FIXATION AND HABITUATION OF BEHAVIOR TECHNIQUES

Although incentives sought and behavior techniques used are both regulated by cultural requirements and rewards, there is considerable variability within any complex culture and for any individual within that complex culture. Through processes of socialization we learn what we should value and how we may go about achieving our goals. We learn very early, for example, that money is important, but we come to learn also that we are expected to obtain it only in certain ways. We find out that it is important to protect ego from damage, but we are seldom given personally satisfactory instructions as to how this is to be accomplished. Consequently, no matter the level of complexity, we invariably encounter at least some conflict whenever we strive to achieve our goals. From the simplest to the most complex goal striving, man anticipates and predicts the consequences of his behavior. The frame of reference he uses to judge the effectiveness of any of his goal-striving behavior is twofold: level of satisfaction in goal achievement and level of satisfaction in the goal-striving behavior itself.

Although in the early stages of development we may try many techniques in goal striving, once we find certain ones to be reasonably satisfactory we tend to use them over and over again. In other words, our goal-directed responses become more and more fixated, habituated, canalized. Eventually such behavior processes may become so ritualized that we are no longer aware of many of the ways in which we are actually behaving. For example, when a person first drives to his new place of work he is very aware of streets, houses, and signs along the way, and he attends to them carefully. During the first few days he may vary his route in search of one that is more efficient. Having settled on one, and after many trips, however, he no longer needs to think about the streets, houses, and signs in order to arrive at his destination; it is all carried out without much conscious effort. If he were to change his place of residence or work so that a different pattern of behavior were required, his ritualized behavior techniques would, of course, be useless, perhaps even detrimental, since they may interfere with the acquisition of new appropriate responses. Even with rats, for example, it has been shown that overlearning and the consequent mechanization of a response pattern decreases their tendencies to attend to and to learn about changes in the characteristics of a maze (Bruner, Matter, and Papanek, 1955).

Similarly the techniques we learn to use in attaining satisfactory or quasi-satisfactory ego-protection may become so mechanized that they are used without awareness. An individual may be unaware, for example, that he habitually withdraws or lowers his goals when he experiences a failure. In fact, his present behavior may be so obviously unsatisfactory that he is socially ridiculed for giving up so easily. But if the technique was successful at an earlier time it is likely that it will continue to be used for some time before it is discarded and replaced by a more satisfactory one.

In the next chapter we will discuss in greater detail the factors responsible for the development and maintenance of these aspects of our social behavior.

VI

Learning
and Socialization

Socially significant human behavior is learned. Every child is faced with the task of learning to think, want, believe, and act in ways similar to those of his elders.

If this book were concerned primarily with the social behavior of insects there would be no need for the present chapter, since insect behavior is controlled primarily by natively determined neurophysiological factors and sensory stimulation. The soldier ant does not have to live in a militaristic society and undergo special training in order to qualify for his job. His qualifications seem to result, rather, from a combination of genetic, nutritional, and hormonal conditions.

The task of the human parent would no doubt be less exasperating as well as less rewarding if children's behavior were known to be unaffected by parental guidance. Most parents believe, however, that they must and can influence and shape their children's social behavior; and in most human families tremendous effort is spent in this process of socialization. As Bugelski has commented:

From infancy on, the to-be-civilized human being is subjected to a training process calculated to make him an acceptable member of society. He is taught where and when to sleep, eat, wash behind the ears, read, write, and calculate, to earn his living, and to even grow old gracefully, or die nobly, depending upon how the great divisions of society are getting along with each other at the time. (1956, p. 1)

Although humans must learn to behave as humans, there is no assurance that any particular human can be taught to behave exactly like any other particular human. Watson once proposed to take any one of a dozen well-formed, healthy infants and train him to become "any type of specialist . . . doctor, lawyer, artist, merchant, chief and . . . even beggarman and thief, regardless of his talents, penchants, tendencies, abilities, vocations, and race of his ancestors." (1930, p. 104) This claim is viewed with skepticism for two reasons. First, there is considerable evidence that certain capacities are to a large extent controlled by heredity. No amount of environmental influence can, for example, overcome innate intellectual deficiency. Second, although much is known about the learning process and training techniques it is doubtful that the techniques are refined enough to enable anyone completely to control the socialization process. While there is little doubt that doctors, lawyers, and thieves are products of socialization, there is still much to be learned about the ways in which the social environment actually influences and determines social behavior. The term "socialization" designates a particular kind of behavior change, one in which the behavior of individuals comes to approximate that expected by other individuals.

THE NATURE OF LEARNING

All changes in animal behavior, whether temporary or permanent, are functions of the requirements of environmental situations. Not all behavior changes are adaptive, however, since adaptation must always be evaluated ecologically. Often the animal's environment changes so that acquired behavior which was previously adaptive becomes maladaptive. The dog that learns to beg for food may find that excessive begging is considered to be in "poor social taste" by another master and, as such, grounds for punishment. Similarly, the young child is continually confronted with changing sets of rules. Crying is appropriate behavior for babies but inappropriate for older children. Behavior change *may* be adaptive but changed behavior may not always remain adaptive.

Our attempts to understand the processes of learning underlying behavior change are complicated by the fact that any given behavior is determined jointly by many processes. Behavior may change for many reasons. The task facing the investigator is that of distinguishing those changes in behavior that are produced by changes in motivation, fatigue, illness, drugs, receptor sensitivity, and other factors affecting performance, from those that are due to the residual effects of past experience, or learning. Since we can observe only performance, any statements we make about learning must be based upon inferences. Learning cannot be directly observed; it must be inferred. When we say that Johnny has learned to talk, or write, or ride a bicycle, we mean that his behavior has changed, and that we assume the change is due to experience or practice, rather than to other possible factors. Why experiences can modify behavior is the major problem facing the learning theorist and one of the most important issues in contemporary psychology.

At a neurophysiological level, Hebb (1949) has suggested that learning is mediated by structural or biochemical changes in the neural elements activated by the particular stimulus situation. Such changes would provide a physiological basis for the behavior change that is observed. If Hebb's or some similar model is substantially correct it may be possible some day to study learning at a purely physiological level, that is, without observing behavior. Such a possibility, although highly intriguing from a theoretical point of view, is not, however, a necessity. We do not have to know what happens at a physiological level in order to know that learning has occurred; provided, of course, we have been careful in making our inferences.

Many psychologists have attempted to understand the learning process by investigating the behavioral-environmental conditions necessary to produce learning. Behavioral theories of learning, as contrasted with physiological theories, can be assessed without recourse to neurophysiological measurement. Ultimately, however, the two types of theories should lead to the same kinds of predictions about behavior. For the present discussion we will not attempt to evaluate either of these approaches to the study of learning; rather, we will present evidence to support some generalizations that can be made concerning the nature of learning.

Tolman (1932) and Woodworth (1958) have argued quite convincingly that learning consists of becoming acquainted with the environment, of learning what leads to what. According to this point of view, learning consists not in the tendency to make particular overt responses in the presence of particular stimuli, but rather in the acquisition of knowledge about the objects and events encountered. The implication of this cognitive view of learning is that organisms come to behave appropriately to the degree that they have acquired the correct information about the environment.

The Learned Response

A number of attempts have been made to derive general principles of learning from the basic results of Pavlov's investigations of conditioned response learning (1927). Pavlov's general procedure consisted of presenting a neutral stimulus (such as the sound of a metronome) to a dog shortly before the presentation of a small quantity of powdered food. After a number of paired presentations the dog was observed to salivate to the sound of the metronome, prior to the presentation of the food. The response of salivating to the previously neutral stimulus has been termed a "conditioned response" and the eliciting stimulus a "conditioned stimulus." The original response of salivating to the food is referred to as an "unconditioned response," and the food as an "unconditioned stimulus." In other experiments, many different stimuli have been used as conditioned stimuli; many responses other than salivation have been studied, and many other stimuli (e.g., electric shock) have been used as unconditioned stimuli. Unfortunately, the results of these studies have frequently been misinterpreted as indicating that learning is a matter of simple stimulus substitution—a process of substituting a new (conditioned) stimulus in place of the old (unconditioned) stimulus. Such a theoretical view of learning is inaccurate. Conditioning consists of learning the *meaning* of the conditioned stimulus. Careful investigations have shown, for example, that conditioned responses are typically *different* from unconditioned responses. In rats, the unconditioned responses to a shock are typically jumping and vocalizing, while the conditioned responses are crouching and suspension of breathing. On the basis of these and similar observations, many investigators have argued that the conditioned response is typically preparatory; that the animal behaves as though it were preparing for the forthcoming unconditioned stimulus. Zener has described the anticipatory or preparatory nature of responses made by a dog which had experienced the presentation of food following the onset of a bell:

Except for the component of salivary secretion the conditioned and unconditioned behavior is not identical. (a) During most of the time in which the bell is reinforced by the presence of food, chewing generally occurs with the head raised out of the food pan but not directed either at the bell or into the food pan, or at any definite environmental object. Yet this posture never, even chewing alone occasionally, occurs to the conditioned stimulus alone. Despite Pavlov's assertions, the dog does not appear to be eating an imaginary food. (b) Nor is the behavior that does appear an arrested or partial unconditioned reaction consisting of those response elements not conflicting with other actions. It is a different reaction, anthropomorphically describable as looking for, expecting the fall of food with a readiness to perform the eating behavior which will occur when the food falls. The effector pattern is not identical with the unconditioned. (c) Movements frequently occur which do not appear as part of the unconditioned response to food: all the restless behavior of stamping, yawning, panting. (Hilgard and Marquis, 1940, pp. 39–40)

Thus, it appears that even conditioned response learning, which many psychologists have pointed to in attempting to emphasize that learning is simply acquiring particular responses, really consists of learning what leads to what rather than the fixation of simple, rigid, mechanistic responses. If an investigator focuses his interest on only one aspect of the response, the conclusions regarding what has been learned are likely to be at best misleading and at worst quite inaccurate. If a trained subject is tested only under the training conditions it is impossible to tell what the subject has actually learned about the experimental situation. Zener could tell that his dogs had learned (an inference from the behavior changes) and that the conditioned responses were unlike the unconditioned responses in many details. In order to find out what has been learned subjects must be tested under many different conditions.

The answer to the question, "What has been learned?" depends on the way the question is asked. Liddell (1942) has reported an experiment in which a sheep was first trained to flex his foreleg at a signal preceding a shock to the leg. Following this the sheep was placed on its back and the signal was presented. When this was done the foreleg was not flexed; all four legs were stiffened and the animal attempted to lift its head. In another experiment reported by Liddell (1942) a dish of oats was used as a signal that a shock was to be applied to the foreleg of a sheep. At first the sheep ate the oats when they were presented. After training, the appearance of the dish was followed by a vigorous flexion of the leg. The sheep was then tested to see if it would eat from the dish under other circumstances. It was placed in the barn with several other sheep and the dish of oats was placed in the center of the floor. Although the other sheep clustered around the dish and ate, the sheep for which the oats meant shock carefully avoided the dish. Clearly, the learning consisted of more than mere leg flexion. The sheep had learned that eating from the dish was followed by shock and it behaved appropriately.

These, along with many other studies, demonstrate that what is performed, as distinguished from what is learned, depends upon many factors. For example, Ritchie *et al.* (1950) have shown that in the early stages of learning a simple T maze, rats can acquire dispositions to go to a particular place in the maze for a food reward even if they are required to make different turning responses on successive trials in order to get to the same place. They argued, on the basis of their findings, that such learning is based in the early stages on the acquisition of a place disposition. However, with continued practice of the learned response they found that a specific turning habit developed. Thus it seems that with overtraining, cognitive dispositions may give way to specific routine responses. With practice, habituation sets in. What is learned depends, then, not only upon what question is asked but upon the conditions, stage, and degree of training as well. Ritchie also found that when the highly trained turning response of some animals was disrupted by introducing a three-inch gap in the floor of the maze at the choice point, there was hesitation, after which they jumped the gap and then went to the previously rewarded place in the maze. Thus, interference with the response habit allowed the original place disposition to determine alley choices once again.

As these studies indicate, learning is not simply a matter of acquiring specific responses. Learning consists of acquiring dispositions to behave in terms of the requirements of the environment. Adequate adaptive behavior requires a knowledge of the environment as well as the ability to make responses appropriate to the environment.

The Nature of the Stimulus

If we are to understand behavior we must distinguish between the physical environment and the psychological environment of the individual.

Any attempt to answer the question, "What is the stimulus (or portion of the environment) eliciting the response?" requires that we keep this distinction in mind. We cannot assume that the stimulus is simply that feature of the physical environment which the experimenter considers important.

Discrimination Learning. Many studies with children and infrahumans have shown that the psychologically effective stimulus in a simple discrimination learning task may be the relationship among the stimuli rather than the specific characteristics of any of the stimuli in the task. If a subject is first rewarded for choosing the darker of two grey cards, and then is offered a choice between the previously rewarded grey and a still darker grey he usually selects the darker grey (Kohler, 1929). Such transposition (sometimes referred to as a specialized case of stimulus generalization) of behavior along any stimulus dimensions seems to be a fundamental characteristic of learning. Ordinarily, transposition occurs only when the testing stimuli are not too different from the training stimuli. For instance, in a brightness discrimination experiment such as just discussed, subjects do not necessarily continue to choose the darker stimulus if the testing stimuli are extremely dark. Johnson and Zara (1960) have shown, however, that the range of transposition can be increased by emphasizing the relationship between the stimuli. Nursery school children simultaneously trained on two size discriminations transposed more than children trained on only one pair of stimuli. The emphasis upon the relationship seemed also to enhance the learning; the children trained on two pairs also learned faster than those trained on only one pair.

Riley (1958) reports that the effective stimulus in discrimination learning is the relationship between the various parts of a stimulus complex. He found that transposition could be obtained even with stimuli quite different from the training stimuli as long as the relationship between the brightness of the two stimuli and the background remained constant. Subjects continued to choose the brighter of two stimuli as long as the ratio of the brighter stimulus to the darker one to the background remained constant. Correct transposition was not obtained when the brightness of the background was not varied along with that of the two stimuli.

The conclusion to be drawn from these transposition studies is that the psychologically effective stimuli in a learning situation cannot always be identified merely by examining a restricted portion of the physical environment.

Motivation and Learning. The basic assumption of the cognitive view of learning emphasized in this chapter is that learning is a process of finding out what leads to what or, more generally, of finding out about the environment. In transposition experiments, such as the first discussed above, the animal learned the general principle that the darker of two doors led to a food reward. Presumably the darker door was then chosen because of the *value* of the food for the hungry animal. According to this view, rewards act by controlling what is done, not what is learned. Although there is considerable evidence that identifiable rewards are not necessary for learning, (Thistlewaite, 1951), it seems clear that what is learned does depend upon the organism's motivational state. What is learned about any situation depends to a large degree upon the extent to which the individual attends to the various aspects of the situation.

Several experiments (Spence and Lippitt, 1946; Kendler, 1947; Kendler and Menscher, 1948) have shown that animals may not learn the location of food in a maze if they are trained while thirsty and rewarded with water. In one experiment, for example (Grice, 1948), thirsty but food-satiated rats were trained to run in a T maze at either end of which was a water reward. The floor of one of the goal-boxes containing water was covered with food pellets. When the animals were then deprived of food and satiated with water, they failed to choose the alley that led to the food pellets. Apparently they did not respond to the irrelevant incentive (food) while they were thirsty. Other experiments, however, indicate that thirsty rats will learn the location of food if they are not rewarded with water while in the maze (Strange, 1950) or if the food is not placed near the water source in the maze (Thistlethwaite, 1952; McAllister, 1952). Contact with a motivationally appropriate incentive apparently acts in some way to narrow the field of attention.

Attending to one stimulus apparently results in a lessened ability to attend to other stimuli. Studies with humans indicate that over-all efficiency of performance is substantially impaired when subjects are required to attend to two or more tasks requiring either the same or different senses (Broadbent, 1952; Mowbray, 1952). As Berlyne has commented, "There is a legend that Julius Caesar could read, talk, write, and think about different topics at once. . . . We can safely assume that if Julius Caesar was capable of this feat, few other human beings have been able to emulate it. (1960, p. 13)

Incidental Learning. The effect of attention on learning is perhaps most clearly illustrated by studies of incidental learning in humans. In these experiments the attempt is made to find out what subjects learn about a task or set of materials in the absence of any explicit instructions to learn. These experiments are particularly relevant for social psychologists since, in comparison with typical learning experiments in the laboratory, the incidental learning experiments approximate more closely the conditions under which most human social learning occurs. Children are seldom specifically instructed to learn that people like "us" are good and people unlike "us" are bad. Somehow children learn such things without the aid of specific instructions.

Woodworth was one of the first psychologists to emphasize the importance of set, or instructions, in determining what is learned even incidentally. The following is Woodworth's description of his pioneer experiment on incidental learning:

I read a list of twenty pairs of unrelated words to a group of 16 adult subjects, instructing them beforehand to learn the pairs so as to be able to respond with the second of each pair when the first should be given as a stimulus. But, after reading the list three times, I told them that they should, if possible, give also the first word of the following pair on getting the second word of the preceding pair as stimulus. I then read the first word of the list, waited five seconds for the subjects to recall and write the second word; then read this second word, and waited the same time for them to recall and write the third word, namely, the first word of the second pair; and so on through the list. The results were most definite; the second members of the pairs were correctly recalled in 74 per cent of all cases, but the first members were recalled in only 7 per cent of the cases. The subjects reported that this great difference was apparently due to the fact that they had examined each pair with the object of finding some character or meaning in it; whereas they had neglected the sequence of pairs as being of no moment. . . . (1958, p. 225)

In another early experiment on incidental learning (Jenkins, 1933), students acting as experimenters read lists of nonsense words to subjects (other students) who had been instructed to learn the words. The following day both the experimenter and the subjects were asked to recall the words. The subjects, not too surprisingly, recalled more words than did the experimenters. Although several experimenters reported that they deliberately attempted to learn the words, the fact that those who did not attempt to learn also remembered many of the words indicates that some learning does occur without intent to learn. Nevertheless, with an equal degree of exposure to the materials, intentional learning appears to be superior to incidental learning.

In more recent experiments, Postman and his associates (1955) have shown that the difference between the amount learned under incidental and intentional learning conditions depends to a large degree on the characteristics of the task to be learned. If the items in the task are very easy to discriminate, intentional learning may be no better than incidental learning. However, if the items in a task are unfamiliar and difficult to discriminate, intentional learning is typically superior to incidental learning. (Postman, Adams, and Phillips, 1955)

These and many other similar experiments indicate that what is learned in a given situation depends jointly upon the nature of the situation and the motivation of the subject; sheer exposure to stimuli without motivational significance is, for both rats and men, no guarantee that learning will occur. The motivational significance can be controlled either by instructing the subject or by using stimuli of known value. In either case, more is learned about the environment when the subject's attention is directed to the features of the environment that are to be recalled later.

THE NATURE OF SOCIALIZATION

Studies of rats in mazes and humans learning nonsense syllables have revealed what most parents have painfully discovered without help from psychologists: frequency of exposure to a stimulus situation is not necessarily positively correlated with the amount learned. If it were, children would need only to be required to observe adults in order to learn "appropriate" behavior. If "appropriate" behavior has little interest or meaning to the child it is doubtful that much learning will occur. Most children have ample opportunity to observe their parents' eating behavior, but it is the rare child who attends to their eating behavior, and still rarer the child who seriously attempts to imitate their behavior in detail. On the other hand, if the parent's behavior is somehow of interest to the child the parent may be surprised to find that the child has not only learned some of his behavior but takes delight in imitating it. The same child who seems constitutionally unable to learn "Mary had a little lamb" may have no difficulty in acquiring and repeating a few swear words or even a fairly complicated off-color joke.

If the child is to become socialized, he must somehow learn what is expected of him. More important, however, he must also behave in a manner expected of him. Appropriate behavior does not always result from knowledge of what is appropriate, however. The child may know that he is expected to clean his plate, wash his ears, brush his teeth, love his brothers and sisters, and study diligently in school. These social expectations may not, however, correspond with what the child wants to do. Socialization implies more than learning; it implies the acquisition of tendencies to behave in certain ways. It implies the control of performance as well as the acquisition of knowledge. As one writer has put it, the term socialization refers to ". . . the whole process by which an individual, born with the behavioral potentialities of enormously wide range, is led to develop actual behavior which is confined within a much narrower range— the range of what is customary and acceptable for him according to the standards of his group." (Child, 1954, p. 655)

Early Experiences

Although socialization is a continuous process, one that goes on more or less throughout an individual's lifetime, there is little doubt that early experiences have particularly profound and lasting effects on subsequent behavior.

Imprinting in infrahumans provides a striking demonstration of the long-term effects of early experiences. For many years, ethologists have observed that the young of many species, particularly wild birds, will, when reared by humans, develop a strong attachment for their foster parents. Birds reared by humans may later tend to avoid members of their own species and may even respond to humans with courtship and mating behavior typically evoked only by the opposite sex of their own species. From an adaptive point of view birds imprinted on humans are clearly unsocialized. Recent experimental studies of imprinting (Hess, 1962) indicate that it typically occurs quite early in the life of an animal. It has also been shown that animals can become imprinted to a great variety of stimulus objects. In one experiment, Hess (1959) exposed very young chicks to moving colored discs for a short period. Twenty-four hours later when each chick was tested in a situation where the object on which it had been imprinted was exposed along with several discs not previously seen, they tended to follow only the disc to which they had been exposed previously. Additional evidence indicated that various objects resembling an adult chicken (e.g., a ball with wing and tail-like structures attached) were less effective imprinting stimuli than a simple round ball. Even more surprising was the finding that a stuffed leghorn rooster was the least effective stimulus of all those tested.

In a similar study Gray (1960) was able to imprint chicks to motionless black circles and triangles. The chicks were first hatched in isolation compartments and then exposed to either a circle or a triangle for a 24-hour period. In later tests with both stimuli present each chick showed a preference for the stimulus to which it had been exposed. This finding indicates that movement of the stimulus and following the moving stimulus are not essential for effective imprinting. Rather, the essential condition seems to be the perceptual salience of the stimulus. In this experiment a black figure against a grey background provided a relatively dominant stimulus in an otherwise austere visual environment. Gray's conclusion that "probably anything that will make an object stand out in the chick's visual environment will be a factor in imprinting" (p. 1834) seems justified by the bulk of the evidence. Under ordinary circumstances the dominant perceptual figure to a newly-hatched chick is an adult chicken. Imprinting this tends to insure that the chick will be attached to a stimulus that will aid in his survival. It is probably atypical that animals in their native habitats become imprinted on potentially dangerous objects. If this happened frequently the species would soon disappear. Although there is evidence that imprinting differs in some ways from typical associative learning (Hess, 1959, 1962), results of the imprinting studies emphasize the importance of the salience of the imprintable stimulus. Any stimulus contrast condition which helps to set the imprinting object off from the rest of the environment facilitates imprinting. In this respect imprinting is similar to the types of learning discussed previously. If the object is perceptually salient the probability is increased that it will be noticed, and if it is noticed learning is apt to occur.

In most studies of imprinting, the dependent variable is some measure of the animal's tendency to approach or follow the imprinted stimulus. Such evidence could be interpreted as showing merely that imprinting consists of the acquisition of a simple approach response. Peterson (1960) has shown, however, that ducklings will learn to perform a response when it is rewarded only by a presentation of a previously imprinted stimulus. Young ducklings were exposed to an imprinting stimulus (a yellow cylinder moving continuously back and forth in a black box in a slight swaying and twisting motion) for six 45-minute periods during the first and second days after hatching. They were then taught to peck a plexiglas disc which controlled the presentation of the imprinted stimulus. With this procedure the duckling pecked the disc at a very high rate. Further, unlike the result of similar experiments where food and/or water are used as a reward, the rate of pecking did not decline with increasing presentations of the reward—the imprinted stimulus. This finding is understandable in terms of our previous discussion of incentives. Food and water lose their incentive values because the intensity of hunger and thirst drives is gradually reduced. As far as we know, there is no corresponding drive that is reduced by presentations of the imprinted stimulus (Moltz, 1960).

Harlow's studies of the development of affection in monkeys, discussed in Chapter V, have shown that affectional responses develop according to a pattern similar to that found in imprinting with ducklings and chicks. This should not be too surprising in view of the findings that other mammals such as sheep and guinea pigs are quite readily imprinted (Hess, 1959). In all species investigated to date imprinting is most effective during a period shortly after birth (or hatching). Similarly, affectional responses in monkeys are more readily established and longer lasting if the baby monkey has contact with its surrogate mother shortly after birth.

Observations of maternal behavior in goats indicate that the experiences of the mother during a period shortly after the birth of the kid are critical in the development of maternal behavior. Normally, a mother will nurse only her own offspring and will vigorously reject other kids. Hersher *et al* (1958) separated newborn kids from their mothers for a short period of time (one-half to one hour) shortly after birth (five to ten minutes). The kids were then returned and permitted or helped to nurse their own mothers. Mothers in a control group were allowed to follow the normal caretaking pattern without disruption. Tests of mother-kid interaction were then given two and three months later. Each mother was observed with three kids, her own and two others, for fifteen minutes. In comparison with the control mothers the separated mothers nursed their own kids less and nursed the other kids more. The short separation following birth had long-term effects on maternal behavior. The "normal" preference of the mother for her own kid seems to depend upon experiences during a critical period. Imprinting seems, then, to work two ways.

These studies of imprinting and the development of affection in infra-humans provide clear evidence that early experiences are particularly important in the development of social behavior. Evidence for a "critical period" in the development of social attachments in humans is unfortunately somewhat less impressive. Note, however, the difference in the "critical period" for ducklings and monkeys. For ducklings the critical period is over within a few days after hatching. For monkeys, the period seems to extend for several months. In view of the slower rate of development of humans, even when compared with the monkeys studied by Harlow, the critical period (or periods) for humans might be expected to extend over a period of many months, or perhaps even several years. Since children in our culture are ordinarily nurtured by one person, the mother, throughout infancy and childhood, it is no surprise from any point of view that strong affectional ties are ordinarily developed with that person. Clinical evidence indicates that individuals deprived of affection during infancy and childhood may have difficulties in showing affection later in life. There is no clear evidence as yet, however, that any one particular period during infancy and childhood is more important than any other in the development of affection. In spite of the lack of evidence for the importance of a critical period for later social behavior, there is little reason to doubt that early experiences *are* important. The fact that early experiences are the first experiences an individual has is reason enough to expect that they will be particularly important. Studies of proactive interference in learning indicate the difficulty of changing responses that have already been learned. Early learning is thus important if only for its effects on ease of subsequent learning.

Early experience may also be important because of the frequency with which the child is likely to experience objects and events in his environment. Mothers are seen more frequently by the preschool child than when he later attends school. In addition, the entire daily routine is likely to be more constant for very young children. Although frequency is no guarantee of learning, children are more likely to learn about the things they encounter frequently.

Perhaps more important for social behavior, however, is the fact that most of the behavior patterns the child learns are temporary. His future life will be filled with discontinuities. The child is faced with a constantly changing set of rules. Eating and toilet habits must change. The previously effective response of crying now comes to elicit punishment. Dependent behavior, once solicited by the parent, becomes grounds for rejection. The requirements of socialization thus seem almost to guarantee that the child will become at least somewhat confused; he has to learn to behave in an unstable, changing environment.

Any given behavior pattern is only *likely* to be approved or disapproved. This is the reason for Brunswick's thesis (Postman and Tolman, 1959) that conclusions based on results of learning studies in which subjects are consistently rewarded are not applicable to "real life" learning. But if, as we have suggested, learning is the process of finding out about the environment, then environmental instability is just another category of knowledge that must be acquired for purposes of survival. How individuals perform after such knowledge is acquired is a problem of motivation.

Limitations of Socialization Research

Parents use many and varying techniques in their attempts to rear children so that they will become adequate members of their culture. And most parents, even those from primitive cultures, claim that they are able to evaluate the relative effectiveness of socialization techniques. These evaluations may range from such clichés as "spare the rod and spoil the child" to complex psychological theories of personality. A thorough, comprehensive evaluation of the relationship between socialization techniques and resulting behavior would require a tremendous body of articulated data. But, as one authority has commented, "The plain fact is that this body of accumulated knowledge is not yet in existence. . . . There is no hard core of well-established and interrelated principles around which the study of socialization is focused. There are, rather, a large numer of ill-assorted concepts and very tentative hypotheses." (Child, 1954, pp. 656–657)

Thus, although adults of any society may believe they know how to socialize their young, behavioral scientists who have examined available socialization data in detail are much more reserved and skeptical. This skepticism does not stem from any doubt that socialization can be investigated by scientific method. It results, rather, from a knowledge of the nature of the data on socialization that have been collected as well as the observation that so far these data do not adequately fit into a truly comprehensive theory of socialization.

The experimental method is, for many reasons, the preferred method of scientific investigation. Unhappily, this approach cannot be used by social psychologists who are interested in long-range socialization processes at the human level. To illustrate, let us suppose that we were interested in the effects on adult social behavior of short-term separation of human infants from their mothers. Such a study would be of critical importance in view of the work on imprinting in lower animals. To investigate the problem experimentally some infants would need to be separated from their mothers. Other mothers would be required by the experimental design to stay with these infants during the separation period. It would be necessary to insure that the two groups of mothers and infants did not differ systematically in any other characteristics which might be expected to produce differences in adult social behavior. This could be attempted (but not guaranteed) by selecting mothers according to either a random or a systematic procedure. The latter would involve attempts to insure that the two groups of mothers were alike with respect to intelligence, age, socio-economic status, and other relevant factors. Further complications would of course arise if age of the infant at time of separation and duration of the separation period were to be systematically investigated. For obvious reasons, human experimentation of this type is impossible.

Since rigorous experimental procedures cannot be used to study human socialization, the only methods left are those involving observation without manipulation. Psychologists interested in problems of human socialization must resort to correlational procedures. Interpretations of the results of correlational studies, however, must be made with great caution. For example, let us suppose that an investigator has reported finding a substantial correlation between severity of toilet training (as reported by mothers) and aggressiveness during adolescence. Obviously, it would be premature to conclude that adolescent aggression results from severe toilet training procedures. As Child points out, "What [the scientist] has called severity of toilet training, for example, might conceivably be only a measure of the mother's frankness in admitting her severity to an interviewer and not at all related to actual severity, and the mother's frankness may grow out of general personality characteristics which have an important influence on the child." (1954, p. 659) Another possibility, typically overlooked, is that maternal and child aggressiveness may be related as a function of similarity in genetic makeup. There is, as a matter of fact, some evidence that human temperament is regulated in part by genetic factors (Fuller and Thompson, 1960). What are sometimes thought to be socialization-produced behavior patterns may actually be due to hereditary factors or, perhaps, an interaction between genetic and environmental factors. For example, a constitutionally active, excitable child is apt to do things which are disturbing to his parents. If the parents are easily annoyed then the child is apt to be frequently punished. Inactive children, by the same reasoning, would be less likely to receive punishment for their behavior. Thus, correlation between severity of punishment in childhood and later emotionality might be due partially to genetic factors and partially to interaction. It seems that this probable interaction has been largely neglected by socialization research. The technical limitations in human socialization research are such that the contributions of hereditary factors to social behavior are extremely difficult to assess. The fact that environmental factors are easier to measure and control should not, however, result in neglecting the possible role of genetic factors as important in the control of socially significant behavior.

Another limitation upon the results of available socialization studies has to do with the nature of the measures used. Rarely does the investigator have the opportunity to measure both the actual socialization treatment and the actual behavior of the subject at a later time. Typically the investigator is able only to obtain reports of socialization techniques used at an earlier time. These reports may be made either by the socialization agent (a parent) or the individual who has been the recipient of the socialization procedure (the child). If there has been a lapse of time between the actual occurrence of the treatment and time at which it is reported to the investigator, the validity of the data is open to serious question. Combined errors of omission and commission may easily result in reported treatments quite unlike the events as they actually occurred. Even under ideal conditions the possibility of distortion is great whenever an event is reported from memory (Bartlett, 1932; Allport and Postman, 1947). When conditions are less than perfect, either due to a time lapse or to the use of questions potentially great in motivational significance for either parent or child, the chances of obtaining valid reports are apt to be quite low. Even more subject to biasing influences, perhaps, is the technique of obtaining information both about socialization treatment and behavior of the child from the parent. Such data may sometimes yield interesting information about the parent, but may quite easily lead to false conclusions about the child.

The individual learns many things in the process of becoming socialized. He learns not only how to behave—the most obvious dependent variable— but he learns also what to believe and what to want. Since behavior depends so much upon motives many researchers have focused their interest on the socialization of attitudes and motives. The value of such research depends of course upon the validity of the measures used in assessing these genotypic variables. One serious danger in this type of research is that evidence of the lack of relationship between a socialization technique and a given motive or attitude does not necessarily indicate a lack of effect of the technique. It may very well be that in such an instance the motive or attitude had been inadequately assessed.

Environmental Influences

One of the most frequently used methods in the study of socialization is that of measuring the relationship between environmental influences on the one hand, and attitudes, motives, or behavior on the other. In studies of this kind attempts have not been made to assess the extent or nature of the subject's contact with the socialization agent. For example, one potential environmental influence is parental attitude. Since it is impossible to measure the actual degree of contact that a child has with that part of his parents' behavior that is indicative of particular attitudes, again such studies are limited to an investigation of the relationship between attitudes of parents and attitudes of children.

Studies of this type have found the relationship to be generally low but positive. For example, one study (Hirshberg and Gilliland, 1942) found positive correlations ranging from .29 to .59 between the attitudes of college students and their parents. Thus, although the relationships are not substantially high, they do suggest that parental attitudes are probably often very influential in the development of children's attitudes.

The mere fact that parents reveal their attitudes to their children does not necessarily mean, however, that their children will adopt them uncritically. For instance, the study by Cooper and Blair (1959) reported in detail earlier, suggests that parent-child attitude similarity probably varies with the attitude of the child toward the parent. College students who had unfavorable attitudes toward their parents indicated that their social ideologies were quite dissimilar to those of their parents, while those students who had favorable attitudes toward their parents indicated that there was little discrepancy between their social ideologies and those of their parents. As Krech and Crutchfield have commented:

To say that the family is important in shaping attitudes or beliefs is not equivalent to saying that the child will take over attitudes and beliefs ready-made from the parents. The influence is possible, but whether the child will develop or not develop the same belief as his parents hold depends upon the importance and meaning of that belief for the child himself. . . . In some instances the effect of the parents' influence can be seen to account for the rise of a belief or attitude that is in opposition to the parents' belief. (1948, pp. 181–182)

Thus it seems clear that in the learning of attitudes, as well as in the learning of other kinds of knowledge, sheer exposure is not enough. Children may learn what their parents' attitudes are, but this is no guarantee that they will adopt them. Whether or not they come to share their parents' attitudes depends upon many factors, including their fondness and respect for their parents and, perhaps, more important, the dominant attitude expressed by other socializing influences. After all, parents represent only a portion of the environment for any child. As Murphy, Murphy, and Newcomb have pointed out; "While parents are the immediate sources of attitudes and patterns of social behavior, they are also mediators of values and emphasis in the culture as a whole. . . ." (1937, p. 371) If the attitudes of parents are consistent with those expressed by other socializing agencies, the likelihood is increased that their children will share their attitudes.

Prevailing parental attitudes are not the only or even, perhaps, the dominant attitude sources. The importance of the child's contact with prevailing community attitudes in the development of his own attitudes cannot be overstressed. Physical contact with minority group members is not necessary for the development of negative attitudes toward such groups. Radke and Sutherland (1949) found, for example, well-developed attitudes toward Jews and Negroes in midwestern children who had had little if any contact with either group. And Rosenblith (1949) found that in spite of the complete absence of Jews and Negroes in a particular region of South Dakota, prejudice scores of subjects from that region were higher than those obtained by other investigators in areas where subjects had extensive contact with members of these minority groups. On the other hand, contact with minority group members is no guarantee that favorable attitudes will develop. In his classic study of the development of attitudes toward Negroes, Horowitz (1936) found that boys from New York City were about as prejudiced toward Negroes as were children from Georgia and Tennessee. On the basis of this as well as other findings of his study, Horowitz made the following comment:

In the course of this presentation, it has been found necessary to contradict many of the oft-repeated cliches current in the discussion of the race problem. Young children were found to be not devoid of prejudice; contact with a "nice" Negro is not a universal panacea; living as neighbors, going to a common school, were found to be insufficient; Northern children were found to differ very, very slightly from Southern children. It seems that attitudes toward Negroes are now chiefly determined not by contact with Negroes, but by contact with the prevalent attitude toward Negroes. (1936, pp. 34–35)

Socialization involves the acquisition of acceptable behavior. The attitudes that are picked up are likely to be those to which the child is exposed. As long as movies and television portray Negroes as simple-minded servants, and as long as ethnic jokes about Negroes are part of a child's approved social environment, negative prejudice toward this minority group will no doubt continue. Children do not need to be told which attitudes are acceptable. What parents fail to communicate, other communication media —newspapers, magazines, friends, neighbors, and sometimes even the church and school—will provide. There are many effective socialization agencies.

Socialization Techniques

Let us now turn briefly to a consideration of the specific socialization techniques used by parents. We have already discussed one technique, simple exposure to attitudes and behavior. As we saw, the effectiveness of this technique depends upon many factors. Usually, however, parents do not place much faith in passive socialization. Rather, rewards and punishment are almost universally used by parents in the attempt to increase their degree of control over children's behavior. It is typically assumed that controlling behavior is a simple process; children will come to behave properly, it is argued, if they are rewarded for appropriate behavior and punished for inappropriate behavior. But rewards and punishment are not forces that regulate behavior. To the child they are environmental events, experiences that accompany certain kinds of behavior. The effectiveness of rewards and punishments in regulating behavior depends, of course, upon many factors. Most important of these factors are: the nature of the event that is called a reward or punishment; the affective consequence of the event for the child; and, in the case of punishment, the value of the incentive the child is attempting to obtain by means of inappropriate behavior as well as the availability of alternate ways of obtaining the same incentive.

In a large-scale study of parental behavior by means of intensive interviews, Sears *et al.* investigated the child-rearing practices of 379 mothers from two New England communities. Although these data are subject to limitation since they are based solely upon the mothers' reports of their own as well as their children's behavior, the conclusions regarding the effectiveness of punishment as a socialization technique are unambiguous:

> Punitiveness, in contrast with rewardingness, was a quite ineffectual quality for a mother to inject into her child training. The evidence for this is overwhelming. The unhappy effects of punishment have run like a dismal thread through our findings. Mothers who punished toilet accidents severely ended up with bedwetting children. Mothers who punished dependency to get rid of it had more dependent children than mothers who did not punish. Mothers who punished aggressive behavior severely had more aggressive children than mothers who punished lightly. They also had more dependent children. Harsh physical punishment was associated with high childhood aggressiveness and with the development of feeding problems. Our evaluation of punishment is that it is ineffectual over the long term as a technique for eliminating the kind of behavior toward which it is directed. (1957, p. 484)

Thus, according to this study, punishment not only fails essentially to produce control over the child's behavior, but it produces many undesirable side-effects as well. As was pointed out, one serious result is increased aggression. Although the aggression may be directed at the punishing parent (much to the increased annoyance of the parent) the fear of additional punishment from the parent may result in the child displacing his aggression to some less threatening recipient. The following example of a mother's comment taken from the report of Sears *et al.* is illustrative:

> . . . she seldom turns around and is directly defiant. If she can't get what she wants or if she is angry about something, she'll walk by, and she'll probably fight the first person she comes in contact with. She doesn't usually turn around and defy us or take it out on us. Usually she'll go out and fight with anybody she sees, or she'll turn around and slap the dog on the leg. (p. 232)

Another consequence of punishment is the arousal of anxiety resulting from the anticipation of punishment. If the anxiety is great enough it may inhibit performance of the punishable behavior. If the incentive for the undesirable behavior is great, however, the child might misbehave in spite of the fear of punishment. Thus, one reason punishment is ineffectual in eliminating responses is that it teaches the child only that certain behavior will result in unpleasant consequences. If the behavior is rewarding in other ways, punishment merely induces conflict. Spanking a child, for example, is not likely to be effective in keeping him from asking for popsicles on hot summer days.

If the child learns that he is punished only when he is caught, he may soon learn either to be very careful not to be detected or he may learn to lie about his behavior. In other words, the child may learn various methods of avoiding the punishment while continuing to behave in the same way.

Under some circumstances punishment may be effective in helping to eliminate undesirable behavior. Typically, punishment tells the child what he is expected not to do. If there are alternative ways of achieving the same goal, punishment may, by inhibiting behavior, increase the probability that a more socially accepted behavior may result. Thus the positive effects of punishment operate indirectly.

So far in our analysis of punishment we have been concerned only with its effects in controlling behavior. There is some evidence that punishment as a socialization technique has long-term effects on behavior. In a study by MacKinnon (1938), male college students were given the opportunity to cheat in a problem-solving task. Those subjects who did not cheat were found to have stronger guilt feelings than those who did cheat. More important for the present analysis was the finding that the students who did not cheat reported that their parents tended to use "psychological" punishment rather than physical punishment. Such punishment consisted of letting the child feel that he had fallen short of some expectation or that he had hurt his parents and was, as a result, in danger of being less loved by them. On the basis of cross-cultural data, Whiting and Child (1953) found further evidence that love-oriented punishment is positively related to strength of guilt feelings. The Glueck and Glueck study (1950) of factors associated with delinquency provides further evidence of the importance of types of punishment used in socialization. On the basis of interviews with the parents of delinquents and nondelinquents, they found that parents of nondelinquents tended to use love-oriented punishment while parents of delinquents tended to use physical punishment. These studies, taken together, suggest that the type of punishment (love-oriented vs. physical) is a significant variable in long-term socialization.

One other problem of punishment requires some comment. We have discussed punishment as though it were some tangible variable. The effect of a given treatment may, however, be quite different for different individuals. For example, most students do not want to receive an F on a college examination. One of our colleagues has reported, however, that one of his students was delighted by F's on several midterms in succession. The reason for the elation was the fact that her parents refused to allow her to marry her fiance as long as she remained in school. Flunking the course (as well as all others) would mean that she could no longer go to college and as a result would be free to marry. Clearly, predictions of the effects of any treatment must take into account the meaning of the treatment for the individual concerned.

Although punishment may seem to be the major socialization technique, we also attempt to control and to socialize our children by rewarding them for behavior we consider desirable. In comparison with punishment, rewards are considerably more effective techniques. The reason for the differential effects of rewards and punishments can be understood quite readily in terms of the information they provide. Punishment tells the child what not to do. Rewards tell him what to do.

The effect of rewards on behavior depends to a large extent upon the type of reward that is administered. In a study of factors related to the development of achievement motivation in children, Winterbottom (1953) found that of three types of rewards—physical affection, verbal praise, and awarding of a special treat or privilege—physical affection was the most closely associated with the development of motivation for high achievement. This finding parallels those discussed above and indicates the importance of love-related punishment in the development of feelings of guilt.

In the development of socially relevant motivation the most effective types of rewards and punishments seem to be those involving the administration or loss of emotional support. These findings are consonant with the view expressed throughout this book, that emotional satisfaction is an important regulator of human behavior. As we have indicated repeatedly, learning consists of finding out about the environment. Behavior is regulated, however, by the affective consequences provided by objects and events encountered.

VII

Communication
and Language

Since all serious students of human affairs have expressed interest in language it is no surprise that social psychologists have given so much attention to the problem of communication in general and language in particular. Currently, some 20 per cent of the publications which are classified in the *Psychological Abstracts* as social psychology are concerned with communication and language.

The reasons for the wide social psychological interest in communication and language are obvious. Since social psychologists study the individual within an interacting social context, the question of the means by which the individual interacts with other individuals is basic. In the very broadest sense, all interaction is communication. In a more refined sense, communication is highly specialized in every species, maximally stereotyped at the lower end of the phyletic scale and minimally stereotyped at the higher end of the phyletic scale. At the very top of the phyletic scale is man, whose communication is, on the one hand, most specialized and complex, and, on the other, least stereotyped.

In the broadest biological sense every animal is in a constant adaptation process. Physical events such as changes in temperature, illumination, and pressure are constantly being recorded by the organism through its sensory channels, and it is constantly using this information as a basis for bodily adjustment. These adjustments, we must assume, are homeostatic, even if they do not in all instances actually aid survival. Part of the environment includes other animals of similar and different species. Some of the stimuli which one organism dispenses are of a direct contact type, as when one animal pushes against another; and this, in the broadest sense, is communication, since one animal is responding to information provided by another.

At relatively complex levels of animal life specialized systems have emerged that permit remote exchange of such information. For example, when the gravid female stickleback enters the courting male's territory, he responds by a zigzag swimming motion in her direction. Her presence in his territory is a signal that releases a specialized pattern of behavior in him. In turn his zigzag motion is a signal that releases further stereotyped behavior in her; and so on until the fertilization process is completed. What is meant by remote communication is a system of signaling which is not dependent upon direct bodily contact, such as pushing. Remote systems are natively set in many of the lower animals, and survival and adaptation are as dependent upon them as upon the internal physiological systems of the individual animal. In fact, these signal and releaser systems are, in most of the lower species, native neurophysiological equipment upon which the individual is dependent just as much as it is dependent upon metabolic exchanges.

Since all animals are at least to some degree social, communication is adaptively indispensable. It seems probable that every species has its own unique communication system which is basically determined by genetic factors. At the same time, it appears that in the more complex social species, it is necessary for the individual to engage in these communication patterns relatively early. The individual must learn to use his native communication equipment. Otherwise, even though he is in a social situation in maturity, much of his communication equipment is inaccessible to him. For instance, if a lamb is taken from its mother at birth and raised by hand for even a short period, it will never become an adequate communicating member of the flock. Even though confined within the same pasture area it will not respond to the same social stimuli as the others, nor will it respond in ways which will release specialized, species-specific behavior in the other sheep. In such instances it seems, as we have suggested before, there is an early critical period during which native communication patterns must be practiced. Denied this, an animal is deprived of an important part of its potential adaptability.

At the human level we encounter an amazingly complex communication potential. Man communicates through a greater variety of channels than does any other species; he vocalizes, gestures, writes, draws pictures, shapes inert matter, fabricates and plays musical instruments, and communicates at a conscious level with himself. Of these, and other less obvious channels, vocalization is, of course, used by far the most. Vocalization is the most variable and manipulable means of human communication as well, since it is used as language—a unique human phenomenon. The potential expressions of language are incalculable. The total number of combinations of sounds the human voice can produce and the human ear can discriminate is unknown. When we add to this the meaningful syntactic arrangements into which such auditory combinations can be organized, an accounting would be astronomical. Any person, even the most accomplished linguist, can have used but a minute fraction of his human vocal potential. He could have been reared in many other cultural settings, any one of which would have provided him with entirely different sound patterns and syntactic combinations which he would have learned instead. Man's potential for language is virtually unlimited, though the particular form the individual's expression and receptive understanding will take depends upon factors other than his biologically determined capacity.

The adaptively important means of communication which are available to man must, however, be brought into use by social stimulation. And, especially with language, it seems essential for practice to start early. While an optimal or critical period is yet to be identified, some students of this subject are convinced that there is such a critical period, and that unless the child is afforded language opportunity at such a time, he will never develop an adequate social adaptation though he learns later to speak. Modern man's social life and capacity to understand himself in terms of his surroundings depends so much upon his use of a socially appropriate language that the only conclusion we may draw is that language is of survival value to man just as much as the natively stereotyped "signal" and "releaser" communication patterns are to the stickleback fish.

Communication in the broadest sense is inter-organism behavior. The study of communication is, then, probably the most direct approach to the study of the individual in a social context. Whether at infrahuman levels or at the human level, interaction of one animal with another or many others is a pattern of communication. Such patterns of communication can be studied, and the information such study provides increases our understanding of the dynamics of social behavior. This chapter will examine very briefly five problems in communication which are of special interest to social psychology. In some instances little more than the problems themselves exist, with scanty theory and a paucity of empirical information. In others, there are bodies of theory and fact that are sufficiently complete to be looked upon as levels of valuable understanding.

First, we will examine the similarities and differences between infrahuman and human communication. Since we have dealt with this problem before, it will only be necessary here briefly to review our previous comments and to cite some additional examples. Of particular importance is the unique property of language which sets it aside as an emergent phenomenon at the human level. The remainder of the chapter will deal with problems pertaining specifically to language.

Second, we will review the principal theories that have been proposed to account for the emergence of language.

Third, we will describe several approaches to the study of language. Of particular interest, of course, will be those which are most specifically psychological.

Fourth, we will examine the development of language in the child. Many studies and theoretical descriptions of the ontogenesis of language are available. Thus, only a sketchy review of what we take to be the more important contributions will be undertaken.

Fifth, we will consider the reciprocal role of language as a determiner of thought and at the same time as determined by the nature of human nature. This is one of the most significant aspects of language, and it again raises the question posed by Comte: How can man be both the cause and consequence of society?

FROM INFRAHUMAN COMMUNICATION TO HUMAN LANGUAGE

Language is a particular and highly specialized type of communication. As such it represents one of the most significant human psychological emergences. This thesis rests upon evidences from the comparative study of communication at various phyletic levels. Let us briefly cite examples of communication used at three of these levels: bees, birds, and chimpanzees.

The typical member of an infrahuman species possesses certain natively determined responses—gestures, sounds, glandular reflexes—that when brought into action seem also to act as stimuli to which other typical species members may respond. Certain patterns of response to these stimulus signals are also natively determined. Such signal systems have adaptive value. As we have pointed out before, the higher we go on the phyletic scale, the less rigid and stereotyped are these species-specific codes. Also at the lower levels communication signals are much more interjectional than referential; that is, they indicate more about the state of the signaling animal than about objects in the outside environment.

As Roger Brown has pointed out (1958), referential communication behavior is clearly demonstrated in many species, particularly in highly social species. At the same time, one of the essential characteristics of language is still different; in infrahumans reference to outside environmental objects depends essentially upon instinctive patterns of signaling and responding, not upon inventiveness and shared experience. One of the characteristics of language is that it is "shared behavior." These shared behavior patterns vary from language group to language group and are not dependent for content upon native propensities. We will return to this point after we have commented upon reference communication in the three species.

Bees

For many years Karl von Frisch (1950) conducted studies of communication in bees. One line of his interest centered on the fact that when a rich source of food has been located by a bee, other bees from the same hive soon come to the source. How is this accomplished? The broadest guess was that somehow bees are able to communicate with reference to a given object. Von Frisch constructed a hive in such a way that the surface of a honeycomb could be seen through glass. He discovered that the returning bees perform what he called "dances," and that some of the bees on the comb gather closely around and follow the dancer. The follower bees soon leave the hive and fly to the food source. Somehow, von Frisch theorized, the scout bee communicates the location of the food to the others. By way of an ingenious series of experiments he was able to identify the principal communication variables responsible for this extraordinary social behavior. One dance (circling) indicates that the food is only a short distance away; the other (wagging) indicates that the food is a great distance away. In the latter dance, the number of turns indicates the distance very precisely; the fewer the turns the greater the distance. In addition, the direction of the food from the hive is indicated by the dance. In this case, the wagging dance gives the cue. During this dance there is some straight running, and the direction this takes in reference to the location of the sun is the important variable. The odor of the nectar or pollen is also important to the follower in locating the particular food source. The vigor of the dance provides the cue as to the food supply. A very slow dance correlates with a scanty supply, a vigorous dance with a plentiful supply.

Birds

Let us look next at referent communication in European crows, called jackdaws. They are monogamous from the second year and live almost as long as man. Among many of the interesting and important characteristics of this bird's social behavior is its species-specific social communication system. For one thing, it uses native, specific calls to activate others to fly away or to fly back. In addition, one of its most curious and at the same time obvious calls is associated with danger. According to Lorenz's descriptions (1952) the black jackdaw will attack any animal (human or infrahuman) that carries a black, fluttering object. Once when Lorenz picked up a young jackdaw, for instance, he was attacked by Jock, his favorite and faithful pet jackdaw. Again, when he came from the river one day after a swim with his black swimming trunks dangling from his hand, he was attacked by several jackdaws. These and other similar incidences convinced Lorenz that a black, fluttering object is the native signal for attack upon the creature carrying it. When such an attack occurs the jackdaw emits a rattling noise. This induces other jackdaws not only to join in the attack but also to emit the rattling noise. The object of the attack then and thereafter tends to become an object of attack in and of itself without the fluttering black object. While this substitute stimulus learning may not be set permanently on the first occasion, Lorenz is of the opinion that two or three such occurences are sufficient to stamp a given person or animal as a jackdaw's enemy for life. Once a target is so identified, whenever the jackdaw sees it he "scolds" with his rattling noise, and other jackdaws that have had no previous experience with that given target learn to identify it as "an enemy."

Lying back of this important phenomenon is the curious fact that the jackdaw, unlike many other infrahumans, seems to have no native enemies. A naïve jackdaw will not run from an approaching cat. Only when the cat seizes the naïve bird do other naïve birds begin an attack with their accompanying rattle. The cat then becomes a "learned enemy," and other naïve jackdaws learn to identify the enemy cat vicariously if there are initiated birds around to "tell the story" when the cat is in view. Roger Brown has summarized the communication significance of this unusual social behavior in the following way: "The jackdaw can share its knowledge and, in effect, tell others that this is an enemy. This is the nearest thing I know among animals to a linguistically conveyed item of cultural information." (p. 162)

Chimpanzees

The chimpanzee is at least as close to man as any of the infrahumans. Since this animal is so much like man in anatomical structure it is easier to identify various of its body movements as of communication significance than it is with species quite different from man. The chimpanzee shows by gesture and grimace much about himself which is of communication significance. Chimpanzees are capable, as well, of intricate and varied vocalizations; they are not essentially limited linguistically by an inadequate vocal apparatus. Chimpanzees have been taught to say a few words instrumentally; that is, a word can come to be used by a chimpanzee to indicate desire for a given object. For example, when hungry, a chimpanzee might use the word "cup" to indicate the object he wants—a cup filled with food. He can also be trained to comprehend words and phrases. However, when these words and phrases are syntactically reassembled, comprehension fails. For instance, a chimpanzee can be taught to kiss the experimenter upon the command, "Kiss me," and to fetch a toy upon the command, "Bring me the toy." If, however, the command, "Kiss the toy," is given, nothing happens. The use of language requires not only the comprehension of words and phrases, but the use of words and phrases in combinations that describe both the felt-states of the individual and his impressions of the nature of outside objects. Chimpanzees are extremely adept in vocal communication. The fact that they cannot use words and phrases syntactically is the limitation that denies them the possibility of language.

What, then, is there in the chimpanzee's behavior that indicates reference communication? First, chimpanzees show an extraordinary capacity to identify other chimpanzees and particular humans. Attachment for another animal is clear indication of selective reference. However, unless this referent is used to communicate something about the referent to others it is not true referent communication. There are descriptions of chimpanzees that have had strong attachments for other particular chimpanzees. When they were reunited after separation there was every reason to believe that the two animals clearly identified each other, as evidenced by their display of affection and attention. Insofar as could be determined, however, there was neither an attempt on the part of either "saddened and deprived" animal to communicate his feelings about himself nor an attempt to "say" anything about the "other" animal that would clearly meet the criterion of referent communication.

Because social behavior stereotypy is considerably less in the higher anthropoids than in lower species, we would not expect to find as much set, species-specific reference communication among them. There are, however, a few reported instances of nonspecific referent communication behavior, aside from the humanly taught vocal examples cited above.

Gesture.   Vocalization is only one type of referent communication and in chimpanzees gesture seems to be a better channel for referent communication. Crawford (1937) taught hungry chimpanzees individually to pull in a weighted box which contained food. Then two trained animals were put into the same cage. Following this, two ropes were attached to the box and the weight was increased so that it took simultaneous pulling on the part of both to draw it within reach. The animals eventually learned to pull together for which, of course, they were always rewarded by food. A crucial test of cooperation was then made. Before introducing the two animals to the testing cage one animal was fed to satiation while the other was kept hungry. Under this condition the hungry animal would direct the satiated animal's attention to the other rope and solicit its aid. On such occasions the satiated animal cooperated even though the food was of no reward value.

In still another study (1941) Crawford taught one chimpanzee to push against four colored plaques in a certain order. Then the cage was divided in two by bars leaving two of the plaques out of reach. Another chimpanzee, who knew how to push the plaques but did not know the correct order, was placed in the barred-off side. In order to be rewarded the trained animal needed the assistance of the naive animal. Such assistance was solicited by begging gestures and movements directed toward the plaque which should be pushed next in the sequence. While these two studies were designed primarily to examine the possibility of cooperative behavior in chimpanzees, they also provided very clear and important evidence of referent communication. In both instances, one animal "pointed to" an object and conveyed information about the object to another animal who, in turn, often comprehended the information. While these instances are extremely simple when compared to referent communication in man, they incorporate the basic ingredients of referent communication. These are, of course, examples of referent communication through gesture, rather than through vocalization, but they demonstrate syntactically complex referent communication.

Advances over Lower Species. Social communication in chimpanzees shows certain differences and advances over lower species. Four of these are quite apparent. First, whereas referent communication in bees and jackdaws is species-specific, we witness in chimpanzees a variety of responses being used syntactically with the evident purpose of solving a novel problem. It is to be noted that these are operant responses, and they are to be contrasted with respondents which are used exclusively by lower species such as bees and jackdaws. Second, the message receiver shows indication of comprehending some of these syntactically novel operant responses. Third, chimpanzees show inventiveness by referring to the object in such a way that it takes on a novel and intended meaning for the other animal to whom it is directed. The sender "ties" the object in reference together with the anticipated and desired behavior on the part of the receiver. The receiver "ties" the meaning conferred upon the object by the sender to the possibilities of his own behavior. Fourth, it seems apparent that chimpanzees are at the verge of language. They do not invent language. Neither do they record such meanings for future reference. On the other hand, on occasion, they do, by gesture at least, engage in one essential phase of the immediate language process. Since they cannot communicate symbolically by vocalization and cannot record such symbolic meanings, chimpanzees are denied the use of language as we understand human language.

Hebb and Thompson (1954) maintain that there are three levels of communication. The first is *reflexive communication*. Since there is no indication of purpose or intention at this level, some students (Maier and Schneirla, 1935) have maintained that this is not true communication. This does not seem to be justifiable. The remarkable social signaling behavior of bees is an example of this reflexive level, and we see no reason at all to conceive of it as anything other than communication. That it is stimulus bound, and that the scout bee shows no deliberate intention to "tell" particular other bees about the food source have nothing to do with its being or not being communication. Such reflexive and stimulus-bound social interaction serves to exchange information which is of vital importance to the species. Thus, in order to avoid a semantic problem, in order to avoid the creation of an insoluble communication problem by the magic of language itself, it seems appropriate to classify all information exchanges as communication. The point is that communication varies in complexity. The second level is *purposive but nonsyntactic communication*. The jackdaw's "rattle scolding" of the learned enemy, or the "broken wing" feigning of the grouse which is used to draw the enemy away from its young, are examples of communication behavior which changes as the situation changes. This is to say that the sender gives evidence of purpose or intention in that its behavior changes as the receiver's behavior changes. This does not mean, however, that this second level is communication any more or less than the first level. The third level is *syntactic or true language communication.* Only man uses language. The essence of syntactic communication is the novel combination and recombination of symbolic acts which convey unique meanings. As we have seen, chimpanzees and probably certain other mammals as well are capable of a limited amount of syntactic communication behavior. They are limited just short of language, however, since their syntactic communications cannot be conveyed vocally, nor can they be recorded.

THE ORIGIN OF LANGUAGE

The question of how language began can be viewed from two standpoints. First, we may study the development of language in children. This is the ontogenetic approach; that is, the attempt is made to understand how the child comes to learn a language. Second, we may inquire into the phylogenetic origin of language itself; how language emerged as a phenomenon. It is to this second perspective that we will direct our attention now.

While the question may be stated quite easily and precisely, it cannot be answered with equal ease and precision. As a matter of fact only theoretical and speculative answers are available. Whereas the phylogeny of body structure has been fairly well recorded, the phylogeny of behavior has not been recorded at all. One student of language behavior has gone so far as to declare that all theories of the origin of language are actually myths which deal with the basic "nature of language and meaning" rather than with the historical aspect of language development within the human species" (Brown, 1958, p. 135). It is quite true that there is no way empirically to demonstrate the origin of language, and it is highly improbable that a way will ever be discovered. On the other hand, we may make some educated guesses about the jump from prelinguistic man to linguistic man. Such guesses must be based upon one primary source of information: the comparative study of communication in the lower animals with reference, of course, to language communication in man.

As we have said, communication can be classified into three levels: reflexive, purposive but nonsyntactic, and purposive-syntactic. At the highest level, operationally described by man using language, spoken and written words and phrases are representational of both felt states (interjectional), and of objects (referential) and their essences. In addition, normal, social humans not only comprehend such stimuli, but also produce them. Essentially, then, when some species advanced neuroanatomically to the point that these functions were possible, a new level of communication appeared—language. Whether language began with australopithecines primitive hominids of the Pleistocene (Washburn and Avis, 1958), or with some more advanced creature we do not know. Whatever the species may have been it is evident that the use of language began in some particular way. What this way was has been a matter of great theoretical speculation. Of the many theories of the origin of language we will mention four of the best known (Klineberg, 1954).

As a preface to these four theories one basic psychological process should be examined. From a social standpoint, language must be looked upon as a tool, as a means of manipulating the environment. Man seems to be the only animal capable of fabricating tools; tools to be used in a great variety of ways to accomplish a great variety of ends. In this sense, words and phrases are used by the sender to manipulate the social environment, and are used by the receiver in a similar way. Certain sound patterns, then, must have been concocted by certain individuals and reinforced by indications of comprehension by others; thereby they were learned by both senders and receivers. What this all means is that operant learning must have been the psychological process which gave impetus to the beginning of language. There is good reason to believe that the recording of language and meaning came much later; but there is no reason to believe that recording was not started in the same psychological way.

An interesting inference from this is found in the writings of Cassirer (1944) who makes a distinction between propositional and emotional language. These are, respectively, what we have called referent and interjectional communication. For our purpose, his important point is that propositional language is "tool communication." Underlying any psychologically important theory of the origin of language is this theme: however words and phrases came into social use, there must have been some form of reinforcement which tended to fix them and foster their perpetuation. Thus, the theories we are now going to cite all have a common theme. Where the original sounds came from is relatively unimportant, since we can never know them. That sounds come to be used by individuals as tools to effect certain ends seems obvious. This has been experimentally demonstrated even in infrahumans (Ginsburg, 1960). Lower animals cannot, however, even with special human training, develop unique socially reciprocal vocal patterns that can be used for representational communication purposes. Clearly this is a limitation that makes language impossible.

Onomatopoetic Theory

Of the various origin theories, probably the best known is *onomatopoetic*. This theory holds that words developed as imitations of natural sounds, that meanings came to be attached to these words, and that gradually a language emerged. There is no doubt that some words are imitations of natural sounds, but their number is very small, and it seems most improbable that these few imitative words are sufficient as a basis for the origin of the meaningfully rich and diverse languages of man.

Interjectional Theory

A second is the *interjectional* theory. This theory maintains that language emerged out of vocal expressions concerning the state of the person. Such sounds as "ugh" and "whew" are often used to indicate felt states; and, as we have pointed out before, many of the lower animals have native vocal patterns, such as the dog's growl, that indicate present states of the organism. There is no reason to deny that interjectional expressions play a role in language. On the other hand, it seems only remotely possible that language had its origin in introjection since, it must be remembered, language also incorporates reference to outside objects.

Natural Ringing Theory

Third is the *natural ringing* theory. The contention here is that outside objects which are sensed produce natively determined resonance impressions upon the body which then flow into predetermined vocal expressions. This theory has been almost completely abandoned by scientists since it has no empirical basis at all.

Gesture Theory

The fourth, and most plausible, theory is the *language of gesture* theory. We know, for example, that the deaf use gesture language quite adroitly and are able to communicate at a symbolic, conceptual level very adequately. Theoretically, sign language gave way to vocal expression, since vocal expression is much more parsimonious, refined, and energy conserving. Earlier in this chapter we referred to referential communication by gesture in chimpanzees. Upon the basis of controlled observations of their gesture communication we stated that the chimpanzee is on the verge of language. It is only a step from such syntactic gesture communication to true language. True language involves the use of vocal expression as a substitute for expression by gesture. We might well assume that once man developed neurologically to the point that he could produce and comprehend varied and syntactically arranged vocalizations as substitutes for communicationally significant gestures, he was on his way to the development and use of language.

One of the problems in any attempt to reconstruct the origin of language lies in the fact that there is no empirical evidence that can be brought to bear upon any of the theories. In view of this, we must content ourselves with the most plausible theory, and it is our contention that upon the basis of comparative evidence the gesture theory is the most plausible. Of course, we must remember that the origin problem is of background importance, not of critical importance. Contemplation of and serious concern with the origin problem is of great concern to those who are deeply interested in man's role in nature. At the same time we should remind ourselves that the most important and critically significant problem is that of cognitive organization and the role that language plays in organizing and conveying human thought. It is to this general but significant psychological problem that we will devote the remainder of this chapter.

THE DEVELOPMENT OF LANGUAGE IN CHILDREN

The study of language development in children, the ontogenetic approach, is to be contrasted with the phylogenetic approach to which we have already referred. While the ontogenetic approach is, strictly speaking, tangential to the problem of language origin, it is our contention that some important insights into the origin of language may be gained by examining certain of the findings of the students of this subject. Specifically, however, the ontogenetic approach is intended to provide information concerning how, from infancy to maturity, the human acquires language. It is to this question that we now turn.

First, let us reemphasize the assertion that language is man's most parsimonious and precise means for manipulating his social environment. Again, we may suppose that, from the broadest perspective, language is instrumentally learned. That is, words and phrases are emitted responses which are socially reinforced and hence fixed, although, of course, their syntactic combinations are virtually infinite. Thus, though we are not discounting the importance of the role of language in thought, we take the position that words and phrases are learned responses that are used as tools to effect certain ends. From a broad biological standpoint this does not differ from the rat in the Skinner box that learns to depress a lever in order to receive pellets of food. On the comprehension side, learning to respond to words and phrases appropriately, social reinforcement plays its role also, since the individual comes to respond to the language symbols of others in ways that maximize the probability of gratification.

The human infant is born with equipment to vocalize in intricate and varied ways. Even before birth the fetus is able to emit vocal responses (Carmichael, 1933). At birth vocalization begins in the birth cry. While its function seems to be purely physiological and without cognitive meaning, it is of special significance to the neonate since now for the first time in its life the vocal apparatus is used in a free environment. The neonate cries and babbles. He cries indiscriminately when cold, hungry or in pain; he babbles with alacrity when in his waking state he is warm, full, and free from pain. These vocalizations are replete with rich sounds, a few of which will later be ordered to a fairly strict structure—one, or even a few, languages. It has been said that babbling is "the vocal stone-quarry of all human language." (Lindesmith and Strauss, 1956.) These basic sound productions are maturations, some of which will later come to be organized into words which, in virtually infinite syntactic arrangements, can be used to maximize that individual's probability of control over his social environment. By imitation of the vocal sounds of his elders the developing infant comes to use only those sounds from his total repertoire that are socially reinforced. He is now on his way to learning a language—the most complete social behavior in which he will ever engage.

Human infancy is usually defined as the first twelve months of postnatal life. The word "infant" is derived from the Latin words *in* (not) and *fari* (to speak). It is, at least in our culture, not until about the thirteenth month that the child begins to use his first words. From this time through the fourth year normal children establish the basic use of language. Through the channels of the language that are available to the child he begins his intellectual life and most of the ways he perceives both the inanimate and animate creatures about him. His cognitive organizations are largely shaped by this developing facility. There is no doubt, too, that personality is in many ways organized around the give and take of his developing language behavior. The early impressions which words and phrases leave upon the psychological makeup of the developing individual must be taken into any account of cognitive-personality organization, since words and phrases are essentially convenient tools by which events and objects are categorized and accorded basic evaluations.

Many students of the ontogeny of language have attempted to identify possible developmental stages that are common to all normal members of the species. This is a potentially productive undertaking in view of the fact that man's major behavioral systems pass through fairly regular developmental stages. Longitudinal and cross-sectional studies of the ontogeny of language have revealed certain uniformities. In broadest outline, language begins in babbling, moves into an imitative stage, and then progresses to adult verbal behavior in which thought is both shaped and expressed by shared verbal meanings and rules of syntactic organization.

Dorothea McCarthy (1946) has reviewed the findings of eight comprehensive ontogenetic studies and has conveniently tabulated the times at which various selected language items appear, as reported in the eight studies. In all she listed 126 such items. These items were arranged in order of their appearance. Examples, by number, are: 1. vocal grunt, 9. attends readily to speaking voice, 26. vocalizes in self-initiated sound play, 55. responds to "bye-bye," 85. says two words, 98. names two objects, 123. uses simple sentences and phrases. Item 1 was reported as appearing at approximately seven days and item 123 at 24 months. Again there is a progression from simple, largely interjectional expression to complex, comprehending referent language. Obviously there are individual differences, and these findings are actuarial, though they represent a straightforward picture of the basic progression of language development. These 126 items were then grouped into 43 categories, which may be thought of as increasingly complex language achievement stages through which the normal child passes during the first two years of life. An overall view of these 43 categories lends the clear impression that language development is not a simple progression from one clearly defined stage to another, and then to another. Rather, it is a progression that builds upon itself, one activity merging into greater complexity with emergent phenomena appearing all along the way. For example, the day comes when the child first imitates words (mean, 11.7 months); however he imitated sounds much earlier (mean, 6 months). Thus, while imitation itself starts quite early it is not until later that it comes to be used as a means of forming words, the most effective social tools available for environmental manipulation and control. Gradually, then, maturational and learning progress permits the developing child to take possession of the language of his social organization, and the door is slowly opened to his own cognitive world and to the cognitive worlds of those about him.

A comprehensive, though quite impressionistic, summary description of these 43 language progression categories may be suggested. For convenience, they may be compressed into six arbitrarily designated stages. First is the birth cry. As we have suggested, this is the actual beginning; the time at which the first use of the vocal apparatus is made. This is purely maturation and the foundation for progressive maturation and learning. Second is the category of prelinguistic utterances of infancy—infancy defined as the period without speech. At the beginning of this period the babblings and reflexive vocalizations are without meanings; though by the fifth week some interjectional meaning begins to appear and by the end of the first year many of these prelinguistic sounds have taken on very clear, but personal, meanings. The third period is that of imitation. While, of course, it overlaps with the prelinguistic period considerably, it does seem that by the twelfth month true imitation of words has begun. This means that the child is now maturationally equipped to acquire the basic language tool units which his social elders are using to manipulate their environments. Overlapping the imitative era is a fourth progress category often referred to as the beginning of language comprehension. It is clear that at about the end of the first year the child shows signs of understanding some of the language of his elders, though he is unable to produce language himself. Thus, comprehension seems a prerequisite to production. Obviously, imitative behavior is involved here—imitation of the words and phrases that he must use in order to interact on "equal terms" with his elders. This comprehension of the language of others opens up a new world to the developing child. He now begins to look into the mental life of others and into his own mental world. By this process he begins to establish his own psychological identity. This presages the emergence of ego from which he can never escape and, like a protective façade, to which all of his subsequent behavior is to be dedicated.

Sixth is the period of first words. At about the beginning of the second year single referent words come to be used. Again, this is not a neat, clear temporal period; it overlaps with others and refers only to a process that articulates with the others. The single referent noun is used to telescope a syntactically complex functional meaning. For example, the one-year-old may say the word "dog." This may mean "Where is the dog?" or "I want the dog," or "I see a dog." We cannot doubt, however, that referent meaning is intended, and that the child is only one step short of expressing the syntactic, functional meaning that true language will soon make possible. Finally, then, comes the beginning of socially interactive, "filled in" syntactic arrangements of words; words arranged into novel organizations that convey explicit and implicit meanings in accordance with the underlying nature of human thought and the rules of language that his culture has provided for him.

The literature on the ontogeny of language is vast, and it is difficult to decide what information to cite and what to neglect in our attempt to describe the social psychological significance of language development in the child. For instance, it would be interesting to pursue such a comprehensive theory as that of Piaget (1926). Piaget takes the position that language lays bare the child's thinking processes, and goes on to theorize that there are, developmentally, two types of speech in the child's language. First is egocentric speech in which the child talks for his own pleasure and makes reference, at least by inference, to his emerging ego. Second is socialized speech, by which the child begins to make contact with others and in so doing begins his referent communication. The substance of Piaget's theory has stimulated a vast amount of research and controversy which has been of great value to our understanding of the ontogeny of language in particular and the social psychological nature of man in general. Of specific interest to one of the principal theses of this book is the light Piaget throws upon ego development.

Other areas of interest in the study of language development in the child are such problems as vocabulary and grammar progression, the use of questions, the relation of language acquisition to intellectual growth, and the differentiation of parts of speech. In addition, there is a large, interesting, and important literature pertaining to the way in which individual differences play their roles in language acquisition. There are also many fascinating findings with reference to the effects of the environmental situation upon language development.

LANGUAGE AND THOUGHT

"I'm having a hard time trying to educate you and your fellows in the matter of race relations. Segregation, integration and violence between the races flow naturally from the frequent use of racial terms in public discussions. Think race and you have the evil of racial bias. Talk race and you get violence between the races. The way to get rid of racial bias is to quit talking about it." (San Francisco *Chronicle,* 1960.) This letter to the editor of a large metropolitan newspaper is replete with important and interesting implications for the problem of language and thought.

At face value the statement may be taken to endorse the view that social behavior is a function of words, that without certain words certain actions would be impossible. Taken literally, thinking about the referent in a comparative-evaluative way produces bias, and talking about bias produces violence. In reverse, then, violence could be eliminated by eliminating the words which stand for violence; and the words which stand for violence could be eliminated by the prohibition of thought about good and bad races. This short letter to the editor points, at least inferentially, to some theoretical issues of great psychological importance.

One of these issues is concerned with objects, things, categories, and the words used to refer to them. Since the writer of this letter did not fill in any theoretical detail we cannot know, but we may interpret what he says to mean that some objects, things, and categories are not real, do not exist in fact. But, since there are words that are used in socially shared ways to refer to such nonexistent objects, things, and categories, the words do, nevertheless, play important phenomenological roles, and some behavior is predicted upon them. An atheist declares that there is no such thing as God, that reference to God is reference to an unreal, mythical object. He may then proceed to the thesis that by eliminating the word God, the concept of God and hence the behavior related to the concept can be eliminated. The words "race" and "God" are speech elements, sounds that can be emitted by the human voice; and, as well, by the voice of a parrot. In the case of man, however, imaginary objects can be conjured up and named. Once named, the name and the conjured object may be socially shared. We might suppose, however, that unless the object is in fact imaginary it will not just go away simply by refusing to accord it referent status through the process of naming it.

Another issue which our letter to the editor raises has to do with meaning, the problem of semantics. As we have said, we cannot be sure just what the author of the letter means. For instance, when he says, "Segregation, integration and violence flow naturally from the frequent use of racial terms in public discussions," we cannot be sure that the meaning and meanings these words and the statement itself create for us are the same as the intended meanings of the author. On first reading,we took the tenor of the letter to mean that segregation and violence are socially iniquitous and that integration is socially virtuous. However, upon careful rereading of the sentence just quoted, it was noticed that what we understood to be the two social iniquities and the one social virtue, the author asserts come from the same source. There are other quandries which careful analysis of the letter will produce, though this is sufficient to illustrate the semantic issue.

A third issue that the letter raises has to do with the extent to which thought is dependent upon words and syntactically arranged groupings of words. As we have noticed, it is the author's claim that without such words as "race" and such terms as "racial bias" not only would the concepts lying back of such words and terms disappear, but overt behavior patterns that "flow naturally" from them would disappear as well. To follow the first part of this line of reasoning we would be forced to conclude that conceptual categories are dependent upon words. While there is substance to this argument, since words are tools used for manipulating one's social environment, it does not follow that without words there is no thought, no conceptual classification and evaluation of the physical and social environment. The mental world of the blind and mute person is not necessarily without rich conceptual content. When taught a tactical-kinesthetic "language," such a person is introduced to a social-mental world that is rich in content and facility. An aphasic may no longer be able to say such words as "race," "bias," "Negro," although he may retain his Negro prejudice as strong as before his affliction. Thus, the depedence of thought upon words, and words upon thought, is no simple relationship contained in simple words themselves.

The fourth important issue that this illustrative letter suggests is that of linguistic relativism. This refers to one aspect of cultural relativism, the thesis that one's thought and behavior are functions of the social context, rather than the determiners of the nature of the social context. The impression is that the author of the letter is in substantial agreement with the linguistic relativism view. He would agree, we must suppose, with the thesis that individuals in our culture hate members of various minority groups because the culture has a language apparatus that includes the concept of discriminative hate and the words to describe the concept. A child reared in a culture in which such a concept and its words did not exist would not develop prejudice. More specifically, the way the child learns to think and behave, the categories he discriminates and the evaluations he places upon them, are determined, according to this thesis, by the words and phrases provided by the language to which he is introduced.

The letter to the editor which we have been discussing has suggested four issues: the elements of language, language and meaning, the dependence of thought upon language, and linguistic relativism. To each of these problems we will give some systematic attention. Before we do this, however, let us make brief reference to the principal avenues of approach to the study of language, each bearing upon the problem of language and thought.

Speech is composed of elements that may be organized in a great variety of ways to convey meanings. One such organization, guided by rules of grammar and syntax, is said to be *a language*. As we know, there are scores and scores of different languages with their own dialect differences. A person who is master of several languages is usually referred to as a linguist. He may, however, be little interested in language structure, the organic relationships between different languages, or concepts that may be used to explain the nature of all languages.

Descriptive linguistics is concerned with the analysis of speech and the structure of language. The *descriptive linguist* is a behavioral scientist, oftentimes an anthropologist. His position is comparable to that of the musicologist who thoroughly understands the history, theory, and structure of music without necessarily being an accomplished musician. The term "psycholinguistics" is often used to designate the study of human behavior and experience through the avenue of language. Perhaps, however, as some believe, this psychological interest is better described simply as the psychology of language.

The most widely separated approaches to the study of speech and language are the neurophysiological and the semantic. The former is concerned with the neurological and physiological bases for the formation of speech sounds and the control of word and phrase production. This approach is interested in the reception and comprehension side of the problem as well. The latter approach, semantics, is interested, essentially from a philosophical standpoint, in the meaning of language; or, as it is sometimes put, in the meaning of meaning.

The psychology of language has been assisted by all of these approaches, one of the most important being descriptive linguistics. Descriptive linguistics soon focuses upon genuine psychological problems, and many times cannot be distinguished from psychology. As we have pointed out, the basic psychology of the language problem is one of trying to understand man's psychological nature by way of his use of language. There are really two aspects to this problem: the influence of language upon man's thought, and the influence of man's neurophysiological-psychological nature upon the structure of language.

The Elements of Language

Any language is a social communication system in which meanings are exchanged with reference to objects in accordance with certain commonly understood procedural "rules." The mechanics by which the successful use of a language is accomplished is of secondary importance from the standpoint of social psychology. However, a few basic features of these mechanics of speech are of background importance to the student of the social psychological nature of language. These may be referred to as the *elements of language.*

In sign language certain movements of parts of the body have referent meanings. These are usually visual signals or signs. While vocal language may have emerged from some such visual signaling system, it is much more efficient. For one thing, the hands are free for other purposes, and, for another, it is possible to incorporate much greater detail, refinement, and speed in a vocal system. While these tiny speech elements have quite restricted meanings in isolation, when organized into complex and comprehensive sequences they take on the function and structure of a language.

Descriptive linguists have spent great time and effort in the study of the basic elements of language and have provided some basic terminology to encompass the conceptual nature of these basic elements. The analysis of the elements of language is extremely difficult since it is necessary to use language to study language. It is not the referent, such as "table," but the process of using the word "table" to refer to the object *table* that is studied. Thus, the descriptive linguist is referring to the process of referring and in so doing is attempting to extract the meaning of language elements.

Phonemes. The vowels and consonants we use in our speech "are not single invarient sounds, but rather categories of varied individual sounds (phones)." (Brown, 1958, p. 23) That is, the phonetic elements of our language are patterns of phones which we represent pictorially by symbols called letters. One such symbol may, however, be pronounced in more than one way; the pattern of phones is not necessarily the same in different contexts. The letter "p" which is commonly thought of as a phonetic symbol in our language may be pronounced as in "put" and as in "up." The phonal contents of these two pronounciations are quite different. Any given language makes use of but a limited number of the total phones that are available to man. In a given language not all phonetic elements are contrasted with every other; not all of them make a difference to those who use the language. In English we perceive a difference between "b" and "p" not just because they are phonetically different but because they can be shown to convey differences in meaning by those who use the language. Such sound elements which a language uses as a code to convey differences in meaning are referred to as "phonemes." The English-speaking person demonstrates that "b" and "p" are both phonemes since, for example, prefixed to "in" differences in meaning are conveyed ("bin" and "pin"). Such a phonetic difference may not be perceived and hence not used to convey a meaning difference in some other language. In that case the letters "b" and "p" are referred to as *allophones* and are the same phoneme. Hockett (1958, p. 26) summarizes the meaning of phoneme as follows, "The phonemes of a language are the elements which stand in contrast with each other in the phonological system of the language."

Morphemes. The next step on the scale of language element complexity is the morpheme, connoting shape or form. The morpheme has been defined as "the minimal semantic unit." (Bruner, Goodnow, and Austin, 1956, p. 263) That is, morphemes are the smallest meaningful language elements; the smallest units that convey information. The morpheme is sometimes, but not always, a word. "The free morpheme is a word not susceptible of analysis into smaller semantic units." (Bruner *et al.*, 1956, p. 263) The word "horse," for instance, is a free morpheme; but "horses" is not a single word morpheme, since it can be analyzed into the free form "horse" and the bound form "-s." A bound morpheme (i.e., always bound to another morpheme) never stands alone. In this illustration it conveys information about plurality. Thus, the words we use in speech are either single or multiple units of meaning. Sometimes the order in which morphemes are arranged in hyphenated words conveys surplus meaning. "Blue-green" means, for instance, that the stimulus object is green with a bluish cast; and, "green-blue" means that the object is blue with a greenish cast. In descriptive linguistic analysis probably the most psychologically important unit is the morpheme.

Parts of Speech. Words are put together into phrases, sentences, paragraphs and then into larger and more complex organizations. And, although we are unable to give "word" the precise definition that we would like, we know that words are used to serve different meaning purposes. Conventionally these meaning-purpose categories have been called parts of speech and parts of speech have been traditionally defined semantically; that is, they have been defined in terms of the classification of meaning they are supposed to handle in the sentence structure. The noun, for example, "names a person, place, or thing." One departure from the traditional definition of parts of speech has made use of the "linguistic frame" to assess the role of words or the parts words play in conveying thought (Fries, 1945). The linguistic frame is a complete sentence, an utterance which completes a referential thought. Thus, the role a given word plays in such a frame is described operationally. According to this procedure there are four basic and large functional categories of words: nouns, verbs, adjectives, and adverbs. They correspond roughly to the traditional parts of speech. For example, take the frame: "A _____ is small." Many different words can be placed in this blank space with the result that the frame completes a referential thought. However, only a word which names something can be used to accomplish this. The information provided by the completed utterance may be at variance with socially agreed-upon experiential fact ("A *giant* is small"), but the assertion is grammatically acceptable to one who speaks English. Thus, the word combinations of a language permit certain things to happen, even though at variance with fact; and other things are not permitted to happen.

The permissibility of discrepancy between "fact" and linguistic frame points to certain interesting and important features of language and thought. For one thing, it is possible that freedom of utterance represents the essence of imagination. In thinking and in the decoding of referential thought there is stimulus freedom; the human clearly shows that he is not stimulus-bound (Doob, 1960). For another thing, that grammatically correct assertions are so frequently at variance with fact is the principal reason for developing a "language of science." As Hockett (1954, p. 123) has put it, ". . . speech-habits were revised to fit observed facts, and where everyday language would not serve, special sub-systems (mathematics) were devised." That one can talk about something does not mean that that something is existent in the empirical world. It may mean, if the assertion is seriously intended, however, that the something is phenomenologically real, and therefore of great importance to the speaker and to those interacting with the speaker. Also, the fact that grammatically correct frames do not have to conform to empirical reality makes possible the use of metaphor, a most important ingredient of esthetics. Even the language of science often uses metaphor. Metaphorical language is a beautiful illustration of man's capacity to lift himself from the facts of the empirical, physical stimulus world and, with perfectly acceptable grammar, discourse meaningfully at a level of abstraction which does not demand direct, empirical reference to the referent he is describing.

Language and Meaning

Ernst Cassirer has commented that, "There is perhaps no more bewildering and controversial problem than 'the meaning of meaning.'" (1944, p. 145) Ancient philosophers and modern semanticists have grappled with this problem with such vigor, obscurity, and diversity that one may wonder whether it is not a pseudoproblem. That it is much more than this we may be sure, but we are still in no position to provide satisfactory answers to this very large and perplexing question. We do not believe we are begging the question when we say that the ancient philosophic quest for meaning in itself unattached to any sentient quality represents a problem which lies outside the bounds of modern science. The ultimate and irreducible essence of meaning as an object which lies beyond human experience may very well be a legitimate metaphysical problem, but it is not a problem which submits itself to an empirical approach. That one may pose a question in perfectly correct and acceptable grammatical form does not mean that there is an answer to that question; in fact, it does not even mean that the question defines a problem.

If, on the other hand, we state the problem a bit differently, it may be possible to demonstrate that it is meaningful, and to suggest a way to examine it from a psychological standpoint. A psychologically proper statement of the problem must take into account referent objects, experiencing humans, and language. Since language is found only at the human level, we may rule out the infrahumans, and leave to others the question of whether or not they experience meaning. The question then is, do the words we learn to use in grammatically correct and syntactically different ways convey to us and to those who listen to us particular meanings with reference to the objects of our discourse? Provided we can state operationally what we mean by meaning, our answer is yes. Let us remind ourselves, again, that this is not the metaphysical "meaning of meaning" question, for now we are including the experiencing human organism.

Symbolism. "All words are symbolic." (Scheerer, 1954) They are generalizations with reference to objects, events, and modifying conditions, that have been in some way experienced by the individual. A word represents a concept. Even the name of a particular person is conceptual since only certain characteristics of that person are known to the user of the name. There are many attributes of which the namer knows nothing, but there is a relatively stable core of attributes that taken together as a constellation provides meaning. The referent object (a person) is experienced by another person, who uses a language element (a word) conceptually to sum up his experiences of the named person. The concept has meaning for the namer since he now possesses expectancies with reference to the named. With sufficient experience the name itself may take on a "free-floating" meaning which describes for the namer any person with a similar pattern of characteristics. The nickname "Joe" is often used to tab an undistinguished, ordinary, run-of-the-mill male. The name has taken on meaning; it tells something.

Another example of the conceptual, meaning-laden nature of words is found in the naming of colors. While there are some seven and one-half million just noticeable differences in the color solid, we have only about eight commonly used color names (Brown, 1958). When looking at the end of the spectrum that is composed of very long wave lengths we use the word "red" to designate the color experience. When we move slightly toward the middle where the wave lengths are a bit shorter the word "orange" is used; and so on to the very shortest visible wave length area, which we call "violet." Now between the extremes, if wave length, brightness, and saturation are taken into account, there are millions of different colors. We name them by categories, but the categories are very few and crude by the standards of human sensory experience. A different type of naming may be used if it is desired; a much more refined type. That is, we can specify any exact color by mathematical measurement reference. However, for everyday language reference purposes such refinement is unnecessary, and for most of us "red is red" and "blue is blue," and neither the language of the scientist nor that of the artist is required for purposes of experientially adequate reference communication. For the artist "blue" is far too vague a reference word; he must give it greater refinement in order to express his highly refined meanings.

Thus, whether naming categories of things, designating processes, or defining the surplus attributes of objects, words are used to convey the individual's "encoded" experience by a process of "decoding." The decoding (use of words) evidences the significance which the referent has for the speaker; this is the *meaning* the referent has for the speaker. Many such meanings have sufficient social commonality of reference category (cat, run, pretty, slow) to make language possible.

Before leaving the subject of meaning we should mention two theories that have been used to explain how it is that word meanings arise (Brown, 1958). If one cries "fire!" we may suppose that the word is intended to convey to others a warning with reference to a dangerous object. The word as heard by the listener may be reacted to emotionally in much the same way as though he had seen the dangerous flame. The question has often been raised as to whether the referent word creates in the listener an image of the referent, or whether the meaningful experience set off in the listener is simply the experience he has learned to associate with that particular auditory stimulus.

In the extreme form of the native image theory it has been thought by some that there are particular words which are naturally the sound referents of particular objects. The onamatopoetic theory of the origin of language is such a theory, as is the "natural ringing" theory. There is some slight evidence to the effect that particular sounds are more frequently than by chance chosen as referring to size, brightness, and other referent category magnitudes and qualities (Newman, 1933). Just what this means is quite unclear, and we are inclined to the view that these results neither lend confirmation to the image theory nor suggest a native correspondence between referent phenomena and human speech elements.

The alternative to the native image theory does not attempt to establish the origin of language. And, aside from a limited number of interjectional sounds which seem to convey relatively uniform meanings, there seem to be no native, preestablished articulations of sounds and meanings. This view is disappointing from the standpoint of the desire to know the relationship of words to empirically demonstrable fact. We are all charmed and often enchanted by vocal sounds—the magic of words. So often in our experiences, words produce the effects of narcosis, exhilaration, ennui, effort, or the sharp image of some important event. The poem of beauty impresses one with the closeness of sound and fleeting impressions of reality, or of what things really mean. Still, if we are to pursue the scientific quest, we are obliged to look to another thesis.

The thesis which seems most appropriate from the standpoint of our present knowledge is the following. We sense a great variety of objects; some are pictures and persons; others are objects available only to tactition, and others are sounds. All of these are real in the sense that they are available to perception. At this point we are most interested in sounds. Being sensory-perceptual experiences, sounds are as real as any other category of sensory-perceptual experience. However, unless painful or distracting, sounds in and of themselves have no meaning. Objects sensed by the visual equipment are no different; there are no intrinsic meanings attached to them. Only through experience with reference objects, whether sounds or masses, do reference objects take on meanings.

The sounds we produce as language do not have intrinsic meanings. They take on meanings as the result of experiences with reference objects. At the highest levels of psychological complexity, sounds themselves become reference objects. This capacity to use language itself as a reference object has important social implications, particularly in the areas of politics, religion, esthetics, philosophy, and science.

Thought without Language

We have frequently alluded to the thesis that normal human thought is dependent upon language. There are at least two approaches to the examination of this view. One is to study the role that a given language—with its conceptual poverty or wealth, its novel encoding and decoding properties—plays in the thinking of those who use that language. The other approach is that of studying human thought in the absence of language. That is, what kind of thinking goes on when the individual is without language? And what happens to thinking when such an individual comes to learn a language? It is this second approach, thought in the absence of language, which we will deal with first.

Research into the problem of thinking in the absence of language, and the nature of thinking once a language is learned, is necessarily limited. No one would suggest that we should socially isolate children in order to experiment with the role of language in thought before and after learning a language. However, we must admit that this moral limitation upon research restricts our understanding of the role of language in thought. There have been two, though quite inadequate, avenues of investigation. The first is the study of feral children. The second is the study of the deaf and blind. These approaches are essentially nonquantitative and impressionistic, and their stated results are difficult to evaluate.

Feral Children.   The feral child approach is of most questionable value. As pointed out earlier, the authenticity of the original data of most of these reports is suspect. The essential problem here is that we can never know the origin of these children. Were they actually reared from infancy by wolves, or had they been abandoned by their parents only a few days before they were found? If they were abandoned—and this is the better thesis—were they abandoned because they were in some way abnormal? These are crucial questions from the standpoint of a scientific position. They cannot be answered.

Of the studies of feral children, the one which has greatest importance for a theory of language in general, and for the significance of language in thought in particular, is that of Itard, who attempted to teach the French language to what he believed to be a feral child, and then described the development of thinking in this child as the language acquisition process went on.

Toward the latter part of the eighteenth century a boy of eleven or twelve years was found surviving through his own devices in a French forest. Though he resisted capture he was brought to Paris and exhibited like an animal in a zoo. The boy proved to be more than a curiosity, however, since much scientific interest soon centered upon him. Could he be taught civilized ways, even though presumably his childhood had been completely without human social interaction? The great psychiatrist Pinel examined him and declared him to be feeble-minded, and predicted that he would not profit from any type of training. Dr. Itard, who was physician in the deaf and blind school in Paris, was of a very different opinion. He believed that the boy, whom they called Victor, could be civilized and that he could even be taught to speak French.

Itard did have some success in training Victor in the use of language, although the boy learned to comprehend better than to speak. The process of instruction which Itard used has been conveniently summarized by Brown (1958). There were seven basic steps in Victor's language training. First, Itard assumed that it would be useless to try to teach meanings until the boy had learned to identify certain speech sounds. Therefore, he started out by teaching Victor to distinguish one vowel from another. He was trained to identify each of the five French vowels by raising a particular finger when a particular vowel was enunciated. Though Victor learned to play this game, he was never able to master it.

Next, Itard switched to a game designed to teach the boy to identify words visually. The same words were written on two blackboards, though in different orders. As the teacher pointed to a given word on one board his pupil was to point to the same word on the other board. When Victor made a mistake, they would both point to the letters in the two words and spell together until they came to the letters that were different. By this procedure Victor was able to learn to recognize quite a few words that superficially appeared to be very similar.

Third, Itard began the task of teaching his pupil the meaning of words. He used several objects, such as a book, a key, and a box, all of which he placed on a shelf. Under each object was a card with the printed name of the object. These printed words Victor had already learned to identify. Before long he was able to match the printed names with the correct objects; and when the objects were placed in a distant corner in the room he could take a name card from his teacher, go to the corner and select the correct object.

Fourth, Itard removed all of the specific objects Victor had learned to identify, but saw to it that the same kinds of objects were present in the room. At first, when Victor was given a card with the word *"livre"* on it, for instance, he would go to the place where the particular book he had learned to identify was usually located; but not finding it there he gave up his search, showing no interest in other books. Obviously, Victor had learned to identify words with specific objects, not with categories of objects.

The fifth step was to teach Victor to use words to refer to categories rather than simply to specific objects. For each of the familiar objects, Itard now brought to Victor's attention other objects that were in certain respects different but which belonged to the same category. For instance, Victor was shown many different keys along with the original key. The ability to recognize new instances was the test of Victor's understanding of a category.

The sixth step was that of training Victor to understand referent qualities and relationships as distinguished from objects which have shape and mass. Itard began by taking two books, one large and one small, and spreading Victor's hand over each, showing him that his hand could not cover the one but could cover the other. Then, by use of cards again, one labeled *grand livre* and the other *petit livre,* he taught Victor to match them with the books. This was repeated for various other objects the names of which he already knew.

Seventh, he undertook the task of teaching Victor about verbs. Here he took some object familiar to the boy and made it the object of some process or action such as dropping, opening, or hitting. The test as to whether or not Victor had learned the meaning of a new verb was whether or not he could name the action when it was applied to a variety of objects with which he was already familiar. This he was able to do reasonably well after sufficient training. Although Itard's ingenious teaching methods were productive, and Victor learned to read many words and phrases, to follow the simple directions of written instructions, to use word cards to indicate certain of his wishes, he was never able to produce vocal symbols sufficiently well to use language in the full sense of language. Itard concluded that Victor was intellectually subnormal; otherwise, he would have profited fully from the instruction and would have become an adept user of language.

While we have no way of knowing whether Itard was correct in his final appraisal, there is one cardinal point which his training methods emphasized that pertains to the basic nature of language and thought. This is that language is a social communication system by which reference is made to categories of reference objects, not just to specific reference objects. As with the millions of identifiable colors, words are not sufficient to identify the specific, unique objects in the world about us. It is necessary for us to categorize, to classify objects according to particular attributes which give them a core identity. There are billions of books, and no two are precisely identical; but all books have certain common attributes: pages, printing, stiff or semi-stiff covers, a generalizable shape, and so on. Since Victor took on the appearance and manners of a civilized child, it was believed that part of this metamorphosis was the result of new ways of thinking and that his new ways of thinking were principally the result of his learning the rudiments of language. He had learned a way to organize and catalogue many of the objects in his environment in a way that had been unavailable to him before. In addition to this he had learned to make some of these concepts known to others and had learned to recognize and act appropriately when stimulated by certain referent signs. There is very good reason to believe that language frees the mind to explore the world in new and limitless ways.

The Deaf and The Blind.   The other approach to the question of the nature of human thought in the absence of language is through the study of the deaf and blind. As we know, many such unfortunate people have been taught to use language with considerable success. The question is, does their language acquisition, by their own accounts, bring about a change in the way they think? The answer is almost too obvious, but let us look at a little evidence.

In discussing reasoning, William James made the point that language is a unique human property, and that humans who use language think differently from those who do not. In support of this assertion he commented on "the exceedingly interesting account which Dr. Howe gives of the education of his various blind-deaf mutes . . ." Since James speaks better for himself than any paraphraser, here is his brief comment:

He began to teach Laura Bridgman by gumming raised letters on various familiar articles. The child was taught by mere contiguity to pick out a certain number of particular articles when made to feel the letters. But this was merely a collection of particular signs, out of the mass of which the general purpose of *significance* had not yet been extracted by the child's mind. Dr. Howe compares his situation at this moment to that of one lowering a line to the bottom of the deep sea in which Laura's soul lay, and waiting until she should spontaneously take hold of it and be raised into the light. The moment came, "accompanied by a radiant flash of intelligence and glow of joy"; she seemed suddenly to become aware of the general purpose imbedded in the different details of all these signs, and from that moment her education went on with extreme rapidity. (1902, pp. 355–358)

For our purpose, one point that James emphasizes is of special significance: Laura became aware of the *general purpose* of the details, the little signs that are the encoding and decoding structure of language. She had, all at once, learned that a tiny sign represented a whole category of stimulus units. She was no longer stimulus bound; she could deal with her fellows at a conceptual level which freed her from denotatively touching each referent object she wished to know about or tell about. Now, not only could she think about, but she could tell about concepts; and she could grasp the conceptual meanings of those about her.

Helen Keller's own account of how she learned to use language confirms the same thesis. She had been blind and deaf from the age of two. Shortly before her seventh birthday she was given a teacher who was to train her in the use of language. Miss Keller has referred to the day her teacher came as the most memorable of her life. It was a day which connected two lives, one of vagueness and conceptual emptiness, the other of ideas and social communion.

The essential events which brought about this personal revolution Miss Keller has described in a very interesting way. From her own account, the following points are of greatest psychological significance. On the first day her teacher presented her with a doll. After she had played with it for a time the teacher spelled the letters "d-o-l-l" into her hand. The child found this an exciting game and immediately tried to imitate her teacher's finger movements. When she finally was successful she ran to her mother and proudly spelled the letters "d-o-l-l" into her hand. For the next few weeks her teacher was content to teach her new words this way; some nouns and some verbs. But Miss Keller is very careful to point out that these were not words in the sense of language, that her associative imitations were only parts of a game unrelated to the comprehension of meaning which words can convey. Finally the day came when her teacher began the next step. This was to teach her that a word stands for more than one specific object. While she was playing with her new doll, her teacher put her old rag doll into her lap and spelled "d-o-l-l" into her hand. This introduced confusion and her emotional upset was such that she threw the new doll on the floor, breaking it. She reports that this act of destruction was not followed by remorse, but by a feeling of relief, since the source of confusion had been removed.

With this her teacher brought her hat, and she knew by this that they were about to go outside for a walk, something she always enjoyed. They strolled to the wellhouse where someone was drawing water. Her teacher placed one of her hands under the spout, and while the cool water ran over that hand the teacher spelled "w-a-t-e-r" into the other, first slowly then more rapidly. "Suddenly," she says, "I felt a misty consciousness as of something forgotten—a thrill of returning thought; and somehow the mystery of language was revealed to me." (1954, p. 36) We may call this insight if we wish, but whatever it was at that moment, Miss Keller declares she realized that everything has a name, and that each new name gives birth to new ideas. She goes on to say that this was the moment that set her free. Now she had a new and efficient means for organizing her stimulus world, comprehending the mental worlds of others and telling others of her own. For the first time she felt remorse, and her eyes filled with tears as she tried vainly to put the pieces of her new doll back together. She could now relate to objects and to other humans in a new way; she was now in communication at a social-conceptual level. When she went to bed that night, for the first time in her life she longed for the next day to come.

While we cannot be sure that Miss Keller's description of her "mental revolution" is psychologically accurate in detail, there is good reason to believe that her account is conceptually accurate, and that the essential nature of the transition from a world without language to one with language is insightfully described.

In commenting on Miss Keller's remarkable description, Lindesmith and Strauss say, "It is extremely significant that Miss Keller describes the changes which language brought in her life as both an intellectual and emotional revolution." (1956, p. 137) The intellectual revolution was one of learning to conceptualize, to categorize reference objects, to think at an abstract level which transcends specific objects of reference. The emotional revolution was that of coming to know herself. With her new-found language she could now "talk to herself" and categorize her own feelings out of her previous confused mental void. Now she could compare herself with those about her, and by this she could for the first time experience empathy. Although this account is far less empirical than we might wish for and does not meet the control standards the scientist wishes to impose upon his data, there is good reason to believe that it describes in broad outline the nature of thought before and after language. It substantiates our belief that normal thought, within a normal social context, is guided and directed, in other words determined, by the language which is available. We say, "determined," since this introduces our other problem. To what extent is our thinking a function of the kind of language available to the individual?

Linguistic Relativism

Linguistic relativism is one aspect of cultural relativism, the thesis that one's thought and behavior are functions of the social context, rather than the determiners of the nature of the social context. In addition, cultural relativism espouses the view that behavior and experience as reported are to be evaluated and understood only in light of the culture context of which the individual is a part. In polar contrast to the linguistic relativism position is what we may call "linguistic isomorphism," the view that the world of objects is the same to all normal people. This position holds that "the world is there and you see it just as I see it." According to this view, since all of us perceive the world identically (encoding), we all describe it (decoding) identically. The "linguistic isomorphism" position is the popular position; that is, it seems quite reasonable to most people. Such admonitions as, "Why don't you talk English?", "Spell it out," and "Just tell me the facts," are examples of the isomorphic view that "The world is there and you see it the same way that I do." This popular view is one which distinguishes between message and code; the message is always the same, only the codes are different. What one has to say about referent objects is the same that anyone else in the same stimulus situation has to say; it is only that the decoding processes (languages) which the two employ are different.

From one standpoint, this popular view may be questioned upon the basis of a comparison of literal and liberal translations of one language passage into another. Often a literal translation is, by the standards of those who use the language into which the translation is being made, ludicrous and absurd. The habitual users of one language often make sport of the "ridiculous" coding techniques practiced in another language. We may hazard a guess that most of these points of humor revolve about the order of action and modification in sentence structure much less than about the reference objects themselves. In English we say, "Bring me the cup." In other languages it might be said, "The cup to me bring." Whether or not these morphemic and syntactic differences really mean that the native users of English and German perceive and describe (encode and decode) the stimulus world in different ways psychologically cannot be decided upon the basis of standard syntactic arrangement or grammar. Certainly, the lexicons of some languages are larger than those of others; some languages are rich in ideational content and others are poor. Obviously, that which we can tell others (decode) about our experience with reference objects depends, just as with Victor, largely upon the coding techniques we have been taught. On the other hand, is our way of thinking, the items in the stimulus world we perceive, as with Laura Bridgman and Helen Keller, dependent, too, upon language?

While the history of the linguistic relativism position can be traced back as far as the eighteenth century, it was not precisely stated until recently. Today it is usually referred to as the Sapir-Whorf hypothesis (Mandelbaum, 1949; Whorf, 1952). These two scholars, Edward Sapir, an anthropologist, and Benjamin Whorf, a lay student of linguistics, independently formulated a general hypothesis that stated the linguistic relativism thesis in such a way that it could be examined scientifically. Both scholars contributed empirical evidence in its support.

Hoijer asserts that, "The central idea of the Sapir-Whorf hypothesis is that language functions, not simply as a device for reporting experience, but also, and more significantly, as a way of defining experience for its speakers." (1954, p. 93) And, as Fearing has put it, ". . . according to Whorf language shapes our ideas rather than merely expressing them." (1954, p. 47) The "linguistic isomorphism" position, as we have named it, or the "natural logic" thesis—". . . that the cognitive processes of all human beings possess a common logical structure . . . which operates prior to and independently of communication through language . . ."—is contested by the linguistic relativism hypothesis and held to be erroneous. (Fearing, 1954, p. 47)

While Whorf seems to recognize a very basic kind of common experiencing which is germane to all normal humans, transcending the structures of culture and language (this he calls *apprehension*), conceptualization is something more and is dependent upon the structure and content of the language available to the individual. Concepts are, then, in part functions of language, and one's view of the world could not be expected to be the same as that of another person whose language is different. As Whorf has said, "We are thus introduced to a new principle of relativity, which holds that all observers are not led by the same physical evidence to the same picture of the universe, unless their linguistic backgrounds are similar, or can in some way be calibrated." (Whorf, 1947, pp. 214–215)

The empirical evidences Whorf cites in support of linguistic relativism are many, most being taken from his studies of the Hopi language. One example is drawn from conceptions of time. He asserts that the Hopi language is "timeless." It recognizes "psychological time," or duration; though this varies from person to person, one duration never being thought of as simultaneous with another, and it has no dimensions. By the phrase "no dimensions" is meant that Hopi time (duration) cannot be divided into units and parts of units. There is, for example, no plural for day. If referring to a visit, the speaker would say, "I left on the fifth day," rather than "I stayed five days." Hopi verbs do not indicate distinctions between present, past and future. This, according to Whorf, illustrates a view of the universe very different from our own. In Western European language and thought we divide time in many ways. Our type of physical time measurement makes possible our whole conception of science; without such measurement our view of the world would be very different. Thus, the language system into which the child is born determines not only the linguistic expressions he will use, but the reference objects he will perceive and the ways he will think about them. In our own Western European culture Whorf finds the rigidity of language an obstruction to the creation of new world views, especially in the case of the development of scientific theory. And he has suggested that only by the development of a new language can these obstructions be removed.

The types of evidence which have been brought to bear upon the linguistic relativism hypothesis are neither complete nor thorough enough either to accept or reject the hypothesis as stated by Whorf and Sapir. Some evidence actually contradicts the hypothesis. For example, the Finns speak a language which is very unlike and unrelated to most European languages, yet the Finns appear to "think" in a European culture way (Bruner *et al.*, 1956). However these evidences may be evaluated, we are certainly in no position as yet either to accept or reject the linguistic relativism hypothesis in its extreme form. The great service the hypothesis has rendered to those who are interested in the psychological implications of language is that it has cautioned us against the naive acceptance of the other extreme hypothesis, linguistic isomorphism.

Perhaps as stated by Whorf and Sapir, the linguistic relativism hypothesis can never be completely accepted or completely rejected. By examining human thought in the light of this hypothesis, however, we have come to a more liberal view of the role that language plays in determining our thinking habits. No doubt both extreme views overstate their cases, and a theory of language and thought which takes both into account will some day emerge, since while the two can be contrasted they are not antithetical.

For social psychology the most direct contribution made by the linguistic relativism position is its insistence upon a phenomenalism. Strictly interpreted this is a "sociological phenomenalism"; that is, it applies to the linguistic culture group rather than to the individual. As Whorf puts it, language "represents the mass mind." (Fearing, 1954, p. 52.) Nevertheless, this emphasizes that the individual tends to perceive and interpret his world in light of the language structures which are made available to him by his linguistic culture. And within a given linguistic culture we would expect no two individuals to use the language structure in identical ways; no two people would be expected to experience the world in the same semantic frame of reference.

Klineberg has said that "Language serves as an instrument of thought and of communication, as a means of controlling the actions of others, and as a force which unites the members of a particular community, at the same time separating them from others." (1954, p. 58) One of the important agents in social organization very obviously is a common language. Not that those who use the same language necessarily live in cooperative harmony. But, with Klineberg's final phrase, it is important to recognize the fact that common understandings, meanings, value orientations, and even perceptions are rendered more divergent by language differences. There is good reason to believe that the most calamitous breakdown of social organization, war, is in many respects a function of misunderstandings which result from profound psychological differences which, in turn, are results of language differences (Cooper, 1955b; Lazarsfeld, 1952; Behanan, 1948). One of the approaches to the problem of social organization and disorganization, from the interpersonal level to the international level, is through the study of the role of language in thought. We would propose the thesis that human life would be drab were there only a single language and that the development of and subscription to a single language would not in itself effect our goal. Rather, we need to train ourselves to the realities of language as a determiner of thought (Fearing, 1953), and recognize that a human ethics which will provide social adequacy for all must not be based on any particular, traditional language system. It must be based upon an empirically tested theory of human nature. If we can agree upon this we can make any language our servant in understanding others, and free ourselves from the bonds and strictures our native tongues so often impose upon us.

VIII

Social Organization

The purposes of this chapter are to examine social organization as a function of individual behavior and experience, and individual behavior and experience as functions of social organization. While human society with its institutions and traditions exists by virtue of individuals, the biological existence and the behavioral-experiential propensities of individuals are shaped by the nature of society.

RESEARCH ON SOCIAL ORGANIZATION

In recent years social organization has received much research attention. Literature on the subject ranges from the strictly speculative and mystic to the rigidly experimental. There are many reasons for this. For one thing—and probably most important—social organizations are unwieldy. Except in those instances where the group is quite small it is impossible to observe the whole for a given period of time. In the case of large groups, a picture of the whole may only be surmised since only small fragments can be observed at any given time. What goes on within the group may be known, after all, by way of observation of what individuals do, and only so many individuals can be simultaneously observed. In last analysis, what we choose to call a social organization is a system of behavioral interrelationships which have some degree of stability and regularity. Only the fact of multiple individuals is palpable; the functional interrelationships that are observed or believed to exist constitute the organization. These described interrelationships of statuses, roles, beliefs, expectations, behavior patterns, are at a level of abstraction over and above the palpable.

Another reason for the inadequacy of systematization of the literature on groups and social organizations is semantic. Terminology is relatively loose and frequently vague. Much of the terminology is borrowed and much is concocted. Although this is necessary in the early stages of a science, it can lead to confusion.

Still another reason for the difficulty in systematizing the field lies in the diversity of problems studied, populations used, and study designs employed. In commenting on the difficulties in codifying the many studies of social structure, Riecken and Homans have emphasized these points, while at the same time they have maintained that ". . . there are no such things as contradictory findings." (1954, p. 829) Results which superficially appear to be contradictory may be seen as coordinate when it is realized that they were reached in different circumstances. In view of the fact that the research in this field is so confused and extensive, these same authors have suggested a kind of empirical research moratorium during which codification and close examination of theoretical implications would be carried out. Subsequent to this suggestion several such publications have appeared (Stogdill, 1959; Hare, Borgatta, Bales, 1955; Lorge *et al.*, 1958; Mann, 1959). Despite this lack of adequate codification and the presence of considerable confusion, there is much of basic importance in the literature. It is not the purpose of this chapter to review this vast literature. Rather, this chapter represents an attempt to draw from the literature only certain findings which we believe throw light upon the fundamental social psychological problem.

GROUP PROCESSES

When we see sheep grazing on a hillside we may simply take it for granted that their relative positions are determined only by chance. If our observation continues long and carefully enough we discover that there is considerable group regularity and uniformity in their patterns of movement. And if we carefully study a flock over an extended period of time, this group uniformity is not only describable but certain interorganism variables responsible for it come to be understood. In observing the formation flight of certain migratory birds we are impressed by the precision and orderliness of the group process. That it represents organization goes without saying.

Of course, organization is not always so easy as this to detect. Since we assume, however, that in some way at least all animal life is social, we are always justified in looking for organization since any social process implies organization. To pursue this point just a bit further: biologically adaptive social behavior (whether within a species, or between and among species) implies some kind of organization. Nonadaptive social behavior implies disorganization. Such a broad biological interpretation, then, places adaptive social organizations on a continuum from those that are tight-knit and compact to those that are loose and vague. At the human level, for example, a closely-knit family might stand at one end of the continuum and geographical groups of the earth's human population at the other. In order for individual animal organisms to adapt biologically and for species to adapt and survive many types of organization are essential.

Group Behavior

One of the problems which has persistently plagued students of collective behavior processes has centered around the distinction between *group* and *organization*. The term "group" has been used in a variety of ways, most definitions emphasizing some single aspect which in one way or another conflicts with certain other definitions. Social psychologists have tended to describe groups in three ways: a number of individuals described by a given physical environment; an association of individuals (human) operating in an organized way; and a collection of individuals who subscribe to some common symbol or loyalty. In commenting on these descriptions, Lorge *et al.* point out that social psychologists have tended to think of "the group" as possessing a tradition, ". . . i.e., a cooperative association of individuals whose members have progressed through the states of coming together in physical proximity, of organizing for common goals, and of accepting commitment for the group's purposes." At the same time, they go on to say, social psychologists who have studied groups have usually worked with *ad hoc* groups; assemblages of people brought together by experimenters ". . . to work together mutually and cooperatively on some specific and externally assigned task. . . . A common and dangerous practice is to generalize the principles valid for *ad hoc* groups to traditional groups." (1958, p. 338) In view of this important observation these writers have suggested that the types of groups which psychologists and sociologists study can be placed on a continuum from "artificial" to "real."

This continuum consists of six steps. First, there are traditional groups. Such a group is an association of individuals whose members work cooperatively toward common goals, and accomplish the world's work. Second, there are *ad hoc* groups. These are groups which have been brought together to work cooperatively on some problem or toward some goal but which have no tradition. Once the goal is reached, such a group usually disintegrates. Third are climatized groups. Such groups are composed of persons in physical proximity. In such a group there is discussion among the members of some problem but there is no group solution, no consensus. Each individual "votes" in his own way—it is the operation of a jury. Fourth, there are social climatized groups. Such groups are composed of individuals in physical proximity; but no interaction is involved other than the members observing each other's presence and observing, perhaps, how other members react to certain issues or in terms of certain problems. Fifth, there are statisticized groups. These are noninteracting individuals who are categorized into some classification in accordance with performance on some task. The results from these independent performances are averaged and the individuals who contributed to the average are referred to as a group. Such a group is in no sense an interacting group. Sixth, and last, are concocted groups. As with statisticized groups, individuals who compose such a group neither meet nor interact. In the concocted group each individual's unique contribution goes into the composition of the group product.

Research by social psychologists and sociologists has tended through the years to move from statisticized to tradition group studies. It is obviously more difficult to study traditional groups than any of the others, though the value of studying traditional groups is unquestionably of greatest value if we are interested in understanding and predicting behavior which is socially determined.

This continuum which Lorge *et al.* have described, it must be remembered, is actually a classification of the "types" of groups which the students of group processes have set up or found to work with. Its primary value lies in the fact that a research result may be more adequately evaluated when the nature of the group studied is known. This description is a partial answer to the proposal made by Riecken and Homans, that since it must be assumed that "there are no such things as contradictory findings," (p. 829) *apparent* contradictions may be resolved if the circumstances under which the researches which produced them are known and understood.

Of greatest importance to social psychological understanding is the traditional group. Of next importance is the *ad hoc* group. Of less value are the next two types, climatized and social-climatized. Of questionable value are the last two types, both of which are noninteracting, non-face-to-face. Under some circumstances, however, even in these last two instances, if the individuals who are "counted" or "averaged" into noninteracting, non-face-to-face groups perceive social pressures and social possibilities during the time in which their performances are being measured, group effects are surely in action. For example, a subject may be asked to make a judgment under conditions of social isolation. The fact that he is asked to do this by another person (who has some unique status) and the fact that he may suspect that other individuals will be making the same kind of judgment, constitute for that subject a group situation from a phenomenological standpoint. Thus, while such a classification is helpful from the standpoint of interpretation of research findings it should not be used as a discrete set of "types of groups." Rather, it should, as its authors suggest, be thought of as a continuum helpful from both heuristic and interpretative standpoints.

Organization

We have pointed out that many students of group processes have found it difficult to distinguish between *group* and *organization*. Since this chapter is concerned with what we choose to call *organization,* before we go on we should give some specific attention to this matter. The continuum which Lorge *et al.* have described suggests organization throughout—organization as most obvious at the "traditional" end and least obvious at the "concocted" end. The points along the continuum, however, are very difficult to identify. From the standpoint of the student who is interested in knowing something about the dynamics of groups, and in what ways these dynamics affect the individual's behavior, a further refinement of the Lorge *et al.* continuum is necessary.

Our suggestion is that the group should be treated as generic, and organization should be treated as specific. That is, only some groups are organizations—some groups are not organizations, or, at least, are little organized. This point has been well made by Stogdill, who says, "A special kind of group is the *organization.* An organization may be defined as a social group in which the members are differentiated as to their responsibilities for the task of achieving a common goal." (1959, p. 125) This seems to be a valuable definition if the phrase "responsibilities for the task of achieving a common goal" is broadly interpreted. We would want to define organization in such a way that it could be used at the infrahuman as well as at the human level. Thus, the terms "responsibilities" and "common goal" need clarification.

If role can be used to designate the meaning of responsibility, there is no trouble. The queen bee, for instance, has a particular role to play within the colony, but we would not think of this role in the human sense of "accepting responsibility." If the meaning of "common goal" is broad enough to include the biological meaning of adaptation, and does not necessarily require the connotation of conscious intent and conscious planning, this definition of organization can serve a very useful purpose. We insist upon this broad interpretation since it is important to view human social organization against a background of infrahuman social organization. In this way we may be able to identify and understand certain features of human organization that are emergent and therefore unique.

Stogdill has also commented upon the practical problem of identifying the characteristics of a human social organization. While he cautions that it is frequently difficult to determine at what point a group becomes an organization, his useful suggestions are as follows:

A group may or may not have leaders. If it does have leaders, it is an organization, for at least some of the members are thereby differentiated from the others as to responsibility, or role expectation in relation to some common purpose. The members of a group may or may not have mutual responsibilities for a common task. If the members do have differentiated responsibilities in relation to common goals, then the group is an organization—a particular kind of group. The continued presence of leaders and of responsibility differentiations in relation to group goals are indicative of organization (1950), p. 3).

Thus, when certain members of the group play specific roles which are related to group accomplishment, such a functioning group may be thought of as an organization; we may say then, that the individuals who constitute the group are organized.

Role in Adaptation.   Without social organization the survival of most species in the animal kingdom would be impossible. At infrahuman levels adaptation success is the only criterion that can be used in judging the efficiency of any organization. Adaptation success is not simply the result of organizational complexity, for in many excellently adapted species social organization is relatively simple. On the other hand, there are many striking examples of excellent adaptation which depend upon great organizational complexity. The intricately complex organizations of some ants, for example, have remained virtually unchanged for millions of years. This demonstrates extraordinary adaptation. It must be remembered, however, that a highly structured, complex and unchanging social organization may easily result in species extinction if ecological conditions are seriously altered. Social organization, whether it is simple or complex, can be evaluated only in terms of its adaptation efficiency within its environmental context.

Evaluation of Social Organization.   At the human level we are faced with certain problems over and above those at the infrahuman levels. The most difficult and serious, of course, is that of evaluating the products of social organization. While adaptation is obviously a basic criterion, since without survival there is nothing to observe, man's efforts create "products" which are more than of simple adaptation-survival value. Man plans, imagines, creates works of art, enjoys contests and literature, worships, and engages in many activities that become more important to him than simple physical survival. These and many other behavioral and experiential processes are, one or another or several, viewed by some humans at some time and place as the reasons for social organization, as the criteria by which social organizations should be evaluated. Thus, when Stogdill speaks of "common purpose" we must view "common purpose" not only from the human standpoint but also from the general adaptation (biological) standpoint. Man, as any other species, is dependent upon social organization for individual physical survival, and for species adaptation. At the same time, man creates a great variety of social organizations in order to achieve values which transcend the biological adaptation level.

Institutions.   From a very broad standpoint the values which come to have greatest meaning in the individual human's life are the outcomes of human interactions—interactions which have great organizational stability. We usually refer to these as institutions: family, church, school, fraternity, lodge, political party. The fact is that most of the values toward which we strive are literally provided for us by institutional types of groupings. They are anything but random assemblages of people. And, as we have said, the substance of an organization is a complex of interactions. While the individual interacts with other people within such organizations, his behavior is to be thought of as a function of his motivations and his expectations—what he wants, and what he believes is possible. He has learned about organizations as instrumentalities, and organizations have provided him with motives and social reinforcements (both positive and negative).

SOCIAL ORGANIZATION AT THE INFRAHUMAN LEVEL

From the lowest forms of animal life to man there is a general reduction in the degree of stereotypy of social groupings. In accordance with Stogdill's definition only some of the lower species could be strictly classified as representing social organization, since in many there is little or no indication of leadership or differential responsibility. However, if it is remembered that only some social groups are organizations we still find that nonorganized social groups often play vital roles in both individual and species survival and adaptation. Thus, while the social organization concept may need to be reserved for only certain of the higher forms, social grouping rigidity varies tremendously from the lowest to the highest species. In most, if not all, of the lower forms, groups of individuals conform to highly specific, stereotyped, virtually nonvariable social group patterns. Given standard ecological conditions, there may be nothing unique about any given group within a given species—they may all be alike. By the time we reach the lower mammals, however, specializations in group behavior are sometimes found, and the organization concept is somewhat easier to employ. At the human level, of course, organizations have become so complex, unique, variable, and nonstereotyped that they defy satisfactory classification. As suggested previously, we propose to use the term social organization in the broadest sense—in a sense that will include certain of the infrahumans as well as humans. Such a comparative perspective provides a better view of those organizational properties that are unique at the human level. We propose, then, briefly to describe organized social behavior in a few representative infrahuman forms. We will attempt to show that organization is essential to adaptation and that as animal forms become more complex their social organizations become more intricate and variable.

The Sponge

Typically, sponges reproduce by budding; they form branching, nonmotile colonies of connected individuals. Adaptation is accomplished purely at a physiological level rather than at a behavioral level, since they are incapable of movement. From a species adaptation standpoint such a colonization represents a vague type of organization since the species is protected by sheer number in physical union. While an individual may survive for a period of time, colonial grouping is typical and represents a vague pattern of organization—though without individual specialization more than "parent" and "budding offspring." From the standpoint of "social change" the sponges are probably as close to a zero point as can be found. Generation after generation these organizations are formed and the organizational pattern of any generation is virtually identical with that of every other generation. A "purpose" is served by such an organization, but the organization is purely a function of genetic characteristics contained within a given ecological situation. The individual plays no specialized role in an unchanging organizational pattern.

The Paramecium

It is customary to think of multicellular animals as more complex than unicellular animals. However, various of the unicellular species have social organizations which are amazingly more complex than some of the multicellular species. A good example of this is the paramecium, a single-celled animal of the class *Infusoria* and phylum *Protozoa*. These single-celled but highly complex animals have cilia which they use to propel themselves about in the water with great facility, a "mouth" for the acceptance of food, and a "gullet" which might be thought of as analogous to a stomach in the higher animals. The paramecium is a versatile and active organism. For instance, it swims with its rounded end forward. However, it has been observed that when it encounters some irritating substance or an obstacle, its cilia reverse their action and it swims backward. This is the essential principle of trial and error behavior and there is some evidence to support the contention that such trials and errors leave semipermanent effects which may legitimately be called learning.

As with all animals, the various species of paramecium are in various respects social. The degree of sociality which these animals demonstrate is not random and unorganized; some amount of organization is observable. On the one hand, such organization may be said to be caused in part by the nature of the individuals; and on the other hand, the nature of the individuals may be said to be caused in part by the nature of the organization. Two examples will illustrate the meaning of this assertion.

First, reproduction in the paramecium occurs ordinarily by way of fission. When a single individual is isolated in suitable water with ample food it divides in two in about ten hours; the two new individuals divide again in about ten hours; thus the population is increased at a very rapid rate. Such division produces what is called a "pure line," (Thompson, 1935) since there is no nuclear interchange with other individuals. The population is essentially the same individual in many identical parts. After the population has increased to a given size, however, individuals begin to show signs of deterioration; they become less active, consume less food, and exhibit a condition biologists call "depression." Thus, the behavior of the group may be understood in terms of physical conditions which result from individual behavior (fission) and physiological processes (giving off wastes).

Second, when individuals from such a depressed population are shifted to another population a different type of organization emerges. Instead of restricting themselves to isolated fission, individuals begin conjugation with the new individuals. This is a quasi-sexual reproductive process in which two individuals come close together in a union of mouths and some amount of nuclear interchange takes place. While new individuals are not created in this way, conjugation promotes new vigor and variability, thus increasing the viability of the species.

Paramecia do not represent social organization complexity which in any way approaches the complexity of higher organisms. At the same time, it is an organization, since a structure can be identified and modifications in ecological and individual conditions correlate with social structure (organization). If an isolated group remains in isolation for a long period of time it degenerates, but if it is able to associate with another group there is a reorganization and this is conducive to individual vitality. Again, in the light of Stogdill's definition of social organization at the human level, paramecia evidence virtually no specialization and no suggestion of responsibility. Nevertheless, such infrahuman groupings are organized and the efficiency of adaptation seems to depend heavily upon the nature of the organization (Jennings, 1931).

The Insect

In the class *Insecta* of the phylum *Arthropoda* are found some of the best examples of social organization, organizational complexity, individual specialization, and social stereotypy in the animal kingdom. Social organizations in some of the insects are so complex, rigid, and adaptively adequate that some entomologists have referred to them as "republics" and have come to think of insect societies as the prototypes of human societies in a homological sense (Maeterlinck, 1939). Reminiscent of Hobbes' concept of society as a super-organism is the view of some entomologists who point to the elaborate interplay of the highly specialized individuals who compose a "working body." The "working body" is analogous to a single human with his various parts (digestive, respiratory, nervous, etc., systems) working harmoniously in the interest of living efficiency. In a termite colony, for example, there are castes and developmental stages that fit together into a kind of super-organism. There are queen, king, eggs, nymphs, supplementary reproductive animals, alates (male and female winged reproductive animals), reproductive nymphs, soldiers, and workers. These highly specialized individuals perform highly specialized functions which make possible the existence of the colony. And in this sense the colony does represent a great organism. Each individual has its specific function to perform and, ecological conditions being stable, it performs those functions unerringly. While it cannot be denied that any individual may modify its behavior slightly as a function of its previous responses, the principal reasons for an individual's specific behavior are to be found in its structure. The entire specialization of individual performance and sterotypy of social organization may be accounted for by genetic characteristics, even though many of the details are still inadequately understood.

We cannot avoid the conclusion that the stability of social organization among various of the insects is much greater than among most, if not all, of the higher organisms. However, this is one of the basic propositions we must recognize in studying human social organization. While with some species social organization is rigid, individually specialized, and unchanging from generation to generation, in man we typically find diversity, rapid change, and invention. Of course, in individual instances, termites and other insects vary their behavior in a wide variety of ways. For instance, the solitary "ant lion" will remove pebbles from its pit in different ways, depending upon the size and location of the pebbles (Wheeler, 1930). Its behavior can be adapted to the requirements of the situation. However, there are limitations, and when we view the over-all life pattern of such "solitary" species we are impressed by the fact that behavioral variation is minimal, that a given animal behaves in ways almost identical with every other. The same conclusion is to be drawn with reference to the social organizations of the social insects. If the species can be identified, an exact prediction can be made with reference to its social organization.

One of the clearest distinctions between the social organizations of the social insects and those of most other forms (including mammals) is to be found in individual structural differentiation. Whereas in various of the termite species there are several classes (or castes), each performing a highly specialized function and each individual in some way dependent upon the behavior of the other classes, in the great majority of other species there are only three classes: male, female, and young. In such class-limited species we would expect less specialization and much more overlapping of function. If the individuals within a social grouping have little task specialization by virtue of genetically determined characteristics we would expect the organizational structure of such a social grouping to be relatively flexible, and we would also expect considerable variation from one socially organized group to another within a given species. Again, this is the case with many of the higher animals; and with man it is eminently true. We must caution ourselves in the temptation to use the assumption that there is a basic and set structure to human organization comparable to the social insects.

The Mammal

A fourth example of social organization is taken from the mammalian level. For this example we will briefly describe one feature of the social life of small mammals. The aspect of social organization we will touch upon here is referred to as territoriality. Rats exemplify territoriality well since they distribute themselves over a given area in a systematic way, ordinarily digging burrows and rearing their young in the burrow location as a kind of colony. When the young mature some of them may find the food supply inadequate, move out into a new location that is not inhabited, and there burrow and rear young themselves. Ordinarily, the members of one burrow colony will not tolerate encroachment upon their territory by individuals from other colonies. This indicates a high degree of socialization since the endemic members of a colony "get along" whereas "strangers" are "bluffed out" or actually attacked. Another interesting aspect of this is that the "stranger" who wanders into a foreign territory usually retreats when bluffed, even though in a neutral area he might be much the superior fighter. To put it anthropomorphically, the individual feels brave and behaves courageously when at home, but acts in a timorous way when away from home.

Rats probably represent the most successful modern rodents, perhaps equaling or outnumbering the human species. They are rugged, adapted to a wide variety of foods, and highly fecund. While not all rats live in burrows, some strains living typically in the holds of ships or in the walls of houses, there are many strains that burrow and colonize in particular terrestrial areas. Systematic studies have shown that there is an organizational pattern in the social life of these burrowing animals.

The female comes into estrus approximately every five days and while out of the burrow at that time copulates with one or more males over a short period. After fertilization she is no longer sexually receptive, and in due time selects some burrow area where parturition occurs about 23 days after fertilization. Her attention to the young is complex and continues, under optimal conditions, until the young are able to explore and take solid food. But, as we have said, because of space and food requirements it is necessary for the young to move out and locate in areas which will support them. Their chances of survival seem to depend upon two principal factors: a location which is not already occupied by another colony, and an adequate food source. If either or both of these conditions are absent, their survival chances are reduced and the probability of females producing young that will survive is greatly reduced. The study of such phenomena in native habitats is obviously difficult. However, controlled observation and experimental techniques have been used to throw light upon territoriality and the general problem of social organization in burrowing rats (Calhoun, 1948, 1950, 1952; Calhoun and Webb, 1953).

In one experimental study the investigators constructed a rat pen of 10,000 square feet, 100 feet to the side. Into this pen they introduced a few animals that had been trapped from a given location, thus assuring that they were from the same general population and that they were familiar with each other. With strange animals it would be expected that there would be considerable fighting, that this itself would be an important factor in the establishment of social organization in general and territoriality in particular. Another important factor was that an unlimited central food supply was provided. Under similar circumstances, save that an unlimited rather than a restricted space were provided, it was estimated that after a period of two years a population of 50,000 individuals would have been produced. And had the same nucleus been introduced into standard laboratory cages with a total space of 10,000 square feet, after two years the population would have reached about 5,000. Under the conditions of this experiment, however, the total population reached less than 200 in the two-year period. In other words, these animals developed an organization which literally controlled the population size. Several factors seem to have been important in determining this impressive result. For one thing, and probably most important, the animals "staked out" specific territories for their burrows and as litters came along the new individuals tended to stay within their natal territories. When they ventured into new territories they were rebuffed and when strangers came into their territory they chased them away. There were no observed instances of carnage, since bluffing seems to have been sufficient for running strangers away. Those colonies that developed close to the central food supply seemed to have greater social stability, whereas the outlying colonies were less protective of their young since their problems of obtaining food involved crossing "foreign territory." Of course, in time, even the young produced close to the central food supply would have had increased survival problems since they were subject to bluffing by older animals. In the outlying areas even the reproduction rate decreased and the young were more subject to insect attack and were provided less maternal care. Reduced maternal care apparently was a function of the mothers' increased needs to spend more time in procuring food. Essentially, then, a stable population developed as a result of the social organization that evolved. Thus the species can maintain itself, although many individuals barely survive and many others do not survive. In the evolutionary process these genetically determined social characteristics have undoubtedly played a vital role in species adaptation.

One other of the studies these investigators conducted should be mentioned here. This was a field study of small mammal populations. They trapped animals in a given area and then counted the number of animals that came into the area just depopulated by trapping. Calhoun and Webb describe the result as follows:

Were there no invasion from surrounding areas, the resident population would be essentially removed at the end of 10 days. . . . Since small mammals move into the denuded area so rapidly, it is suspected that shifting the place of habitation is a response directly related to the relative intensity, frequency, or both, of perceiving neighbors at a distance. . . . Whatever the exact mechanism underlying the response, those animals living just peripheral to the area subject to continuous trapping do move into it. As soon as the shift occurs, the next group living still farther away must move into the area just vacated by the previous group. Through this process a biological chain response is established whereby a simultaneous movement toward the central depleted area extends for a considerable distance away from the periphery of the trapping area. (1953, pp. 358–360)

These studies are important for several reasons. For one thing, food supply plays a definite role in determining the level of organization a colony may maintain, or the degree of disorganization to which it may descend. Whereas the termite queen continues to lay eggs until she starves to death, with no indication of moving toward a food source, the female rat tends to neglect her "maternal duties" when the food runs short, although, as Warden (1931) has shown, she demonstrates a drive for the newborn which is stronger than any of the other drives. This unusually strong drive seems to give way when the young are a bit more mature and living under the field conditions Calhoun describes.

Another reason these studies are important is found in the reciprocal factors of familiarity with colony territory and mates, and unfamiliarity with new territory and new individuals. As pointed out earlier, if lethal fighting were an intraspecies rule, a species would not survive. Here is a point in reference. Upon encounter, these small mammals do not ordinarily fight and kill. One signals and the other responds to the signal by an avoidance response. Thus, the territory is divided; space is "assigned." This type of social organization has evolved and has become adaptively well established. When there is a distributed food supply and sufficient room for territorial expansion, other things equal, these small mammals demonstrate an amazing degree of social organization, an organization which is clearly conducive to species adaptation. The converse of organization—disorganization—results when ecological conditions are significantly altered. From one standpoint, instances of social disorganization may represent a process of reorganization. By this is meant that some individuals are eliminated and reproduction is restricted, thus providing more food and territory for a few. This has the tendency, in the long run, to stabilize and strengthen a small population. Thus, from the standpoint of a restricted physical environment, it is adaptive.

The Infrahuman Primate

Except for man, infrahuman primates demonstrate the greatest docility among the terrestrial members of the animal kingdom, and here we should expect to find social organization at a very high level of complexity. Depending upon what we mean by complexity, this is both true and false. On the one hand, social organization in the many subhuman primate species is quite vague. On the other hand, since as individuals these animals are so complex, the social organizations they develop produce intricacies and constant changes which in some ways are more variable and complex than those found in lower animal orders. The primates do not demonstrate clear-cut, rigid social organizational structures which hold up under changing environments. Rather, they demonstrate social organizations which "change with the times," organizations which are adaptive from the standpoint of modifying the environment a bit rather than permitting genetic and environmental factors to determine behavior entirely. However, except for man, primate capacity to survive by environmental manipulation has not been impressive. Most primates have barely "hung on" and some genera are now reduced to virtual extinction. Since, however, the primates are quite modern animals, this is exactly what the theory of organic evolution would lead us to expect.

Howling Monkeys. One of the field studies of social organization in the primates was conducted by Carpenter (1934, pp. 1–168), who investigated howling monkeys on an island in the Panama Canal Zone. This species represents a sprawling type of society, yet one with real organizational cohesiveness. Again, it is to be supposed that genetic factors are primarily responsible for the basic social organization which Carpenter has described. Behavioral variability within the group and nonspecificity, however, seem to be responsible for the type of social organization these animals manifest. When we describe the social organization of termites, there is no difficulty. It is stereotyped, and every individual in the organization has its specific role to play. When we describe rats, the roles are much less specified in terms of the individuals that will play them. At the primate level the difficulty of describing social organization is even greater, since there is increased overlapping of individual function and considerable variability in group behavior.

The howling monkeys are beautifully adapted to a tree-top life, where they find their food (fruit, leaves, small twigs) and where they sleep. They live in groups ranging from about four to thirty-five individuals, the average band being seventeen. Adult populations are composed roughly of 30 per cent males and 70 per cent females. Food taking and infant care seem to be their principal preoccupations. They arise in the early morning and wander about until they find a food-laden tree. There they remain to eat until about mid-day. They usually rest from that time on until late in the afternoon when they commence taking food again. As darkness approaches they assemble in a tree and sleep. This is the daily routine for the band. Whether or not bands are biological families is a question, though they probably are.

One of the most significant observations about howling monkeys is that they virtually never fight. As the name implies, vocalization seems to be a substitute for fighting. Encroachment of one band upon the territory of another is prevented by unison roaring by the males.

Scott (1958, pp. 163–168) has summarized the Carpenter study, and we will follow his outline in describing other features of the social organization of howling monkeys. He has described social organization in terms of the types of "interindividual" (male, female, and young) relationships which are possible.

With reference to female-young relationships, the most evident feature is a strong tie between mother and young. The mother carries her young everywhere, feeds it, protects it from the weather, retrieves it when it falls, and affords such solicitous behavior until weaning when the young animal is about two years old. Adult females form a sort of group of their own which, of course, includes the young. Though specific leadership seems to be absent, the female group tends to move along after the male group.

Male-male relationships are much the same, save for the fact that the males tend to seek out food, working independently, and when one does locate a supply, he emits a kind of clucking sound which calls the others, males and females, to share it. Although males do not fight among themselves, they roar in unison when threatened by outsiders, and this appears to be of mutual defense value. As with females, leadership seems to be absent.

Male-female relationships are typified, as we have said, by relative group isolation. That is, the males tend to stay together and the females tend to stay together, the female group being larger than the male group. This sex disproportion is typical among the infrahuman primates according to field counts (Nissen, 1951). Reasons for it amount essentially to speculation, though some of the speculations are most interesting. When a female is in estrus she goes to a nearby male and presents. The male stays with the female until satiated, at which time the female moves on to another male. This estrus behavior lasts for several days. There seem to be no variables which account for the selection of one male over another, with the possible exceptions of adulthood and proximity. Fighting among females or among males over the opposite sex does not seem to take place. Although the adult males pay little attention to the young animals, when one of the young falls from a tree they set up unison howling and evidence considerable excitement. Again, this probably represents warding off or defense behavior. On occasion adult males pick up unattended young.

The young are in fairly close association since they stay close by their mothers. They play a great deal, chasing each other about through the trees. Some of this behavior, biting and wrestling, is simulated fighting—though it seems to be the closest thing to real fighting in the howling monkeys. Play, including the simulated fighting, may sometimes reveal degrees of dominance. Otherwise, behavioral differentiation among the young is virtually lacking.

An over-all view of the social organization of howling monkeys is one of generalized relationships. Except during the time of mother-infant association, there is nothing in the way of behavioral specialization which gives a sharp picture of lasting individual-to-individual relationships. The individual seems to relate to the group more than to other individuals. Males, females, and young do, of course, contribute differently to the social organization; and in this sense we observe behavioral differentiation or specialization. Males, as a group, take the lead in searching for food, but particular males do not seem to lead or dominate the others.

This type of social organization is in clear contrast with many others in which there is high individual specialization, dominance hierarchies and individual-to-individual attachments of long duration. On the one hand, one might interpret the howling monkey organization as scarcely an organization at all since these intricate interindividual relationships do not seem to exist. On the other hand, the interpretation might be made that the howling monkeys represent an enormously complex social organization, the cohesive subtleties of which escape our detection.

For purposes of studying and attempting to understand social organization, two principal impressions may be gained from the howling monkeys.

First, when we attempt to make specific and precise descriptions of the social organization of a high order species (in this case at the primate level) we find that individual behavior variability is so great that it is difficult to make specific statements about what "the male" or "the female" or "the young" do within the social organization. Thus, the concept of social organization at higher levels of animal life must be broadened to include extremely loose, variable, and subtly controlled social processes. At this level we are dealing with animals that are not "stimulus bound," animals that are not behaving simply reflexively. At this level, a type of social organization has emerged which cannot be understood solely upon the basis of genetic factors. Experience and situational variation must also be taken into account.

Second, the howling monkeys represent a type of social organization in which an individual evidences strong attachment for its own group, but relatively weak attachment for other individuals making up the group. This is not true of many species. The gibbon, for instance, apparently mates for life and this male-female attachment is the family nucleus. This family nucleus is the basic social organization unit and may include one or two young. The adult male or female drives the maturing young of opposite sex out of the family when the young reach about two years of age. By contrast, then, this is a much more structured social organization, and in ways seemingly simpler than that of the howling monkeys. Thus, if we are to ask what kind of social organization is typical of primates, we must answer that from species to species there are great differences, and that successful species adaptation does not necessarily depend upon any basic prototype. In this there is a hint for us at the human level. While man is enormously more complex and creative than any of the lower primates, it is conceivable that particular social organization features which provide the developing individual with certain interpersonal experiences are more conducive to successful adaptations than others. The study of the socialization aspects of social organization at the human level seems imperative if we are to throw light upon this important problem.

Social Disorganization

In contrast to social organization which is conducive to adaptation, there is social disorganization which is detrimental to adaptation. However, as we have said, disorganization may be interpreted as movement toward organization if we view it from a long-time perspective. Disorganization, at least by analogy, is a kind of social homeostatic process which moves toward the re-establishment of a social equilibrium which is adaptively favorable. Before we leave the infrahuman primates, let us cite one illustration of social disorganization. Let us bear in mind that a given species, under given conditions, goes about its social disorganization process in an organized way. That is, a given species tends to use particular disorganization techniques.

The baboons are usually pictured as domineering and vicious, constantly venting their hostility upon other members of the group. That this is not true of troops of baboons in their native habitats has been stressed by Washburn and DeVore (1961), who have found that under native conditions there is indication of care-giving and a minimum of fighting and domination by the older males. However, some years ago, when the London Zoo brought 100 baboons into a 6000 square foot enclosure, fighting was rampant, and after two years there were only 59 animals left, most of these being males. At this time 30 females and five young males were introduced. A general melee followed, the older males not only fighting each other but tearing some of the females to pieces. Three years later the "colony" was reduced to 39 males and 9 females. During that time only one infant survived. There was some organization in this general disorganization. Under conditions of restricted space and unfamiliarity these animals moved socially to a reduction of numbers. We might suppose that under these conditions of territory restriction an adaptive organization could never be developed. And it might further be supposed that were all baboons required to live under such changed physical circumstances the species would die out. Thus, social organization must be viewed as adaptive only under certain circumstances. Given these circumstances, the type of social organization which has evolved is adaptive and the species flourishes.

SOCIAL ORGANIZATION AT THE HUMAN LEVEL

We have seen that infrahumans' social organizations are relatively stereotyped, that generation after generation the social organization of a given species is virtually the same. We have also suggested that there is a rough positive correlation between the morphological complexity of the individual species member and the stereotypy of social organization for that species. But when we reach the level of man we find ourselves dealing with an organism of such complexity that we would expect him to organize himself socially in even more complex ways. The human individual's role within an organization is determined by much more than simple genetic factors. Factors determined by experience, both for the individual and for other members of the organization, play a greater part in assigning the individual his role than they do with any of the infrahumans. Admittedly, this is a matter of degree, of relativity. However, the gap between man and even the highest primates is so great that role occupancy and mobility seem, at the human level, to have taken on a new quality.

In Chapter III we made reference to several human-infrahuman behavioral analogies which point to the fact that at the human level there are certain emergent psychological capacities. These capacities—such as language, systematic curiosity, and esthetics—are basically important in characterizing man as different from any of the lower species. We would expect such emergent capacities to determine in many ways the types of social organizations man develops. And it follows that any psychological analysis of human social organization will require constant reference to various of these emergences. For instance, no adequate psychological analysis of a human family organization would be adequate without attention to such variables as language, attitudes, taboos, and ethics. These variables would not be considered in analyzing the gibbon family structure since, to the best of our knowledge, they are absent. While, of course, it is not necessary to recount and describe each human emergence each time we examine the psychological nature of a given human social organization, it is necessary to remember that the essential psychological variables which are responsible for any form or instance of human social organization are different from those which support infrahuman social organizations. The study of infrahumans and their social organizations assists in identifying these unique human variables, but infrahuman social organizations are by no means the human prototypes.

Controlling Factors

In the broadest sense, both individual behavior (role) within the group and the dynamic pattern of the organization itself are determined by two sets of controlling factors: individual and situational.

Individual Factors. These fall into two categories: genetically determined and experience-determined. For example, in the usual family, the father-husband role (not only this designation as such, but also how he plays that role) is determined by the fact that he is male and by the ways he perceives himself and the other family members. He has developed these ways of perceiving by experience. Of course, there is a dynamics here. The genetically determined fact of maleness tends to channel his premarital experiences into ways of perceiving himself as a possible father-husband, and later as a father-husband in fact. The assumption of certain responsibilities and the use of certain accorded privileges represent the man's way of using his role. He may interact with his wife and children in a high-handed, authoritarian way, demanding deference, respect, and economy. Or he may be submissive to the point of neglecting to accept the status, privileges, and duties to which the role ordinarily entitles a male in our culture. Thus, there are both biological and experiential variables which determine the position an individual occupies within any social organization. With reference to the individual's organizational role, then, biological factors are relatively less important and experiential factors are relatively more important at the human level than at any infrahuman level.

Situational Factors. These, as the term implies, are factors which lie outside the individual. They are commonly called "the environment." However, it is to be remembered that the environment includes people and lower animals as well as the inanimate physical world. While the total environment has no psychological meaning in and of itself—it has psychological meaning only as it is perceived and responded to by individuals— it represents situational control which may be viewed in at least three ways.

First, there are culture factors, such as traditions, language, and institutions, which surround the individual and make their various impositions upon him. Whether the individual rejects or accepts them all or in part, he cannot avoid being greatly influenced by them. If he were reared under a different set of environmental conditions he would be a different person psychologically and his behavior within organization would be different. Second, there are inanimate physical factors which are either assembled by other humans or are parts of the unmodified physical environment. A prison or a conference room are examples of a part of the physical environment assembled by man; a mountain or a tropical rain forest are examples of the unmodified physical environment. Such factors obviously affect the types of organizations which develop individual behavior within such organizations. Third, there are phenomenological factors, which may be thought of in part as external-environmental. What is meant here is that the way the individual perceives the outside world has much to do with his behavior as a group member. Psychologically, the physical world of reality is what the individual perceives it to be, not necessarily what standard physical measurements reveal it to be. While there is reason to think of phenomenological factors as individual rather than situational we prefer the situational classification at this point, since it permits the tying of situational factors to individual factors. Thus, the individual's behavior as a group member will be in part a function of the nature of the environment as he perceives that environment in his own unique way.

This individual and situational category classification represents one way of conceptualizing the variables which we believe can be shown to account for individual behavior within human social organizations. Into both broad classifications we can order infrahuman phenomena also. However, at the human level it will be noted that there are additional variables in both categories. With reference to individual control factors, it is necessary that we give much greater attention to experience factors than at the infrahuman level. With reference to situational factors, in contrast with the infrahumans, it is necessary to consider culture factors and in addition to give greater attention to phenomenological variables. For man even more than for infrahumans, attention to the physical environment, as described in physical measurement terms alone, is insufficient.

Adaptation success is the only criterion by which the adequacy of social organization can be evaluated. At the human level this is a most difficult and involved problem. It requires the use of criteria other than purely biological criteria. Certainly, in modern man's brief appearance on this planet, and with the present rapid increment in his population, we can but conclude that he has been a biologically adaptive success. However, because of man's several unique emergent capacities, we have need to ask some questions with reference to the adequacy of certain types of social organization. We assume that at the human level these unique capacities require outlets that provide ego-protection for the individual. We further assume that individuals who are denied such adequate outlets will tend to behave in ways that are inimical to the freedom of action of others. Under such conditions the efficiency of the social organization is reduced and the organization moves toward the other end of the continuum—disorganization. On the positive side, the total biological meaning of adaptation is met best when social organizations into which humans are thrust, or into which they move, facilitate the use of man's emergent capacities by providing adequate social channels through which they may be constructively expressed.

SYSTEMATIC STUDIES OF HUMAN SOCIAL ORGANIZATION

This concluding section will describe a few studies that have identified and examined certain human organization variables. Here we are principally concerned with the effects various types of organization may have on individual behavior. It will be recalled that Lorge and his coworkers emphasized that studies of group performance have moved from artificial to real. "Recent work," they say, "is moving toward work with people in real situations." (1958, p. 367) While some of the studies to be cited have used noninteracting groups, most have made use of groups which involved at least some degree of interaction, if only for the duration of the study.

The studies to be described will be divided into two major categories: those emphasizing *independent variables* and those emphasizing *dependent variables*. The independent variables are: history of the individuals composing the group, type of task set for the group, and size of the group. The dependent variables are: judgment, learning, social facilitation, problem solving in nonrealistic and realistic situations, memory, productivity, and ideology.

Studies Emphasizing Independent Variables

There are many independent variables which could be cited, though we have chosen only three for discussion here. Also, we could discuss all variables as either independent or dependent. When we choose to view independent variables we seek to pay particular attention to the nature of the group as a behavior determining variable; and when we look at dependent variables we seek to pay particular attention to behavior as a function of the group. These may be viewed either way, though we find it more convenient to use the classification just described. Figure 1 will help to draw this distinction and clarify the examples we are about to cite. To interpret this figure, look at the box on the left and ask, "What will happen to the dependent variable if something here is varied?" Then look at the box on the right and ask, "What independent variable is responsible for this phenomenon?"

INDEPENDENT VARIABLES   DEPENDENT VARIABLES

Examples: history of group, task set, size.	Examples: increase or decrease in productivity, change in authoritarianism.
(These vary from group to group.)	(The phenomenon.)

FIGURE 1

History of Individuals (Composition of the Group). It is obvious that the individuals who make up the organization have much to do with the functions of the organization in general and the behavior of its members in particular. A group of children, for example, performs quite differently from a group of adults. The adult scout leader who is interacting with cub scouts will behave in ways different from the way he behaves at the office where he works each day. This fact is so obvious it scarcely needs elaboration. However, there are studies which have systematically altered the independent variable and have demonstrated the point empirically.

One such study, which involved several experiments, was patterned on a model developed by Kurt Lewin specifically designed to study frustration. However, it involved social organization. This study demonstrates how slight changes in the composition of the group can result in changes in the behavior of individuals who are members of the organizational group (Barker *et al.,* 1947).

Essentially the experiments incorporated in this study amount to quantitative comparisons of child behavior under conditions of frustration and nonfrustration. Observations were first conducted of children in a standardized playroom, in which they were permitted unrestricted, free play. Second, they were observed at play in the same room with the same toys, but with the additional feature of "a number of more attractive, but inaccessible toys present." The more attractive toys were on the other side of a wire-net partition through which they could be easily seen but not reached. In the first series 30 children, ranging in age from 2 to 6, were observed individually. In the second series 78 other children (same age range) were observed in pairs.

The nonfrustrating situation may be described as follows. Sets of standardized play materials were placed on the floor of the playroom. The experimenter brought a child (or pair) into the room and demonstrated the toys. The child was then left to play for 30 minutes while the experimenter sat at a corner table and surreptitiously recorded the child's activities. The frustrating situation was as follows. A partition was lifted at one end of the room making the room now twice as large. Almost all of the previously used toys were now incorporated into a more elaborate array which before had been hidden behind the partition. All of the subjects showed immediate interest, began to play with these new toys, and were allowed freedom (and in some cases demonstrations by the experimenter of toys unnoticed) until it was evident that they had become thoroughly involved in play (from 5 to 15 minutes). The experimenter then collected all of the old toys which had been used in the first half of the room and distributed them in the original half as they had been when the subject was first brought in. He then said to the subject, "Now let's play at the other end," and the subject either went or was led to the original half. The experimenter then lowered a wire-net partition separating the old from the new section with its much more attractive toys. The subject was now again free to play as he wished; the experimenter sat at the table recording as before, remaining aloof from the subject's situation. The experimenter entered the situation only by his being in the room and by answering subjects' questions as well as possible. After 30 minutes the experimenter suggested they leave, and after assuring himself that the subject was in agreement with this suggestion he raised the partition and allowed the subject another opportunity to satisfy his desire to play with the more attractive toys.

Without entering into the details of the treatment of the data, the results may be summarized under five headings. The first of these concerns the "average constructiveness of play in the nonfrustrating and frustrating situations." Constructiveness was rated by the experimenters on a scale (2–8) of 7 points. "The mean constructiveness of play for an experimental session was determined by assigning the proper scale value to each play unit, multiplying by the duration of the unit, summing these values for the whole record, and dividing by the total time of play during the session." (pp. 285–6) These mean constructiveness ratings had a reliability coefficient of .88, and correlated with mental age .73. The mean constructiveness of play in the nonfrustrating situation was 4.99 whereas in the frustrating situation it dropped to 3.94. The mean mental age regression was 17.3 months.

The second result concerns the strength of frustration. This factor was measured by "the proportion of the total experimental period occupied by barrier and escape behavior." (p. 287) Of the 30 subjects in the first series, 20 were judged to be relatively strongly frustrated and 10 to be relatively weakly frustrated. In the case of the strongly frustrated subjects a significant drop in play constructiveness, equivalent to 24 months in mental age, occurred. In the case of the weakly frustrated subjects the drop in play constructiveness was so slight that it was not statistically significant.

The third result is the emotional factor. Emotional expression changed with the shift in constructiveness of play. These changes were greater for the strongly than for the weakly frustrated subjects. When subjects were frustrated, happiness decreased; motor restlessness and aggressiveness increased.

The fourth result is the factor of "social interaction." In the change from nonfrustration to frustration two significant shifts in social behavior were noted. Cooperative behavior (both children in pair striving toward common goal and assisting each other) increased from a level of 38.2 per cent during nonfrustration to 50.4 per cent during frustration. Social conflict (subjects aggressive to each other) decreased from a level of 14.9 per cent during nonfrustration to 6.9 per cent during frustration. These results point toward increased "interdependence and unity" as functions of frustration.

The fifth result is the factor of friendship strength. On the basis of previous observation, 18 pairs of subjects were known to be strong friends, and 21 to be weak friends. These strong and weak friend-pairs closely resembled each other in their interpersonal activities in the nonfrustrating situation. During frustration, however, changes in social behavior were more marked for strong friend-pairs than for weak friend-pairs. Comparisons of strong with weak friend-pairs showed significant increases in cooperativeness and decreases in conflict for the strong friendships as compared with the weak. It is also interesting to note that strong friend-pairs showed more hostile action against the experimenter (47 per cent) than did the weak friend-pairs (31 per cent) during the frustration period. This difference is even greater when the matter of direct physical attack (attempts at hitting with blocks, tearing his records, etc.) upon the experimenter is noted. Here 26 per cent of the strong friend-pairs engaged in such attacks as compared with only 4 per cent of the weak friend-pairs.

The authors summarize their findings in the following way. Frustration resulted in a) an average regression in intellectual functioning, b) increased unhappiness, restlessness, and destructiveness, c) increased intragroup unity, and d) increased aggression against outsiders. The degree of intellectual function regression and increase in negative emotional response were positively related to the effective strength of frustration. Under the frustration condition, the degree of intragroup unity and outgroup aggression were positively related to friendship strength. In view of these findings the authors hold that tentative conformation of the hypothesis which they set out to test is established. This hypothesis was: ". . . strong frustration causes tension which leads to emotionality and restlessness, to de-differentiation of the person, and hence to behavioral regression." (p. 290)

For our present purposes, the history of the individuals who are members of an organization have much to do with the operation of the organization as well as the behavior of the individuals themselves. Certainly, though our knowledge is meager, we must conclude that a group of people *per se* means little or nothing from the standpoint of knowing what that group of people will do. The independent variable must be specified in greater detail than simply identifying its composition as human. We must know much about the backgrounds of the members of an organization in order to achieve any understsanding of its operation or the behavior of its members.

Task of the Organization. This independent variable must assume the restrictions of the one we have just discussed. Certainly, a group of cub scouts would not be able adequately to deal with an international political issue. Thus we must assume in dealing with this type of variable that the composition of the organization in question is known and stable. With this settled we are able to look at the task assigned to the organization, or the task the organization has assigned itself, as an independent variable which may be studied as possibly responsible for the behavior of its members. Simply stated, the independent variable here is, What is to be done?

Group production as a function of group decision on goals will serve to illustrate the point that the behavior of an individual may, under certain conditions, be a function of the tasks the organization sets out to accomplish. Maier (1955) has reviewed a study reported by Alex Bavelas in which changes in production (individual behavior) were shown to be functions of group decisions with reference to specific goals or tasks to be accomplished. In an industrial situation in which groups of men worked as teams in producing units for which they were paid not by the hour but by the piece-rate method, a coordinating group of workers met with the plant psychologist to discuss problems of production. Upon the suggestion of the psychologist they unanimously decided to strive for a higher production goal. At the time the production output was 60 units per hour. The decision was to increase this to 84 units. This goal was reached in five days. At a later meeting a goal of 95 units was decided upon. This goal was not achieved, though their production became stabilized at about 87 units per hour.

The question arose, of course, as to whether or not this significant increase in production might have been the result of some factor other than the goal set by group decision. Two other teams of workers held interview sessions with the plant psychologist. In these sessions the same types of friendly discussions were held, though production goals were not decided upon. Production increases did not follow the sessions for these groups. In addition, all three groups were, at a later time (after the first group had reached its high production level) given assurance that increases in production would neither result in less pay per unit nor establish a higher quota which they would have to maintain. This reassurance had no effect upon production of any of the three groups.

The conclusion to be drawn, under the circumstances of such an organizational situation, is that the task to be accomplished will be accomplished more adequately by groups that agree upon a relatively high level of aspiration; that is, by groups that concertedly set goals for themselves. What is to be accomplished, if known and agreed upon by the members of the organization, will affect individual output. Thus, the nature of the organization, from the standpoint of task to be accomplished (an independent variable) must be taken into account as a determiner of individual behavior (the dependent variable).

Size of the Group. This third independent variable seems of obvious importance in affecting the behavior of individual members. Any college student knows that in a very large class his behavior is different in many ways from his behavior in a small class. His instructor, too, acts differently under the two conditions. Several studies designed to test this assumption scientifically and to identify such differences have been conducted. In summarizing his review of such studies with specific reference to morale and productivity, Blum comments, "In general it has been found that size is inversely related to industrial morale and productivity." (1953, p. 55) This statement supports the thesis that group size is a determining factor, and that some of the behavior items involved can be identified.

One of the studies which throws important light on the determining role of group size and identifies certain behavior items which are affected by size was reported by Hemphill (1950). In this study, each subject was asked to respond to a variety of questions concerning the behavior of leaders in an organization to which he had belonged, or did at the time belong. Among other things, each subject was asked to designate the size of the group he intended to answer questions about. A group was considered small if it contained 30 or less members, and large if it contained 31 or more members. One feature of this study which deserves comment is that "traditional" groups were used. It will be recalled that students of organizational behavior have insisted that there is a need for studies which use interacting, face-to-face organizations that have a tradition of working together.

Of five hundred respondents, 365 reported the leaders of their groups either "good" or "excellent," and only these 365 were used for the analysis we are reporting here. Each respondent rated each of 70 brief behavior descriptions with reference to how frequently the leader of his group displayed it. The first statement, for example, was, "He was lax with the group." The rating responses were divided into three categories: 1) always or frequently, 2) occasionally, seldom or never, and 3) does not apply or don't know. It should be remembered that the data from this study are phenomenological in that they represent judgments (social perceptions) made by members of groups. They do not represent physically "objective measurements" by count of the actual frequencies of such behavior items. On the other hand, they represent psychological objectivity; and this is a basic requirement of psychological research.

The results of this study indicate, as common sense would dictate, that successful leaders of large groups behave differently from successful leaders of small groups. However, common sense will not necessarily tell what the specific behavior characteristics are that distinguish successful large-group from successful small-group leaders. Table I designates a sample of behavior items which are typical of successful large-group leaders as distinguished from successful small-group leaders. These are all statistically significant differences. Hemphill concludes from his study that two hypotheses are suggested: 1) demands upon the leader's role are increased with an increase in size of the group; 2) members of the group become more tolerant of the leader's occupancy of the "center of the stage" as the group becomes larger. These hypotheses suggest, again, the importance of group size, an independent variable. We might conclude that, among other things, the practitioner needs to look to the size of his group as a determining factor in making predictions about its potentialities.

ITEM NO.	BEHAVIOR DESCRIPTIONS OF SUCCESSFUL LARGE-GROUP LEADERS
13	Informs members about things concerning them
29	Makes rules and regulations clear
32	Apparently enjoys ruling the roost
51	Is easy to talk to
67	Makes decisions for the group, not for individuals

TABLE I

Studies Emphasizing Dependent Variables

A dependent variable, it will be remembered, is behavior that is a function of some other (independent) variable. In this case the independent variable is the group, and the dependent variable is the behavior that that group's interaction produces. Unfortunately, the independent variable is not the same from study to study; thus it is not possible to make comparisons with the precision we might wish. Knowing the general nature of the group used in a given study, however, it is possible to compare behavior as a function of that group with behavior as a function of social isolation, a different independent variable.

Judgment. The essence of social behavior is interactional influence. Most of us are interested in the opinions of others and often we adopt them ready-made, or change our opinions once we have learned about the opinions of others. When one is required to make a judgment he often looks to those about him for help, or waits for another's estimate before revealing his own judgment. Several studies have been conducted for purposes of determining the individual's accuracy of judgment as a function of his being within a group.

In one study (Dashiell, 1935), individuals were asked to make judgments concerning a variety of problems. The results were then summarized and reported to all the members for discussion. Following the discussion the individuals were asked to make their judgments again. Improvement in accuracy resulted; the individuals who contributed least to the discussion improved the most, relatively. Under such circumstances it seems that judgment can be improved when individuals are able to compare their judgments with those of others. Whether or not such judgment modification (in this case, improvement) results in part from an individual desire to conform or from careful reappraisal is not known. It is known, however, that under other social circumstances an individual's judgment may be significantly distorted, that the accuracy of his judgment would be greater were he allowed to operate in social isolation.

One series of experiments which demonstrates the distortion effect upon individual judgment that a group situation may have has been reported by Asch (1958). Groups of face-to-face noninteracting subjects were asked to match the length of a particular line with one of three other unequal lines. One individual in such a group was unaware that the other members were in collusion; that they previously had been instructed to designate a given line as the matching line, though in fact it was nonmatching in length. Thus the subject whose judgment was under investigation was placed in a position of conflict with the other group members. Each member of the group made his judgments known publicly. Through a long series of experiments Asch varied the independent variable in many ways, each time recording changes which resulted in the dependent variable. However, let us extract from these studies one part which clearly demonstrates that the dependent variable—in this case yielding to another or others, or not yielding—is in part a function of the nature of the designated independent variable (what the group is doing).

Asch varied the size of his face-to-face noninteracting groups. For example, some groups were composed of only two (i.e., a naive subject and one in collusion with the experimenter), while others were composed of as many as fifteen persons. The results were that some naive subjects yielded to the others and some subjects did not. When called upon to choose the one of three lines which was closest to the standard line, some subjects did in fact select the objectively correct one. Others did not. Thus, when we view the behavioral result we must look to the independent variable—in this instance, size of group—for an explanation. Table II summarizes the results.

Independent Variable	Size of Majority	Control	1	2	3	4	8	10–15
Dependent Variable	Mean No. of Errors for Naive Subject	0.08	0.33	1.53	4.0	4.20	3.84	3.75

TABLE II

Table II indicates that subjects who were paired with other naive subjects (control) made virtually no errors in judgment—only .08 for all the tests. The same was true of those naive subjects who were paired with one other person who was in collusion—only .33 errors for all the tests. When a naive subject was judging with two others who were in collusion, however, he fell off in accuracy considerably—to 1.53. With a stooge majority of three, inaccuracy increased to 4.0; beyond a majority of four it seemed to drop slightly, though not significantly.

It might be asked whether or not these subjects who were naive were saying to themselves, "I don't believe this, but I can't disagree with so many people." This question has nothing to do with the fact that they acted as they did, though it has much to do with their personal experiences. In social situations, in situations in which people respond and then others respond in terms of their actions, *behavior* is of most importance. A former Nazi stormtrooper may now declare that he really did not agree with Hitler at the time he helped put Jews into concentration camps. The fact is, however, that he did. Our interest is in understanding the types of psychological forces which pushed him into these deeds of atrocity, not just in understanding the avoidance-avoidance conflict that tormented him.

We do not have sufficient cross-cultural information to assert that the Asch findings are universally germane. We also know that some individuals do not behave as most do within our own culture. We may conclude, however, that most people within our culture behave in this way. Judgment of physical dimensions, as well as social relationships, is modified by the need to be in rapport. This we contend is another illustration of the universal human motive for ego-protection. Human judgment is not alone the product of an impartial, cold, rational creature. It is in part a function of the way a human perceives the world of other people who surround him. Thus, an individual's judgment is to be accounted for in part by the nature of the group in which he is operating.

Learning. The question here is essentially whether individuals learn more efficiently in isolation or in group situations. Again, we are looking at the dependent variable, learning; though it is always necessary to specify the independent variable in its various forms. Several studies designed to throw light on this question have been reported in the literature. The groups used in most of these studies have been small—they can be called small working groups. That is, they are small enough so that there is ample opportunity for interaction, and since they work toward goals they may be thought of as organized groups.

In general, the results of these studies indicate that group learning situations are slightly, though consistently, superior to isolation situations. It is important to note two qualifications here: the groups must be relatively small (perhaps not over 10 or 12) and the learning must be of a problem solution type (ranging from maze learning to learning to make accurate judgments with reference to human conduct). For example, Gurnee (1937) had groups of about 10 subjects learn a maze. On successive trials subjects voted at each choice point whether to turn left or right. Although the over-all time to learn was great because of the voting procedure, the number of errors to criterion was less than for the average individual learning the maze by himself.

A more recent study by Perlmutter and de Montmollin (1952) adds support to Gurnee's view that group learning is superior to individual learning. Several three-person groups memorized two lists of nonsense words. One list was learned individually, though in the three-person group setting. The other list was group-learned, a requirement being that agreement should be reached on each word before being voiced as the group's choice. The subjects were asked not to assign certain parts of the list to certain group members. In terms of recall scores the groups were equal to, and in some cases superior to, the best individuals.

These small group results are not readily understandable and it is not our purpose here to attempt an explanation. Several possibilities have been suggested, however. For instance, group consensus seems to be more critical, by use of evaluation and rejection, than individual decision. This is supported by the fact that groups used relatively few concocted and modified words. It may also be suggested that despite the fact that subjects were instructed not to make assignments of parts of the list of certain members, nevertheless this may have been done unwittingly. Whatever the explanation, we may conclude that an organized group may, under certain circumstances, evidence superiority in learning over individuals. It is just possible, though we think not probable, that social facilitation, the variable we will consider next, plays a role in facilitating learning.

Social Facilitation. Lorge *et al.* describe social facilitation as "the effects on an individual of working at a task in the presence of other individuals but independently of them, i.e., not interacting with them, although they may be face-to-face in an audience or classroom." (1958, p. 352) The social facilitation concept has a long history and has been used in many ways. It is by no means a precise concept, and unless used with caution, may come close to the "group mind" concept, or the innate competitiveness concept, or the "mutual aid" concept. Used cautiously, however, there is no need to shy away from it.

The Lorge *et al.* description is adequate as an operational definition, though we may be left to wonder what really goes on psychologically. There are many possibilities with reference to the psychological involvements. Perhaps introspectively one is able to understand this better than by making reference to a scientist's operational description, empirically sophisticated as it may be. While in the presence of others, most all of us have experienced cognitive-affective states that prompted us to work harder, produce more, demonstrate our talents. On the other hand, we have sometimes felt the need to withdraw and not produce. It would seem that our tendencies to produce above level or below level are not determined simply by the presence of others. There are also many instances in which the presence of others affects us little, if any. How one perceives others who are present in terms of his goal achievement, and the possibility of goal achievement as a function of their presence, seem to be the variables of most probable basic importance. This is to say again that in the study of psychological phenomena we must give careful attention to phenomenological variables. The psychological fact is not the physical dimensions of the stimulus object. The psychological fact is the perceptual use an individual makes of the stimulus object.

Griffith (1921) published the results of a study of grades made by college students in relation to their seating positions in the classroom. He found that students who occupied seats toward the front center of the room made grades which were significantly higher than students who sat in outlying areas. One interpretation of this finding lies in the social facilitation construct which conceives of the audience as more facilitated at the center than at the periphery (Murphy and Murphy, 1931). And some educators have concluded that the position of the student in the classroom may have a facilitating or retarding effect upon learning (Morrison, 1931). The social facilitation construct incorporates the view that the individual's amount, and sometimes quality, of performance is increased by his perception of others about him; the more he perceives the greater the facilitation.

One reasonable interpretation of Griffith's findings is that individuals who have strong achievement motivation will, given the opportunity, move into central group positions; and those with lower achievement motivation will tend to occupy those positions which are easily available, most probably in outlying areas. A technique to test an aspect of this interpretation was devised by Jones and Cooper (1938). If students are required to sit in regularly assigned positions (alphabetically determined), those of high achievement aspiration will be randomly distributed throughout the classroom and not concentrated in a central position. This being so, any positional concentration of high achievement could still be postulated as a function of social facilitation, but seating position selection as the determining factor would have to be ruled out.

They tested this proposition by studying college students' achievement in an elementary economics course over a period of twelve semesters. In all, there were some 5,000 students, for each semester a class of slightly over 400. Students were always assigned seats alphabetically, the same instructor delivered all the lectures, and students were assigned grades on the basis of objective achievement testing results. Although there were great individual differences there was a consistent, though minimal, decrease in mean achievement scores from front to rear. Students who sat at the front made an average score slightly higher than those sitting in the middle; and the students sitting at the rear made an average score slightly lower than those sitting in the middle. Though these differences were slight, they were consistent, and it might reasonably be concluded that proximity to the source of information was the essential factor responsible for this slight gradient. Were the social facilitation factor operating, then the front-central part of the group should have been highest in achievement. Since this was not the case we are inclined to conclude that factors other than social facilitation were principally responsible for this result. The most parsimonious explanation is that those who sat close to the instructor heard him better, were thus able to take better notes, were less distracted by those over whose heads they had to look, and in general were more in perceptual contact with the requirements of the course. It seems improbable that social facilitation can explain even this meager gradient of difference. Humans may facilitate each other under certain interactional circumstances, though under the circumstance of simply being spatially together social facilitation may have little if anything to do with individual production. In any case, a mystic interpretation of social facilitation is to be rejected.

Studies of the part social facilitation may play in individual performance have provided varying results. For example, F. H. Allport concluded that "it is the *overt* responses, such as writing, which receive facilitation through the stimulus of co-workers. The *intellectual* or *implicit* responses of thought are hampered rather than facilitated." (1924, p. 274) The effects of social facilitation may be dissipated over a period of time, as was shown specifically in one experiment (Abel, 1938). Subjects who worked in pairs tended to show greater efficiency at first, but as time went on subjects working in isolation did as well as those working in pairs.

From the various studies of social facilitation, it can be concluded that the mere presence of others, even though all may be working at the same task, will not *per se* guarantee any particular change in behavior. Social facilitation is not a blind mystical force which either increases or decreases performance.

Problem Solving. Problem solving overlaps learning considerably and no clear distinction between these named processes will be attempted. Whereas learning is essentially concerned with changes in performance as a function of experience, problem solving refers more typically to an end result which provides an answer, and if possible a correct one, to a question. Most studies of this dependent variable (problem solution) as a function of group action as contrasted with the individual working alone (independent variables) have been relatively unrealistic. Most of the problems given groups and individuals to solve have been in the nature of puzzles, riddles, and information-type questions. These are problems quite far removed from those encountered in real-life situations. For the most part, the groups used in these studies have been *ad hoc,* and though they meet our definition of social organization, they do not represent tradition which ordinarily has so much to do with group behavior. For these reasons, generalizations from these studies to every-day group problem solving situations are not warranted. Let us look briefly at one of these problem-solving studies.

The game "Twenty Questions" was used by Taylor and Faust (1952) to compare individual with *ad hoc* group performance. Subjects in groups were allowed to discuss each question before asking it, and they were motivated by knowing that they were competing against other groups. The results were that groups required fewer questions to reach solution and also required more man-hours to reach solution. Thus, from the standpoint of arriving at a correct solution with a minimum of errors, the group situation (independent variable) was superior. However, from the standpoint of time-efficiency the individual situation (independent variable) was superior. Many other independent variables are at work in such situations. For example, subjects used in this study were college students who, it should be supposed, have relatively similar levels of information. Were the group composed of grammar school children the results would, no doubt, have been very different. Or, if the groups had been composed of one erudite and the rest ignorant subjects, the results would probably have been different. We might conclude, however, if the problem to be solved is within the comprehension and knowledge range of the subjects, the probability of its solution is increased under a group situation. On the other hand, since time is consumed when members of the group must pool their information and make decisions, some individuals working alone will reach correct solutions faster. Slow but relatively sure is the way of the group; fast but often inaccurate is the way of the individual.

Memory. Studies of the effects upon recall (memory) of group versus individual learning situations are few. As with group learning or problem solving versus individual learning or problem solving, the effects are very difficult to appraise. For one thing, if we regard memory as that which the individual retains of that which he has learned, we are confronted by several problems we did not ask for in the first place. Nevertheless we cannot avoid them if we insist upon asking the question: Is one's memory of an event better if he learned about an event in an organized group than it would be had he learned about it in isolation? From the scant literature on this subject let us describe one study which was designed to discover whether or not the memory for meaningful material is better in a group or an individual situation.

This study by Perlmutter (1953) investigated individual versus group memory for a story which was read to sixteen groups and to ten individuals. Among other things the study was concerned with a comparison of the principles that govern changes in group memory with those that govern individual memory change, and whether or not individual memory is superior to group memory.

The first of these questions arose in terms of certain generalizations that Bartlett had made in his classical studies of memory (1932). For instance, Bartlett had concluded that in a literal sense reproduction accuracy in the individual is rare. Perlmutter found that pooled (group) memory was likewise inaccurate in a literal sense. Another of Bartlett's inferences with reference to individual memory was that the general form of a story will tend to persist once it has been recalled. Again, Perlmutter found that his groups conformed to this principle. The third Bartlett generalization was that omission and increased simplification of details, and transformation of information into more familiar structures, will progress during successive recall sessions; that is, such memory changes become more pronounced as time goes on. In this, too, Perlmutter found confirmation. Since these conclusions which Bartlett drew from his studies of individual performance were found by Perlmutter to operate in group memory situations as well, he states an hypothesis which may be taken as his tentative conclusion: ". . . there are general principles that describe both group-*qua*-group and individual-*qua*-individual behavior." (1953, p. 365)

The other question which Perlmutter raises is the more obvious: Is individual memory superior to group memory? He found that groups achieve somewhat better memory scores, though the difference between group and individual scores is of slight statistical significance since individual scores were so variable. Individuals require significantly less time to recall.

Any over-all generalizations from this study would be premature. At the same time, one tentative conclusion that we made with reference to problem solving may be drawn here. An informed group may be somewhat more accurate, though it will be somewhat slower than an informed individual. The other and perhaps more important tentative conclusion is that group memory does not differ qualitatively from individual memory. The implications of this second tentative conclusion are of great social psychological significance, since they throw light upon the group-mind theory. Perlmutter's findings support the view that the group product is not the result of an emergent, nonempirical force which comes into being when a group is formed, but rather is the function of interacting individuals who compose the group. The differences in measured productivity are to be thought of in terms of interpersonal production and perception factors that are open to empirical investigation.

Productivity. Productivity, as measured by work-output, as we all know, varies from situation to situation. There are many studies of the effects of alterations in the independent variable upon production (the dependent variable). Many of these studies have been conducted in industrial settings, thereby having two advantages over many other investigations of group processes. For one thing, these are real life situations in which subjects are working toward livelihood goals. For another, production measurement is quite precise, since units of production per unit of time may be accurately determined and compared. We have already made reference to a study by Bavelas (Maier, 1955) in which he was able to show that production changes in a factory were increased by the introduction of group decisions. This study throws important light upon the present issue; namely, production can be shown to be a function of the nature of the group.

In one of the most famous of all research programs concerned with human factors in industrial production, the Western Electric Research Program brought to light some most important relationships between production and the nature of the group (Roethlisberger and Dickson, 1939). Pigors and Myers (1951) summarize the program as follows:

This research program is especially significant, because the investigators allowed their center of attention to move, as new facts came to light, from primarily mechanical and physiological factors to the human element. The successive stages by which the inquiry developed were as follows:

At first, investigators carried out their experiments in the production departments and tried to test the effects on output of changes in a single variable, such as light intensity. The results of these experiments were negative. Employee output went up during the test periods regardless of whether the value of illumination was increased or decreased. The observers concluded that, in a regular operating department, there were so many factors affecting the reactions of workers that it was impossible to evaluate any one by itself. Consequently, it was decided to put a small group of workers in a room apart from the regular working force, where their behavior could be scientifically studied.

However, the experiments with several such test groups showed that the logical approach of setting up a controlled experimental situation was not productive here. Even though there had been no alterations in work methods and materials, the investigators had unwittingly introduced a very signficant change. The experimental situation was no longer that of a standard shop department but that of a small special unit that soon developed characteristics of its own. Observers quickly recognized that changes in the evolving social situation were more significant than the new experimental conditions that they introduced at various times. These social developments may be summarized under three headings: (1) development of a primary group, (2) development of social participation with an increased sense of personal dignity and status, and (3) improved relationships between workers and supervisors. (pp. 538–539)

Of course, productivity cannot always be measured in units of output per unit of time. In such fields as science and esthetics productivity must be estimated in relatively subjective ways, and quantitative statements concerning the relationships between group variables and production variables are, upon the basis of quantitative research, impossible to make. However, there are many studies of the types we have cited which clearly indicate that measurable group productivity is a function of certain characteristics of the group. Although our knowledge is not great concerning these subtle and complex intervariable relationships, we do have some definite information about group factors which will result in low productivity, and some information about group factors which will result in high productivity.

Personality and Value Systems. It is generally agreed that the nature of the adult individual's personality is greatly influenced by the social organizations of which he has been and is a part. This statement is not to be taken as a downgrading of the importance of genetic factors which also undoubtedly play important roles in shaping personality. However, our interest here is with social organization and therefore we will not concern ourselves with genetics. With reference to personality structure as a function of social organization, one of the most vexing problems lies in the fact that in a complex culture, such as ours, an individual has membership in many different organized groups. Thus, when we attempt to account for the dependent variable—personality structure—we encounter difficulties whenever we look to any specified group as the antecedent independent variable. At the same time, we cannot doubt that some groups play more important roles than others. Examples in particular are family, church, and school. With reference to what we choose to call "value system" or "ideology" we are dealing with rational-affective personality content, essentially what the individual believes. Here again, what the individual believes (his fundamental beliefs), we have reason to suppose, is in large measure a function of the belief-systems of the organized groups of which he is a part. Since this problem has been dealt with previously, our purpose here is but to emphasize the importance of group organization as a complex of variables that in part determine the individual's personality structure and value system.

Many studies have been concerned with personality as a function of group organization practices. Some of these are strictly psychological, as for example the study by MacKinnon (1938) in which personality characteristics of violators and nonviolators of social prohibitions were investigated. The thesis of this study was that personality is in part a function of the family organization and, more specifically, certain family organization variables which may be used to characterize a given family. In MacKinnon's study male college students were asked to solve problems, some of which they could obtain help on by referring to a booklet containing all the solutions. Those who obtained help only on the designated problems and refrained from looking up solutions to those they were asked to do on their own, were compared with the violators. The violators were those who were seen by a concealed observer to obtain help on the problems they had been asked to solve independently. In the comparison it was found, among other things, that the nonviolators seemed to have received relatively more "psychological punishment" (i.e., were made to feel guilty when they transgressed) than the violators. Amount of psychological punishment used is to be thought of as a part of the family organization, and in line with MacKinnon's findings it may be supposed that this is an independent variable in the determination of certain personality characteristics. In addition, the violators evidenced little feeling of guilt for having cheated, whereas the nonviolators evidenced much stronger guilt feelings in terms of contemplating breaking rules.

A study that illustrates the nature of family organization impact upon personality content has been reported by Dickens and Hobart (1959). They were interested in discovering whether or not high and low *ethnocentrism* (what we are calling here "personality content" or "ideology") may in part be a function of the nature of the family organization. Ethnocentrism in their college student sample was measured by the Bogardus Ethnic Distance Scale. Mothers of the high- and low-scoring subjects were given the Shoben Parent Attitude Survey (Shoben, 1949). This scale taps three features of parents' demeanor toward children within the family organization: possessiveness, dominance, and aloofness. It was found that those college students who were high in ethnocentrism came from families that were excessively possessive of their children and/or dominant in their relationships with them. It was also found, perhaps contrary to common sense, that most of the high authoritarian students came from aloof families, families whose attitudes toward their children were "ignoring" in nature, who regarded the good child as the child who demands the least time, and who tended to disclaim responsibility for their children's behavior. The effects of parental behavior upon the child's ideological system are phenomenological. This means that a given child may respond to parental dominance by developing a nonauthoritarian personality—although this is the exception. There was found to be a substantial positive correlation between parental dominance and authoritarian personality structure and content.

Certainly, personality structure and content are greatly influenced by the nature of the family organization. What the relationship may specifically turn out to be cannot be determined upon the basis of present knowledge.

However, some of the factors which determine adult personality organization and content may be sought in social organizations—one of the most important being the family. One of the tasks of contemporary psychology is to discover the interrelationships between the individual's personality development and organization, and the organizations of which he is and has been a part. The examples we have cited here have been concerned only with the family as an organization, and, at that, with only one small aspect of this type of organization.

IX

Leadership

The interest of social psychology in leadership is closely allied to its interest in social organization. As we have seen, many social organizations incorporate distributions of influence and power. Influence and power positions within a social organization are conveniently referred to as positions of leadership, and individuals who occupy these positions we call leaders.

The term leadership is an abstraction that refers to a particular kind of social expectation. It is a phenomenon which humans observe. As a consequence of social experience, we come to expect certain regions within social organization to be power-laden and the individuals who occupy such regions to wield power. For example, one expects a college to have an office known as the presidency, and the person who occupies that office to be president. Beyond this, it is expected that the president will exercise the power of that office. Thus, the office is a perceived region of the social organization, and from that region certain performances are expected. That such performances are not always forthcoming, and may be far out of line with that which is expected, supports the view that *leadership* and *leader* are not synonymous.

Types of Leadership

Distribution of power within human organization has both adaptive and survival value and is analogous to the distribution and specialization of function so clearly found among many of the infrahumans. Many instances of such distribution and specialization are, of course, individually destructive, and conducive to social disorganization. Leadership and leaders, however, are indispensable to human adaptation and survival.

"Push" Leadership. Although the genesis of human leadership phenomena is not to be found in lower species, in the broadest perspective, the same basic, necessary social phenomenon is evident among all the social animals. Within a colony of animals there may be marked differences in status. With many species of birds there are "pecking orders" which are scrupulously observed by members of the flock. Dominant males have greater access to both food and females. Very subordinate males may

constantly refrain from approaching females even though the dominant male has been removed. And dominant hens permit mating less often than subordinate hens. In reviewing the literature on the establishment and maintenance of dominance, Collias has concluded that a dominance-submission relationship between two species members is usually established during the initial encounter or during a series of early encounters. Fighting, bluffing, or passive submission appear to be the most important variables in determining the outcome of such early encounters, and "success in initial encounters depends upon a variable complex of factors and is generally favored by maturity, maleness, familiarity with the locale, help from other individuals, high social status in the home group, isolation from dominating individuals, experience in winning, signs of fear or unaggressiveness in the opponent, body weight, endurance, skill, endocrine balance, good health, and various unknown factors." (1951, p. 392) Douglis (1948) has shown, for instance, that a hen that was rotated systematically from one flock to another established and maintained a different status in as many as five different flocks simultaneously. Obviously, for many infrahuman species dominance-submission relationships are important social organizational features, and the behavior of individuals may be better understood if we know something about the establishment and use of these relationships. Leadership within such dominance-submission relationships may be characterized as the "push" type.

"Pull" Leadership. In addition to the "push" type there is also the "pull" type among some of the infrahumans. By the "pull" type is meant one or several animals out in front followed by another or many others. Again, among many migratory species of birds, one bird is first in formation with others following. With sheep, typically ". . . the old female with the largest number of descendants consistently leads the flock." (Scott, 1958, p. 170) As with "push" type leadership, this, too, is adaptively important behavior since those species that demonstrate leader-follower ("pull") type interrelationships seem to have "imprinting" propensities. The young have a native capacity for learning to follow particular moving stimulus objects. This aids survival since those objects are likely to help provide conditions (e.g., nourishment and shelter) necessary for survival. For instance, the young lamb nurses and the gosling is brought into areas of food supply.

Of course, with both types—"push" and "pull"—there are many subtleties which are not understood. For example, why do members of a "push" type organization stay together? While it is not our purpose to pursue questions of this sort here, we believe it is important to emphasize that many, if not most, social organizations incorporate power differentials. The members of a social organization are, of course, not all necessarily alike in terms of the reasons for their responses to social influences. Some group members may respond in particular ways because they are afraid of others, and pattern their social behavior largely in terms of avoidance of those a) they have learned to fear, and b) those who are afraid of them. In other instances, animals follow other animals, we might suppose, because of previous affective satisfaction. At the lower animal level, these two principal conditions of leadership seem reasonably evident. But at the human level leadership phenomena are comparatively complex because of the emergences to which we have so frequently alluded.

At the human level we also find "push" and "pull" leadership phenomena. It is by no means as clear, however, as at the infrahuman level. In broadest perspective, human goals are ego-related. In his constant ego-protection striving, man, in common with many of the lower species, learns to use others as "tools." In some instances he bows to the behavior of others, and in some he is bowed to. However, man's social behavior is typically a confused mixture of the two. He may simultaneously bow and be bowed to, and he usually has some complex planning which lies behind the complex, multiple role he is playing.

In previous chapters we have suggested several human capacities that characterize man as psychologically unique among the many species. It was further suggested that the unique nature of social organization at the human level is partly a function of these unique human capacities. The same may be said of human leadership. Man's capacities for religious experience, esthetic appreciation, political thought and action, systematic inquiry, and language, to mention some of his more important unique capacities, add new dimensions to human leadership. But it is by comparing human leadership with examples from the infrahuman levels that these new dimensions may most clearly be seen in relief.

While there are both "push" and "pull" leadership processes at the human level, just as there are at infrahuman levels, there are additional features. For the "pull," something more than simple imprinting or reward training operates. A human may generate enthusiasm for, or an affectively-toned desire to follow, another. In addition he may develop a highly structured cognitive organization to support his desire to follow. At the human level "push" type leadership also evidences certain unique features. Its uniqueness lies principally in two human features. First is man's tremendous capacity to anticipate, to plan. Humans are capable of behavioral logistics that find them often even "willingly" being dictated to, directed, and pushed into behavior they very much dislike. Second, man is capable of showing signs of interpreting a situation as pull, when in reality he interprets it as push. The human may act as though he admires the person in command and professes a desire to follow, though in reality he may be working out a compromise. Being pushed around now in order to gain a favorably anticipated position later is common practice among humans. While some few descriptions of infrahuman behavior somewhat similar to this have been recorded, principally among chimpanzees (Hebb and Thompson, 1954), man's capacity to use it is so great by comparison that it may be considered unique at the human level.

CLASSICAL LEADERSHIP THEORIES

Psychologists are by no means alone in their interest in leadership. Philosophers, historians, political theorists, theologians and others have given much attention to this social phenomenon. Long before psychology was established as a science scholars had developed theories of leadership and some students of social-political processes had explained in detail rules for successful leadership. For instance, as early as the sixteenth century Machiavelli, the Florentine statesman and political writer, had described in great detail the ways by which the head of state could rule effectively and the machinations he must employ in order to maintain his position of power. Philosopher-statesmen such as Francis Bacon and Thomas Hobbes showed an active interest in the problem of leadership and wrote extensively on the subject. Down to the present time men of learning have been fascinated by leadership phenomena. On the one hand, there have been attempts to explain leadership by the development of theories. On the other hand, practical guide lines have been sought by which leadership positions may be obtained and consolidated.

As a background it is helpful to look to the main lines of classical theory which have served as basic orientations for contemporary psychological approaches. In broadest outline, two basic leadership theories grew out of the thinking of the early political-philosophers. They are usually referred to as the "great man" (sometimes, "hero") and the "times" (sometimes, "history") theories. In their extreme forms, these theories are in direct op-position to each other. As J. F. Brown (1936) pointed out some years ago, each represents either-or thinking and they are analogous to the traditional nature-nurture dichotomy. In general, the "great man" theory has received the greater amount of attention and support in western society. This is quite understandable when we stop to think that the intellectual elite in western society has, for the most part, come from privileged societal groups. Since this elite has in the past written most about leadership, we should expect that most writers would have sought to show natively-determined characteristics as responsible for the occupancy of leadership regions. We have but to examine the chronicles of history to realize that most history has been written around particular leaders. To say the least, the "times" theory has been given much less attention, and since the variables which support it are relatively difficult to identify, it is much less appealing and personally related than the "great man" theory.

Great Man Theory

In general, the "great man" theory holds that particular individuals are natively endowed with characteristics that cause them to stand out from the many and permit them to guide, direct, and lead the majority. This is a view that fits well the doctrine of the divine right of kings. It is not uncommon to any elite, whether economic or intellectual. In its extreme, this theory views social organization and social change as functions of unusual foresight and action on the part of a select few. The select few are natively endowed with qualities that make their leadership possible; and their responsibility is to guide society and direct the behavior of the many. This position is the general thesis which underlies the thesis of Plato's *Republic*.

Times Theory

The "times" theory views leadership as a function of the given social situation. At a particular time, a group of people has certain needs and requires the services of an individual to assist it in meeting its needs. Which individual comes to play the role of leader in meeting these needs is essentially determined by chance; i.e., a given person happens to be at the critical place at the critical time. The particular needs of the group may, of course, be met best at a given time by an individual who possesses particular qualities. This does not mean that this particular individual's peculiar qualities would thrust him into a position of leadership in any other situation. It means only that the unique needs of the group are met by the unique qualities of the individual. It has often been said that had Hitler espoused his doctrine in the United States rather than in Germany, he would have been committed to a mental institution. It may very well be that the need to "escape from freedom" was so great in post-World War I Germany that a majority seemed to believe that their needs could be met only by a person who held the megalomaniac views and action plans Hitler espoused. The "times" theory is somewhat less rigid than the "great man" theory, since it does assume a part of the great man theory. It agrees that humans are not all alike—that there are individual differences, and that the unique characteristics of a given person may at a given time meet the needs of a given group most adequately.

CONTEMPORARY LEADERSHIP RESEARCH

Contemporary psychological studies of leadership have tended to use one or the other of the two classical leadership theory orientations. Contemporary research approaches can most generally and conveniently be classified into one or the other of two categories: *trait* and *situation.* The trait approach is the descendant of the "great man" theory, and the situation approach of the "times" theory.

Trait Approach

Industrial psychologists have achieved considerable success in the development of personnel selection and placement techniques. The general pattern of their research and technology has been to identify the particular skills and aptitudes needed for a certain job, then to select an individual with these skills and aptitudes and place him in that job. Great economic savings have been effected by following this relatively simple design. The criterion in this instance is a relatively simple and stable one by which to judge selection techniques. In the general study of leadership this same approach has been followed many times. However, it has not been as successful. The reason for its relative lack of success lies partly in the fact that the criteria for judging effectiveness are many and relatively unstable. The requirements for being an effective leader in one situation are not necessarily the same as they are in another situation.

The trait approach has followed this research design so successfully used in industry. The principal idea is that leaders are those individuals who possess certain skills and aptitudes, and that such individuals are drawn into leadership positions because of these particular talents. Before we examine some examples of trait theory research, we should emphasize its basic theoretical deficiency. That a given trait or cluster of traits is universally appealing from the standpoint of leadership is to be discounted on two grounds. First, studies show that no given trait or trait-cluster invariably makes the person possessing it a leader. Second, effective leadership varies from situation to situation; the traits which make for good leadership in one situation may be totally inadequate in another situation.

Leadership Traits. One student of leadership has said, "It is a fair assumption that almost any approved trait in excess of the average might be used to characterize a leader." (Young, 1947, p. 229) Most terms that describe traits—such as "cultured," "competent," "mature"—are vague. This means that they are difficult to quantify and deal with objectively. One review of leadership studies (Bird, 1940) listed the adjectives that some twenty trait-designed studies of leadership found to be leader-identifying. In one or another of these studies adjectives such as the following were found as descriptive of effective leaders: "ambitious," "clever," "mature," "reliable," "stable," "vigorous." In all, 79 such traits were listed. What surprised the author of this review was that there was so little trait overlapping from study to study. Clearly, almost any culturally approved trait could be taken as the key leadership variable. That is, a given leader in a given situation may be thought by some observers to be the leader because he is competent, or just, or poised, or stable, or possesses some combination of such traits. And there may be no doubt in a given instance that the leader is the leader by virtue of possessing one or another, or a particular combination, of such traits. However, the possession of a given trait or traits is an inadequate basis for predicting that the individual will be a leader in some other situation. Among other things, the number of leadership regions available will have much to do with region occupancy. For instance, the leader of a given group will ordinarily not be replaced even though a newcomer may in fact possess traits more in key with those acceptable to the position. In the United States, the incumbent in an elective office ordinarily has an advantage, even though his challenger may be more qualified by the standards of the voters. In many organized groups there is considerable reluctance to "turn an old-timer out to pasture."

Validity of Studies. Most of the studies of leadership which have followed the trait design have used high-school and college students as subjects, since these groups are readily available. This, of course, is a serious limitation if generality from these studies is expected. Traditional groups are much more difficult to investigate. The specific pattern of this research design is to identify the frequent and the nonfrequent leaders and, treating them as two independent samples, discover the traits the leaders possess that the nonleaders do not possess (or vice versa). In one study it was found that college campus women leaders differed from nonleaders in possessing greater ability to express their thoughts in the language of the group, in making higher grades, and in greater participation in campus activities (Maurer, 1947). In another similar study campus leaders demonstrated relatively great self and social adjustment, as measured by the California Test of Personality (Alexandra, 1946).

In line with this approach, Drake (1944) has, on the basis of his research, advanced the thesis that there is good argument for thinking of leadership as a manifold-trait concept. His study indicated that the elements in such a manifold are: originality, aggressiveness, common sense, cheerfulness, humor, emotional stability, trustworthiness, tact, persistence, and desire to excel. On the other hand, he found the following trait-manifold characteristic of nonleaders: anger, conceit, introversion, selfishness, pure-mindedness, quick-oscillation, occasional extreme depression, and excitability.

Obviously, it is difficult to evaluate the conclusions drawn by the authors of such studies. What is their generality? How do they correlate with the findings of other such trait studies? And, granted that these findings are valid for the samples studied, we might question their predictive efficiency. That is, knowing that a given individual possesses such a manifold of traits, would the prediction be accurate that that individual will become a leader if placed within the group that composed the study sample? Of course, this last question cannot be satisfactorily answered by an examination of the literature, since methodological limitations have prevented the adequate testing of such an hypothesis. One might even speculate that some of these named traits develop in those who become leaders in such groups, rather than that they were possessed beforehand and were responsible for elevation to leadership positions. While these questions cannot be answered in definitive ways, some attempts have been made to review the studies that have used the trait approach.

An excellent literature review study by Stogdill throws considerable light on these questions. He abstracted the details from a large sample of studies designed to identify traits and personal factors associated with leadership (1948). He included for evaluation only the traits that had been treated by a minimum of three investigators.

In discussing the findings from these studies, Stogdill concludes that there are five factors which seem consistently to be associated with leadership: capacity, achievement, responsibility, participation, and status. These general factors, each of which includes specific traits and capacities, are meaningless, however, unless they are viewed in light of *the situation*. As Stogdill puts it:

A person does not become a leader by virtue of the possession of some combination of traits, but the pattern of personal characteristics of the leader must bear some relevant relationship to the characteristics, activities, and goals of the followers. . . . It becomes clear that an adequate analysis of leadership involves not only a study of leaders, but also of situations. (1948, pp. 64–65)

Evaluation.   The trait approach calls our attention to the necessity of looking to the unique capacities of particular individuals in particular situations in order to understand leadership phenomena. However, it is not sufficient to list the traits leaders in a given situation possess. There is no doubt that the particular traits or capacities of an individual have much to do with his elevation to a leadership position within a particular group situation. However, this cannot be pushed too far.

In addition, although a given constellation of traits may be found typical for leaders and its absence found typical for nonleaders, it is still not possible to predict accurately that a given person who possesses such a constellation will become a leader in any particular situation. There are too many fortuitous factors involved; he may not be identified, he may not be in the right physical location, he may bear the "wrong name," he may not want to be a leader.

Finally, it is well known that research studies that find no differences for a given variable between two samples find their way into print less frequently than those investigations that do discover differences. This being the case, we might wonder as to the adequacy of the sampling that a review of the literature on leadership traits affords. Although this question is speculative, we should not too readily conclude that the leadership trait constellation reported in a given study is to be taken as valid for other comparable social organizations.

The trait approach is not to be discounted, though it does incorporate some serious limitations. On the one hand, particular traits and capacities do, without doubt, contribute to the success of an individual in operating as a leader. This does not mean, however, that these particular traits and capacities are the ones which make for "good" leadership. For example, participation, which has been found to be a characteristic of successful leaders, may be a description of persons who move into group situations with stealth and vigor, become leaders, but lack the capacity to protect ego by means other than operating from a position of power. And, again, we might pose the question: Do successful leaders demonstrate certain qualities of behavior because they possess certain traits, or do these certain traits come into operation as a result of occupancy of a leadership position?

Situation Approach

The situation approach to the study of leadership is somewhat less precise than the trait approach. It is much more difficult to observe and to quantify the variables that constitute a group situation. The situation approach does not devaluate the importance of particular individual traits; it simply insists that traits are important only as they relate to the particular group situation.

Field Leadership Theory. Before discussing some representative studies which have used the situational-interaction approach to the study of leadership we will make reference to two studies that, while not designed specifically to assist in the development of situational-interaction (or field) leadership theory, show the importance of field theory as a broad base for the development of situational-interaction leadership theory. These studies are pioneering from the standpoint of basic theory. They were designed in part to test particular tenets of field theory; most specifically, that the group atmosphere created by a leader may exert an important influence upon the individual's behavior within the group.

One of these field theory studies dealt specifically with the training of leaders (Bavales, 1942). It was designed to discover if leadership effectiveness could be improved by democratic methods of leadership training. Playground recreation leaders were offered a democratically organized training course. The specific content emphasis of the course of study was directed toward showing, by participation, how democratic techniques can be used by recreation leaders. A follow-up showed that, by contrast with leaders who had not participated in the course, those recreation leaders who instituted democratic procedures in their programs found subsequent changes in the behavior of those who were under their leadership. These changes included greater amounts of voluntary participation, greater enthusiasm, longer group membership, and more self-discipline.

The other study (Levine and Butler, 1952), conducted in an industrial situation, was designed to discover which of two group methods (group discussion or lecture) is more effective in getting supervisors to improve the accuracy of their personnel ratings. In general, supervisors had been subject to the "halo effect"; workers in the lower job classifications were consistently underrated and the skilled workers were consistently over-rated. It seemed that the foremen tended to rate the grade of the job rather than the performance of the individual worker. Three groups of foremen were organized for comparative study: a) those who received no instruction, b) those who gathered together for instruction followed by discussion and decision-making with reference to improvement, and c) those who met in a formal lecture room and listened to a lecture on rat-ing theory and validity. The instruction-discussion-decision-making group showed the greatest improvement. The control group showed no change. The only change in the lecture group was that of "toughening up," and rating lower all along the line. As Kurt Lewin has emphasized (1958), once an individual is allowed to participate in making a decision his sub-sequent behavior is much more apt to follow that decision.

In the direct study of leadership, Pigors (1935) stated the basic thesis of this position years ago when he pointed out that the study of leadership must attend to four things: a) the nature of the leader, b) the individuals who compose the social organization, c) the functional nature of the organiza-tion, and d) the particular situation which obtains at the given time. It will be noticed that these are in essence concerned with what we are calling here the total situation. He does not neglect, however, the particular traits of the individual as a functioning leader.

Studies in Situational Leadership. A general and fair appraisal of the situational research approach has been made by Jenkins when he says, "Advances in methodology in this field are definitely not striking." (1947, p. 75) However, some students of leadership have been able to show that the nature of the situation is as important as traits from the standpoint of attempting to develop a comprehensive theory of leadership.

In a military study, Stone (1946) found that the adjustment of individuals to squadrons resulted in the development of a social system in which status and leadership expectancies were based upon criteria quite different from those the same men used in civilian situations. In his study of adolescent gangs, Deutschberger (1947) was able to show that the nature of leader-ship in such groups is unique, and can be understood only in terms of the goals of the individuals who compose such groups.

Several studies have tended to confirm the plausible hypothesis that in groups in which there is at least some freedom of choice, changes in group requirements are frequently accompanied by the emergence of new leaders who can better serve those needs. Singer and Goldman (1954) conducted a study that contrasted authoritarian and democratic atmospheres in group therapy. During early sessions they found that those subjects who partici-pated in an authoritarian atmosphere made more relevant comments than did those who participated in a democratic atmosphere. As time went on, however, though the democratic group had at first been relatively disorganized and irrelevant in communication, it surpassed the authoritarian group in morale and cohesiveness as measured by action and verbalization. Such results seem to point to three important matters. First, a given type of leadership may direct an important influence upon the history of a group. Second, the dynamic nature of a group seldom remains the same over an extended period of time; goals are reached and new goals and obstacles emerge. Third, different leader characteristics are needed from time to time; that is, the nature of the situation may define the type of leadership required.

Another study that throws light on the needs of the group (the particular situation) as determining factors in leadership selections was conducted by Crockett (1955). He observed that the appointed or designated leader of a group may, under certain circumstances, give way to another person who emerges as an "operational leader." On the basis of observations of 72 business, government and industrial organization decision-making conferences, the principal conditions that lead to such emergent, operational leadership were identified. The most general finding was that when there were definite goals to be attained leaders emerged and operationally replaced designated leaders under one or more qualifying conditions. These were the following: a) when designated leaders were relatively inactive in setting goals, seeking information, and proposing problems; b) when there was considerable motivational variability and the existence of cliques; c) when those who emerged as leaders were generally known to have relatively high rank and expertness in the larger organization; d) when there was relatively high motivation on the part of those who emerged as leaders; e) when those who emerged as leaders were perceived as needed by rank and file members.

A very pertinent study dealing specifically with leadership changes as they relate to changing group needs was reported by Sterling and Rosenthal (1950). They studied an organized group composed of sixteen persons from the ministry, labor, and academics over an extended period of time. On the basis of psychometric measurement and clinical observation, they predicted that particular individuals would move into leadership roles as, if, and when particular group needs arose. These particular need situations the authors referred to as "psychological phases of group process." As different psychological phases arose, they were able to predict which individuals would take over as leaders. For example, when a phase of the group process that could be described as aggression arose, the most aggressive individuals assumed leadership positions.

Wolman (1956) has specifically emphasized the importance of the situational approach in the study of leadership. Essentially, he maintains that leadership phenomena are to be found in three basic types of social organizations: a) instrumental groups, b) mutual acceptance groups, and c) vectorial groups. This is one of many ways of classifying social organizations at the human level, but it rests solidly upon the assumption that a given social organization at a given time constitutes a unique situation. The instrumental group is one to which an individual adheres because he perceives it as an instrument in the furtherance of his own goals. The mutual acceptance group is an organization to which individuals belong on a "give and take" basis, because of the desire to be with friendly people. The vectorial group is the sort of organization that propounds lofty goals, and people join because of their desire to help others. While the validity of such a classification might be questioned, there is reason to agree that it does rest upon operational differences which, in turn, permit us to define the situation. Wolman maintains that an individual's status within an organization is a function of his power as the other members perceive it and the degree to which he is accepted. Wolman's formula for status is: $S = f(P,A)$, when S = status, P = power, and A = acceptance by others. In a free situation in which members can choose their leaders as they wish, this formula may be used to define leadership simply by thinking of leadership as a type of status; thus $L = f(P,A)$.

By using this theoretical formulation of leadership Wolman was able to hypothesize concerning the relative contributions of P and A to leadership status in each of the three types of social organizations. In the case of the instrumental group, for example, he hypothesized that leadership is more a function of power than of acceptance. He tested this hypothesis by setting up a small instrumental group in which problems were to be solved by the members working together. Two of the members were given special role-playing instructions beforehand, but unknown to the others. One was given the information necessary to solve all the problems, and was instructed to play the role of a strong, knowledgeable, unfriendly person. The other was to play the role of an incompetent though warm, helpful, friendly person. Even though he knew the answer to a question he was instructed to give a wrong answer. Of course, one of the "rank and file" members or the "hostile, but knowledgeable" member always corrected him. Wolman found that the "powerful" (P) person was accorded the status position of leader, whereas the acceptable (A) person was denied this role in the instrumental type of organization. While this study may seem to be an oversimplification of the leadership problem, it does handle some of the basic variables. In this specific instance when a group member is interested in achieving some specific goal for himself, it is only reasonable to suppose (within the context of our culture) that he will turn for leadership to that person who seems to him most capable of helping him achieve that goal. He may like another person more, but he will usually turn to a person he dislikes for help and leadership if he perceives an important personal advantage from such a situation.

Another study which throws light upon the importance of *the situation* in the attempt to understand the leadership construct gives special attention to the matter of leadership and friendship. (Hollander and Webb, 1955) On the basis of peer nominations by 187 Naval Aviation Cadets, answers to two basic questions were provided. These questions were: a) "In what way, and to what degree, is followership related to leadership?" and b) "In what way, and to what degree, is friendship related to leadership, and how does this compare with the relationship, if any, between friendship and followership?" By use of a sociometric-type device, each cadet was asked during his last week of training to make three nominations: the three cadets from his section best qualified to lead; the three cadets from his section he would like most in his unit were he the leader; and the three cadets from his section whom he considered to be his best friends. Table I shows the correlational results.

CORRELATIONS AMONG LEADERSHIP, FOLLOWERSHIP, AND FRIENDSHIP SCORES

CORRELATED VARIABLES	R
Leadership—Followership	.92
Leadership—Friendship	.47
Followership—Friendship	.55

TABLE I

It will be noted first that a very strong relationship between leadership and followership was found. This may be interpreted to mean that those who were regarded as good leaders were also regarded as good followers. The corollary of this would be that those who are regarded as poor leaders are also looked upon as poor followers. Second, both leadership and followership nominations are relatively independent of friendship. For our purposes the leadership-friendship relation is most important. As was found by Wolman, in an instrumental group, subjects seem to look more to the capacity of the individual to accomplish a task than to his desirability as a friend in reaching a decision with reference to his leadership capacity. It seems that evidence of this type supports the contention that the situation has much to do not only with the type of leadership that is most appropriate, but also with the selection of leaders to accomplish particular tasks.

Interaction Theory. Recently, some students of leadership have approached the problem from the standpoint of interaction theory and have conducted experiments that have thrown considerable light on the interrelation between leader and followers. Interaction theory rests upon the assumption that a leader's behavior is in part a function of the nature of the group, and that the behavior of the group is in part a function of the nature of the leader. This is the broadest statement of the situational approach, since it assumes that little is to be gained in the study of leadership unless the characteristics of the leader and the present nature of the group are articulated. There seems little doubt that this approach will furnish the principal research design in the future.

One of the best examples of the interaction research design has been reported by Haythorn and his co-workers (1956, 1958). The purpose of these studies was to examine the interactive effects upon group behavior of different personality variables. Only one of these studies will be described here. The aspect of personality used as the independent variable was level of authoritarianism. The dependent variables were such features of group problem-solving behavior as the leader's sensitivity to others and the follower's striving for equal participation.

Sixty-four male college students served as subjects; thirty-two were high and thirty-two were low in authoritarianism, as measured by the California F-Scale. The high authoritarians were all "conservative" and the low authoritarians were all "liberal" as measured by the Cattell Q^1 Scale; and all subjects were "relatively normal" as judged by the Minnesota Multiphasic Personality Inventory. Sixteen working groups of four men each were established. In each group a leader was appointed upon the basis of his authoritarian classification. Thus it was possible to study four types of organizations. These are shown in Table II.

All groups were given the task of writing the dialogue for a proposed film on improving human relations. First, a film on improving human relations was shown the group. Following this the appointed leader and

	High F leaders	Low F leaders
High F followers	4 groups	4 groups
Low F followers	4 groups	4 groups

TABLE II

the three other group members discussed the film and then went on to the task of writing the script. Four trained observers watched through a one-way vision mirror and recorded their observations according to a schedule of criteria within several behavior categories. In addition, when the group's working session was over, the subjects filled out a postmeeting reaction sheet, designed to elicit impressions from group members as to the general effectiveness of their group.

Obviously, such an elaborate design afforded a wealth of data which were studied from many perspectives. We will indicate here only some of the results, and organize them under three headings. The first concerns the effects of varying leader personality: appointed authoritarian leaders versus appointed equalitarian leaders with reference to rating of leader behavior by trained observers, evaluation of leaders by followers, and evaluation of leaders by the trained observers. The trained observers rated the authoritarian leaders (without regard as to whether the group composition was authoritarian or equalitarian) as low in equalitarian behavior, low in effective intelligence, and low in sensitivity to others. The followers evaluated the authoritarian leaders as relatively efficient. The trained observers evaluated the authoritarian leaders as failing to permit equal participation in their groups, maintaining relatively great group structure, being less motivated toward the goal than the equalitarian leaders, and fostering less opinion variance.

The second general set of findings may be termed the effects of varying follower personality. Here the groups composed of authoritarian followers were compared with those composed of equalitarian followers. The trained observers rated the leaders of authoritarian followers as promoting greater frequency of individual prominence, being more aggressive, and as being more autocratic. They rated the authoritarian followers as being less equalitarian, striving less for goal achievement, and demonstrating less effective intelligence than equalitarian followers. The followers' post-session evaluations of their groups indicated that authoritarian followers tended to increase definiteness in leadership, strive less for equal participation, produce more, be more dominated by the appointed leader, and show greater satisfaction with the appointed leaders.

The third, and last, group of findings dealt with the effects of varying homogeneity of leader and follower personalities. That is, what are the effects of having the leader and his followers similar with respect to the authoritarian personality variable, as compared with a personality difference between leader and followers? The observers rated leaders of homogeneous groups (i.e., personality similarity between leader and followers), whether high or low in authoritarianism, as relatively low in submissiveness, more aggressive, and more autocratic. The followers in homogeneous groups were rated by the observers as striving more for group approval, having higher morale, and being relatively little personality conflict with their leaders.

Evaluation.   The over-all results of these significant studies suggest that the situational approach to the study of leadership is a great improvement over the trait approach *per se*. Specifically, the interaction type study, in line with field theoretical constructs, is the most powerful tool so far devised for the study of leadership. As the studies by Haythorn and his coworkers clearly show, the behavior of a leader is not simply a function of his characteristic traits. While his behavior is in part a function of his characteristic traits, it is also in part a functon of the group-situation in which he is operating. Conversely, the collective trait composition of a group makes an important contribution to the pattern of its behavior, but the leader has much to do also with that pattern. What the leader perceives the group situation to be will affect his interaction with the group, since he is constantly monitoring and modifying his own behavior. The interaction type study of leadership lends strong support to a phenomenological field interpretation of social behavior.

DEFINITIONS OF LEADER AND LEADERSHIP

A leader is a person who performs particular acts, the nature of which places him, by the perception of others, in a particular category. Leadership is a social process. Leadership designates the essence, the commonality, the least common denominator of the acts of many people who have been perceived as leaders. In addition we are dealing with expectancy—what the potential followers believe should be done within a region they perceive as a given leadership region.

In reviewing the many psychological definitions of leader and leadership we will follow an outline provided by Gibb (1954), who has conveniently organized the various contemporary definitions into seven categories.

The Leader as an Individual in a Given Office

This is a convenient, operational way to define leadership. It is particularly well-suited to a highly structured organization, such as some branch of the military. Although such a definition is a good starting place for a theoretical consideration of leadership, it is vague in that it involves such a vast assortment of relationship variables that it is of limited scientific value as a research model. A more analytic approach is necessary. This definition does, however, designate the central reference point—the person who is, in fact, recognized as the leader, at least by title and power delegation. Starting with such a reference point, the student of leadership is then in a position to inquire into the conditions responsible for such leadership and the conditions which could change the nature of the leader's behavior or remove the leader from his position.

The Leader as Focus for the Behavior of Group Members

This is a very particular picture of the leader, developed by Redl (1942). He has reserved the term "leader" for the individual who is loved by the group members, and whose personality comes to be incorporated into the "ego ideal" of the followers. The principal emphasis of this definition is upon the emotional relationship between leader and followers. One of the essential limitations of this definition is that it is quite restrictive in that it eliminates many situations ordinarily thought of as leadership. Also, the necessary information for the study of leadership, within such a restricted framework, is virtually impossible to obtain. On the other hand, this definition describes in some detail one of several situations which may be thought of as leader-leadership.

The Leader as a Sociometric Choice

Sociometry, as a technique for assessing the interpersonal attitudes of members of relatively small human groups, has been used by several researchers as a tool for studying the structure of leadership in small groups. Each member may be asked to identify the most influential person, the person who is the "real leader," the best liked person, or any such question pertaining to the characteristics of other group members. There is some evidence, for instance, that group members are better able to identify leaders within their own groups than are outside observers (Wherry and Fryer, 1949). Those who are most enthusiastic about sociometry feel that these techniques provide a truer picture of leadership than do observational procedures. Though individual A may be the designated leader of a group, individual B may be pointed to by his fellow group members as the person who provides the most ideas, attracts the greatest respect, actually directs individual A's behavior, and is best liked. On the basis of this information it might be argued that B, rather than A, is the "real leader." That this is a poor argument may be seen in the fact that this is really a way of avoiding the problem. The most adequate way of dealing with the problem this raises is to return to the first definition: the leader is an individual in a given office. This simply means that the expectancy region is occupied, and by occupancy alone individual A is the real leader, even though he may be very ineffective, disliked and incompetent. The "power behind the throne" may, in fact, be individual B. The task of the student of leadership is not only that of analyzing the functional structure of a group in terms of interpersonal influence, but also of interpreting the power and restraints which perpetuate particular leadership statuses for particular individuals. That individual A is in the leadership status, though he plays the role inadequately, depends upon important variables which must also be identified and considered. Sociometry is of great value in the study of the dynamic nature of groups, though it is insufficient as a comprehensive definition or theory of leadership.

The Leader as One Who Exercises Influence over Others

In one respect this definition is in agreement with the sociometric definition since it points to the person who is most influential in guiding and directing the behavior of others as the "real leader." There seems to be nothing wrong with this definition insofar as it goes. At the same time, an ineffectual person who occupies a leadership expectancy region is by definition, if nothing more, a leader. There may be others in the group who exercise greater influence; and, in this sense, they, too, are leaders. It is then more a problem of describing the dynamics of the group than of trying to defend the position that a given person, and no other person, is the real leader.

The Leader as Differentiated from the Head

Gibb (1947) has for some time maintained that leadership, headship, and domination should be distinguished. He believes that one meets the true definition of a leader only when the influence he exerts is accepted voluntarily by others, or when it is in "a shared direction." Again, this is an arbitrary definition of leadership which says, in effect, only the "pull type" influence process is leadership. However, according to Gibb, we should think of influence exerted by one person over another or others as lying somewhere along the leadership-headship-domination continuum.

Such a theoretical scheme permits several combinations or overlappings. The real leader may also be the legally appointed head. A good example of this is the military officer who occupies a leadership-expectancy region by virtue of his legally bestowed rank. To the men over whom he has this jurisdiction, he may also be respected, and his men might wish to follow him with no regard to his leadership status at all. This condition, Gibb points out, ". . . is the assumption which underlies the selection of military officers." The fact that such appointments do not always turn out so happily brings us to a second combination. The military officer may, instead of being voluntarily accepted as a "real leader," be a dominator. He may influence his subordinates only by punitive acts and threats. Third, an individual may be a "real leader," though he has no rank, no headship status. Workers may take their leads from another rank and file worker and pay only lip-service to the foreman. Fourth, the head may be completely ineffectual, neither "real leader" nor dominator. Yet, he is head by virtue of an external power that maintains him in office. History is replete with accounts of monarchs who have fallen into this category. Finally, there is the dominator who influences the behavior of others by virtue of his own power. The "self-made" tycoon who controls powerful financial networks and politics by virtue of the fact that he is feared is a type well known to all through fiction and film.

The value of Gibb's scheme is great from the standpoint of functional analysis. It represents a framework for describing interpersonal influence combinations. At the same time, there are two apparent limitations. First, there is a semantic problem. What Gibb chooses to call leadership could more profitably be referred to as a type of leadership. Domination behavior also influences the behavior of others, even though our preference for democratic behavior leads us to dislike and try to prevent domination.

Second, group processes are fluid, dynamic. A given individual may play a variety of roles and occupy different positions of status within a given group over a period of time. One is reminded of J. M. Barrie's play, *The Admirable Crichton,* about the butler who, during a crisis, became the truly respected, high status leader of the household. Once the crisis had ended he returned to his butlership, and influence again emanated from the employer. The parent generally is leader to his child. He has status—is "head of the household." At times he is loved and respected by his child, and at such times the child wants to follow. At other times the father may dominate his child, and his dominant behavior may be motivated from a punitive basis or from the standpoint that the child must be forced to do a certain thing for his own good.

Our preference is to think of influence effectively exerted on others as leadership. From this we may then go along with Gibb and agree that at any given time interpersonal influence may be voluntarily accepted in a shared direction (common motivation), or it may be domineering in nature and result in resentful acquiescence. In either circumstance the person doing the influencing may or may not command a headship status. Finally, in some situations influence may be exerted only symbolically; that is, a leadership expectancy region is merely occupied by an individual who actually exerts no influence, either as a person others want to follow or as a dominator. These are conditions of leadership that must be studied in the light of their unique psychological characteristics and constant fluidity.

The Leader as an Influence upon Syntality

Syntality is defined as the performance of the total group. According to this definition, leadership may be operationally identified by measuring the amount of change in production as a function of an individual's (leader's) performance. Theoretically, this is a very appealing definition; but, as is inherent in the classical "great man" vs. "the times" controversy, it is virtually impossible to isolate precisely a single variable responsible for social changes. Also, this view of leadership seems more sociological than psychological, since it defines leadership in terms of what the group does, and neglects the psychological relationships between leader and follower.

The principal theoretical strength of the syntality definition lies in its insistence upon including under the general term "leadership" many specific types or conditions of leadership. As long as an individual influences the behavior of others—whether he is loved or hated, uses bribery, threat or physical coercion, is looked upon as virtuous or iniquitous—he is a leader. The psychologist's job is one of studying these various conditions of leadership from the standpoint of trying to understand them, and, upon such a basis of understanding, being able to make accurate predictions and to suggest effective controls. This definition of leadership merits serious respect since it refuses to quibble about good and bad social influences as leadership criteria. Rather, it emphasizes the importance of the conditions responsible for social influence.

The Leader as One Who Engages in Leadership Behavior

This final definition has much in common with some of the others. Its main distinction lies in its attention to two points. First, it holds that a leader is one who sets up a structure within the group which then flows into group action. That is, a leader is one who is able to organize (though not necessarily with reasoned intention) his group in such a way that group behavior changes follow. Second, it is a statistical definition in the sense that having observed a given person's behavior sufficiently in the past, his future leadership performance can be predicted at a level above chance. Or, some individuals are leaders upon frequent occasions; knowing this it can be predicted that they will more probably be leaders in future situations than will certain other members of the same group. This definition of leadership has much to recommend it. Again, its chief limitation lies in the fact that the type of information needed to test its strength is virtually impossible to obtain.

The Use of Definitions

These definitions Gibb has categorized have much in common. Interestingly, Gibb's own theory is most at variance with the others. In our comments on these seven definitions we have indicated our disagreement with his definition. Essentially, we cannot accept his definition since he sets up an idyllic situation, a goal toward which those who adhere to democratic principles strive, and since he holds only this to be leadership. We, too, believe that democratic leadership is preferable to authoritarian leadership. However, it seems reasonable that effective interpersonal influence is the essential ingredient of leadership, and that there are several ways by which this can be effected. The psychological task is one of studying these several ways in order to understand them. We have no argument with Gibb's total theory. It only seems that the statement of his theory is less parsimonious than it should be. There are those who are liked, respected, and therefore followed. There are those who occupy leadership-expectancy regions and, for no other reason than this, are followed. And there are those who dominate and coerce; not to follow them (and we must remember that "follow" does not always mean to come happily behind) is perceived as dangerous. All three conditions must be studied in order to understand interpersonal influence and the nature of human social organization.

PERSONALITY APPROACHES TO LEADERSHIP

These definitions we have just reviewed do not exhaust the psychological views of leadership which are to be found in the literature. They represent, perhaps, the most systematic modern definitions or theories. There are others, however, that approach the psychological study of leadership differently. Two of these are of importance for our purpose. Both are personality approaches: a) psychopathological and b) authoritarian.

Psychopathological Approach

The psychopathological approach seeks to find the factors responsible for the person's leadership role in personality disturbance. Freud (1916), for example, studied the life of da Vinci in search of personality depth factors that might have been responsible for his extraordinary creativity and demand for knowledge. Freud concluded that da Vinci suffered severe early sexual repression from which he never recovered; therefore, his libidinal energy was supposedly sublimated into these potent strivings. A more recent example of the psychopathological approach is found in the writings of Bluemel (1950). His general thesis is that many prominent world-known leaders occupy their positions because of particular psychological disturbances. Especially significant, according to Bluemel, is the obsessive-compulsive syndrome, in which an individual fixates on some particular panacea and is excessively compulsive in striving to cure the ills of the world through his particular panacea.

The psychopathological approach is theoretically intriguing, and there seems little doubt that the particular personality characteristics of certain individuals are at least in part responsible for the assumption of positions of leadership as we define leadership. At the same time, the needs of the social situation must be such that the potential leader's obsessive-compulsive behavior is perceived by followers as an adequate answer to the needs. A good example of this is found in post-World War I Germany, when Hitler came to be perceived by many Germans as the answer to their needs. Bluemel concludes his analysis of Hitler with these comments: "Hitler is sometimes referred to as a monster. This is unfortunate, for no one understands monsters. From a psychiatric viewpoint Hitler was a schizoid individual, egocentric, juvenile, and paranoid. He had obsessive-compulsive traits and in certain moods he was pathologically aggressive. He was a phenomenal individual in history but a commonplace person in psychiatry." (1950, pp. 88–89) Circumstances were such that these bizarre personality characteristics were perceived as useful to the social striving of many Germans.

The psychopathological approach is no global, comprehensive theory. It is useful in interpreting a few, but by no means all, leader-leadership phenomena. For one thing, it deals only with some of the variables involved. There are many other types of leadership situations that employ quite "normal" personalities; persons who neither strive for social recognition nor avoid it, but who are drawn into leadership roles by virtue of certain well-developed talents that have been tested by potential followers. Also, it is virtually impossible to obtain enough exact information concerning the needs of those who compose the group and the personality nature of any potential leader to look to these variables as functionally related in a causal sense. Finally, this theory is dramatic and fascinating since it selects its data; finding a "beautiful case," it is easy to become rhapsodic and generalize to all other leadership situations. While it is most descriptive of some leadership situations, it is certainly not descriptive of most.

Authoritarian Approach

A much more pinpointed personality trait approach to the study of leadership has been through the authoritarian syndrome variable. We have already referred to studies that found interesting differences between the behavior of both leaders and followers who are high and low in authoritarianism. The high or low authoritarian composition of groups was also found to affect the nature of group interaction. Since we will necessarily make detailed reference to the authoritarian personality syndrome in our discussion of prejudicial attitudes, it is premature to elaborate on the nature of its theoretical structure here.

While, as will be seen, the authoritarian syndrome is most complex, high authoritarians evidence more and stronger stereotypes, more positive and negative prejudices, and less keenness in social perception than those who are low in authoritarianism (Christie and Cook, 1958). However, simply knowing that an individual is high in authoritarianism is not sufficient to predict *what* his stereotypes will be or toward *which* groups his prejudices are directed.

The same is true with reference to authoritarianism as it relates to leadership. That a person is high or low in authoritarianism is an insufficient independent variable upon which to predict that he will most usually be a leader or a follower. In summarizing their review of the literature on authoritarianism as a variable in leadership determination Titus and Hollander comment: "On theoretical grounds, the use of the F scale in studies of leadership appears entirely appropriate. In point of fact, though, the meaningfulness of the empirical data obtained is not always evident. One may even say that, since both variables are so complex and diffuse, we are correlating one unknown with another." (1957, p. 58)

The authoritarian syndrome cannot, however, be discounted; it is an important independent variable in the study of leadership. One characteristic of people high in authoritarianism is acceptance of a hierarchical social power structure in which the authoritarian perceives himself as occupying some position on a power continuum. From this position he looks with manifest deference to those above himself, and with disdain at those below himself. In view of this, we would expect an individual's level of authoritarianism to play a part in determining his response to leadership as such. In fact, there is some evidence to support this expectation. For example, Jones (1954) found that men who were low in authoritarianism perceived forceful leaders as more powerful, and passive leaders as less powerful, than did men who scored high in authoritarianism. This empirical finding can be taken to mean that persons who are low in authoritarianism are relatively more sensitive to the personal characteristics of others, whereas, those high in authoritarianism look more to the institutional status a person occupies as the basis for evaluating the nature of his leadership behavior. Also, high authoritarians were found to be less critical of individuals in leadership positions than were low authoritarians. Again, it seems that acceptance of the *status quo,* that "this is the way it should be," is characteristic of high authoritarianism. Certainly, the authoritarian variable operates in one way or another in determining the role any given individual plays in the power structure of most of the social organizations in our culture. While the authoritarian personality syndrome is inadequate as a total theory of leadership, it must be considered as an important variable.

EVALUATION OF CONTEMPORARY THEORIES

The essential deficiency of these various theories seems to lie in oversimplification, in attention to only certain aspects, rather than to the totality of power allocation within social organizations. Specific theories seem to neglect psychological variance from social situation to social situation. Since it is evident that the psychological composition of groups varies immeasurably, it follows that no completely valid, global psychological theory of *leadership* can be constructed. Rather, *leadership* is also a sociological abstraction and, as such, is not amenable to vigorous theoretical analysis at a psychological level. A given instance of leadership (ten men in a boat) may be described quantitatively, but it is impossible precisely to equate this instance psychologically with another (even the same ten men dumped from the boat and swimming in the water). Since physical and interpersonal circumstances change from time to time, even the same group of people promotes and demotes its leaders in many ways.

From a psychological standpoint a broad description of leadership seems, at our present stage of knowledge, preferable to any specific theory that is intended to provide the basis for global understanding. We propose the following operational denominator of the human leadership abstraction:

Leadership is a social process by which the behavior of one or more individuals is determined, directly or indirectly, by another individual (or his symbol), or a group of individuals (or their symbol). Although this is a very loose description, it does take into account the fact that leadership may operate in an untold number of psychological ways. Failure to recognize this has confused our thinking about leadership and led to the development of several theories which tend to particularize leadership into a psychological fiction. If we can back away from fiction long enough to accept the simple fact that people may influence each other in countless ways, we are then in a position to identify and study the psychological conditions that underlie what we commonly refer to as leadership. This means, then, that leadership, important as it is, is not to be studied or even thought of as a psychological entity. It is a social phenomenon which the psychologist must try to understand in terms of species capacity, physical circumstance, learning, motivation, and perception. These are the same variables he must consider in studying any other social phenomenon.

X

Attitudes

For many years social psychologists have recognized both diversity and uniformity in social behavior. A given social stimulus object may evoke a variety of social responses; some individuals may respond to it favorably, some may reject it, and others may fail to respond to it at all. Obviously, the social stimulus object cannot be looked to for the sole explanation of social behavior. The individual, as he relates to the social stimulus object, must also be brought into the picture. In contemporary psychology, the attitude construct has been increasingly used in the attempt to understand social behavior.

Before the turn of the century several German psychologists had recognized the importance of the subject's "set" in psychological experimentation. For example, when a subject was ready or set to press a reaction-time key upon presentation of a stimulus signal, he was found to react more quickly than when he was attending primarily to the expected signal. Many terms and phrases were used to designate the general concept of set, each, of course, with its specifically unique meaning: task attitude, conscious purpose, idea of the goal, idea of the relation between the self and the object to which the self is responding, idea of direction, determining idea, mental set, motor set.

Although these shades of meaning all centered around *attitude* they were so embedded in psychophysical measurement that their relevance to a central social psychological concept seems to have been largely neglected by these early German psychologists. By 1900 the construct of "perseveration" (Müller and Pilzecker, 1900) had been used to designate ". . . persistence of attitudes that are totally unconscious. . . ." (Allport, 1954b, p. 44) The painstaking experimental work of these early German psychologists firmly established the attitude (or set) construct in modern psychology. But the vitality the construct needed in order to occupy a central theoretical position in general psychology and serve as a foundation for an emerging social psychology came from clinical quarters. Psychoanalytic theory came to ". . . endow attitudes with vitality, equating them with longing, hatred and love, with passion and prejudice, in short, with the onrushing stream of unconscious life." (*Ibid.*)

Up to this time, attempts to explain regularities and irregularities in social behavior had been made either from instinct theory or social determinism theory. The dynamic attitude concept avoided both of these inadequate extremes and provided a core thesis for social psychology. Obviously, for social psychology, interest resides in attitudes toward social stimulus objects, though we should realize that we all have attitudes toward many objects which have little specific social meaning.

In their discussion of attitudes, Murphy, Murphy and Newcomb have made the following cogent comment: "Perhaps no single concept within the whole realm of social psychology occupies a more central position than that of attitude." (1937, p. 889) The basic value of the concept lies in the fact that it provides much help in understanding the individual's social behavior, and serves as the best basis for the prediction of social behavior thus far devised. If an individual's social attitudes have been comprehensively assessed we are then in a position to know something of his aspirations, his motivations to strive toward his goals, and why along the way he deals as he does with a great variety of social objects and values. In other words, his behavior begins to "make sense." Bizarre as his behavior may appear to the casual observer, from the standpoint of his attitude system it may be perceived as articulated and integrated. In addition, if we know an individual's attitude toward a given stimulus object, other things equal, we will be able to predict his behavior as, if and when that stimulus object confronts him. Furthermore, with such knowledge, his behavior may be predetermined to some degree by controlling the stimulus objects toward which he has attitudes. Thus, from the standpoints of both theory and practice, the attitude construct is of great value.

In the last paragraph we used the qualifying phrase, "other things equal." This is necessary since attitude and behavior do not correlate perfectly. In attempting both to understand and to predict an individual's behavior, his psychological field must also be taken into account. Attitudes do not blindly force behavior to flow into set and rigid patterns. What the individual perceives the social situation to be will have much to do with whether or not he will act in line with his attitude. Even a chimpanzee may respond in a friendly way to a keeper toward whom it has long held a grudge if it perceives denial of some important reward as the consequence of hostile behavior. This is one of the serious limitations of the attitude construct. Knowledge of an individual's attitudes without knowledge of the situation, as that individual perceives it, is insufficient. This brings to our attention the need for caution in the way we use the attitude construct, and the need for supplementary psychological information.

DEFINITION OF ATTITUDE

Literal Meaning

The literal meaning of attitude upon which the psychological meaning rests is of long standing. The core of the concept is that of state of readiness or set. One literal meaning, for example, is that of "position assumed to serve some purpose." This literal meaning has sometimes been used in gunnery to describe the position of a gun, thereby indicating the course the projectile will take. Another literal meaning is "bodily position used to convey a mood or state." This has an important psychological contribution to make in that it points to the fact that we can know an individual's attitude only after observing a sample of his behavior. This is, as a matter of fact, the assumption which underlies all attitude scaling.

One of the most interesting current uses of the attitude construct is in the design of electronic computers. In a symposium on "The Design of Machines to Simulate the Behavior of the Human Brain," Schmitt *et al.* referred to what they termed "preforms." When asked to describe what is meant by a preform, Schmitt replied:

I use this term 'preform' to represent the numerous stylized but slightly flexible patterns of behavior exhibited by the animal or man in response to characteristic combinations of cues, or of nearly equivalent patterns of cues, even if presented in varying sensory modes. These preforms, some innate and some learned, are set in motion by key combinations of stimuli, sometimes called releasers, and are usually very efficient means to a practical end, but occasionally lead to systematically repeated blunders. These preforms are the biological counterpart of automatic subroutines built into computers, such as recorded function tables and the like, but differ markedly in their combination rules and simultaneous compatibility. Subjectively we experience these preforms as 'ideas,' 'principles,' 'approaches,' 'ideals,' 'prejudices,' 'intuition,' and 'skills.' (1956, p. 246)

In essence, then, what a computer will do when confronted by a particular set of stimuli (input variables) will depend upon the subroutines which have been built into the equipment by electronic engineers. When Allport (1935) speaks of an attitude as a ". . . *neural* state of readiness" (italics ours) he emphasizes the importance of thinking of attitudes as states of readiness based upon real changes in nerve tissue. Such neural states are ready to produce particular patterns of behavior when the individual is stimulated by particular stimuli or releasers. At the same time, and analogous to Schmitt's "preforms," such sets are dynamic in the sense that an additional set of cues may alter the output or inhibit it. This takes into account the importance of the *situation* in understanding and predicting what an individual will do as a function of his attitude when confronted by the object of his attitude. The attempt to simulate attitudes is especially difficult since it is necessary to introduce a dynamics: that is, a feed-back system which allows release of a performance only when particular inputs are in operation, even though no two input combinations may ever be the same.

In viewing the computer analogy, it should be recognized that many of the "sets" that are built into computers are rigidly structured and are not modifiable as are Schmitt's "preforms." This is also true in animals. In man, for example, there are many "reflexive sets," such as the neurological mechanism lying back of the pupillary response to light, which are native and rigid. On the other hand, man and many of the lower animals have modifiable neural equipment which is altered by experience. This is the dynamic aspect. Especially in the case of man, experience with an object modifies his neural equipment in such ways as to establish a "preform" or psychological set; and the very same equipment, under different conditions of experience, could have produced a very different set. Thus, the types of sets we are interested in here, attitudinal sets, are learned with neural equipment which could have been used in countless other ways. Attitudinal sets are dynamic in that they are capable of releasing different patterns of behavior under varying conditions of stimulation.

Contemporary Definitions

Although contemporary psychological definitions of attitude differ very little from each other, there are some slight variations in emphasis. Probably the most quoted definition is the one proposed by Gordon Allport in 1935: "An attitude is a mental and neural state of readiness, organized through experience, exerting a directive or dynamic influence upon the individual's response to all objects and situations with which it is related." (p. 810) This classic definition points to the essential psychological aspects of attitude. First, social attitudes are sets, or states of readiness to act. Second, they are learned. Third, they are dynamically organized; that is, they articulate with each other in the individual's cognitive organization. Fourth, they define subject-object relationships: the individual's evaluations of social stimuli.

Another definition which has received wide recognition was proposed by Krech and Crutchfield: ". . . an enduring organization of motivational, emotional, perceptual, and cognitive processes with respect to some aspect of the individual's world." (1948, p. 152) Krech and Crutchfield approach the study of human behavior and experience from the standpoint of a systematic examination of motivation, perception, and learning; and their approach to the study of attitude is consistent with this systematic approach. In order to understand the attitudinal nature of any individual, according to these authors, it is necessary to examine the individual's dynamic psychological field. Such a dynamic field pictures the individual as a) constantly motivated, driving toward and away from particular stimulus conditions, b) perceiving stimulus objects as related to goal attainment, such perceptions being phenomenologically unique for him, c) meeting frustrations and rewards, both of which induce emotion which further helps to fixate and reorganize his perceptions of the related stimulus objects, so that d) in maturity he has a more or less enduring matrix of attitudes, or a cognitive organization, with reference to the many aspects of his world. This cognitive organization is always in flux, is always changing, at least in minor ways; although there is a central core which maintains considerable stability. This central core, we suggest, is what is usually referred to as social ideology, a *stimulus-free* cognitive organization which guides and directs the changing of attitudes, the development of new attitudes, and the maintenance of most of one's already existing attitudes.

A third definition which, like the second, uses field-theoretical constructs, is the following: attitudes are sets with reference to barriers and facilitations which are perceived as affecting goal attainment. The main emphasis here is that sets are directed toward barriers and facilitations. A barrier is any stimulus object which hinders goal attainment, and a facilitation is any stimulus object which assists goal attainment. According to the proposition that man is psychologically homeostatic, we may assume that any human is constantly in a state of relative disequilibrium and constantly striving toward psychological equilibrium. Striving does not imply focal consciousness, and disequilibrium does not imply a constant level of disequilibrium. At one time an individual may be considerably more equilibrated than at another. The cold and ravenously hungry man who is brought into a warm room and invited to eat as much as he wants of his favorite food may, under these circumstances, have the feeling of psychological equilibration; for the time he may have no awareness of the fact that within a few hours he will be cold and hungry again. That at any instant he is in some degree disequilibrated is evidenced, however, by his continued eating, signs of discomfort when he finishes eating, and any of the many activities he engages in during his stay. In fact, any act must be thought of as an answer to a need, a tension, either "real" or imagined. This description pictures a human as constantly on the move, always moving toward a "better environmental fit." The very important assumption we must now make is that certain of the features of his environment are perceived by him as "helps" and others as "hindrances." He cannot avoid living homeostatically, and he cannot avoid perceiving some of the stimulus objects which surround him.

Next, since a human is in the constant process of motivationally interacting with his environment, since whatever he does depends upon the ways in which he perceives at least some of the features of his environment, and since perceiving always means retaining something of that which is perceived, he cannot avoid establishing approach and avoidance tendencies to these perceived features. Any stimulus object which is of sufficient importance to be perceived at all by an individual is accorded at least a slight positive or a negative affective value.

It is obvious that only a limited number of an individual's attitudes can possibly be functioning at any given time. In a given psychological field situation the motivated individual is to be pictured in a limited or specific point in time. At this point in time his behavior is a function of the "field forces" (independent variables) which are impinging upon him. Some of these may be physical structures which may be pushing or pulling or preventing locomotion. Others may be novel stimuli which he is perceiving for the first time. Still others are valence perceptions which he already has of the stimulus objects operating in his present field. Lewin (1936) has used the term *valence* to designate the attractiveness or repellent value which an individual ascribes to a region (stimulus object) in his "life space" (total psychological world—past, present and anticipated future). Thus, the individual's behavior is a function of the valenced objects he perceives. *The valence nature of any object is identical to our conception of attitude content.*

Figure 1 schematically represents a very simplified field situation in which Lewin describes what happens to a boy who wants to become a physician:

The vocational goal of a sixteen-year-old boy (*P*) is to become a physician. . . . The "path" to this goal (*G*) leads through definite stages: college-entrance examinations (*ce*), college (*c*), medical school (*m*), internship (*i*), establishing a practice (*pr*). The boy may have a fairly clear idea of college. Medical school and the following stages may constitute a more or less undifferentiated region "beyond" which lies the goal of being a physician. Of this the boy may have a false but nevertheless a clear picture.

When he passes his college entrance examinations he has made a "step forward" on the way to his goal. This movement is certainly not a bodily one. Nevertheless it is real locomotion, a real change of position in the quasi-social (and as a matter of fact also in the objective social) life space. The examinations have brought him a step closer to his goal. The reality of the change in his position becomes clear when one considers that many things are now within his reach which were not before. He can go to college or university, his time is much more within his own control than before. His social position too is changed: he can play on the college football team, go to the dances, etc. His examinations therefore had for him the character of a boundary between two distinct regions. He had to cross this boundary if he wished to go from the one region to the other.

Had he failed in his examinations, then he would not have made this advance toward his goal. But also in that case there would have been a real change in his life situation. The failure would have changed the barrier between him and the region of college, which was shortly before in his immediate neighborhood. The barrier would seem much more solid, almost impassable. The youth would be thrown back and possibly would seek an entirely new goal. (1936, pp. 48–49)

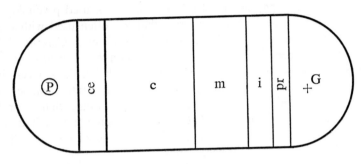

FIGURE 1

(Adapted from K. Lewin, *Principles of Topological Psychology.* New York: McGraw-Hill Book Co., Inc., 1936, p. 48).

This description by Lewin is of a present field in which the person's goals, anticipations of regions, and present appraisal of self are all operating. His behavior at any time is the resultant of the convergence of these forces upon him. At this moment, for example, though college may be negatively valenced, medical school and internship may be so strongly positively valenced that he is willing to enter the unpleasantly anticipated regions of entrance examinations and college. Thus, his attitude toward a given region does not necessarily determine his present behavior. This is often clearly observed in the contrast between children and adults when they are required to take some medicine toward which they have very strong negative attitudes. The adult often takes the medicine as though he likes it since he anticipates the goal of good health. The child, on the other hand, acts out his attitude, since he has no such anticipation of good health in his psychological field.

Although an individual's attitudes are historical psychological facts, an individual's present psychological field may include the functioning of only a very few of his attitudes. His behavior at any time is a function of only a select few of his attitudes. And in a present field situation an individual's behavior and experience are unaffected by most of his attitudes. During the period in which the boy resolved to become a physician he was unaffected by his dislike of his second grade teacher, the Boy Scouts, the Sunday School band, and his favorable attitude toward basketball and girls with blue eyes. These attitudes had nothing to do with his *present* field. Only the attitudes which operated in his present field affected his decision to pursue medical studies.

Correlative Concepts

While the term *attitude* is used most generally in contemporary psychology to designate psychological set, and we find it used psychologically in a generic sense, there are other terms that are often used with the intention of conveying more specific psychological meaning. Certain of these correlative terms seem to introduce more confusion than clarification of the basic concept of psychological set. On the other hand, though certain of these terms are often used in literary ways to convey quite variable meanings they are worth citing since we may safely assume that their long history in the language insures that they have some utility. The terms which are used most frequently as specific variations of the attitude construct are described in the next paragraphs.

Belief. A belief is an attitude which incorporates a large amount of cognitive structuring. Operationally, one has an attitude *toward* and a belief *in* or *about* a stimulus object (Krech and Crutchfield, 1948). One believes in another person, a political concept, or a theory. The stimulus object of a belief is relatively complex even though this may mean that the subject has differentiated the object into smaller and smaller sub-regions. Belief connotes an attitude which involves or identifies the subject deeply with the object. The individual uses his belief as a basis for predicting what will happen in the future.

Bias. Bias literally refers to that which is bent or oblique. A father may be correctly thought of as biased in favor of his own child when he overvalues the child's competitive behavior. In such an instance the outside observer more or less expects this. His evaluation of the father's attitude is that it is based upon incomplete, inaccurate, preconceived or deductive premises. Biases may also be described as weak prejudices, prejudices that do not carry conviction or great potency. Biases are often admitted by the subject; he is willing to admit that his attitude is not based on as firm ground as it perhaps should be. This he has great difficulty doing with a prejudice. Thus, a biased attitude is a perception of a stimulus object from a slightly warped, inaccurate position.

Doctrine. Doctrine literally means that which is taught. Coutu (1949) puts the concept nicely when he says that it refers to that which we are taught and expected to believe; how things should be done and what should be believed. The "doctrine of the Church," "doctrine of the Republican Party," "doctrine of Communism" are teachings, elaborate stimulus objects, toward which individuals have attitudes. A doctrine is a highly involved logical system concerning some complex phenomenon to which an individual subscribes or objects. A doctrine must be accepted or rejected—there are no shades of gray, since it is a way of interpreting an important phenomenon. A doctrine explicitly describes (by codification) the reasons for adherence and the ways those who subscribe to it should behave as a function of its validity.

Faith. Faith is a complex form of attitude involving deep affective meaning. It refers to a system of attitudes that describes a specific and fundamental belief in a person or principle or conception which may or may not be shared by others. "Faith" stands between "belief" and "ideology." It is belief in that it is a prediction, it tells what will happen in the future. It is ideology in that it may be an elaborate cognitive system which purports to explain some phenomenon. On the other hand, one may be said to have faith in a doctrine. Thus, the term is closely associated with other "attitude species" terms. All theologies incorporate faith; in fact, religions are frequently referred to as faiths. Also, faith incorporates personal identification; the individual surrenders self to a predetermined future. While the term is infrequently used in current psychological parlance, it is quite possible that as psychology moves into a more intensive and systematic study of religious experience, the concept of faith will undergo rigorous scrutiny (Dunlap, 1946). If we can agree upon an operational definition there is no reason why faith cannot be measured and dealt with quantitatively.

Ideology. According to Gordon Allport (1954b), the ideology construct can be traced back to Francis Bacon's "idols." In this sense an ideology is an elaborate cognitive system which may be used to justify certain forms of behavior—or, is a means of rationalization. Historically, ideology connotes hypocrisy. For example, the term was used by Marx and Engles to describe the elaborate system of "false logic" used by the capitalists to justify their favored socio-economic positions. These writers would never have referred to "communist doctrine" as an ideology. By the same token, it is common practice for non communists to refer to communist doctrine as an ideology, thereby connoting something unsavory. In this sense a person would never use the term ideology to describe his own religious doctrine, though he might freely use it to describe another religious doctrine. Thus, the term is secular from the individual's standpoint. In recent times there has been a shift in the meaning of ideology in the direction of eliminating the negative connotation. Democratically oriented persons may now occasionally refer to belief in democracy and the rationale lying back of the belief as the "democratic ideology." When he does this he certainly imputes nothing but good and truth.

Newcomb speaks of ideologies as ". . . codifications of certain kinds of group norms." (1950, p. 274) The truth of an ideology may be defended even though there are no criteria by which its accuracy may be tested. Thus, ideology is intimately related to faith, in that an ideology must be accepted as faith.

From the standpoint of the individual, the term ideology may be used with a slightly different meaning. This involves personality structure and content. It would be accurate, for example, to speak of an "authoritarian ideology" without implying adherence to a particular system, such as communism or facism. This use refers to the individual's outlook upon self and society (i.e., other humans). Scales that have been developed for the assessment of authoritarian and nonauthoritarian personality characteristics may be used to describe individual social ideologies. From this standpoint, an individual's social ideology represents a holistic view of his self perception and his perception of society. In a sense it is a generalized, global attitude, virtually a "philosophy of life," though not formally structured.

Judgment.   This is either the process or the result of the process of classifying stimulus objects (including cognitve events) into categories. It is always comparative. In that many judgments are not ego-related, not all judgments can be classified as social attitudes. For example, one may judge one tree as taller than another. Such a judgment incorporates no ego-involvement, no affective property, and no "barrier" or "facilitation" character. On the other hand, one may judge a given person as better than another. Thus, to the extent that a judgment-produced perceptual set has ego-involvement, an affective property, and "barrier" or "facilitation" character it can be properly be thought of as a type of attitude.

Opinion.   An opinion is a tentative perceptual set toward points of view (cognitive organizations) or stimulus objects. An opinion is tentative in that the subject reserves the right to reverse himself and realizes that the cognitive organization or stimulus object he now perceives as a barrier may at a later time be viewed as a facilitation. Opinions play an important role in the thought process in that they represent cognitive summaries along the way. Ideas and constructs are organized during the constant process of cognitive exploration. Once such a summary emerges the individual may then "stand back" and appraise it. To the extent that the appraisal is tentative, nonfixed, it is an opinion.

As with all these "species terms," "opinion" is often used loosely. Often it is used synonymously with the generic term "attitude." Public opinion polling, for example, samples attitudes of which only some are actually opinions. Some are well-fixed prejudices, ideologies, beliefs, values, and judgments. In general, additional information concerning attitude strength will reveal whether the opinion measured is actually an opinion or some other type of attitude.

The popular meaning attached to opinion may take any one of three meanings. First, it may refer to the individual's tentative set itself. Second, it may refer to a point of view or set in the abstract; that is, a possibility to which a person may or may not subscribe. Third, it may have a "collective" meaning. This is to say that the term "public opinion" means an attitudinal consensus at a given time which, it is supposed, may shift at a later time.

Value. The term *value* is used in many ways, though it is never unrelated to the attitude construct. Historically, there have been two basic theoretical approaches to the study of value. One rests upon the assumption that worth resides in the stimulus object, that the stimulus object has an intrinsic worth or importance which is unrelated to man, the user of the stimulus object. The other rests upon the assumption that stimulus objects do not have intrinsic worth, that an object's worth is only a function of the ways humans perceive it. According to this position, a given stimulus object could be of great worth to a person at a particular time, though at another time he might perceive it as a barrier. The ancient story of King Midas is evidence that this second position is much more in line with human behavior and experience than the first and that the distinction we are pointing out is not something new. The second view holds that the worth an individual ascribes to an object is its value for that individual. Thus, a given object has as many values as there are humans with varying worth ascriptions to perceive it.

Field theory has made much of the value concept. While field theory denies neither the existence nor the importance of stimulus objects, it insists upon assessing their significance properly. As we have pointed out, the individual's ascription of worth to a stimulus object is, to use field terms, assigning it a valence. Thus, for a given individual, a stimulus object with which the individual is familiar and for whom the stimulus object has significance, has a positive or negative valence. As the term is ordinarily used in psychology, this field theoretical interpretation may be applied to the individual's most important life goals.

In a broad psychological sense, Newcomb (1950) speaks of dominant frames of reference which tie together one's attitudes. Such frames of reference are guide lines or maps used to evaluate experience and behavior as being in line or out of line with life goals. When we include the goals it is proper to speak of these as "value systems." And Allport *et al.* (1951) have theorized that there are six possible life values: theoretical, economic, aesthetic, social, political, and religious. A person develops a personality structure and content which uses one or another of these "life themes" as his dominant frame of reference. For example, the "political personality" is preoccupied with social power, and evaluates stimulus objects predominantly from a power standpoint. Or, put differently, for such a person what is most important in life? In this case the answer would be: the attainment of power over others and the use of the stimulus objects about him for this purpose.

The value concept in contemporary psychology is quite broad and often loosely used. The fact that it is used so much should suggest, however, that it does have substance. For our purposes, we propose two uses. First, a *value* is an attitude which is dominated by the individual's interpretation of the stimulus object's worth to him in the light of his goals. Second, a *value system* is an individual's over-all life aspiration (what he really wants to achieve) which on the one hand gives direction to his behavior, and on the other hand is a frame of reference by which the worth of stimulus objects may be judged. In the value system sense, it is an elaborate and articulated organization of attitudes.

MEASUREMENT OF ATTITUDES

A scientific construct is a theoretical description of the underlying dynamics of a natural phenomenon as a scientist or many scientists picture it. When a scientist gives a name to a dynamics which he envisages and believes is responsible for some event or class of events he is pressed to describe it quantitatively. This is to say that he must try to measure it. Until he can measure his construct its validity must be held suspect by the scientific community since quantified infomation is the criterion scientists agree upon as the final arbiter.

Attitudes, like other psychological variables, cannot be measured directly. Rather, attitudes are inferred upon the basis of direct measurements of behavior samples. This is no different from the procedure used in measuring a rat's learning. This may be done by using a maze or some other device to which the rat responds. Since the device is set and stable we can use it as a measuring instrument simply by counting the number of times the rat responds to it before it reaches a given criterion of response. Let us suppose that we have already arbitrarily decided that one errorless trial define learning for a rat in a given maze. On the first trial the rat makes 20 wrong turns, but after 25 trials it runs from the starting box to the goal box without making a single error. Our conclusion is that we have measured a process. The rat's behavior now is quite different from what it was when it was first introduced to the maze. This change in behavior is described and operationally defined by the errors counted on successive trials. In this case the underlying process has not been directly measured. Rather, since the present behavioral events are very different from those we first measured, we infer an underlying process—learning. These remarks are not to be taken as an appeal to reductionism; it may not be necessary to know the biochemical events which have accompanied the learning. We need not reduce the learning process to biochemistry in order to agree that learning has occurred. What was done was to take an unchanging physical device (comparable to a ruler), a maze, and measure changes in behavior in time by "applying" it to the behaving rat. These measurements were then used to describe the rat's learning. Since this device has been shown over and over to measure both validly and reliably, scientists will agree with the conclusion that learning, the modification of behavior as a function of experience, has been measured.

This logic also holds for attitude measurement. We infer that people have attitudes because of the stability of measurement of certain behavior samples. Usually, individuals are asked to state verbally how well they like given stimulus objects. Their verbal reports are taken as measurements of their attitudes toward these objects. Of course, such a report may be invalid if, for instance, the person does not want the interrogator to know how he feels about the stimulus object. However, verbal behavior is just as much behavior as is walking or hitting or anything else; and a human is usually capable of concealing his attitude if he wishes. This is no problem with the rat, except perhaps when in latent learning the rat does not demonstrate all that he has learned until a proper incentive is introduced. But, at least as far as we know, the rat does not deliberately try to confuse the observer.

Measurable Attributes

In measuring attitudes we must first consider what it is about attitudes we want to know. As we have seen, the attitude construct is very complex. In addition, an attitude has several attributes or parameters. If we can provide conditions under which we can be reasonably sure that subjects will respond accurately to an attitude measuring instrument, we are then in a position to design an instrument which will measure one or more attributes. Krech and Crutchfield (1948) have listed the following primary attributes.

Kind. This refers to the nature of the stimulus object. Actually, there is no really satisfactory classification into which all the objects toward which individuals have attitudes can be ordered. It is of some help, however, to classify attitude objects into common perceptual groupings, such as religion, war, politics, family, ethnic group, education. The nature of the stimulus object does not give us any information concerning the individual's attitudes, but it is one way of organizing attitudes into categories for purposes of communication and comparison. From the standpoint of measurement, this attribute designation is not powerful. It only places an object into a category, gives it a name. This type of measurement is referred to as *nominal*.

Content. The content of an attitude is its cognitive structure. The perceptions and cognitions one person has with reference to God may differ considerably from those of another person. Thus, as Krech and Crutchfield point out: ". . . when we attempt to measure the 'same' belief or attitude of different people, we are, strictly speaking, analyzing different beliefs and attitudes. However, we can, with some justification, treat these different beliefs as if they were the same." (1948, p. 159) While we infer that the valence an individual ascribes to a stimulus object is unique in its cognitive content, measured as an attitude it may appear to be no different from the attitude of another person. That is, two individuals may both be favorably disposed toward the Republican party, though for quite different reasons. In respect to the facilitation character of the Republican party which both individuals perceive, there is ostensible identity. Thus, from the standpoint of attitude measurement, content is commonly summarized as direction; that is, whether it is positive or negative toward the attitude object. This is only nominal measurement, but when combined with other attributes it becomes much more meaningful. In order to approach a true picture of attitude content it is necessary to study individual attitudes in depth. An excellent example of this was the study by Smith, Bruner, and White (1956) in which they studied in great detail the "reasons" lying behind the attitudes of ten different persons toward Russia. While direction is usually taken as an indication of content, it is to be remembered that there is much more to what lies behind an attitude than simply whether the stimulus object is perceived as a barrier or a facilitation.

Strength. Once we know an attitude's content we probably will want to obtain more refined information about it. One such additional bit of information is its *strength,* or how favorable or unfavorable the attitude is toward the stimulus object. In field theoretical terms this refers to the power of the valence. As we have defined attitude, it is a measurement of the barrier or facilitation strength of the individual's perception of the attitude object. With this information the attitude's content becomes much more meaningful since a more powerful type of information has been added. This amounts to ordinal measurement, and in some instances to interval measurement. The attitude's content may be compared for strength with another of the individual's attitudes, or it may be compared for strength with another individual's attitude toward the same object. For example, a subject designates from a long list of national groups five toward which he has favorable attitudes; he has a favorable attitude content toward each. Let us suppose now that he ranks these in order of preference as follows: English, French, Swiss, Italians, Germans. From this we know that he likes the English best, the French next best, and so on. Such a rank order is a "more than" or "less than" measurement but it fails to tell us how much more or how much less one group is preferred to another. With a more refined attitude measuring device, such as a Thurstone type scale, the "how much more or less" can be measured. This is measurement of the psychological interval between any two attitudes. It not only tells that the English are preferred by our subject to the French but how much more. In this way the magnitudes of different intervals may be compared. While, as pointed out in Chapter II, measurement of psychological intervals is neither as accurate nor as refined as the measurement of physical quantities, it provides important information concerning attitude strength and is the most powerful type of strength measurement we presently have.

Importance or Salience. This attribute is quite difficult to measure, although it is obvious that some attitudes are much more important to a person than others. For example, an artist may have some very strong, clearly delineated attitudes toward art forms and techniques, whereas he may be virtually without attitudes toward different religious doctrines. Other things equal, and within a social climate conducive to free conversation, the objects about which an individual talks most are the objects toward which he directs his most important attitudes. Unfortunately, it is seldom if ever possible to identify all of an individual's attitudes and then measure their relative saliencies. The Allport-Vernon-Lindzey approach to the measurement of values, mentioned earlier, attacks this problem. Many attitudes from six "life theses" are presented to the subject and he indicates which of these are most important. In general, strength and importance are highly correlated. It is just possible that strength and importance are virtually one and the same psychologically.

Clarity. This attribute refers to the sharpness or precision of the attitude, how precisely the object is perceived. It has been found that strong attitudes are both clear and important (Cooper, 1956). Thus, strength, clarity, and importance seem to be intimately interrelated, and it may actually be that they represent three ways of describing, or three aspects of, the same phenomenon.

Verifiability. Verifiability is not so much an attribute of an attitude as a statement about all or any of the attributes we have discussed. It refers to what are usually called reliability and validity. Reliability is a measurement of attitude consistency over a given period of time. Let us suppose that an attitude scale is administered to several subjects today, and that they are then ranked from high to low according to their scores. Some months later it is administered to the same subjects who in the meantime have had no occasion to think about or deal with the attitude object. Again they are ranked from high to low. If, when the two rankings are compared, no discrepancies are found in rank positions, we are justified in assuming that the scale is highly reliable; that is, that it is stable. On the other hand, suppose we already know our attitude measuring device to be reliable and we use it to measure the attitude of a given subject toward organized religion. Next month it is administered to the same subject and it is found that he scores very differently the second time. In this case, since we know the scale is reliable, we would be justified in concluding that the subject's attitude toward organized religion had changed.

Validity is a different aspect of verifiability. As Green has said, "If a scale is reliable . . . it measures some variable." (1954, p. 340) The problem of validity is to discover what it measures, or whether it measures what it is supposed to measure. As we have stressed before, there is no absolute way of determining whether the individual's behavior is a true indication of his attitude; in a given field circumstance he may deliberately behave in such a way as to throw the observer off the track. However, if we know this is not the case, we are justified in assuming validity of measurement at the time if the measuring instrument has face validity. That is, validity is built into the instrument by virtue of the types of statements used. Green suggests three types of attitude universes: elicited verbal attitudes, spontaneous verbal attitudes, and action attitudes. These are, respectively, what the person says his attitude is when asked, what the person says his attitude is when he feels like making a prediction regarding his future behavior with reference to some object, and what the individual actually does when confronted by the object. If all three of these are congruent, then an attitude scale which taps the first source (elicited verbal report) may be thought of as valid. As Green points out, the classic example of incongruence between verbal report and nonverbal behavior is LaPiere's account (1934) of his accompanying a Chinese couple in their travels across the United States. At the conclusion of their travels LaPiere wrote to the managers of the hotels, motels, and restaurants where they had stayed and eaten, inquiring as to whether or not they would accommodate Chinese. Over 90 per cent replied in the negative. While this was not a controlled study, it suggests the point that verbal reports of attitudes and actual behavior may not be congruent. This is not surprising since our own predictions of our future behavior are frequently out of line with what we actually do when the time comes. And on the other hand, simply because an innkeeper reported that he would not accept Chinese, but had in fact accepted them, is no reason to believe that his verbal report was not an accurate description of his attitude toward Chinese. Had the field been different (that is, had he not needed money, or not wanted to avoid an argument) he would no doubt have refused to accept them. This brings us back to our earlier point that knowledge of attitudes is helpful in predicting future behavior, but it is by no means a perfect basis for prediction. Unless we have knowledge of the individual's present psychological field, knowledge of his attitude toward an object may be of little help in understanding and predicting his behavior toward the object.

Attitude Scales

The many devices which have been developed for the measurement of attitudes are usually referred to as scales. Attitude scales are not as exact as are physical weight and distance measuring scales. Nevertheless, since they are designed to measure attitudes they may be properly thought of as scales, even though they are imperfect.

We have just discussed six attitude attributes which in one way or another are open to measurement. Since it is neither our purpose to describe a wide variety of measurement techniques, nor any one in detail, we will attend only to the types of scales that are used to measure content and strength. For convenience these may be classified as *simple ordinal scales* and *interval scales.*

Simple Ordinal Scales. There are three popular and much used types of simple ordinal scales: rating, ranking, and paired comparison. They require no statistical balancing or weighting to construct and the information they provide is only ordinal in nature. That is, the measurement magnitudes are only relative to each other; as, for example, a subject is found to prefer French to Italians and Italians to Germans. The stimulus objects are simply ordered (lined up) in terms of preference. These scales are very useful in psychological research, particularly exploratory research. Their simplicity of construction is one particular advantage. And when the investigator is concerned with identifying attitude content and relative strength, such simple scales may be used satisfactorily.

The *rating scale* provides a continuum for each attitude object, from strong approval or preference to strong disapproval or dislike. The subject checks a point along the continuum which indicates his attitude content (positive, neutral, or negative) and, if positive or negative, the degree or strength of the content. The further away from the central point (neutrality) the greater the strength. Figure 2 illustrates three items taken from a national attitude rating scale.

The subject who rated these national groups in terms of his preferences

A RATING SCALE

	Like Intensely	Like	Neutral	Dislike	Dislike Intensely
1. English					X
2. French		X			
3. Italians			X		

FIGURE 2

expressed neutrality toward Italians, indicating that he neither liked nor disliked them. This may be taken to mean that he really has no attitude toward Italians since there is neither content nor strength. He also indicated that he disliked the English more than he liked the French.

The rating scale is flexible and may be used for assessing attitudes toward virtually any type of stimulus object. Ordinal comparisons of attitude strength are possible if the attitude objects are of the same kind. There are two principal deficiencies in this type of scale. First, subjects often tend to "halo" all or most of the stimulus objects. That is, there is often a tendency to let the rating given to the first object influence the rating given to the second, and so forth. Second, subjects sometimes "feel guilty" in assigning an extremely high or an extremely low rating to any group. Thus, there is considerable question concerning the validity of rating scales as responded to by some subjects. The best validity check is to use another simple scale, such as the ranking type, in conjunction with a rating scale. If they do not agree for a given subject it is obvious that the measurement is invalid and should not be used.

The *ranking scale* also uses the assumption of a continuum and is truly an ordinal scale since it forces the subject to order the stimulus objects according to his attitude content and strength toward them. The stimulus objects may be presented to the subject in alphabetical order and the subject uses numbers from 1 to n to indicate his preferential attitudes toward them. Figure 3 is an example of such a scale.

A RATING SCALE

3	Austrians
4	English
1	French
5	Germans
2	Norwegians

FIGURE 3

The subject who ranked these stimulus objects in terms of preference placed the French first and the Germans last. Obviously, this does not provide certain important information. The subject may neither really like nor dislike any group on the list. For example, one subject commented after ranking a list of such groups, "I really like all these groups about the same but since you asked me to do this I tried my best." Obviously, this was a spurious measurement, since the validity of the rank order is doubtful, let alone the validity of psychological distances between one position and another. In the example shown in Figure 3 it might be that the subject likes the French more than any other group he knows but hates the Norwegians only a little less than the Austrians, and so on. Thus, there is no way of knowing the relative degrees of strength. Also, there is no way of knowing the content of attitudes as measured by this method except within the context of the stimulus objects included within the scale. Actually the subject may hate or like them all, and a rank procedure in and of itself will not provide such information. The best procedure for checking upon the ranking technique is, as with the rating technique, to use another simple scaling device in conjunction with it; and the reciprocal, the rating device, is a good one to use. If, for example, a subject indicates by way of a ranking scale that he dislikes Germans by listing them last, and also on a rating scale checks the "dislike intensely" position, there is little doubt that his attitude toward Germans is negative in content and of considerable strength. Still, this does not measure the exact "psychological distance" strength of any attitude.

The *paired-comparison* scale has certain advantages over the rating and ranking scales. The principal advantage is that it incorporates in one scale the basic features of the other two. In the first place, each stimulus object is rated against every other; and in the second place, each stimulus object is ranked above, the same as, or below every other. As is shown in Figure 4, the subject is asked to underline the preferred stimulus object in each pair. The frequency of preference for each stimulus object is then tabulated. The result is both a ranking and a rating. For a given subject, the stimulus objects are, by the paired-comparison method, ordered from high to low along a continuum and each is, in effect, rated at some point on the continuum. From the rating standpoint, the varying distances between the stimulus objects amount to the same thing as (or at least very close to) an interval scale.

The four national groups to be compared:
Austrians, Germans, Poles, Swedes

1. Austrians —— <u>Germans</u>
2. <u>Austrians</u> —— Poles
3. <u>Austrians</u> —— Swedes
4. <u>Germans</u> —— Poles
5. <u>Germans</u> —— Swedes
6. <u>Poles</u> —— Swedes

FIGURE 4

In the short example shown in Figure 4, four groups were comparatively paired. Notice that the Germans were underscored each time they appeared, and the Austrians, Poles, and Swedes were underscored only once each. Thus, the scores were: 3, 1, 1, 1, respectively. Ordinarily the pairs are randomized. Reliability is generally satisfactory. In one study in which 10 national groups were used, a test-retest reliability coefficient of .96 was found (Cooper and Pollock, 1959). The essential deficiency of the paired-comparison scaling technique is that it becomes quite bulky as the number of stimulus objects increases. For example, with 10 stimulus objects, there are 45 comparisons to make. Thus, there is a practical limit to the number of stimulus objects the device can handle.

Interval Scales. In Chapter II we used the development of an attitude scale to illustrate technique research. This was the Thurstone equal-appearing interval type scale. It will be recalled that the Bogardus social distance scale used seven statements which constituted a continuum from one extreme of social intimacy to another extreme of social ostracism. Subjects indicate the social distances they wish to maintain between themselves and various groups by checking the statements which most accurately describe such distances. However, since these distances are not necessarily psychologically equal, this rating scale's maximal power is only ordinal. The Thurstone technique is an attempt to increase measurement power from ordinal to interval. Since the Thurstone scale was described in Chapter II as an example of an interval type measurement device, only brief attention will be given here to interval scaling.

The Thurstone equal-appearing interval type scale is versatile and can be adapted to different types of stimulus material. For example, let us suppose we wish to develop a scale to measure attitudes toward the poll tax. First, we would assemble a large number of statements representing a wide range of attitudes toward the poll tax. These statements would then be placed at various positions along an eleven-point continuum (from extremely positive to extremely negative) by judges working independently. Those items that are scattered throughout the continuum, since the judges could not decide upon their meaning, are eliminated, and only those items upon which there is high positive agreement are retained. Each item that is qualified for retention is assigned a score, this being its median position on the continuum. For the final form, items are selected so that each area on the continuum will be represented. Subjects check those items that express their attitudes. The values of the items checked are summed and divided by the number of items checked. This is the subject's score and represents some position along the continuum.

Reliability of the Thurstone type scale is high. The chief advantage in its use lies in the fact that individual attitude shifts and attitude comparisons from one person to another can probably be made more adequately by interval than by ordinal measurement. At the same time, it is always a question as to whether or not the statements have the same meanings for the judges as for the subjects. It has been found, for instance, that subjects who are extremely favorable to some stimulus object tend to judge neutral statements about the object differently from the way subjects who are extremely unfavorable judge the same statements. For example, to the statement, "Organized religion has brought some benefits to civilization," an antireligious judge will usually respond by assigning it a favorable-to-religion meaning. A very religious person, on the other hand, will tend to interpret the same statement as unfavorable to religion. Thus, there are semantic problems which the equal-appearing interval technique is not perfectly equipped to handle. Perhaps the answer to this last problem is to use the subject himself as the judge or evaluator of the statement rather than assign the job of evaluation to others.

Another interval scale developed by Likert (1932) is a partial answer to the criticism of the Thurstone scale mentioned above. It should be noted that the Likert scale is not strictly an equal-appearing interval scale and may more properly be thought of as an internal consistency technique (McNemar, 1946). Items are retained only if they have high correlations with the total score. Thus, the subjects themselves select the items which mean strong approval or strong disapproval of the attitude object. However, judges are not used to place items along a continuum and thereby give the continuum equal intervals comparable to the equal inch intervals on a ruler. In one of these scales—attitudes toward the Negro, for example— the items retained were those that were used by subjects who were highly favorable and those who were highly unfavorable to the Negro. Thus, the statements constitute a continuum, but they fall at the extremes of the continuum. It is by Likert's method of scoring that subjects' attitudes may also fall in the middle of the distribution. The information this measurement procedure provides is actually ordinal; since one subject's score is greater or less than another's, the psychological distance between two scores cannot be designated.

Very briefly, the Likert type scale is constructed as follows. As with the Thurstone type scale, many statements pertaining to a given stimulus object are assembled and administered to a group of subjects who designate strong approval, approval, indecision, disapproval, or strong disapproval to each. These are assigned numerical values of 5, 4, 3, 2, and 1, respectively. Each subject's scale is scored and a correlation for each item with the total score is computed. Those items which have high correlations are retained. A surprisingly small number of highly correlated items needs to be retained. One of the original scales contained only twelve items.

The Likert type scale is tedious to construct, as is the Thurstone. If it has any advantage over the Thurstone type it probably lies in its method of scoring. Reliability coefficients are generally somewhat higher than the Thurstone. In one study, in fact, when Thurstone scales were administered and scored by both the Thurstone and Likert methods, it was found that the reliability coefficients were in the .80's by the former and in the .90's by the latter (Likert, Roslow, and Murphy, 1934).

In evaluation of the simple scaling methods and the two complex interval methods, the advantages of one over the other depend upon what the investigator is attempting to measure or identify. If he is simply interested in identifying persons who have strong attitudes toward given stimulus objects, the simple scales are quite adequate, particularly when used in pairs. On the other hand, if he is interested in measuring attitude change over a period of time, either for an individual or a group, there seem to be some advantages in using one or another of the more complex methods. Also, when but a single attitude object is to be assessed with the intention of providing information with reference to several of its attributes, then the use of a complex interval type scale is indicated.

Other Methods for the Assessment of Attitudes

Many times scaling procedures cannot be used to measure attitudes; and sometimes the type of information sought cannot be obtained by scales. One classification of nonscalar procedures has been developed by Deri *et al.* (1948). They have emphasized the diagnostic aspect of attitude measurement rather than the quantitative and have described techniques that may be used to assess attitude depth factors such as clarity or precision. As well, they recognize that there are reasons for wanting to know about the attitudes of persons who are not available for direct measurement. We will follow their outline in briefly referring to seven nonscalar attitude diagnostic techniques.

Direct Observation. Though direct observation without well-defined control criteria by which such observations are judged is of little or no value, with such controls valuable information may sometimes be obtained. Even provided with such controls, however, it is infrequent that a trained observer finds himself in a spontaneous situation which involves the outward display of important attitudes. One rare example of this is reported by Bettelheim (1947). During his internment in a German concentration camp during World War II he observed the behavior of different individuals and classifications of individuals under extreme stress. Later he described several important characteristics of attitude change as a function of these critical, stressful conditions.

Personal and Public Records. These may be used to assess the attitudes of contemporary public and historical figures. The method most frequently used is that of content analysis. This consists essentially of tabulating the frequency per unit of space with which a particular word, phrase, or statement of opinion is found in a document. Such information may then be interpreted as representative of particular attitudes or related to the occurrence of particular social events.

Performance.   Specific performances may be taken as attitude indexes. The investigation by LaPiere, referred to earlier, in which by letter he interrogated eating and lodging establishment proprietors which he and a Chinese couple had visited, is an example of the specific performance procedure. Observation of specific performances is useful for the purpose of comparing attitudes with behavior. This procedure often forcefully brings to one's attention the fact that attitudes determine social behavior only under certain field conditions.

Sociometry.   Sociometry can be used to assess certain social attitudes. Most frequently each member of a group is individually asked to name that person in the group he likes best or would choose as his leader. Such information may be useful in a wide variety of ways. For example, in industry it is frequently desirable to organize work crews on the basis of sociometric data in order to maximize interpersonal harmony. Sometimes classroom teachers use sociometric information in organizing seating arrangements and study groups.

Interviews.   Interviews may range in complexity from the simple "yes" or "no" type to very intensive "depth" questioning designed to reveal underlying personality dynamics responsible for manifest attitudes. In attitude survey work, one of the chief concerns must be with adequacy of sampling. Therefore, it is necessary to question a representative sample of respondents face to face. Even the national census cannot rely on mailed questionnaires. Interviewing becomes an expensive operation and there are many attendant matters which must be controlled carefully. For example, there have been instances in which hired interviewers concocted answers and did not conduct the assigned interviewing. Also, as the information becomes more complex, so does the problem of processing the data. In order to handle intensive interview information, content analyses must first be made, then these data transferred to some statistical design for interpretation. Even with these limitations, however, the interview is flexible and adaptable to a great variety of attitude measurement problems.

Pictorial Techniques.   These are among the most interesting attitude-assessing procedures. Although pictures may be used in many ways as stimulus materials, the usual procedure is to present the subject with a number of pictures of individuals and then ask him to select the one he likes most, or with whom he would least like to fraternize, depending upon the type of information desired. There are limitations to this technique since only pictures of visible groups can be used when the purpose is to measure relative group preferences. On the other hand, the individual's confidence in his ability to identify people as members of various ethnic and national groups may be nicely measured in this way.

Projective Techniques.   These have been used by several investigators for attitude assessment purposes, though with dubious success. Projective tests are designed to bring to light deep-seated desires and conflicts within the individual's personality. Some ambiguous stimulus object is presented to the subject and he is asked to explain what it means to him. His answer is then interpreted by the examiner in accordance with some theory of personality. Upon the assumption that many of an individual's attitudes are not known to him at a focally conscious level, some psychologists have used projective devices in an attempt to tease out such hidden, latent attitudes. For example, an individual may honestly believe that he likes Negroes, though at a latent level his attitude may be hostile. By interpretation of the symbolism of the subject's perception of the stimulus situation the examiner intends to reveal the existence or nonexistence of such latent attitudes.

In a study titled, "A projective method for the study of attitudes," Proshansky (1943) studied the attitudes of subjects toward labor by way of a method derived from the Murray Thematic Apperception Test (Morgan and Murray, 1935; Murray, 1938). Subjects were shown pictures, most of which involved something about laboring people in social conflict situations. They were asked to write brief descriptions of what they believed each picture represented. Judges then evaluated each description with reference to its attitude content toward labor. A high correlation was found between the projective information and results from a conventional attitude scale toward labor.

There is no doubt that at least some projective information may be used to identify attitudes, and that such information may be rich in detail of a qualitative, impressionistic, clinical nature. At the same time, the very qualitative nature of such information does not lend itself readily to quantitative manipulation and therefore must, at the present, be viewed as of questionable value from an empirical standpoint.

ATTITUDE CHANGE

One of the most important aspects of attitude theory is that of attitude change.

When an individual needs to achieve some goal he perceives goal-related stimulus objects, some old and some new, along the way to his goal. Once such attitudes are established they may persist throughout the remainder of the person's life, or they may change. They may change by becoming extinguished; or they may change in strength. They may even change in content. The violent anti-Semite may become pro-Jewish, and the pro-Negro may come to hate Negroes. The search for variables that are responsible for attitude changes has been going on for many years; and while this has been a very active research field the results, unfortunately, have not been completely enlightening.

Much of the research on attitude change has followed the standard experimental design. Many studies have used "matched control subjects," while many others have used the experimental subjects as their own controls. In the first instance, subjects' attitudes toward some stimulus object are measured. Each subject is then matched with another subject whose score is identical; thus, there are two "matched" groups. To one group (the experimental) is introduced some independent variable such as propaganda, an instructional movie, or a face-to-face experience with the stimulus object. Following this experience both the experimental and control subjects are again measured. Any measured attitude discrepancy between the experimental and control groups is taken to be the dependent variable and is viewed as a function of the independent variable. When the experimental subjects are used as their own controls, any shift in attitude which is revealed by measurement after the introduction of the independent variable is viewed as defining the dependent variable. Again, the dependent variable is considered to be a function of the introduced independent variable. In some experiments additional variables, such as age, have been used. In other studies the nature of the independent variable has been varied, as, for instance, comparing the effectiveness of oral versus written information.

The heterogeneity of the many studies which have been designed to identify independent variables that are effective in producing attitude change is so great that it is most difficult to compare one study with another. Thus, discrepancies between results can be accounted for in most cases only by speculation. Then, too, when some subjects shift their attitudes and others do not, following some experience, we are left with the question as to what additional variables are responsible for the discrepancy. For example, in one study (Murphy, Murphy, and Newcomb, 1937), a considerable increase in pacifist attitudes followed a college campus anti-war campaign. At the same time, some students reacted to the campaign by expressing even stronger militaristic attitudes.

At this time it is, of course, impossible precisely to designate the independent variables that are effective in producing attitude change. Upon the basis of the many studies dealing with this problem, however, some very tentative conclusions may be drawn. Unfortunately, these are mostly at an actuarial survey level and we are left to speculate and develop *post hoc* hypotheses. There is a vast research literature on the subject of attitude change and any attempt to review or evaluate it would take us far beyond our present interest. Briefly, however, from the standpoint of research design, these studies fall into two categories.

First, there are studies in which subjects are classified into categories such as age, sex, or educational background. Attitude change differences among categories, following some common experience such as viewing a propaganda film, are attributed to the differential effects of category membership. In this case, category membership is the independent variable. Second, there are studies which hold the group membership category constant (for example, all college freshmen) and the independent variable is some manipulated agent such as oral versus written propaganda.

One important independent variable which has been studied is chronological age. For example, it was found that systematic curricular information designed to change attitudes toward Negroes in a favorable direction produced different results at the high school and college age levels. Whereas high school students became more favorable toward Negroes after this specialized instruction, college students showed no reliable change (Schlorff, 1930). This finding lends itself to the *post hoc* hypothesis that as one grows older his attitudes become more rigid and less subject to modification as a function of new information.

Another example of this design may be seen in studies which have classified subjects according to the original strength of their attitudes. An analysis of one series of studies was summarized as follows:

Those whose initial attitude was more or less neutral showed the greatest change, and those initially neither neutral nor extreme changed their attitudes the least. This latter group of moderates, in fact, showed a relatively large percentage of negative changes, i.e., in the direction opposite to that of the appeal. Since those who were initially extreme in attitude tended to regress toward moderate positions on the same side of the neutral position, the implication to be applied by those interested in the changing of attitudes by such means is fairly clear; the most significant changes are likely to be made by those whose present position is near the middle of the scale. (Murphy, Murphy, and Newcomb, 1937, p. 966)

Let us turn now to the type of study which compares the effectiveness of different situational variables. It goes without saying that the subject's knowledge of a stimulus object is of unquestioned importance in both the development and change of his attitude. Knowledge is many things, however, and many things to many people. One person hates Negroes because he claims to know them; another likes and respects Negroes for the very same stated reason. The level, amount, nature of, and context in which the knowledge is provided are most crucial factors to be dealt with in any appraisal of the effectiveness of knowledge in changing attitudes. Many studies have been conducted in the attempt better to understand this variable. Most of them have dealt with the relative effectiveness of oral, written, and film methods of information presentation.

A good example of such a study was one conducted by Wilke (1934). The object of this experiment was to evaluate the relative effectiveness of direct speech, radio, and printed material in changing attitudes toward certain social issues. Four social issues were used as stimulus materials; one was, for instance, the need for birth control. Each college student subject's attitudes toward two of the four issues were measured. Then he was presented with propaganda on one of the issues by one of the three methods. His attitudes toward the issues were then measured again. The nonpropagandized issue was used as a control. Differences between amount of attitude shift under the two conditions were calculated. The results, not too surprisingly, were: greatest change followed the oral presentation; least change followed the written presentation. It must be remembered that a modification of the situational context, personality of the speaker, and many other variables could easily reverse these findings. Thus, these results are not to be taken as rule-of-thumb.

Another aspect of the knowledge variable has to do with first-hand versus second-hand information. One study which throws some light on this problem was conducted by the Information and Education Division of the U. S. War Department (1952). White officers and enlisted men were questioned about their feelings toward Negro troops before and after having served with them in combat. Table 1 presents the results which are most pertinent to the question of the effectiveness of first-hand information. It will be noted that both the whites who served with and did not serve with Negroes had quite similar attitudes toward Negroes before introduction of the independent variable (Negro platoons introduced). Then, most of those who served with Negroes changed their attitudes quite radically. This favorable shift, it will be noted, is in line with the general appraisal that Negro troops conducted themselves very well in combat. And these results are in line with an earlier study by Smith (1933), cited by Murphy, Murphy, and Newcomb (1937), in which a group of white adults spent two consecutive weekends in a Negro community visiting in homes, churches, a hospital, and becoming acquainted with many people in the community. Following this experience it was found that there was a decided positive shift in attitude toward Negroes. Several controls were used in this study which lend support to the validity of the findings and general conclusion that first-hand information is effective in producing attitude shifts.

Another variable which must be taken into consideration as a determiner of attitude change is *amount* of information. As one learns more about a stimulus, does his attitude toward the stimulus object change in a particular way? Obviously, the answer to this question is no. It is only when the amount of information is coupled with other independent variables that its determining role can be evaluated. Such other determining variables as type of information (positive or negative), and whether it is gained by way of the individual's own direct motivation or is imposed upon him must be known before its role in attitude shift can be understood or predicted, or the desired change can be controlled. For example, several naval preflight cadets who were required to play and study football for several hours each day over a long period of time came to detest football, a sport toward which they had previously held highly favorable attitudes.

Opinions of White Officers and Enlisted Men in Companies With Negro Platoons

"How did you feel at first about serving in a company that had white platoons and colored platoons?"

Response	White officers Per cent	White noncoms Per cent
1. Relatively unfavorable ("skeptical," "didn't like it," "thought it'd cause trouble," etc.)	64	64
2. Relatively favorable ("willing to try it," "made no difference," "didn't mind," etc.)	33	35
3. No answer	3	1

"How well did the colored soldiers in this company perform in combat?"

1. Not well at all	0	0
2. Not so well	0	1
3. Fairly well	16	17
4. Very well	84	81
5. Undecided	0	1

"With the same Army training and experience, how do you think colored troops compare with white troops as infantry soldiers?"

1. Not as good as white troops	5	4
2. Just the same as white troops	69	83
3. Better than white troops	17	9
4. No answer	9	4

"Has your feeling changed since having served in the same unit with colored soldiers?"

1. No, my feeling is still the same	16	21
2. Yes, have become more favorable toward them, ("feel more respect for them," "like them better," etc.)	77	77
3. No answer	7	2

TABLE I

"Some Army divisions have companies which include Negro and white platoons. How would you feel about it if your outfit was set up something like that?"

	Per cent of white enlisted men who answered:	
	"would dislike it very much."	"very good idea" or "fairly good idea."
1. Cross section of field force units which do not have colored platoons in white companies	62	18
2. Men in same division, but not in same regiment as colored troops	24	50
3. Men in same regiment, but not in same company as colored troops	20	66
4. Men in company with a Negro platoon	7	64

TABLE I (*continued*)

Under some conditions subjects claim to possess much more knowledge about stimulus objects toward which they have strong attitudes than they do in fact possess (Cooper and Michiels, 1952; Cooper, 1951, 1958). This seems to be especially true with reference to attitudes toward human groups; but with nonhuman stimulus objects, such as sports, there is a close correspondence between attitude content and strength as one variable (dependent), and amount of objective knowledge as the other variable (independent). An individual claims to have much information about sports he likes, and when he is tested for amount of objective information it is found that his estimation of his knowledge is highly accurate. Of course, there are reversals, as with the preflight cadets and football. When information is forced upon an individual his attitude toward the object of information may easily become strongly negative. Again, though, with reference to attitudes toward human groups, it was found that subjects claim to be able to recognize members of nonvisible groups toward which they are hostile, whereas they claim much less of such ability with reference to nonvisible groups toward which they are favorably disposed. To add to the picture of intervariable complexity it was also found that individuals who are high in authoritarianism claim exceptional ability in identifying members of both the groups they like and dislike.

While these studies cited deal tangentially with the amount of information variable, some studies have more directly dealt with it. Again, the *amount* of information has generalized importance for attitude change only when it is viewed in context with numerous other variables. An illustration of one of the few studies that was designed directly to assess the importance of this variable was conducted by Cherrington (1934). In this study, eleven different groups were exposed to varying amounts of information, by different methods, about international relations and the causes of war. The exposure ranged from a single lecture to a summer in Geneva hearing international figures explain their views. In general, those subjects who did the most intense studying made the least changes in their international attitudes. Subjects who were exposed to the least instruction made the greatest attitude shifts. It might be tentatively concluded that great amounts of pro and con information may lead either to "confusion" or to such an astute evaluation of the stimulus object that the subject is rendered incapable of moving from the attitude he has had all along.

How the information is presented is another factor of great importance in determining attitude change. Again, there is no rule-of-thumb that is best, since different individuals respond in various ways to information media. As has already been pointed out, the greatest attitude shifts followed face-to-face oral propaganda. The next in effectiveness was the same information conveyed by radio, and the printed presentation was least effective.

Another variable that is a corollary to the mode of presentation is the "personality" of the information source. There is no way to deal with this problem satisfactorily since a given personality is perceived in various ways by various people—with receptivity by some, neutrality by others and rejection by still others. At the same time, no one would deny the importance of personality impact in interpersonal relationships, and hence in effecting or failing to effect attitude change. Kroll (1934) conducted a study in an effort to appraise the effectiveness of different teachers in modifying the attitudes of high school seniors toward social issues. Teachers were identified as radical or conservative, and the students of these teachers were tested for social attitudes at the beginning and end of a semester course. Whereas the students of the radical teachers shifted their attitudes far to the left, the students of the conservative teachers shifted only slightly, and unreliably, in the conservative direction. While this is predictive of very little from the standpoint of the interrelationship of specified variables, the study does confirm the thesis that the personality nature of the person providing information has an important bearing upon the direction and strength of attitude change. For a thorough understanding of such changes as do occur it would be necessary to know a great deal about the phenomenological worlds of the individuals involved.

Majority opinion often plays an important role in modifying attitudes. Many individuals have strong needs to conform and tend to keep their attitudes in line with what they perceive majority opinion to be. This is particularly evident in modern advertising and propaganda campaigns. Advertisers have long known that the "band-wagon effect" is highly useful in developing favorable attitudes toward their products. This is the process of giving the impression that "everyone likes it." While such campaigns incorporate many other features there is no doubt that many people are swayed by the impression that the majority is favorably disposed toward a given stimulus object.

Another variable closely associated with majority opinion is "expertness." It is quite obvious that in many instances individuals develop and change their attitudes as functions of the prestige of the reputed expertness of the source of a verbalized comment. The problem here amounts to: "Who says what?" Several studies have dealt with prestige of authority as a variable in attitude modification. A good example of such studies is one conducted by Kelman and Hovland (1953). They used three different recorded speakers, each of whom delivered the same speech on the need for more lenient treatment of juvenile delinquents, before classes of senior high school students. One speaker was introduced as trustworthy and well-informed, another as untrustworthy and poorly informed, and the third as simply drawn from a studio audience with no further information provided about him. Thus, the intention was for the speakers to represent positive, negative, and neutral prestige levels. For our purposes the results may be summarized as follows: a) The greatest attitude change was produced by the trustworthy speaker and the least by the untrustworthy speaker. b) Three weeks later the students' attitudes were again measured; the finding was that agreement with the trustworthy speaker was now not as strong, and somewhat closer to the untrustworthy speaker. c) At the remeasurement session three weeks later, some of the subjects were reminded of the credibility of the speaker to whom they had listened. This "reinstatement" procedure had the effect of increasing the extent of agreement with the trustworthy speaker and decreasing agreement with the untrustworthy speaker. In fact, three weeks later the "reinstatement" subjects' attitudes were approximately the same as immediately after the original session. While at a common-sense level no one would deny the importance of prestige in changing attitudes, this study expressly demonstrates its effect and shows that it can be measured. Some studies have been designed to assess the relative effectiveness of prestige from majority opinion versus prestige from expert opinion. The general conclusion seems warranted that they are about equally effective as attitude modifiers.

Another variable which is known to be of great importance in attitude modification is *social climate*. While social climate is next to impossible to define explicitly, it may be thought of as the general warmth, congeniality and acceptability of the social organization. Probably the best known investigation of the effects of social climate on attitude change is that of Newcomb (1943). This was a lengthy, comprehensive, involved study, and no attempt to review it will be made here. There was one general finding, however, which has special relevance to the problem of social climate as an attitude determiner.

Over a period of four years, Newcomb studied patterns of attitude change of some 250 students in a small Eastern women's college. The social climate (local atmosphere) of the campus was decidedly liberal. Both the faculty and the student leaders were of decided liberal persuasions, the latter being chosen from among those who had tended to abandon their former conservatism and move in a liberal direction. Most of the girls had come to the college from relatively conservative homes; thus their attitudes tended to be conservative upon entering as freshmen. But, for the great majority, repeated attitude measurement over the four-year period revealed consistent shifts toward a much more liberal position. One of the questions which such findings raises is: How permanent are such attitude shifts? While there is no way of answering this question to our full satisfaction, a follow-up by Newcomb throws some light on it. In 1939 he sent attitude scales to all 1936, 1937, and 1938 graduates. The findings pointed to two tentative conclusions. First, those who had spent the most time in the college changed their attitudes most in a liberal direction. Second, those who had spent the most time in the college retained their attitude changes most persistently after leaving the college community. Thus, the general, though tentative, conclusion to be drawn seems to be that social climate is an important attitude modifier.

Studies by Coles (1953) and Plant (1958a, 1958b) have thrown additional light on the social climate variable. In these studies social ideology was measured by an authoritarianism scale. Coles found that the longer students remained in a liberal arts college the less authoritarian they became. He also discovered marked differences between different curriculum populations. Using the same measuring instrument, Plant found that those students who completed the four years were lower in authoritarianism than those who had entered college at the same time but had withdrawn before graduation. While there are attrition and group membership factors which could not be controlled in these studies, as was the case with the Newcomb study, these findings lend support to the general thesis that the social climate is an important factor in producing ideological shifts which, it is reasonable to believe, lie behind measurable attitudes.

As this brief review of a few attitude change studies indicates, there is much still to be learned. At the same time, some of the most important variables have been isolated. One of the most significant and important problems lying ahead centers around the task of studying the interrelationships of these variables. Up to the present time studies have, for the most part, been designed so as to try to hold all variables constant except the one under investigation. It is obvious that this is actually impossible. To design and conduct studies which can improve on this, and at the same time quantitatively interplay one or more variables with still others, is a stimulating challenge.

CHAPTER
XI

Prejudice

Psychologically, prejudice is an abstraction. But to the prejudiced person and the person toward whom prejudice is directed, it is anything but an abstraction—it is very real. Our interest here, of course, is in the psychological nature of prejudice; and thus we will direct our attention to prejudice as a psychological abstraction.

Individuals behave prejudicially in many ways, and toward many different stimulus objects. Despite great diversity in both behavior and target, psychologically there seems to be something in common from instance to instance, a basic syndrome that predisposes particular individuals to behave prejudicially.

Unless we discover and understand the psychological reasons that force or permit prejudicial behavior, we will remain ill-equipped to deal with it from the standpoint of scientific prediction and control. For instance, in some communities there are legal restraints which may be brought to bear upon those who behave prejudicially. While there are sound reasons to conclude that such restraints are often necessary and effective, there is no reason to believe that overt suppression of prejudicial behavior can automatically eliminate the underlying causes of prejudice.

THE PHENOMENA OF PREJUDICE

Like attitudes, prejudices are both positive and negative. Stimulus objects are valenced as either barriers or facilitations. For present purposes we will attend almost exclusively to negative prejudice, however, since more is known about it and since understanding negative prejudice must be considered as of greater social urgency. While it has been customary to assume that positive and negative attitudes lie at opposite poles on a continuum, there is reason to believe that they are not equally opposite psychologically. An individual's deep hatred for a given ethnic group is rooted in psychological variables which are in many respects different from the variables responsible for his love for some other group. In the first instance he may experience a need to keep certain people away, even perhaps to destroy them; while in the second instance he may experience feelings of affective identification. In support of this distinction there is some slight evidence which suggests that the emotional supports for positive and negative prejudices are different.

Approaches To The Study of Prejudice

Since prejudice develops from many sources, there is no single theory that is comprehensive. Allport (1950) has classified the more evident theoretical and methodological approaches to the study of prejudice into six categories, as shown in Figure 1.

Historical Approach. Various social philosophers who have been interested in prejudice have attempted to explain it in terms of long-range social changes, usually from the standpoint of power shifts. Karl Marx's theory of prejudice is a good example of the historical approach, although it is but one of several such theories. Any historical theory is based upon a survey of a sequence of social events; it interprets antecedent events as responsible for contemporary events. Thus, the present display of prejudice in a given community is traced back to some origin. While there is little psychological theory in most historical accounts as such, there is no question that an understanding of the broad social events that have gone before throws important light upon a present situation in which prejudice flourishes. No psychologist could possibly hope to understand the nature of anti-Semitism in Nazi Germany without taking into account the long flow of historical events which preceded Hitler's rise to power.

Socio-cultural Approach. Another approach to the problem of prejudice is socio-cultural, used principally by sociologists and anthropologists. This has much in common with the historical approach, differing from it essentially in that the socio-cultural approach finds some special aspects of the historically-determined social context as the causal agent of prejudice. Allport uses the sociological studies of urbanization as an example of this approach. The basic thesis is that humans have been forced to live in massive, tightly-knit socio-geographical units. This forces upon man a type of living which he hates. Since he cannot escape from it he fixes upon some group as being responsible for his unhappy state. The need to conform directs his aggression toward particular proscribed groups.

While there is no doubt about the value of this approach, it is insufficient as a total theory. For example, it does not explain why some majority members do not develop and employ prejudices against the groups toward which most prejudice is directed by other majority members.

Situational Approach. There are many theories that look to the contemporary social setting (sociological variables) to discover the prevailing attitudes, motivations, and tension-producing conditions which lie back of prejudice. One such theory looks to the level of frustration as a function of economic deprivation (Hovland and Sears, 1940). For example, lynchings of Negroes in the South increased during economic stress periods with the conclusion that these lynchings reflected the economically-caused frustrations of the whites. This situational approach has much to recommend it, even though it is not inclusive enough to account for more than a limited part of prejudice and hostile behavior. Its essential psychological deficiency lies in its inability to account for the fact that the same stimulus conditions which seem to produce prejudice in one person fail to produce it in another.

THEORETICAL AND METHODOLOGICAL APPROACHES TO THE STUDY OF THE CAUSES OF PREJUDICE.

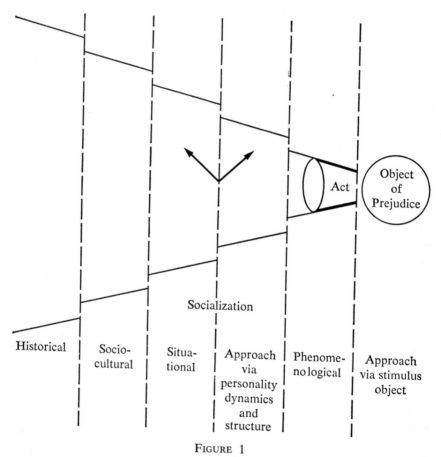

FIGURE 1

(From G. W. Allport, "Prejudice: a problem in psychological and social causation," *Journal of Social Issues,* Supplement Series, No. 4, 1950).

Psychodynamic Approach. The next approach emphasizes the importance of psychodynamics. One traditional theory holds that man has a native "dislike of the unlike." (Klineberg, 1954, p. 512; Giddings, 1896) It holds that this is a propensity common to all human personalities. Thus, prejudice is inevitable; man comes to identify with his own group, becomes ethnocentric, and cannot avoid hatred for and distrust of members of other groups. Another example of a psychodynamic theory is one which looks to frustration as the causal agent. Dollard (1937) has suggested that when an individual becomes frustrated he becomes aggressive, and this aggression may be directed either to the actual frustrating agent or displaced upon some nonretaliating agent. The latter is commonly known as scapegoating.

Of the first theory—dislike of the unlike—little can be said other than that there is no support for such a universal mechanism. Although there is no doubt that many individuals learn to identify with their own groups completely, and at the same time learn to distrust all others, this does not point to the existence of a universal mechanism. Rather, it describes only interpersonal behavior which sometimes occurs in conjunction with other psychodynamic properties such as anxiety. The frustration theory, too, describes the expression of prejudice, though there are many displays of prejudice which it cannot explain, and frustration does not, by any means, always lead to prejudice or to its expression.

Phenomenological Approach. Like the psychodynamic approach, this is a purely psychological approach. The phenomenal question, it will be recalled, is simply: What is there? That is, what does the individual perceive before and around him? It is assumed, of course, that what he perceives is determined primarily by antecedent conditions such as sociocultural and personality structure. These converge at a point in time and in a given situation; they focus through the "lens" (Figure 1) upon the stimulus object and tell the subject what is there. The act in which he then engages is a function of what he perceives the object to be and what he perceives the rest of the immediate situation to be.

While from a psychological point of view the phenomenological approach is indispensable, it must be used in conjunction with the other approaches in order to make its maximum contribution to our understanding of prejudice and prejudicial behavior. What the individual perceives is to him psychological fact. However, we must also search for both the antecedent and contemporary events which produced the perception.

Stimulus Object Approach. Finally, there have been attempts to approach the study of prejudice by way of the stimulus object itself. The significance of this approach is extremely difficult to appraise. On the one hand, we know that there are differences within and among various types of organizations—religious, national, political, ethnic, familial, economic. On the other hand, such differences are by no means apparent to all observers.

The "earned reputation" theory is an example of this approach. It holds that the way a group is perceived by others depends upon the way it has behaved in the past. Ordinarily, the reputation of a group is as much that which is attributed to it as that which it is in fact. This is not to say that all groups are blameless. Some have committed atrocities and are remembered for them; others are presently behaving in antisocial ways. In the first instance such groups may be suspect not for their present intentions or behavior, but because of the deeds of their ancestors. In the second, group members may be behaving in socially damaging ways because a more dominant group has created a social-physical situation which could elicit no other kind of behavior.

An examination of the earned reputation theory brings to light one of the most pernicious and stubborn characteristics of prejudice: the process of inferring that because a person is identified as belonging to a given group he is motivationally the same as all the other members of that group. This, of course, assumes a "good or bad" group nature which, again, is usually an ascription, not an empirical appraisal. While any individual must generalize in order to survive, overgeneralization is as dangerous as not to generalize at all. When a small child becomes angry with his playmate he often extends his wrath and abusive remarks to his playmate's entire family. On the other hand, we may learn by long experience that a given person is not to be trusted. This is not prejudice—it is not prejudgment; we have drawn this conclusion on the basis of empirical experience. If, however, we assume that since this single individual is not to be trusted, the other members of the group with which that person is identified are not to be trusted, without knowing anything more about them, we are prejudiced.

Obviously, an adequate theory of prejudice, one which will provide an understanding of prejudice and prejudicial behavior, must be multidimensional. It must view prejudice from all six perspectives which Allport has classified. Each of these approaches is important—perhaps equally important. Since, however, we are concerned here specifically with psychological involvements, we will limit ourselves in defining and examining prejudice to those variables which the individual brings most directly into his phenomenological focus upon the stimulus object.

Expression of Prejudice

Prejudice expresses itself in many ways. Broadly, the prejudiced person either directs his hostility outward or inward. While outward-directed hostility is by far the more common, there are instances of displacement upon self. In such an instance, the person finds no outside target upon which he feels it is safe to vent his feelings and resorts to some type of self-damage. Since these expressions seem to be rare and little relevant clinical information is available, we will confine our discussion to outward-directed hostility. As we know, outward-directed hostility is ubiquitous and of unlimited social importance.

Gordon Allport (1954a) has classified prejudicial expression into five categories which represent a hierarchy of expression intensity (ordinal measurement). From the standpoint of the person who expresses prejudice and those against whom prejudice is expressed, such measurement is no doubt somewhat inadequate. For the person against whom prejudice is expressed, to be avoided may be as psychologically painful as to be attacked physically. To the observer, however, there is a marked difference in expression intensity between the two displays. Allport's five levels of "prejudicial energy" place the expressions of prejudice into the following categories.

Antilocution. This is the practice of expressing antipathy toward other groups verbally. Among friends an individual may say that he feels Jews are responsible for the economic or moral distress of his community. This is not to say that an individual who operates at the antilocution level will not, under certain circumstances, operate more aggressively. However, many prejudiced people do not go beyond this level of hostility expression.

Avoidance. Here the particular feature is that of staying away or withdrawing from the prejudice target. This may result in considerable effort and expense to the prejudiced person. An anti-Negro family may sell their home and move elsewhere when a Negro purchases a home in their neighborhood. A parent may send his child to a private school rather than have him attend a public school that admits pupils from all ethnic groups.

Discrimination. At this level the prejudiced person takes active measures to remove the object of his prejudice rather than removing himself from preferred areas. Acts designed to exclude others from certain neighborhoods, employment, churches, beaches, swimming pools, hospitals and other such facilities are discriminatory.

In many places discrimination is legally sanctioned and enforced. In these instances it becomes an integral part of the cultural-political organization. In such institutionalized instances, conformity pressures are very great and prejudice modification is difficult and slow to effect.

Though this is graded at only the third level of intensity, there are many reasons to believe that it is the most resistant of all to change. Over relatively long periods of time, organized discriminatory practices have usually led to serious social disorganization.

Physical Attack. At this level prejudice is triggered off into acts of physical violence against the stimulus objects or their symbols. It may take the indirect form of desecration of a church or cemetery or the bombing of a home. Its direct form flows into physical attack upon the stimulus objects themselves. This may be directed toward particular individuals as, for example, in a lynching. Or, it may be "free floating" aggression against any person who is identified as belonging to the stimulus object group. The following quotation describes such an example.

FIREBOMB BURNS BUS OF "FREEDOM RIDERS"

BIRMINGHAM, Ala. (AP)—A bus was destroyed by a firebomb and several members of a racially mixed group of "freedom riders" were beaten as they tried to bring their test of bus station color barriers to Alabama Sunday. . . .

All told, 13 persons were taken to hospitals Sunday—12 for smoke inhalation suffered when someone in a crowd of angry white men threw a fire bomb into a stalled bus outside Anniston, and one for head cuts suffered at the hands of white men using pipes for clubs at a Birmingham bus station.

Two other persons required medical attention. None was hurt critically.

No arrests were made in Anniston or Birmingham.

. . . .

When the Greyhound bus arrived there, the bus station was closed and an angry crowd of about 200 white persons milled around.

Members of the crowd smashed some bus windows with bars and lengths of pipe.

The driver headed for Birmingham, but six miles outside Anniston the bus had a flat tire. A crowd of white men who had followed in cars sought to board it.

They were blocked by Alabama state investigator, Ell M. Cowling, who had ridden the bus from Atlanta on a tip.

A fire bomb—believed to have been a soft drink bottle containing gasoline—was thrown through a window of the bus. (*Palo Alto Times,* 1961, p. 1)

Extermination. This is any systematic program designed to eliminate great numbers, if not all, of the stimulus group. We do not include lynching here, even though it is extermination, since it is much less systematized and is directed only toward specific members of the target group. The history of the human species is replete with programs of mass extermination; and in every instance the underlying psychological dynamics may be shown to be prejudice. From Pharaoh's systematic plan to exterminate the Hebrews by ordering the midwives to kill all the newborn boys, to Hitler's systematic genocide, prejudice may be shown to be the psychological source of such human catastrophes.

Prejudice As A Human Emergence

In no other species is there behavior which fits the pattern of prejudicial expression, nor is there any evidence that species other than Homo sapiens experience prejudice. While there are analogues of prejudice among the infrahumans, nothing which meets the criteria of human prejudice has been identified.

Studies of territoriality in rats (Scott, 1958) reveal that members of a given colony will attack members from another colony that venture into their territory. In other words, an individual rat has little tolerance for members of its species other than those who belong to its own colony. Intra-species displays of hostility, however, are usually limited to bluffing; seldom is there mortal combat, since this would be nonadaptive and a disservice to species survival. Then, too, among the infrahumans there are no cultural traditions which hand down dislike for other species member groups from generation to generation. The type of communication which is necessary for the development and use of prejudice is found only at the human level. Prejudice, crude and destructive as it is, requires a very high level of conceptualization. Probably the only qualification the infrahumans, even the great apes, have for prejudicial experience and expression is emotionality (Hebb and Thompson, 1954).

Emotionally similar to man as is the chimpanzee, it is incapable of social group generalization and long-range anticipation of consequences, both of which are important ingredients of prejudice. Though chimpanzees display striking positive attachments for certain chimpanzees and long-lasting hostility toward others, these are directed toward individuals, not toward groups which are perceived as groups as a function of a conceptualized generality. It takes a very high level of intellectual capacity to be prejudiced, and it takes an unusual intellectual sophistication to avoid being prejudiced.

It is conceivable that at an early stage in the development of Homo sapiens, prejudice played an adaptive role. One reason to believe this is that according to organic evolution theory, psychological as well as structural characteristics have played some role in the adaptation history of each species. The time comes, of course, when certain of these characteristics play a nonadaptive role. If there is any substance to this postulate, modern prejudice is a case in point. The time has come when prejudice plays a nonadaptive role.

What adaptation role could prejudice have played in the early period of man's history? It is unreasonable to suppose that so unique and prevalent a capacity developed purely by chance. Granted, prejudicial experience and expression do not represent a trait, but rather a complex capacity that may have resulted from the coalescence of several trait-like capacities. With a primitive affective system and a new powerful intellectual system, Homo sapiens emerged as "an animal with a potent predisposition to the genesis of internal conflict and anxiety." (Freedman and Roe, 1958, p. 461) He now could categorize other humans, group them perceptually, and, over long periods of time and tradition, direct his anxiety-produced hostility toward certain of these groups. The individual did not have to experience directly the aggressive acts of another group. With language he could be told of the dangerous other group. This amounted to a warning system which, it may be supposed, many times prevented mutual destruction—at least, as long as it remained at the avoidance level.

This, it might be speculated, became man's social analogue of bluffing behavior, so adaptively important among many of the infrahumans. While there was ample intergroup slaughter, it is quite possible that this warning mechanism served a survival and hence evolutionarily adaptive role in man's early history. It may have given some groups time to consolidate and populate increasingly large territories. This line of theorizing seems plausible when we stop to think that man is a predatory animal, given to cannibalism even today under certain circumstances.

The coalescence to which we have referred provided the elaborate capacity to be prejudiced, and this warning system may have divided groups sufficiently to permit population survival and increase into modern times. Once the species was well established over wide land mass areas, this very capacity became a threat to the social organizations that would permit the most adequate social and individual development. According to this view, then, prejudice is atavistic; it is a detrimental vestige of an earlier evolutionary struggle to survive.

Since we are living in but a brief moment in the total history of man, we must not look to evolution as a mechanism which will bring about the elimination of prejudice. Evolution has worked slowly and it is just possible that man's organic evolution is over. This is not a teleological assertion. Man has now stabilized himself sufficiently and is so capable of understanding nature and his position in nature that whatever changes we may expect to experience as a species within foreseeable time will depend upon man's capacity for intelligently planned change. What we refer to, then, as non-organic social evolution—the only foreseeable change—will be a function of man's capacity for intelligent, planned social change.

It is obvious that one of man's most recent social developments is ethics. Man has provided himself with enough leisure to ponder his future as a living person, to conjure with the possibilities of life after death, to evaluate the significance of social reward and punishment. Many humans have learned to empathize and are able thereby to imagine their own feelings if placed in the situations of others. These capacities make an ethics possible. Man's capacity to condone and condemn is the capacity that makes prejudice obsolete.

Man is now in a position to eliminate an ancient, atavistic vestige; a vestigial capacity which may have permitted man's survival as a species but which now does a disservice to his survival. Man's great intellectual capacity permits him to understand the inadequacy of prejudice, even though biologically he still possesses the potential. It seems reasonable that just as an individual can learn to behave prejudicially, he can also learn to behave nonprejudicially. If this period in man's history is to be controlled more by what he can conceive and learn than by changes in genes, there is no reason to believe that he cannot reduce prejudice to a point where it will cease to plague him and render his existence precarious. We might conclude, then, that while the capacity for prejudicial experience and expression is humanly unique, it is a threat with which modern man must deal. The hopeful aspect of all this is that modern man is also in possession of capacities to control it, reduce it, and thereby increase the probability of his personally productive existence.

Definition of Prejudice

Prejudices are social attitudes which are developed before, in lieu of, or despite objective evidence. The principal criterion by which an attitude is judged to be prejudiced is that of objective evidence. Granted, there is no precise point along the continuum of objectivity-fantasy at which prejudice may be said to begin. However, prejudices are seldom difficult to identify, and the most readily available identifying feature is the ascription of characteristics to members of a group which, in fact, the group does not possess. An individual may reveal his prejudice toward Jews by such a statement as "Jews control all the banks." This statement is used as a reason for his negative attitude toward Jews. This is part of his derogatory perception of Jews and indicates that he perceives them as a barrier. But beyond this, Jews do not in fact control the banks; and individual differences among Jews are as great as will be found in any comparable type of grouping, a fact that this anti-Semite tacitly denied by his statement. In effect, his assertion was based upon fantasy-unreality. In contrast to this, the statement, "I do not like the Ku Klux Klan because it promotes prejudice and anti-democratic activities," describes a nonprejudicial attitude since it states a factual reason for the attitude. It does not prejudge the intentions of a group and then generalize to all those who are members. Prejudging the nature and intentions of persons who are identified as members of a given group is the hallmark of prejudice.

While we draw a distinction between reality and fantasy, thereby bringing into view the ancient metaphysical problem of reality, the distinction need not be dealt with metaphysically. There are objective facts, and there are phenomenological facts. Usually, but not always, these two types of facts coincide reasonably well. They coincide most frequently with reference to inanimate objects and less frequently with reference to living objects. Leaving out the flora, we observe an increasing discrepancy between the two as we move up the fauna phylogenetic scale. When we arrive at the human level the discrepancy is greatest. In human perception of other humans, what is an empirical, objective fact, as measured by a commonly-agreed-upon measuring instrument, is not perceived by some or many to be as the objective measuring instrument describes it. Distorted as a perception may be from the standpoint of objective measurement, however, to the individual who has the perception it is a *psychological fact*. This is what we have called the phenomenological world of the individual. If he perceives Jews as controlling the banks, then, even though this has been shown to be objectively untrue, this is to him fact; and it is a support for his attitude toward Jews. The person whose attitude is opposed to the KKK because he perceives it as a prejudice-promoting organization has a non-prejudicial attitude. In the latter instance, one of the person's goals is the elimination of prejudice; and the KKK represents an objective barrier to the achievement of this goal.

Social psychologists are not interested only in identifying prejudice, defining its meaning, and describing the ways it operates. They are, more than this, interested in identifying and understanding the variables responsible for its development in the individual.

THE PSYCHOLOGICAL NATURE OF PREJUDICED PERSONS

Some individuals may be called prejudice-prone. They seem to have personality systems which predispose them to develop and use prejudice. In this section we will briefly examine two aspects of this matter. First, we will look into certain personality characteristics that have been found to relate to prejudice development and use. Second, we will refer to certain characteristics of stimulus objects which have been suggested as rendering some relatively more vulnerable to prejudice than others.

Prejudice-Prone Personality

Since publication of *The Authoritarian Personality* by Adorno *et al.* in 1950, there has developed a vast research literature on the authoritarian syndrome, sometimes referred to as the prejudice-prone personality. Within our culture, social psychologists generally agree that this perspective of personality has been extremely helpful in the attempt to understand prejudice. Obviously, this theoretical position and research departure is but one way of viewing personality, and is not to be taken as a completely comprehensive theory of personality. Although there are many points of disagreement among psychologists concerning the dynamic properties of the authoritarian personality (Christie and Jahoda, 1954; Christie and Cook, 1958), it has produced the most unifying view of prejudice so far developed and is an essential part of the psychological approach to the study of prejudice.

Like all great ideas, this one goes far back into our sociocultural past. For a contemporary starting point, though, we may look to the writings of Eric Fromm (1941) and A. H. Maslow (1943a). The title of Fromm's book, *Escape from Freedom,* pinpoints the essence of the concept. There are those who are incapable of assuming critical personal-social responsibility: who, when freedom to choose is given them, seek out a leader to make their decisions for them and thereby escape from freedom. Freedom to some, then, is threatening. Now, in order to effect this escape and turn over personal-social responsibilities to some authority figure, the individual must be of a particular personality structure; and being of a particular personality structure, and bent on surrendering an important portion of his personal sovereignty to a more powerful person or symbol, he must engage in particular patterns of social behavior.

While not fully in detailed agreement with Fromm, Maslow described such persons as in possession of a "logic of their own which integrates all life for them in such a way as to make their actions not only understandable, but from their own point of view, quite justifiable and correct." (1943a, p. 402) Maslow then proceeds to identify the particular facets of such a personality. First of all, such a person sees his social world as a jungle in which most persons are dangerous and threatening. In effect, he can settle for some degree of security by surrendering his central sovereignty to another.

In some detail Maslow then designates the following items as those that characterize such a personality.

1. *The tendency to accept hierarchy:*   This is the view that all humans are arranged in an order of power—those above self (to be feared, resented, and admired), and below (to be scorned and dominated). The individual pictures himself as occupying some position on this hierarchy. Those whom he perceives as above him he perceives as powerful in all things and those below him as weak in all things. The social jungle in which he lives is composed, then, of the "good guys" (strong) and the "bad guys" (weak), since power is the measure of human social value. His attitude toward a powerful figure is ambivalent; there is both resentment and admiration. This has important consequences for the child-parent relationship. This view of the superior and the inferior, relative to self, leads to an overgeneralization. The superior are superior in all things, and the inferior are inferior in all things.

2. *Need for power:*   The authoritarian has an excessive need for personal power. The power he seeks is, in the last analysis, power over others. Thus he seeks prestige and status that show externally and that, as power, may be used ruthlessly. As Maslow puts it, "power, used in this way, is the symptomatic expression of thwarting of the person's basic needs for safety, belongingness, or love." (1943a, p. 405) Therefore, while the authoritarian seeks power directly and regards it as an end in itself, his "unconscious

striving" is for personal security, or escape from anxiety; and power is mistakenly perceived as security.

3. *Hostility, hatred, prejudice:* These are probably the best-known authoritarian characteristics. The object of hostility, hatred, or prejudice is chosen by accident. Hostility toward a given group is not a necessary attribute of authoritarianism; what is necessary is such feelings toward *some* group. Socially approved norms usually identify the object for the subject.

4. *Judging by "externals" rather than by "internals:"* The authoritarian takes external signs of strength, such as titles, family name, and similar symbols, as criteria for distinguishing the strong from the weak. The authoritarian's generalization of "all goodness" to the prestigeful may be accompanied by self-abasement since the strong are perceived as having the power to hurt him. To put it another way, the prestigeful, powerful figure is not identified for the actual qualities he possesses or does not possess; rather, the external label he wears is all that matters to the authoritarian.

5. *A single scale of value:* Since the authoritarian has difficulty in scaling others on anything but the power continuum, he tends to view the worth of all human endeavors as equal. He defers to the winning politician even though the devices the politician uses are immoral; since the politician is strong, he is "good." The top man in almost any other enterprise is similarly respected, not for the social or intrinsic value of his work, but for his power. The object of his respect is not the excellence of some human enterprise but the display of dominance in any human enterprise. Also, the authoritarian perceives anyone who bases his evaluations of others on the nature and quality of their work, as much as on their dominance in it, as a threatening person. This is perhaps because alien variables are introduced into his orderly, single value world.

6. *Kindness means weakness:* Authoritarians tend to regard kindness and generosity in interpersonal activities as signs of weakness. Harshness and displays of authority mean strength. Maslow's metaphor is that since the "authoritarian is actually living in a psychological jungle, then the lamb who trusts the lion, who believes what he says, who is kind to him, is in actuality an idiot, and such behavior is in actuality dangerous." (1943a, p. 407) Again, this is an indication of personal weakness; and indications of weakness are viewed by authoritarian personalities as degenerate.

7. *Others are tools to be used:* In that authoritarian personalities are prone to perceive others on a power scale, they need to use other humans as tools to effect their wishes. In extreme instances, authoritarians may regard their "inferiors" as not quite human, and are thus well-equipped to justify exploitation of "inferiors" and the miserable conditions forced upon "inferiors". On the other hand, those who are perceived as holding positions

of relative power are perceived, too, as tools. To accord deference and servility to powerful people is the authoritarian's calculated venture, his gamble in a bid for a more powerful, secure social position.

8. *The tendency toward sadism-masochism:* The authoritarian personality displays a strange juxtaposition of contradictory tendencies. On the one hand there is a need to hurt others, and on the other a need to hurt self. This is actually another way of stating the last point. There is a need to be harsh and cruel when dealing with those below, and self-debasing, even self-destructive, when dealing with those above. In Hitler's Germany it was the purpose of the thorough Nazi to punish the Jews and to die for the fatherland if necessary.

9. *The limitation of satisfaction:* The authoritarian's need for power is insatiable since the only complete "satisfaction would be power over everyone in the world and even then one would be threatened by the resentment of slaves, lack of friends, the inability to trust anyone, and of course also by the biological exigencies of life—illness, old age, and death itself." (1943a, p. 409) Thus satisfaction is not even theoretically possible for the authoritarian personality. Happiness is never of long duration since he is constantly ambitious for greater power and is usually, then, gripped by disquieting anxiety.

10. *Conflict and guilt feelings:* In our western culture there are many conflict-producing agencies. For example, there is militarism and there is the Christian ethic. The authoritarian must believe in physical power of which military force is the ultimate representation. If he has been reared in the Christian ethic he has been taught the immorality and wickedness of physical violence. Thus, such a person must behave in an authoritarian manner in order to gain power, but he harbors feelings of guilt about his behavior since it is contrary to divine teaching. In order to contain his guilt feelings he must develop or adopt a cognitive superstructure which makes excessive use of defense mechanisms, especially rationalization. It may be necessary, for instance, to conceive of certain minority groups as less than human. If this is possible, the harsh treatment he would accord them is in minimal conflict with the divine morality in which he believes and to which he defensively claims to subscribe.

Level of Authoritarianism. Several scales have been constructed to measure the individual's level of authoritarianism. One of the most widely used of these is the E-F Scale, in which E stands for "ethnocentrism" and F for "antidemocratic trends" "Fascism". (Gough, 1951) It consists of thirty statements which relate to the core characteristics of authoritarianism, and to which a subject responds by indicating his degree of agreement or disagreement with each statement. Although it is possible that some subjects deliberately dissemble in answering some items, it seems safe to say that subjects who score very high are authoritarian or antidemocratic in personality makeup. On the other hand, all those who score low are not necessarily democratic. Thus, it seems safest to avoid the temptation to think of authoritarianism in political terms and confine ourselves rather to a strict personality level interpretation.

The hypothesized relationship between authoritarianism and prejudice has been the subject of many investigations; and, as we have pointed out, a substantial relationship has been consistently found. It might be argued that since prejudicial experience and behavior potential are built into the authoritarian personality construct we should expect those who are highest in authoritarianism to have the most and strongest prejudices. While this is, in fact, what is expected, it is of considerable importance that measuring instruments have been constructed which are reasonably efficient in assessing the level of authoritarianism, and that there is a substantial correlation between amount of authoritarianism and amount of prejudice. For one thing, the tendency for personality to be organized into an authoritarian syndrome is measurable, and from such measures certain reasonably accurate predictions can be made. For another thing, such scales provide support for the theory which describes "the authoritarian personality." The psychological ingredients of authoritarianism cluster into a pattern very much like the pattern described by Maslow. If these personality ingredients are known, it then becomes feasible to study the genesis of the ingredients and the total pattern; the conditions, for example, which produce anxiety, power seeking, the perception of kindness as weakness.

Statistical studies of the E-F Scale reveal a high level of reliability; high enough, in fact, to convince some that the authoritarian syndrome is an indivisible organization. While this is an overstatement of the case, there is no doubt that authoritarianism can be measured, even though not perfectly. It should also be remembered that the level of authoritarianism, as measured by one or another of the standardized scales, is in part a function of the culture context and cannot be understood apart from it. In addition, the individual's level of authoritarianism does not predict the particular prejudice targets except, again, within the culture context. And, from the standpoint of prejudicial behavior, it is to be remembered that the individual's prejudice flows into overt action, at one or another of the levels we have described, only under particular field conditions. Thus, measurement of authoritarianism has its limitations. To repeat, the measurement of authoritarianism makes its chief contribution to the study of prejudice by adding to our knowledge of prejudice-prone personality dynamics (Christie and Cook, 1958).

In commenting on the authoritarian personality structure and prejudice, Christie says:

Those persons who view the world as threatening and unpredictable tend to be less tolerant of minority groups than those who are more at ease with their social environment. . . . The relationship between personality variables and ethnic prejudice is not simple, however. The dimension of authoritarianism apparently cuts across customary personality scales and scoring categories. Although it bears little relationship to more frequently utilized personality variables, it is closely related to certain items on personality inventories which reflect suspicion of others and hostility toward the world. (Christie, in Christie and Jahoda, 1954, p. 194)

Therefore, the authoritarian syndrome is not to be equated with any of the customary nosological categories of psychopathy. This supports the contention that in our culture those high in authoritarianism are not regarded as mentally ill; that, as a matter of fact, authoritarianism is looked upon as quite normal and is frequently an actual asset in social achievement. This indicates the extent to which feelings of prejudice and their evidence in behavior are integral parts of our socio-economic system. If by magic all authoritarian personalities were suddenly to become nonauthoritarian, it is possible that our socio-economic system would be thrown into such chaos that we would be forced drastically and quickly to overhaul our entire social organization in order to survive.

Relationships between Personality and Prejudice

We turn now to a brief review of some studies that have dealt with certain of the variables that theoretically compose the authoritarian personality syndrome as they relate to prejudice.

Anxiety. The authoritarian may be referred to as the "anxiety archtype." If he looks upon society as a jungle in which he must constantly struggle for existence, he must then be constantly anxious—anxious about being "stabbed in the back," about losing his social position, about gaining and consolidating a more secure social position. If this part of the theory is accurate, this critical feature should be measurable, and it should be possible to state on the basis of measurement whether or not in fact authoritarians are more anxious than nonauthoritarians.

A study by Siegel (1954) tested this assumption directly. He administered the E-F Scale and the Taylor Manifest Anxiety Scale (1951) to a sample of college students. The E-F Scale was used as the measure of authoritarianism, and the Taylor Manifest Anxiety Scale as the measure of anxiety. As predicted by the hypothesis, subjects who were high in authoritarianism tended also to be high in anxiety.

Another study which throws light on this apparent relationship between authoritarianism and anxiety made use of a less direct measure of anxiety (Cooper, 1956). In this study a modified E scale (Adorno *et al.,* 1950) was used to measure authoritarianism. Anxiety was measured by the number of statements a subject made with reference to anticipated loss or gain in his social status if he were to associate with members of groups he disliked and groups he liked. As expected, subjects who were high in authoritarianism expressed more prejudices than did the low authoritarian subjects. And, directly to the point, authoritarian subjects expressed significantly more status anxiety by indicating that they would lose or be prevented from gaining status if they associated with groups against which they held prejudices. As well, they indicated that they would gain status if they associated with groups they liked and respected. These findings also provide support for the contention that high authoritarian personality are excessively anxious.

In reviewing the authoritarian personality construct as described by Maslow, one of the prominent features, it will be remembered, was that authoritarians perceive a hierarchical world of power; there are those more powerful and those less powerful than themselves. Thus there are two, and only two, categories into which humans must be compulsively classified. Since such classification of humans is empirically impossible, the authoritarian is constantly forced to use a system of classification which is in constant conflict with the empirical world in which he lives. Since such categorizing is very difficult, and constantly in conflict with other features of his empirical world, he is excessively anxious about creating order in or imposing it upon his world. This is *his* order, not an order which adheres to any given esthetic, theological or scientific system.

This all means that the authoritarian is intolerant of ambiguity. That which is ambiguous is threatening since, being ambiguous, it does not easily fit into one or the other of the categories. At the social-personality level intolerance of ambiguity seems evident; it seems clear that authoritarians need to designate the "good guys" and the "bad guys." Some psychologists have gone further in this, however, and have postulated that intolerance of ambiguity is a general personality trait which is more than the need to order social variables. We will cite three studies which throw light on this postulate. The first uses nonsocial stimulus material, and the other two deal with human interaction variables.

In the first study (Fisher, 1951), subjects were briefly shown a drawing of a truncated pyramid, as shown in Figure 2. Immediately following this they were asked to draw it from memory. For both those high in prejudice and those low in prejudice, approximately 40 per cent drew the figure symmetrically, centering the middle rectangle. After four weeks the subjects were asked to draw it again from memory. This time 62 per cent of the highly-prejudiced subjects drew the figure symmetrically, whereas only 34 per cent of the low-in-prejudice subjects did so. Since it is known that those who are high in prejudice are also high in authoritarianism, the assumption

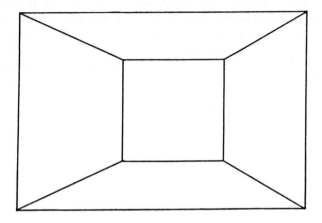

FIGURE 2

may be drawn that this finding points to a particular characteristic of the authoritarian syndrome—intolerance of ambiguity. This simple finding is at least a hint that the authoritarian is constantly driven to impose order upon the stimulus world (at least his memory of it), to organize the stimulus world neatly and into traditional forms. His compulsiveness to structure points to a constant anxiety, not limited to social stimuli alone. It seems reasonable to suppose that his compulsive structuring affords him a semblance of order which, in turn, tends to reduce his anxiety.

In another study of ambiguity (Siegel, 1954), a set of sixteen pictures and sixteen statements was used as stimulus materials. The pictures were selected at random from an out-of-date magazine. The statements were randomly selected from other sources. An example of the statements was, "I count only the sunny hours." Subjects were instructed to match as many statements with the pictures as they felt they could. The result was that high authoritarians matched significantly more statements with pictures than did those low in authoritarianism. This result is evidence, again, in support of the thesis that the authoritarian is compulsively driven to impose structure upon the stimulus world, to categorize, to reject ambiguity.

An even more direct approach to the relationship between authoritarianism and intolerance of ambiguity was made by O'Connor (1952). She used two scaling devices: one to measure ethnocentrism (authoritarianism) and the other to measure intolerance of ambiguity. The former was a modification of the E-Scale, and the latter was a scale which had been developed by Walk (1950) for the specific purpose of measuring intolerance of ambiguity by direct verbal means. Subjects' scores on the two instruments were correlated and a substantial positive relationship was found.

On the basis of findings of the type referred to here, there seems little doubt that the authoritarian personality syndrome incorporates the compulsive need to structure, the need to convert that which is ambiguous into something unambiguous. The authoritarian imposes a structural dimension upon his social world which permits him easily and clearly to perceive the strong and the weak. His attitude toward the weak is most often prejudicial in nature.

Still another aspect of anxiety is conformity. According to authoritarian personality theory, the authoritarian, who is, of course, anxiety-ridden, tends to conform, and as a matter of fact, in some areas to over-conform. For instance, in a study (Cooper, 1956) which used a California college student population sample, it was found that Mexicans, Negroes, and Filipinos were ranked lowest on a prejudice scale. The high and low E-Scale quartiles (N = 26 each) were studied for adherence to this prejudice pattern. Whereas the low-E-scoring subjects (low quartile) were evenly divided with reference to adherence to the pattern, only one of the high-scoring subjects failed to conform. On the basis of this finding it seems justifiable to refer to those who are high in authoritarianism as "antipathy conformers."

At this point in the development of a theory of prejudice, there is sufficient evidence to support the thesis that the authoritarian syndrome is prejudice-prone, and that such personalities are driven to prejudicial experience and behavior partly as a function of high levels of anxiety. This is not to argue that anxiety, *per se,* produces prejudice.

Social Perception. One of the ways the authoritarian personality structure may be viewed is from the standpoint of social perception. That is, authoritarians seem to ascribe special meanings and evaluations to social stimulus objects. The perception question is, What does the individual take his social stimulus world to mean? Is it accepting and friendly, or is it hostile and threatening? Essentially, as Maslow stresses, the authoritarian seems to perceive his social stimulus world as hostile and threatening. Studies which relate to the authoritarian's social perception, of course, overlap in many respects with studies of other authoritarian personality facets. However, there are many studies which throw important light on the unique nature of the authoritarian's social perception.

In one study (Scodel and Mussen, 1953), pairs of subjects, high and low in authoritarianism, were brought together to discuss a variety of topics. Following this they were asked to fill out the E-F Scale as they believed their partners would. Whereas the high authoritarians scored their low authoritarian partners about as high as themselves, the low authoritarians scored their high authoritarian partners as significantly higher than themselves. This study is representative of many that have pointed to the conclusion that high authoritarians are perceptually obtuse with reference to social stimuli. If this is so, as it seems to be, we would be drawn to conclude that those who are high in authoritarianism are lacking in empathy, are forced to perceive others principally in their own images. This may mean that since the high authoritarian perceives himself as a pawn in a power struggle, and feels constantly forced to improve his position, he is constrained to perceive others as engaged in the same business. This personality characteristic prevents the authoritarian from identifying fully with others and denies to him feelings of genuine warmth and affection.

Another aspect of the authoritarian's social perceptual process may be viewed from the standpoint of stimulus generalization. It has long been known that in the early stages of conditioning, subjects will respond to stimuli that are slightly different from the conditioning stimulus. As training proceeds, of course, subjects become more and more discriminating until finally they respond positively only to the specific conditioning stimulus. The tendency to generalize stimuli, the failure to note the refined features which distinguish one stimulus pattern from another, seems also to be more characteristic of some persons than others (Brown, Bilodeau and Baron, 1951). This tendency, it may be supposed, is important in prejudicial experience and behavior since, to be prejudiced, one must ascribe features and attributes to individuals on the basis of group affiliation rather than upon the basis of the empirical nature of individuals. Upon the assumption that authoritarian personality structure is prejudice-prone, and that over-generalization is a necessary part of prejudice, Arnhoff (1956) studied the possible relationship between authoritarianism and stimulus generalization. To measure authoritariansm he used the E-Scale, and to measure the degree of stimulus generalization he used a visual discrimination task. The correlation between the two variables was positive. Those subjects who were highest in authoritarianism tended to over-generalize.

Authoritarian perception has also been looked at from the standpoint of stereotypy. Katz and Braly conducted a study to discover if there is consistency in ascription of characteristics to various ethnic and national groups. Among other things, they found high agreement as to preferences for the groups; and they found that their subjects were in close agreement as to the characteristics which distinguished each group. For example, 84 per cent of their subjects agreed that Negroes (much disliked) are superstitious, and 78 per cent agreed that Germans (much liked) are scientifically minded. These investigators concluded that, "Racial prejudice is thus a generalized set of stereotypes of a high degree of consistency. . . ." (1947, p. 210)

While there is no doubt that prejudice involves stereotypic perception, the question might be asked whether or not the authoritarian personality structure, which we theorize is prejudice-prone, does in fact display an exaggerated tendency toward stereotypic perception. This is another question raised and examined in a study referred to earlier. Siegel (1954) hypothesized that those who are high in authoritarianism are also given to excessive stereotyping. The E-F Scale was used to measure authoritarianism and a picture-nationality matching test to measure stereotyping. In the stereotyping test it was assumed that the more national-ethnic names a subject assigns to pictures of persons, none of whom were members of any of the groups named, the greater would be his tendency to perceive stereotypically. The statement, "Yes, he looks like an Englishman, and he looks like a Jew," represents stereotyping since, in fact, there are no physical features which distinguish such groups. It is, rather, as Walter Lippmann (1922) put it, that "pictures in our heads" are used to represent certain groups, not the objective nature of the groups. As hypothesized, subjects who were highest in authoritarianism were found to be highest in stereotyping.

With reference to social perception, it is important to notice the intimacy of the two aspects we have just discussed—over-generalization and stereotyping. In order to stereotype it is necessary to generalize stimulus differences, to knock off the rough edges of stimulus objects. If these rough edges can be smoothed, then the "pictures in our heads" can be imposed upon objectively different stimulus objects, and they can all be perceived as essentially alike. Again, the anxiety archtype, the authoritarian, is forced by his jungle ideology to impose structure upon his environment so as to "spot the enemy." In order to do this he must overgeneralize and use readymade stereotypes. In so doing he engages in prejudging, and this, of course, is prejudice.

Prejudiced persons not only stereotype the objects of their prejudices but are relatively confident of the accuracy of their stereotyped perceptions. That is, they believe they can identify individuals as members of groups against which they direct prejudice. Several studies have been reported which deal with this problem and upon which this conclusion is drawn.

The conclusion from one of the first studies that dealt with this problem (Allport and Kramer, 1946) was that those who are anti-Semitic are able to identify pictures of Jews more accurately than those who are not anti-Semitic. These investigations attributed this finding to the probability that prejudiced persons learn to identify facial features and expressive behavior so well that they can easily spot the "enemy." The results of another study not only confirmed this finding but indicated, as well, that prejudiced persons have greater confidence in their identifications than do the nonprejudiced (Lindzey and Rogolsky, 1950). However, the contention that the prejudiced are in fact able to identify their targets with relatively great accuracy was seriously challenged (Elliott and Wittenberg, 1955). In a partial replication of these two studies, it was shown that those who were not anti-Semitic refused to commit themselves to as many identifications as the prejudiced subjects. Put differently, the prejudiced subjects checked "Don't know" less than the nonprejudiced. Therefore, since the prejudiced responded more often to the pictures, half of Jews and half of non-Jews, they made higher scores. When all subjects were instructed to respond to all the photographs, i.e., when there were no "Don't know" responses allowed—the prejudiced subjects were unable to identify the pictures with any greater accuracy than those who were not anti-Semitic. There are two important conclusions to be drawn from these studies. First, prejudiced persons are no more accurate in identifying pictures of members of a group against which they are prejudiced than are the nonprejudiced. Second, though the prejudiced are just as inaccurate as the nonprejudiced, they believe they are accurate. The fact that they go ahead and make identifications without hesitation supports this phenomenological fact. And there is little doubt that within the dynamics of prejudice what an individual believes to be true is *at least* as important as that which is empirically true.

One of the problems we must face in an attempt to examine the nature of the objects of prejudice and the perception of the objects, lies in the fact that there are "visible" groups and "nonvisible" groups. There is no doubt that certain classifications of humans are based upon external, evident physical characteristics. Although any such classification incorporates great variability, there is within it a central tendency which not only creates the classification but also permits relatively easy perception. For instance, skin pigmentation is used principally as the identification device that *creates* the Negro group in the United States. The ease and accuracy by which such group members may be identified are often used as prejudice supports. But, with the nonvisible groups or classifications this is not the case. There is, for example, no trait or characteristic which identifies Jews. Thus, it is necessary to create "out of thin air" an image of *the Jew* if one is to be prejudiced against Jews. The stimulus object must have substance, even though it is only phenomenologically substantive.

One study which dealt with this thesis directly made use of paper and pencil scaling rather than pictorial stimulus materials (Cooper, 1958). Subjects were asked first to rate sixteen visible and nonvisible groups on a preference scale. They were then asked to rate the same groups with reference to how easy or difficult it would be to recognize each. In addition, the E-F Scale was administered. There were three principal findings. First, subjects claimed relatively high ability to recognize members of the groups toward which they had expressed negative prejudice. On the other hand, they claimed relative inability to recognize members of the groups toward which their attitudes were strongly positive. This seems to mean that, for most, close ties and friendly association dissipate the tendency to overgeneralize and stereotype. Second, groups that are in fact relatively visible received, as expected, high ease of recognition scores from both those who were hostile and those who were favorable toward them. This finding points to the conclusion that objective visibility is by no means the sole determiner of hostility. That it may be an assistance, though, is suggested by the fact that subjects who were negatively prejudiced toward certain visible groups claimed a slightly greater recognition ability toward them than did the subjects who felt no such prejudices. Third, subjects who were high in authoritarianism, in contrast to those who were low in authoritarianism, claimed relatively high ability to recognize not only members of groups they disliked but, as well, members of groups they liked. Thus, we are led tentatively at least, to conclude that highly authoritarian personalities do tend to overgeneralize and stereotype, since to do otherwise would be to neglect both the threats and opportunities which are constantly present in their "social jungle."

These studies of recognizability of the stimulus objects of prejudiced persons lead to certain tentative conclusions. First, objective visibility is a definite support for prejudice; if a person may be easily recognized, he is all the more accessible as a target of the prejudice the subject already has. In addition, visibility makes it easier to establish human classifications, such as Negro and Oriental, and, by ghetto procedures, to perpetuate them. Without classifications, prejudice, positive or negative, could not exist. Second, it seems clear that those who are prejudiced feel that they perceive the objects of their prejudices easily and confidently. The perceived object is not a function of its empirical content; it is, rather, a function of a phenomenological content that is part of the beholder, not of the beheld. Third, the person who is high in authoritarianism is in possession of a phenomenological world which is at odds with the empirical world. Since, in effect, this is irrationality in the extreme, any approach to bringing his phenomenological world into closer articulation with the empirical world will require approaches that are seldom available in our culture.

Another perspective of the perceptual nature of prejudice has to do with the role of knowledge. In some respects this may be thought of as quite similar to the recognition variable. Belief in one's ability to recognize is actually one aspect of this more comprehensive variable; how much the individual believes he knows about the object of his prejudice.

On the basis of the findings of his classical study of the development of white children's prejudices toward Negroes, Horowitz (1947) concluded that "it seems that attitudes toward Negroes are now chiefly determined not by contact with Negroes, but by contact with the prevalent attitude toward Negroes." (p. 517) This conclusion was based in part upon the finding that children who had had opportunities to associate with "nice" Negroes were no less prejudiced than children who had never had such contacts. This finding suggests that objective knowledge probably plays a minor role in prejudice development, use, and modification. From the standpoint of the stereotypes used to describe and identify various groups, Katz and Braly

(1947) were led to conclude that the conception by the prejudiced of a group against which their prejudice is directed is "so stereotyped that it cannot be based upon actual contact with or direct knowledge of the groups in question." (p. 210) Again, then, the importance of the phenomenological nature of the stimulus object, in addition to its physically objective nature, seems apparent.

Some studies have been conducted with the specific intention of throwing more light on the role of knowledge in prejudice (Cooper, 1951; Cooper and Michiels, 1952). In one study subjects were asked to rank 30 alphabetically-listed national groups in terms of preference. Following this, they were asked to rank the same groups in terms of how much they knew about them. It was hypothesized that subjects would claim relatively great amounts of knowledge about both the groups they liked and those they disliked. For the groups toward which relative neutrality was indicated, it was hypothesized that subjects would claim very little knowledge. Whether or not such claims and denials of knowledge were in line with objective fact was not a concern of this study. The theoretical assumption was that either a feeling of positive identification or hostility would be backed up by a cognitive organization—a rationale. As expected, there was a strong tendency for subjects to claim relatively great knowledge about the groups toward which they expressed positive attitudes. While their claims to knowledge were not as great for the groups toward which they expressed hostility as toward the groups they liked, claimed knowledge about the disliked groups was great in comparison with claimed knowledge about the neutral groups. As a partial check on the cogency of the general hypothesis, the same procedure was used on a different classification of stimulus objects. It was postulated that the need to buttress positive and negative attitudes with a cognitive organization (knowledge) should be great when the stimulus objects are human, and little when the stimulus objects are nonhuman. The other stimulus object classification was sports. Again, subjects were asked to rank 30 alphabetically listed sports with reference to preference and to presumed knowledge. The results in this instance were quite different. Subjects claimed much knowledge about the sports they liked, less for those toward which they were neutral, and still less for the ones they liked least of all. Obviously, sports are quite different from human groupings, and we would not expect attitudes toward nonhuman objects, even though of great social significance, to be the same as attitudes toward human objects. This finding, it seems, points to one of the possible differences. Perhaps, it might be argued, humans feel less called upon to support their attitudes toward nonhuman objects by cognitively-contrived rationales. Toward nonhuman stimulus objects, there is obviously less ego-involvement.

A second study was conducted with the intention of discovering whether or not this apparent difference between attitudes toward human and non-human stimulus objects is a function of variance in ego-involvement. If attitudes toward highly ego-involved objects require relatively great cognitive support, then an assessment of the degree of correspondence of presumed and objective knowledge should help in answering the question. This second study replicated the first, but in addition it measured amounts of objective knowledge (demographic and sociographic) about the human groups and the sports. An objective test was constructed for each of the national groups and for each of the sports. The test results indicated that subjects did in fact overestimate their knowledge of the national groups they disliked, and also of the groups they liked. For the groups toward which they expressed neutrality, their estimates of knowledge about them were factually accurate. Subjects' estimates of their knowledge about sports were consistently accurate. The sports they liked, they knew much about, and vice versa. While there is no doubt that these studies have limitations, there is no question that persons who claim high levels of information about some national group should be expected to have reasonable amounts of this sort of information. Such a person should have picked up this type of information as a function of his apparent concern about the group. With reference to the sports, the objective test results indicated that subjects were highly accurate in estimating their objective levels of knowledge. We might suppose that the urgency for supporting one's liking or disliking for a nonhuman stimulus object classification is much less than the urgency to find and use a rationale for his human affinities and antipathies.

We might conjecture, then, that prejudicial attitudes are supported by rationalization. By definition, we have reserved the term "prejudice" for attitudes toward human stimulus objects. The findings we have just cited lend support to the validity of this reservation. We might suppose further that since a human is capable of "seeing himself mirrored" in other humans, he is capable of projecting his own feelings of guilt or greed, warmth or love, upon other humans. To do this in a systematic way he must have cognitive supports, reasons. Lacking these, he is capable of fabricating them, or borrowing them from others. While this involves us in personality problems we cannot deal with here, we are sure that in the matter of prejudice, psychological facts are at variance with objective facts. At a psychological level it is virtually useless to argue physical objectivity with a prejudiced person, since to him "truth" is what he perceives in his own phenomenological world.

Once these prejudicial social perceptions become fixed they are unusually resistant to change. One aspect of this may be seen from the standpoint of emotional defense. It has been found that when relatively strong prejudices are held up to threat or contradictions, subjects' galvanic skin responses are relatively great (Cooper and Singer, 1956; Cooper and

Siegel, 1956; Cooper and Pollock, 1959). (See Chapter II for details of these studies.) This finding was taken to point to several things, three of which were the following. First, it seems probable that since prejudicial attitudes are based upon fantasy and therefore cannot be supported adequately by reference to empirical evidence, individuals who must defend their prejudices find themselves faced with emergency. Emotionality is the common answer to emergency. Second, since prejudices seem to be emotionally supported, as perceptual sets they can probably be changed more effectively by emotional appeals than by cognitive-rational appeals. The prejudices themselves are but symptoms. The elimination of the tendency to be prejudiced requires basic personality reorganization. Otherwise, as one symptom is eliminated, another replaces it. It has been shown, for example, that an individual's prejudice toward a particular group may be altered without changing in the least his prejudices toward other groups (Murphy, Murphy and Newcomb, 1937). Third, positive prejudicial attitudes which are held up to contradiction seem to be supported by less emotion than negative ones. In view of this, we might suspect that while positive and negative prejudices may be loosely thought of as opposite, they should not be thought of as equally opposite in a psychological sense. The psychodynamics which produces hostile feelings does not, we suspect, require an equal amount of love to balance it off. As authoritarian personality theory holds, there is a need for the high authoritarian *only to identify* with those who are strong, and a need to sustain hostility feelings toward the weak.

We have used the authoritarian personality structure as the best single concept for organizing the many aspects of prejudicial experience and behavior. It should not be inferred, as it often is, that the high authoritarians are bad and that the low are good. What flows from high authoritarianism may often be bad, immoral, socially damaging. That this is often so cannot be denied. However, from the standpoint of science we must look at authoritarianism, the prejudice-prone personality, as a phenomenon to be understood. Then, if we evaluate the outcomes of such a personality structure, and evaluate such outcomes as bad, immoral and socially damaging, we need to look for the causes of its development.

PSYCHOLOGICAL CONTRIBUTIONS TO PREJUDICE REDUCTION

There is no accurate way of estimating how many people in the United States are prejudiced, to say nothing of the strength of their prejudices. In commenting on the prevalence of racial prejudice in the United States, Krech and Crutchfield (1948) conclude that at least 80 per cent are prejudiced. When asked, "Isn't every human being a little prejudiced?," Marie Jahoda replied in the following way: "No. Quite a number of people tested are free of prejudice against other groups or persons. Estimates for the United States vary from 10 per cent to 15 per cent of the adult population. My guess is that the true figure is nearer 10 per cent than 15." (1960, p. 94) At any rate, we must unhappily conclude that there is an excessive proportion of prejudiced people in the United States.

We have emphasized before that the prejudice a person manifests is a symptom of an underlying personality disturbance. This all points to the fact that prejudice is a "two-edged sword." One edge damages socially, the other personally. The approach to prejudice reduction, then, must be from two very broad positions. First, it is necessary to create social conditions that make the overt display of prejudice difficult and negatively reinforcing. Second, it is necessary to create conditions that reduce the chances of the development of prejudice-prone (authoritarian) personalities.

Social Prohibition of Prejudice Expression

Many psychologists have been interested in the problem of "unlearning" that which has already been learned. Their studies have consistently shown that what has been learned is lost or extinguished only when it has been unrewarded. A learned response can no longer be elicited if, after a relatively long period of time, it has not been accompanied by an appropriate reinforcement. There are many institutions and social organizations that provide positive reinforcement for prejudicial behavior. Any organization which excludes certain individuals on the basis of ethnic, national, religious, or other such affiliations or origins provides positive prejudice reinforcement to at least some of its members. In fact, the reason for such discriminatory exclusion is that of providing reinforcement. We must be careful to notice that not all who are members of such an organization derive this type of reinforcement, and perhaps most who do are unaware of it. A college student may become a member of a fraternity that by constitution excludes non-Caucasians and be unaware of its discriminatory rule. In fact, there may be some members who are working to eliminate this discriminatory clause from the fraternity constitution. However, there are other members who do derive benefit from identification with an organization which practices this sort of discrimination. Thus, such organizations may provide socially approved channels for the expression and continuity of prejudicial experience and behavior.

Individuals who are "born into" such organizations—families, fraternities, churches, neighborhoods—typically conform to the practices of such organizations without question, since identification with them has ego-protecting reinforcement value. In time, the individual is given "reasons" for the necessity of discrimination by the older members of the organization. This serves as a further reinforcement. The creation and success of any discriminatory organization lies in its "protection" against the intrusions of dangerous outsiders. Such an organization identifies the prejudice targets, creates anxiety about them, and provides socially approved techniques for anxiety containment. Thus, reinforcement is provided in two ways: through identification with the group, and through anxiety containment. This amounts to a closed, circular system which is self-reinforcing.

One way of reducing prejudicial behavior is by reducing the reinforcement value which accompanies it. Obviously, this is more easily said than done. However, if a democratically oriented society is seriously interested in the eventual elimination of prejudicial behavior it must, for one thing, approach the problem from the standpoint of psychological reinforcement. This is not to say that there are no other approaches. Rather, it only means that it is one of the essential *psychological* approaches, and an important element in a total multi-dimensional approach.

While we cannot concern ourselves here with a detailed societal program to deal with the reinforcement problem, we can propose a general solution. The solution we propose is nothing new, since many individuals and organizations have been actively engaged in attacking the problem of prejudice from this position for many years. Our purpose here is to point to its psychological significance and validity.

The general solution to the problem of reinforcement through social organization is that of removing support for those organizations that practice discrimination against individuals on bases of ethnic, national, religious, or other affiliations or origins. This would mean, from a practical standpoint, that those schools, churches, fraternal organizations, political clubs, neighborhoods, housing projects, and any other such social organizations that exclude persons from membership on these *fantasy* bases must be subjected to pressures which will either eliminate their discriminatory practices or eliminate the organizations. In the United States notable strides have recently been taken in this direction by way of legal sanctions against discriminatory practices in school systems, fraternal and military organizations, labor unions, and certain other groups that have long been guilty of fostering the display and perpetuation of prejudice.

Significant reduction in societal support for discriminatory organizations will lead to the elimination by such organizations of prejudicial practices, or the demise of such organizations. Without the reinforcement effects provided by social organizations, individuals are forced to deal with their anxieties realistically, and the expression of prejudicial behavior is thereby curtailed.

The dangers of reinforcement by discriminatory social organizations are obvious. This matter points to a specific psychological involvement in the global problem of prejudice, although it should be emphasized again this is but one aspect of the global problem. However, if we neglect it we miss something that is of basic significance in the learning and performance of all individuals, whether referring to prejudice or to any other socially significant human activity.

By reducing discriminatory organizational practices an additional benefit will accrue. It will be more difficult to stereotype various minority groups, even the visible groups. This will be the result of removing certain of the perceptual supports which make stereotyping and stimulus generalization so easy. If, for example, Negroes were afforded opportunities in employment, education, politics, recreation, housing, religion, and other such social dimensions equal to those enjoyed by the majority members of the community, they would be perceived as much less set apart and separate. Thus, the social prohibition of prejudicial expression, while a big order, goes directly to the problem of democratic living. Prejudicial practices are inimical to efficient democracy, and there are psychologically sound ways of dealing with them.

Avoiding the Development of Prejudice-Prone Personalities

Some individuals are without prejudice. From this fact it is probably safe to infer that the different social conditions under which personalities mature have much to do with the development of prejudice-prone and prejudice-free personality structures. We cannot rule out the possibility that genetic factors play a role in this aspect of personality development, but since nothing is actually known about it we must stay with the social-learning line of inquiry. It seems quite clear that the types of social interactions the child typically experiences leave long-lasting impressions, some of which principally determine the degree of his adult prejudice-proneness.

If it were known what types of social learning are propaedeutic to prejudice-free personality organization, it might then be possible to increase the opportunities for such learning with a view toward increasing the frequency of prejudice-free adult personalities. Obviously, this is no pat solution, and with the paucity of information presently at hand, it must be approached with extreme caution. In our enthusiasm over a small bit of highly promising data we would do well to realize that a panacea has not yet been found.

To date there are several studies which have shown a relationship between child-rearing practices and authoritarian personality structure development. One of these studies (Harris, Gough, and Martin, 1950) investigated the child-rearing practice beliefs of mothers as they related to the prejudices of their high-school age children. The beliefs of mothers of high- and low-prejudiced children were compared. The finding was that the mothers of those high in prejudice were themselves relatively high in rigidity and authoritarianism. On the other hand, it was found that the mothers of the children low in prejudice demonstrated attitudes of "good judgment" and tolerance with regard to child-rearing practices. In another study (Kates and Diab, 1955), attitudes of subjects about child-rearing were measured. It was found, as expected, that those who were high in authoritarianism expressed latent indication that as parents they would behave in a dominant, possessive way, would exercise excessive control over their children's activities, would be lacking in respect for their children's rights, and would subordinate the needs of their children to their own. In another investigation (Dickens and Hobart, 1959), mothers of high and low authoritarian subjects were interrogated with reference to their child-rearing beliefs. It was found that both parental dominance and parental indifference (ignoring the child) were significantly associated with high authoritarianism in children.

The way in which some of these results are stated may give the impression that we know more about what parents *should not do* than what they *should do* in order to promote the development of prejudice-free personalities in children. In a sense, this is true. However, the last of the three studies just reviewed gives a good hint: don't ignore the child. The converse of this is for the parent to involve himself in every item of his child's life; and, as we have seen, this is dominance and leads to authoritarianism. There is probably some middle course, but it must be very hard to steer. Without acute insight into and control over one's own needs and behavior, the balances between dominance and *laissez faire* freedom, cold objectivity and overindulgence, the parent is hard put, even knowing these facts about parent-child relationships, to stay on a central course. The typical authoritarian parent is most apt to reject findings of this sort, if he hears of them, and if he knows nothing of them he will, of course, rear his child in such a way that the probability of his child developing an authoritarian personality structure is very great. All that can be said at this point is that some knowledge is now at hand which throws light upon the independent variables that are responsible for the development of the prejudice-prone personality. How to convert this information into practical, positive programs for the development of prejudice-free personalities is another matter, and one about which we can now only make educated guesses.

From the standpoint of reducing the amount of prejudice we suggest again that a psychological contribution can be made from two broad standpoints. First, it is psychologically sound to foster a program that will deny general societal support for social organizations which discriminate against individuals on the bases of ethnic, national, religious, or other such affiliations or origins. This would reduce the reinforcement value afforded by identification with such groups. Second, there is now sufficient scientifically-developed information to support the thesis that children can be reared in ways that will produce relatively prejudice-free adult personalities. How these psychological contributions can be brought into societal effectiveness is a matter for action research by democratically-intentioned scientists supported by a democratically-intentioned laity.

REFERENCES

NOTE: *Numbers in parentheses refer to page numbers in this volume.*

ABEL, T. M. 1938. The influence of social facilitation on motor performance at different levels of intelligence. *Amer. J. of Psychol.*, 51, 379–389. (202, 282)

ADORNO, T. W., FRENKL-BRUNSWIK, E., LEVINSON, D. J., & SANFORD, R. N. 1950. *The authoritarian personality.* New York: Harper & Bros. (86, 276, 282)

ALEXANDRA, SISTER M. 1946. Personality adjustment and leadership. *Educ.*, 66, 584–590. (215)

ALLEE, W. C. 1951. *Cooperation among animals, with human implications.* New York: Abelard-Schuman, Ltd. (61)

ALLPORT, F. H. 1924. *Social psychology.* Boston: Houghton Mifflin Co. (4, 202)

ALLPORT, G. W. 1935. Attitudes. In Murchison, C. (ed.), *A handbook of social psychology,* Worcester: Clark University Press. (235, 236)

ALLPORT, G. W., & KRAMER, B. M. 1946. Some roots of prejudice. *J. of Psychol.*, 22, 9–39. (286)

ALLPORT, G. W., & POSTMAN, L. 1947. *The psychology of rumor.* New York: Henry Holt & Co., Inc. (132)

ALLPORT, G. W. 1950. Prejudice: A problem in psychological and social causation. *J. soc. Issues,* Supplement Series, No. 4. (267, 268)

ALLPORT, G. W., VERNON, P. E., & LINDZEY, G. 1951. *Study of values.* Boston: Houghton Mifflin Co. (243)

ALLPORT, G. W. 1954a. *The nature of prejudice.* Reading, Mass.: Addison-Wesley Publishing Co., Inc. (271)

ALLPORT, G. W. 1954b. The historical background of modern social psychology. In Lindzey, G. (ed.), *Handbook of social psychology.* Reading, Mass.: Addison-Wesley Publishing Co., Inc. (233, 241)

ANDERSON, J. E. 1946. Methods of child psychology. In Carmichael, L. (ed.), *Manual of child psychology.* New York: John Wiley & Sons, Inc. (80)

ARNHOFF, F. N. 1956. Ethnocentrism and stimulus generalization. *J. abnor. soc. Psychol.*, 53, 138–139. (285)

ASCH, S. E. 1952. *Social psychology.* Englewood Cliffs, N.J.: Prentice-Hall, Inc. (3, 5, 72, 78, 84)

ASCH, S. E. 1958. Effects of group pressure upon the modification and distortion of judgments. In Maccoby, E. E., Newcomb, T. M., & Hartley, E. L. (eds.), *Readings in social psychology,* 3rd ed. New York: Henry Holt & Co., Inc. (198)

BARKER, R. G. 1942. An experimental study in the resolution of conflict by children. In McNemar, Q., & Merrill, M. A. (eds.), *Studies in personality.* New York: McGraw-Hill Book Co., Inc. (112)

BARKER, R. G., DEMBO, T., LEWIN, K., & WRIGHT, M. E. 1947. Experimental studies of frustration in young children. In Newcomb, T. M., & Hartley, E. L. (eds.), *Readings in social psychology*. New York: Henry Holt & Co., Inc. (192)

BARTLETT, F. C. 1932. *Remembering*. Cambridge, England: Cambridge University Press. (132, 204)

BATESON, G. 1941. The frustration-aggression hypothesis and culture. *Psychol. Rev.*, 48, 350–355. (29)

BAVELES, A. 1942. Morale and the training of leaders. In Watson, G. B. (ed.), *Civilian Morale*. Boston: Houghton Mifflin Co. (217)

BEACH, F. A. 1945. Hormonal induction of responses in a rat with congenital absence of gonadal tissue. *Anatom. Rec.*, 92, 289–292. (51)

BEACH, F. A. 1950. The snark was a boojum. *Amer. Psychologist*, 5, 115–124. (95)

BEACH, F. A., & JAYNES, J. 1954. Effects of early experience upon the behavior of animals. *Psychol. Bull.*, 51, 239–263. (49)

BEACH, F. A. 1958. Normal sexual behavior in male rats isolated at fourteen days of age. *J. comp. physiol. Psychol.*, 51, 37–38. (38)

BEHANAN, K. T. 1948. Cultural diversity and world peace. In Dennis, W. (ed.), *Current trends in social psychology*. Pittsburgh: University of Pittsburgh Press. (170)

BENEDICT, R. 1934. *Patterns of culture*. Boston: Houghton Mifflin Co. (29)

BERLYNE, D. E. 1960. *Conflict, arousal, and curiosity*. New York: McGraw-Hill Book Co., Inc. (124)

BETTELHEIM, B. 1947. Individual and mass behavior in extreme situations. In Maccoby, E. E., Newcomb, T. M., & Hartley, E. L. (eds.), *Readings in social psychology*, 3rd ed. New York: Henry Holt & Co., Inc. (254)

BINDRA, D. 1959. *Motivation: A systematic reinterpretation*. New York: Ronald Press. (93)

BIRD, C. 1940. *Social psychology*. New York: D. Appleton-Century Co., Inc. (214)

BLUEMEL, C. S. 1950. *War, politics, and insanity*. Denver: World Press. (229)

BLUM, R. H. 1953. *The study of groups*. Human research unit No. 12., Fort Ord, California. (196)

BOGARDUS, E. S. 1925. Measuring social distance. *J. appl. Sociol.*, 9, 299–308. (17, 252)

BRELAND, K., & BRELAND, M. 1961. The misbehavior of organisms. *Amer. Psychologist*. 16, 681–684. (42)

BROADBENT, D. E. 1952. Speaking and listening simultaneously. *J. exp. Psychol.*, 43, 267–273. (124)

BROWN, J. F. 1936. *Psychology and the social order*. New York: McGraw-Hill Book Co., Inc. (75, 212)

BROWN, J. S., BILODEAU, E. A., & BARON, M. R. 1951. Bidirectional gradients in the strength of a generalized vocabulary response to stimuli on a visual-spatial dimension. *J. exp. Psychol.*, 41, 52–61. (285)

BROWN, R. 1958. *Words and things*. Glencoe, Ill.: The Free Press. (141, 143, 146, 156, 159, 160, 162)

BRUNER, J. S., MATTER, J., & PAPANEK, M. L. 1955. Breadth of learning as a function of drive level and mechanization. *Psychol. Rev.,* 62, 1–10. (116)

BRUNER, J. S., GOODNOW, J. J., & AUSTIN, G. A. 1956. *A study of thinking.* New York: John Wiley & Sons, Inc. (157, 169)

BUGELSKI, B. R. 1956. *The psychology of learning.* New York: Henry Holt & Co., Inc. (118)

BUTLER, R. A. 1954. Incentive conditions which influence visual exploration. *J. exp. Psychol.,* 48, 19–23. (104)

BUTLER, R. A., & HARLOW, H. F. 1954. Persistence of visual exploration in monkeys. *J. comp. physiol. Psychol.,* 47, 258–263. (66)

CALHOUN, J. B. 1948. Mortality and movement of brown rats (*Rattus norvigicus*) in artificially supersaturated populations. *J. of Wildlife Management,* 12, 167–172. (182)

CALHOUN, J. B. 1950. The study of wild animals under controlled conditions. *Annals of the New York Academy of Sciences,* 51, 1113–1122. (182)

CALHOUN, J. B. 1952. The social aspects of population dynamics. *J. of Mammalogy,* 33, 139–159. (182)

CALHOUN, J. B., & WEBB, W. L. 1953. Induced emigrations among small mammals. *Science,* 117, 358–360. (182, 183)

CANNON, W. B. 1939. *The wisdom of the body.* New York: W. W. Norton & Co., Inc. (96, 100)

CARMICHAEL, L. 1933. Origin and prenatal growth of behavior. In Murchison, C. A. (ed.), *A handbook of child psychology.* Worcester, Mass.: Clark University Press. (149)

CARPENTER, C. R. 1934. A field study of the behavior and social relations of howling monkeys. *Comp. psychol. Monog.,* 10, 1–168. (184)

CARPENTER, C. R. 1940. A field study in Siam of the behavior and social relations of the Gibbon (*Hylobates Lar*). *Comp. Psychol. Monog.,* 16, 1–212. (33)

CASSIRER, E. 1944. *An essay on man.* New York: Doubleday & Co., Inc. (147, 158)

CHERRINGTON, B. M. 1934. Methods of education in international attitudes. *Teach. Coll. Contrib. Educ.,* No. 595. (262)

CHILD, I. L. 1954. Socialization. In Lindzey, G. (ed.), *Handbook of social psychology.* Reading, Mass.: Addison-Wesley Publishing Co., Inc. (126, 130, 131)

CHRISTIE, R., & JAHODA, M. (eds.) 1954. *Studies in the scope and method of "the authoritarian personality."* Glencoe, Ill.: The Free Press. (277, 281)

CHRISTIE, R., & COOK, P. 1958. A guide to published literature relating to the authoritarian personality through 1956. *J. of Psychol.,* 45, 171–199. (230, 277, 281)

COLES, G. R. 1953. Ethnocentrism as related to college year. Unpublished. Master's Thesis, San Jose State College, San Jose, Calif. (264)

COLLIAS, N. E. 1951. Problems and principles of animal sociology. In Stone, C. P. (ed.), *Comparative psychology.* Englewood Cliffs, N.J.: Prentice-Hall, Inc. (55, 57, 210)

COMTE, A. 1875. *The positive polity.* Transl. London: Longmans, Green & Co. (1)

COOPER, J. B. 1942. An exploratory study of African lions. *Comp. psychol. Monog.*, 17, 1–48. (52, 56)

COOPER, J. B. 1944. A description of parturition in the domestic cat. *J. comp. Psychol.*, 37, 71–79. (50)

COOPER, J. B. 1951. Attitudes and presumed knowledge. *J. soc. Psychol.*, 34, 97–110. (261, 289)

COOPER, J. B., & MICHIELS, L. J. 1952. A study of attitudes as functions of objective knowledge. *J. soc. Psychol.*, 36, 59–71. (261, 289)

COOPER, J. B. 1955a. Psychological literature on the prevention of war. *Bull. of the research exchange on the prevention of war*, 3, 2–15. (63)

COOPER, J. B. 1955b. Perceptual organization as a function of politically oriented communication. *J. soc. Psychol.*, 41, 319–324. (84, 170)

COOPER, J. B. 1956. Mobility anticipation, class assignment and authoritarianism as field determinants of attitudes. *J. soc. Psychol.*, 43, 139–156. (86, 247, 282, 284)

COOPER, J. B., & SINGER, D. N. 1956. The role of emotion in prejudice. *J. soc. Psychol.*, 44, 241–247. (21, 291)

COOPER, J. B., & SIEGEL, H. E. 1956. The galvanic skin response as a measure of emotion in prejudice. *J. Psychol.*, 42, 149–155. (22, 291)

COOPER, J. B. 1958. Prejudicial attitudes and the identification of their stimulus objects: A phenomenological approach. *J. soc. Psychol.*, 48, 15–23. (261, 287)

COOPER, J. B. 1959. Emotion in prejudice. *Science*, 130, 314–318. (21)

COOPER, J. B., & POLLOCK, D. 1959. The identification of prejudicial attitudes by the galvanic skin response. *J. soc. Psychol.*, 50, 241–245. (22, 252, 291)

COOPER, J. B., & BLAIR, M. A. 1959. Parent evaluation as a determiner of ideoloy. *J. genet. Psychol.*, 94, 93–100. (28, 133)

COUTU, W. 1949. *Emergent human nature.* New York: Alfred A. Knopf, Inc. (240)

CRAWFORD, M. P. 1937. The cooperative solving of problems by young chimpanzees. *Comp. psychol. monog.*, 14, 1–88. (144)

CRAWFORD, M. P. 1941. The cooperative solving by chimpanzees of problems requiring serial responses to color cues. *J. soc. Psychol.*, 13, 259–280. (144)

CROCKETT, W. H. 1955. Emergent leadership in small, decision-making groups. *J. abnor. soc. Psychol.*, 51, 378–383. (219)

DARLING, F. F. 1937. *A herd of red deer.* London: Oxford University Press. (54)

DASHIELL, J. F. 1935. Experimental studies of the influence of social situations on the behavior of individual human adults. In Murchison, C. (ed.), *Handbook of social psychology.* Worcester, Mass.: Clark University Press. (197)

DEEVEY, E. S. 1960. The hare and the haruspex: a cautionary tale. *Amer. Scientist*, 48, 415–430. (62)

DENNIS, W. 1941. The significance of feral man. *Amer. J. of Psychol.*, 54, 425–432. (75)

DERI, S., DINNERSTEIN, D., HARDING, J., & PEPITONE, A. D. 1948. Techniques for the diagnosis and measurement of inter-group attitudes and behavior. *Psychol. Bull.*, 45, 248–271. (254)

DEUTSCHBERGER, P. 1947. The structure of dominance. *Amer. J. of Ortho-psychiat.*, 17, 343–351. (218)

DICKENS, S. L., & HOBART, C. 1959. Parental dominance and offspring ethno-centrism. *J. soc. Psychol.*, 49, 297–303. (207, 295)

DOBZHANSKY, T. 1960. The present evolution of man. *Sci. Amer.*, 203, 206–217. (64)

DOBZHANSKY, T. 1962. Genetics and equality. *Science*, 137, 112–115. (47)

DOLLARD, J. 1937. *Caste and class in a southern town.* New Haven: Yale University Press. (269)

DOLLARD, J., MILLER, N. E., DOOB, L. W., MOWRER, O. H., & SEARS, R. R. 1939. *Frustration and aggression.* New Haven: Yale University Press. (29)

DOOB, L. W. 1960. The effect of codability upon the afferent and efferent func-tioning of language. *J. soc. Psychol.*, 52, 3–16. (158)

DOUGLIS, M. B. 1948. Social factors influencing the hierarchies of small flocks of the domestic hen: Interactions between resident and part-time members of organized flocks. *Physiol. Zool.*, 21, 147–182. (210)

DRAKE, R. M. 1944. A study of leadership. *Character and Personality*, 12, 282–289. (215)

DUNLAP, K. 1946. *Religion: Its functions in human life.* New York: McGraw-Hill Book Co., Inc. (241)

EDWARDS, A. L. 1954. Experiments: Their planning and execution. In Lindzey, G. (ed.), *Handbook of social psychology.* Reading, Mass.: Addison-Wesley Publishing Co., Inc. (14)

ELLIOTT, D. N., & WITTENBERG, B. H. 1955. Accuracy of identification of Jewish and non-Jewish photographs. *J. abnor. soc. Psychol.*, 51, 339–341. (287)

FEARING, F. 1953. Toward a psychological theory of human communication. *J. Pers.*, 22, 71–88. (170)

FEARING, F. 1954. An examination of the conceptions of Benjamin Whorf in the light of theories of perception and cognition. In Hoijer, H. (ed.), *Lan-guage in culture.* Berkeley: University of California Press, 47–81. (168, 169)

FEATHER, N. T. 1959. Subjective probability and decision under uncertainty. *Psychol. Rev.*, 66, 150–164. (109)

FISHER, A. E. 1956. Maternal and sexual behavior induced by intracranial chemical stimulation. *Science*, 124, 228–229. (95)

FISHER, J. 1951. The memory process and certain psychosocial attitudes, with special reference to the law of pragnanz. *J. Pers.*, 19, 406–420. (282)

FRANK, J. D. 1941. Recent studies in the level of aspiration. *Psychol. Bull.*, 38, 218–226. (108)

FREEDMAN, D. G., KING, J. A., & ELLIOTT, O. 1961. Critical period in the social development of dogs. *Science*, 133, 1016–1017. (37)

FREEDMAN, L. Z., & ROE, A. 1958. Evolution and human behavior. In Roe, A., & Simpson, G. G. (eds.), *Behavior and Evolution.* New Haven: Yale Uni-versity Press. (274)

FREUD, S. 1916. *Leonardo da Vinci.* New York: Moffat, Yard & Co. (229)

FRIES, C. C. 1945. *Teaching and learning English as a foreign language.* Ann Arbor: University of Michigan Press. (157)

FRISCH, K. von 1950. *Bees; Their vision, chemical senses, and language.* Ithaca: Cornell University Press. (54, 141)

FROMM, E. 1941. *Escape from freedom.* New York: Rinehart & Co. (1927)

FULLER, J. L., & THOMPSON, W. R. 1960. *Behavior genetics.* New York: John Wiley & Sons, Inc. (36, 131)

GIBB, C. A. 1947. The principles and traits of leadership. *J. abnor. soc. Psychol.*, 42, 267–284. (226)

GIBB, C. A. 1954. Leadership. In Lindzey, G. (ed.), *Handbook of social psychology.* Reading, Mass.: Addison-Wesley Publishing Co., Inc. (224)

GIDDINGS, F. H. 1896. *The principles of sociology.* New York: The Macmillan Co. (269)

GINSBURG, N. 1960. Conditioned vocalization in the Budgerigar. *J. comp. physiol. Psychol.*, 53, 183–186. (147)

GLUECK, S., & GLUECK, E. 1950. *Unraveling juvenile delinquency.* Cambridge, Mass.: Harvard University Press. (136)

GOUGH, H. G. 1951. Studies of social intolerance: I. Some psychological and sociological correlates of anti-Semitism. *J. soc. Psychol.*, 33, 237–246. (280)

GRAY, P. H. 1960. Evidence that retinal flicker is not a necessary condition of imprinting. *Science,* 132, 1834–1835. (127)

GREEN, B. F. 1954. Attitude measurement. In Lindzey, G. (ed.), *Handbook of social psychology.* Reading, Mass.: Addison-Wesley Publishing Co., Inc. (248)

GRICE, G. R. 1948. An experimental test of the expectation theory of learning. *J. comp. physiol. Psychol.*, 41, 137–143. (124)

GRIFFITH, C. R. 1921. A comment on the psychology of the audience. *Psychol. Monog.*, 30, 36–47. (201)

GRUEN, E. W. 1945. Level of aspiration in relation to personality factors in adolescents. *Child Develop.*, 16, 181–188. (111)

GURNEE, H. 1937. Maze learning in the collective situation. *J. Psychol.*, 3, 437–443. (200)

HARE, A. P., Borgatta, E. F., & BALES, R. F. 1955. *Small groups.* New York: Alfred A. Knopf, Inc. (172)

HARLOW, H. F. 1953. Mice, monkeys, men, and motives. *Psychol. Rev.*, 60, 23–32. (99)

HARLOW, H. F., & MCCLEARN, G. E. 1954. Object discrimination learned by monkeys on the basis of manipulation motives. *J. comp. physiol. Psychol.*, 47, 73–76. (105)

HARLOW, H. F., & ZIMMERMAN, R. R. 1959. Affectional responses in the infant monkey. *Science,* 130, 421–431. (103, 128)

HARRIS, D. B., GOUGH, H. G., & MARTIN, W. E. 1950. Children's ethnic attitudes: II. Relationship to parental beliefs concerning child training. *Child Develop.*, 21, 169–181. (295)

HARTSHORNE, H., & MAY, M. A. 1928. *Studies in deceit.* New York: The Macmillan Co. (84)

HAYES, K., & HAYES, C. 1952. Imitation in a home-raised chimpanzee. *J. comp. physiol. Psychol.*, 45, 450–459. (52)

HAYTHORN, W., COUCH, A., HAEFNER, D., LANGHAM, P., & CARTER, L. 1956.

The effects of varying combinations of authoritarian and equalitarian leaders and followers. *J. abnor. soc. Psychol.*, 53, 210–219. (222)

HAYTHORN, W. 1958. The effects of varying combinations of authoritarian and equalitarian leaders and followers. In Maccoby, E. E., Newcomb, T. M., & Hartley, E. L. (eds.), *Readings in social psychology*. New York: Henry Holt & Co., Inc. (222)

HEBB, D. O. 1949. The organization of behavior. New York: John Wiley & Sons, Inc. (119)

HEBB, D. O., & THOMPSON, W. R. 1954. The social significance of animal studies. In Lindzey, G. (ed.), *Handbook of social psychology*. Reading, Mass.: Addison-Wesley Publishing Co., Inc. (52, 58, 145, 212, 273)

HEMPHILL, J. K. 1950. Relations between the size of the group and the behavior of "superior leaders." *J. soc. Psychol.*, 32, 11–22. (196)

HERSHER, L., MOORE, A. U., & RICHMOND, J. B. 1958. Effect of postpartum separation of mother and kid on maternal care in the domestic goat. *Science,* 128, 1342–1343. (128)

HESS, E. H. 1959. Imprinting. *Science*, 130, 133–141. (127, 128)

HESS, E. H. 1962. Ethology: An approach toward a complete analysis of behavior. In Brown, R., Galanter, E., Hess, E. H., & Mandler, G., *New directions in psychology*. New York: Holt, Rinehart, & Winston, Inc. (127)

HILGARD, E. R., & MARQUIS, D. G. 1940. *Conditioning and learning*. New York: Appleton-Century-Crofts, Inc. (121)

HIRSCH, J., & BOUDREAU, J. C. 1958. Studies in experimental behavior genetics: I. The heritability of phototaxis in a population of Drosophila melanogaster. *J. comp. physiol. Psychol.*, 51, 647–651. (94)

HIRSCH, J. 1959. Studies in experimental behavior genetics: II. Individual differences in geotaxis as a function of chromosome variations in synthesized Drosophila populations. *J. comp. physiol. Psychol.*, 52, 304–308. (94)

HIRSCHBERG, G., & GILLILAND, A. R. 1942. Parent-child relationships in attitude. *J. abnor. soc. Psychol.*, 37, 125–130. (133)

HOCKETT, C. F. 1954. Chinese versus English: An exploration of the Whorfian theses. In Hoijer, H. (ed.), *Language in Culture*. Berkeley: University of California Press, 106–123. (158)

HOCKETT, C. F. 1958. *A course in modern linguistics*. New York: The Macmillan Co. (157)

HOIJER, H. 1954. The Sapir-Whorf hypothesis. In Hoijer, H. (ed.), *Language in Culture*. Berkeley: University of California Press, 92–105. (168)

HOLLANDER, E. P., & WEBB, W. B. 1955. Leadership, followership, and friendship: An analysis of peer nominations. *J. abnor. soc. Psychol.*, 50, 163–167. (221)

HOLT, E. B. 1931. Animal drive and the learning process. New York: Henry Holt & Co., Inc. (74)

HOPPE, F. 1930. Erfolg und Misserfolg. *Psychol. Forsch*, 14, 1–62. (108)

HOROWITZ, E. L. 1936. The development of attitude toward the Negro. *Arch. Psychol.*, 28, No. 194. (134)

HOROWITZ, E. L. 1947. Development of attitude toward Negroes. In Newcomb, T. M., & Hartley, E. L. (eds.), *Readings in social psychology*. New York: Henry Holt & Co., Inc. (289)

HOVLAND, C. I., & SEARS, R. R. 1940. Minor studies of aggression: VI. Correlation of lynchings with economic indices. *J. Psychol.,* 9, 301–310. (269)

HUXLEY, J. 1961. Discussion of the paper: Hess, E. H. Effects of meprobamate on imprinting. In Birney, R. C., & Teevan, R. C., (eds.), *Instinct.* New York: D. Van Nostrand Co., Inc. (39)

INFO. & EDUC. DIV., U.S. WAR DEPT. 1952. Opinions about Negro infantry platoons in White companies of seven divisions. In Swanson, G. E., Newcomb, T. M., & Hartley, E. L. (eds.), *Readings in social psychology.* New York: Henry Holt & Co., Inc. (259)

ITARD, J. M. G. 1932. *The wild boy of Aveyron.* (tr. George and Muriel Humphrey). New York: The Century Co. (162)

JAHODA, M. 1960. What is prejudice? *Look Magazine,* May 24, p. 94. (292)

JAMES, W. 1890. *The principles of psychology.* (Vol. I.). New York: Henry Holt & Co., Inc. (106, 107)

JAMES, W. 1902. *The principles of psychology.* (Vol. II). New York: Henry Holt & Co., Inc. (164)

JENKINS, J. G. 1933. Instruction as a factor in "incidental" learning. *Amer. J. Psychol.,* 45, 471–477. (125)

JENKINS, W. O. 1947. A review of leadership studies with particular reference to military problems. *Psychol. Bull.,* 44, 54–79. (218)

JENNINGS, H. S. 1931. *The behavior of the lower organisms.* New York: Columbia University Press. (179)

JOHNSON, R. C., & ZARA, R. C. 1960. Relational learning in young children. *J. comp. physiol. Psychol.,* 53, 594–597. (123)

JONES, E. E. 1954. Authoritarianism as a determinant of first-impression formation. *J. Pers.,* 23, 107–127. (231)

JONES, F. N., & COOPER, J. B. 1938. The relation between college grades and classroom seating position. *J. of gen. Psychol.,* 18, 423–427. (201)

KATES, S. L., & DIAB, L. N. 1955. Authoritarian ideology and attitudes on parent-child relationships. *J. abnor. soc. Psychol.,* 51, 13–16. (295)

KATZ, D., & BRALY, K. W. 1947. Verbal stereotypes and racial prejudice. In Newcomb, T. M., & Hartley, E. L. (eds.), *Readings in social psychology.* New York: Henry Holt & Co., Inc. (285, 289)

KATZ, D. 1950. Survey techniques in the evaluation of morale. In Miller, J. G. (ed.), *Experiments in social process.* New York: McGraw-Hill Book Co., Inc. (15)

KELLER, H. 1954. *The story of my life.* New York: Doubleday & Co., Inc. (165, 166)

KELMAN, H. C., & HOVLAND, C. I. 1953. "Reinstatement" of the communicator in delayed measurement of opinion change. *J. abnor. soc. Psychol.,* 48, 327–335. (263)

KENDLER, H. H. 1947. An investigation of latent learning in a T-maze. *J. comp. physiol. Psychol.,* 40, 265–270. (124)

KENDLER, H. H., & MENCHER, H. C. 1948. The ability of rats to learn the location of food when motivated by thirst—an experimental reply to Leeper. *J. exp. Psychol.,* 38, 82–88. (124)

KING, J. A., & GURNEY, N. L. 1954. Effect of early social experience on adult aggressive behavior in C57BL/10 mice. *J. comp. physiol. Psychol.,* 47, 326–330. (38)

KINSEY, A. C., POMEROY, W. B., & MARTIN, C. E. 1948. *Sexual behavior in the human male.* Philadelphia: W. B. Saunders Co. (26)

KLINEBERG, OTTO 1954. *Social psychology.* New York: Henry Holt & Co., Inc. (29, 147, 170, 269)

KÖHLER, W. 1927. *The mentality of apes,* 2nd ed. New York: Harcourt, Brace & Co. (39)

KÖHLER, W. 1929. *Gestalt Psychology.* New York: Liveright Publishing Corp. (123)

KRECH, D., & CRUTCHFIELD, R. S. 1948. *Theory and problems of social psychology.* New York: McGraw-Hill Book Co., Inc. (6, 113, 133, 236, 240, 245, 246, 292)

KRECH, D., & CRUTCHFIELD, R. S. 1958. *Elements of psychology.* New York: Alfred A. Knopf, Inc. (114)

KROLL, A. 1934. The teacher's influence upon the social attitude of boys in the twelfth grade. *J. educ. Psychol.,* 25, 274–280. (262)

LA PIERE, R. T. 1934. Attitudes versus actions. *Soc. Forces,* 14, 230–237. (248, 255)

LASHLEY, K. S., & MCCARTHY, D. A. 1926. The survival of the maze habit after cerebellar injuries. *J. comp. Psychol.,* 6, 423–433. (92)

LAZARSFELD, P. F. 1952. The prognosis for international communications research. *Pub. opin. Quart.,* 16, 482–490. (170)

LEBON, G. 1897. *The crowd.* New York: The Macmillan Co. (3)

LEVINE, J., & BUTLER, J. 1952. Lecture versus group decision in changing behavior. *J. of appl. Psychol.,* 36, 29–33. (217)

LEWIN, K. 1935. *A dynamic theory of personality.* New York: McGraw-Hill Book Co., Inc. (7, 80, 81, 96, 106, 112)

LEWIN, K. 1936. *Principles of topological psychology.* New York: McGraw-Hill Book Co., Inc. (238, 239)

LEWIN, K. 1943. Defining the field at a given time. *Psychol. Rev.,* 50, 292–310. (109)

LEWIN, K., DEMBO, T., FESTINGER, L., & SEARS, P. S. 1944. Level of aspiration. In Hunt, J. McV. (ed.), *Personality and the behavior disorders.* New York: The Ronald Press Co. (87)

LEWIN, K. 1958. Group decision and social change. In Maccoby, E., Newcomb, T. M., & Hartley, E. (eds.), *Readings in social psychology.* New York: Henry Holt & Co., Inc. (19, 218)

LEWIS, O. 1951. *Life in a Mexican village.* Urbana, Ill.: University of Illinois Press. (29)

LIDDELL, H. S. 1942. The conditioned reflex. In Moss, F. A. (ed.), *Comparative Psychology.* Englewood Cliffs, N.J.: Prentice-Hall, Inc. (121–2)

LIKERT, R. 1932. A technique for the measurement of attitudes. *Arch. Psychol.,* 22, 1–55. (253)

LIKERT, R., ROSLOW, S., & MURPHY, G. 1934. A simple and reliable method of scoring the Thurstone attitude scales. *J. soc. Psychol.,* 5, 228–238. (254)

LINDESMITH, A. R., & STRAUSS, A. L. 1956. *Social psychology.* New York: The Dryden Press. (150, 166)

LINDZEY, G., & ROGOLSKY, S. 1950. Prejudice and identification of minority group membership. *J. abnor. soc. Psychol.,* 45, 37–53. (287)

LIPPMANN, W. 1922. *Public opinion.* New York: Harcourt, Brace & Co. (286)

LITTMAN, R. A. 1961. Psychology: The socially indifferent science. *Amer. Psychologist,* 16, 232–236. (78, 80)

LORENZ, K. Z. 1937. The companion in the birds' world. *The Auk,* 54, 245–273. (36)

LORENZ, K. 1952. *King Solomon's ring.* New York: Thomas Y. Crowell Co. (41, 52, 55, 61, 142)

LORGE, I., FOX, D., DAVITZ, J., & BREMER, M. 1958. A survey of studies contrasting the quality of group performance and individual performance, 1920–1957. *Psychol. Bull.,* 55, 337–372. (172, 173, 175, 191, 200)

MACCOBY, E. E., & HOLT, R. R. 1947. How surveys are made. In Newcomb, T. M., & Hartley, E. L. (eds.), *Readings in social psychology.* New York: Henry Holt & Co., Inc. (14)

MACFARLANE, D. A. 1930. The role of kinaesthesis in maze learning. *Univ. Calif. Publ. Psychol.,* 4, 277–305. (92)

MACKINNON, D. W. 1938. Violation of prohibitions. In Murray, H. A. (ed.), *Explorations in personality.* New York: Oxford University Press. (136, 206)

MACLEOD, R. B. 1947. The phenomenological approach to social psychology. *Psychol. Rev.,* 54, 193–210. (82)

MAETERLINCK, M. 1939. The life of the white ant. New York: Dodd, Mead & Co. (179)

MAIER, N. R. F., & SCHNEIRLA, T. C. 1935. *Principles of animal psychology.* New York: McGraw-Hill Book Co., Inc. (145)

MAIER, N. R. F. 1955. *Psychology in industry.* Boston: Houghton Mifflin Co. (195, 205)

MANDELBAUM, D. G. 1949. *Selected writings of Edward Sapir.* Berkeley: University of California Press. (168)

MANN, R. D. 1959. A review of the relationships between personality and performance in small groups. *Psychol. Bull.,* 56, 241–270. (172)

MASLOW, A. H. 1943a. The authoritarian character structure. *J. soc. Psychol.,* 18, 401–411. (277, 278, 279)

MASLOW, A. H. 1943b. A theory of human motivation. *Psychol. Rev.,* 50, 370–396. (40)

MAURER, K. M. 1947. Measuring leadership in college women by free association. *The Amer. Psychologist,* 2, 334. (215)

MCALLISTER, W. R. 1952. The spatial relation of irrelevant and relevant goal objects as a factor in simple selective learning. *J. comp. physiol. Psychol.,* 45, 531–537. (124)

MCCARTHY, D. 1946. Language development in children. In Carmichael, L. (ed.), *Manual of child psychology.* New York: John Wiley & Sons, Inc. (150)

MCCLELLAND, D. C., & APICELLA, F. S. 1945. A functional classification of verbal reactions to experimentally induced failure. *J. abnorm. soc. Psychol.,* 40, 376–390. (114)

McCLELLAND, D. C., ATKINSON, J. W., CLARK, R. A., & LOWELL, E. L. 1953. *The achievement motive*. New York: Appleton-Century-Crofts, Inc. (96, 102)

McDOUGALL, W. 1920. *The group mind*. New York: G. P. Putnam's Sons. (4)

McDOUGALL, W. 1931. *An introduction to social psychology*. London: Methuen & Co. (73, 74, 79, 95, 99, 105)

McNEMAR, Q. 1946. Opinion-attitude methodology. *Psychol. Bull.*, 43, 289–374. (253)

MEAD, M. 1928. *Coming of age in Samoa*. New York: William Morrow & Co., Inc. (29)

MELZACK, R. 1954. The genesis of emotional behavior: An experimental study of the dog. *J. comp. physiol. Psychol.*, 47, 166–168.

MILLER, N. E., & BUGELSKI, R. 1948. Minor studies of aggression: II. The influence of frustrations imposed by the in-group on attitudes expressed toward out-groups. *J. Psychol.*, 25, 437–452. (115)

MOLTZ, H. 1960. Imprinting: Empirical basis and theoretical significance. *Psychol. Bull.*, 57, 291–314. (128)

MORGAN, C. D., & MURRAY, H. A. 1935. A method for investigating fantasies. *Arch. Neurol. & Psychiat.*, 34, 289–306. (256)

MORGAN, C. L. 1894. *Comparative psychology*. New York: Charles Scribner's Sons. (47)

MORRISON, H. C. 1931. The practice of teaching in the secondary school. Chicago, Ill.: University of Chicago Press. (201)

MOWBRAY, G. H. 1952. Simultaneous vision and audition: The detection of elements missing from over-heard sequences. *J. exp. Psychol.*, 44, 292–300. (124)

MÜLLER, G. E., & PILZECKER, A. 1900. Experimentelle beiträge zur Lehre vom Gedächtniss. *Z. Psychol.*, 1, 1–288. (233)

MURPHY, G. 1954. Social motivation. In Lindzey, G. (ed.), *Handbook of social psychology*. Reading, Mass.: Addison-Wesley Publishing Co., Inc. (64)

MURPHY, G., & MURPHY, L. B. 1931. *Experimental social psychology*. New York: Harper & Bros. (201)

MURPHY, G., MURPHY, L. B., & NEWCOMB, T. M. 1937. *Experimental social psychology*. New York: Harper & Bros. (133, 234, 257, 258, 259, 291)

MURRAY, H. A. 1938. *Explorations in personality*. New York: Oxford University Press. (256)

NEWCOMB, T. M. 1943. *Personality and social change*. New York: The Dryden Press. (264)

NEWCOMB, T. M. 1950. *Social psychology*. New York: The Dryden Press. (6, 241, 243)

NEWMAN, S. S. 1933. Further experiments in phonetic symbolism. *Amer. J. Psychol.*, 45, 53–75. (160)

NISSEN, H. W. 1951. Social behavior in primates. In Stone, C. P. (ed.), *Comparative psychology*, 3rd Ed. New York: Prentice-Hall, Inc. (26, 39, 185)

O'CONNOR, P. 1952. Ethnocentrism, "intolerance of ambiguity", and abstract reasoning ability. *J. abnor. soc. Psychol.*, 47, 526–530. (284)

OSGOOD, C. E., SUCCI, G. J., & TANNENBAUM, P. H. 1957. *The measurement of meaning*. Urbana, Ill.: University of Illinois Press. (89)

PALO ALTO *Times.* 1961. "Freedom riders" (AP), 15 May, p. 1. (272)

PAVLOV, I. P. 1927. *Conditioned reflexes.* (tr. G. V. Anrep). London: Oxford University Press. (120)

PERLMUTTER, H. V., & DE MONTMOLLIN, G. 1952. Group learning of nonsense syllables. *J. abnor. soc. Psychol.,* 47, 762–769. (200)

PERLMUTTER, H. V. 1953. Group memory of meaningful material. *J. Psychol.,* 35, 361–370. (203, 204)

PETERSON, N. 1960. Control of behavior by presentation of an imprinted stimulus. *Science,* 132, 1395–1396. (128)

PFAFFMAN, C. 1960. The pleasures of sensation. *Pyschol. Rev.,* 67, 253–268. (102)

PIAGET, J. 1926. *The language and thought of the child.* New York: Harcourt, Brace & Co. (152)

PIGORS, P. 1935. *Leadership or domination.* Boston: Houghton Mifflin Co. (218)

PIGORS, P., & MYERS, C. A. 1951. *Personnel administration.* New York: McGraw-Hill Book Co., Inc. (205)

PLANT, W. T. 1958a. Changes in ethnocentrism associated with a four-year college experience. *J. educ. Psychol.,* 49, 162–165. (264)

PLANT, W. T. 1958b. Changes in ethnocentrism associated with a two-year college experience. *J. genet. Psychol.,* 92, 189–197.

POSTMAN, L., ADAMS, P. A., & PHILLIPS, L. W. 1955. Studies in incidental learning: II. The effects of association value and of the method of testing. *J. exp. Psychol.,* 49, 1–10. (125)

POSTMAN, L., & TOLMAN, E. C. 1959. Brunswik's probabilistic functionalism. In Koch, S. (ed.), *Psychology: A study of a science.* (Vol. I.) New York: McGraw-Hill Book Co., Inc. (130)

PROSHANSKY, H. M. 1943. A projective method for the study of attitude. *J. abnorm. soc. Psychol.,* 38, 383–395. (256)

QUEENER, E. L. 1951. *Introduction to social psychology.* New York: William Sloane Associates, Inc. (76)

RADKE, M., & SUTHERLAND, J. 1949. Children's concepts and attitudes about minority and majority American groups. *J. educ. Psychol.,* 40, 449–468. (134)

RANKIN, R. E., & CAMPBELL, D. T. 1955. Galvanic skin response to Negro and White experimenters. *J. abnorm. soc. Psychol.,* 51, 30–33. (24)

REDL, F. 1942. Group emotion and leadership. *Psychiatry,* 5, 573–596. (224)

RIECKEN, H. W., & HOMANS, G. C. 1954. Psychological aspects of social structure. In Lindzey, G. (ed.), *Handbook of social psychology.* Reading, Mass.: Addison-Wesley Publishing Co., Inc. (172, 174)

RILEY, D. A. 1958. The nature of the effective stimulus in animal discrimination learning: Transposition reconsidered. *Psychol. Rev.,* 65, 1–7. (123)

RITCHIE, B. F., AESCHLIMAN, B., & PIERCE, P. 1950. Studies in spatial learning. VIII. Place performance and the acquisition of place disposition. *J. comp. physiol. Psychol.,* 43, 73–85. (122)

ROETHLISBERGER, F. J., & DICKSON, W. J. 1939. *Management and the worker.* Cambridge, Mass.: Harvard University Press. (205)

ROMER, A. S. 1934. *Man and the vertebrates.* Chicago: University of Chicago Press. (43)

ROSENBLITH, J. F. 1949. A replication of 'Some roots of prejudice.' *J. abn. soc. Psychol.,* 44, 470–489. (134)

SAN FRANCISCO *Chronicle.* 1960. Letter to the editor, 8 September, p. 28. (153)

SAPIR, E. 1929. A study in phonetic symbolism. *J. exp. Psychol.,* 12, 225–239. (160)

SAWREY, W. L., CONGER, J. J., & TURRELL, E. S. 1956. An experimental investigation of the role of psychological factors in the production of gastric ulcers in rats. *J. comp. physiol. Psychol.,* 49, 457–461. (113)

SCHEERER, M. 1954. Cognitive theory. In Lindzey, G. (ed.), *Handbook of social psychology.* Reading, Mass.: Addison-Wesley Publishing Co., Inc. (159)

SCHLORFF, P. W. 1930. An experiment in the measurement and modification of racial attitudes in school children. Unpublished doctoral dissertation, New York University library. (258)

SCHMITT, O. H., McCULLOCH, W. S., OTTINGER, A. G., ROCHESTER, N., & TOMPKINS, H. E. 1956. Symposium: The design of machines to simulate the behavior of the human brain. *I. R. E. Transactions on Electronic Computers,* Vol. EC-5 (4), 240–255. (235)

SCHNEIRLA, T. C. 1946. Problems in the biopsychology of social organization. *J. abnorm. soc. Psychol.,* 41, 385–402. (31)

SCODEL, A., & MUSSEN, P. 1953. Social perceptions of authoritarians and non-authoritarians. *J. abnorm. soc. Psychol.,* 48, 181–184. (285)

SCOTT, J. P. 1958. *Animal behavior.* Chicago: University of Chicago Press. (36, 43, 45, 54, 62, 185, 210, 273)

SEARS, P. S. 1940. Levels of aspiration in academically successful and unsuccessful children. *J. abnorm. soc. Psychol.,* 35, 498–536. (110)

SEARS, R. R., MACCOBY, E. E., & LEVIN, H. 1957. *Patterns of child rearing.* Evanston, Ill.: Row, Peterson & Co. (135)

SHEFFIELD, F. D., WULFF, J. J., & BACKER, R. 1951. Reward value of copulation without sex drive reduction. *J. comp. physiol. Psychol.,* 44, 3–8. (105)

SHERIF, M., & SHERIF, C. W. 1956. *An outline of social psychology.* New York: Harper & Bros. (106)

SHOBEN, E. J. JR. 1949. The assessment of parental attitudes in relation to child adjustment. *Genet. psychol. Monog.,* 39, 101–148. (207)

SIEGEL, S. 1954. Certain determinants and correlates of authoritarianism. *Genet. psychol. Monog.,* 49, 187–229. (281, 283, 286)

SIEGEL, S. 1957. Level of aspiration and decision making. *Psychol. Rev.,* 64, 253–262. (87, 88)

SINGER, J. L., & GOLDMAN, G. D. 1954. Experimentally contrasted social atmospheres in group psychotherapy with chronic schizophrenics. *J. soc. Psychol.,* 40, 23–37. (218)

SMITH, F. T. 1933. *An experiment in modifying attitudes toward the Negro.* (cited in Murphy, Murphy and Newcomb; see reference above). New York: Teachers College, Columbia University, Ph.D. dissertation.

SMITH, M. B., BRUNER, J. S., & WHITE, R. W. 1956. *Opinions and personality.* New York: John Wiley & Sons, Inc. (83, 246)

SPENCE, K. W. 1937. The differential response in animals to stimuli varying within a single dimension. *Psychol. Rev.,* 44, 430–444. (123)

SPENCE, K. W., & LIPPITT, R. O. 1946. An experimental test of the sign-gestalt theory of trial and error learning. *J. exp. Psychol.,* 36, 491–502. (124)

STERLING, T. D. & ROSENTHAL, B. G. 1950. The relationship of changing leadership and followership in a group to the changing phases of group activity. *The Amer. Psychologist,* 5, 311. (219)

STOGDILL, R. M. 1948. Personal factors associated with leadership: A survey of the literature. *J. Psychol.,* 25, 35–71. (216)

STOGDILL, R. M. 1950. Leadership, membership, and organization. *Psychol. Bull.,* 47, 1–14. (175)

STOGDILL, R. M. 1959. *Individual behavior and group achievement.* New York: Oxford University Press. (172, 175)

STONE, R. C. 1946. Status and leadership in a combat fighter squadron. *Amer. J. Sociol.,* 51, 388–394. (218)

STRANGE, J. R. 1950. Latent learning under conditions of high motivation. *J. comp. physiol. Psychol.,* 43, 194–197. (124)

TAYLOR, D. W., & FAUST, W. L. 1952. Twenty questions: Efficiency in problem solving as a function of size of group. *J. exp. Psychol.,* 44, 360–368. (203)

TAYLOR, J. 1951. The relationship of anxiety to the conditioned eyelid response. *J. exp. Psychol.,* 41, 81–92. (281)

THIESSEN, D. D., & MCGAUGH, J. L. 1958. Conflict and curiosity in the rat. Unpublished symposium paper presented at the Western Psychological Association meeting, Monterey, California. (113)

THISTLETHWAITE, D. 1951. A critical review of latent learning and related experiments. *Psychol. Bull.,* 48, 97–129. (124)

THISTLETHWAITE, D. 1952. Conditions of irrelevant incentive learning. *J. comp. physiol. Psychol.,* 45, 517–525. (124)

THOMSON, J. A. 1935. *Biology.* New York: E. P. Dutton & Co., Inc. (178)

THORPE, W. H. 1956. *Learning and instinct in animals.* Cambridge, Mass.: Harvard University Press. (36)

THURSTONE, L. L., & CHAVE, E. J. 1929. *The measurement of attitudes.* Chicago: University of Chicago Press. (17, 252)

TINBERGEN, N. 1953. Social behavior in animals. New York: John Wiley & Sons, Inc. (41, 51, 57)

TITUS, E. H., & HOLLANDER, E. P. 1957. The California F. Scale in Psychological research: 1950–1955. *Psychol. Bull.,* 54, 47–64. (230)

TOLMAN, E. C. 1925. Purpose and cognition; the determiners of animal learning. *Psychol. Rev.,* 32, 285–297. (99)

TOLMAN, E. C. 1932. *Purposive behavior in animals and men.* New York: The Century Co. (96, 120)

TRYON, R. C. 1942. Individual differences. In Moss, F. A. (ed.), *Comparative psychology.* Englewood Cliffs, N.J.: Prentice-Hall, Inc. (44)

VALENSTEIN, E. S., RISS, W., & YOUNG, W. C. 1955. Experiential and genetic factors in the organization of sexual behavior in male guinea pigs. *J. comp. physiol. Psychol.,* 48, 397–403. (38)

WALK, R. D. 1950. Perception and personality: A pretest. Unpublished study, Social Relations Library, Harvard University (284)

WARDEN, C. J. 1931. *Animal motivation: experimental studies on the albino rat.* New York: Columbia University Press. (183)

WASHBURN, S. L., & AVIS, V. 1958. Evolution of human behavior. In Roe, A., & Simpson, G. G. (eds.), *Behavior and evolution.* New Haven: Yale University Press. (147)

WASHBURN, S. L., & DEVORE, I. 1961. The social life of baboons. *Sci. Amer.,* 204, No. 6, 62–71. (187)

WATSON, J. B. 1930. *Behaviorism.* New York: W. W. Norton & Co., Inc. (118)

WHEELER, W. M. 1930. *Demons of the dust.* New York: W. W. Norton & Co., Inc. (180)

WHERRY, R. T., & FRYER, D. H. 1949. Buddy ratings: Popularity contest or leadership criteria. *Personnel Psychol.,* 2, 147–159. (225)

WHITING, J. W., & Child, I. L. 1953. *Child training and personality.* New Haven: Yale University Press. (29, 136)

WHORF, B. L. 1947. Science and linguistics. In Newcomb, T. M., & Hartley, E. L. (eds.), *Readings in social psychology.* New York: Henry Holt & Co., Inc. (168)

WHORF, B. L. 1952. Collected papers on metalinguistics. Washington, D.C., Dept. of State, Foreign Service Institute. (168)

WIESNER, B. P., & SHEARD, N. M. 1933. *Maternal behavior in the rat.* London: Oliver & Boyd, Ltd. (94)

WILKE, W. H. 1934. An experimental comparison of the speech, the radio, and the printed page as propaganda devices. *Arch. Psychol.,* No. 169. (258)

WINTERBOTTOM, M. R. 1953. The relation of childhood training in independence to achievement motivation. Unpublished doctoral dissertation, University of Michigan. (137)

WOLMAN, B. 1956. Leadership and group dynamics. *J. soc. Psychol.,* 43, 11–25.

WOODWORTH, R. S. 1958. *Dynamics of behavior.* New York: Henry Holt & Co., Inc. (83, 120, 125)

YERKES, R. M. 1941. Conjugal contrasts among chimpanzees. *J. abnorm. soc. Psychol.,* 36, 175–199. (56)

YOUNG, K. 1947. *Social psychology.* New York: F. S. Crofts & Co. (214)

YOUNG, P. T. 1955. The role of hedonic processes in motivation. In Jones, M. R. (ed.), *Nebraska Symposium on Motivation.* Lincoln, Nebraska: University of Nebraska Press. (96, 102)

YOUNG, P. T. 1959. The role of affective processes in learning and motivation. *Psychol. Rev.,* 66, 104–125. (96, 102)

YOUNG, W. C. 1951. Internal secretions and behavior. In Stone, C. P. (ed.), *Comparative psychology.* Englewood Cliffs, N.J.: Prentice-Hall, Inc. (51)

ZINGG, R. M. 1940. Feral man and extreme cases of isolation. *Am. J. Psychol.,* 53, 487–517. (75)

NAME INDEX

SUBJECT INDEX

Adaptation: and behavioral traits, 40–41

comparative perspective, 8

Adaptation efficiency and human behavior, 40

Affect and motivation, 99–105

Analogies in human and infrahuman social behavior, 47–66

Anticipation in motivation, 99

Attitudes (see also prejudice), 11, 233–66

and cognitive organization, 236–38

attributes of, 245–48; clarity, 245; content, 245; kind, 245; salience, 247; strength, 246; verifiability, 247

change, 256–65; as a function of attitude strength, 258; as a function of characteristics of the information source, 262–63; as a function of knowledge, 258–62; effect of chronological age, 258; effect of social climate, 263–64

contemporary definition, 236–40

correlative concepts, 240–44

formation environmental effects, 134

importance of the concept, 233–34

infrahuman, 58–60

literal meaning, 235

measurement, 244–56; direct observation, 254; use of interviews, 255; use of performance indexes, 255; use of personal and public records, 254; use of pictorial techniques, 255; use of projective techniques, 255; use of sociometry, 255; validity, 248

parent-child similarity, 28, 133

scales, 249–54; interval scales, 252; ordinal, 249; paired-comparison, 251; ranking, 250; rating, 249–50

set, 233

valence, 238

Authoritarianism: and college experience, 264

and phenomenological information, 86

and prejudice, 280–85

and social mobility concern, 86–87

in leadership, 230

parental effects in development, 295

"Band-wagon" effect (in propaganda), 263

Behavior disorganization, definition, 60

Behavior emergences and genetic mutations, 48

Behavior genetics: and paleontology, 42–45

and species survival, 42

Belief, 240

Bias, 240

California F scale, 222

California personality test, 215

Communication (see also language): adaptive significance, 138–40

and language, 138–70

in bees, 141–42

in birds, 142–43

in chimpanzees, 143–45

infrahuman, 52–53, 141–46

nonsyntactic, 145

reflexive, 145

syntactic, 146

Conflict, 112–113

approach-approach, 112

approach-avoidance, 113

avoidance-avoidance, 113

Conformity and prejudice, 284

Connotative meaning, 89–91

Contact comfort, 102–104

Critical periods: importance of, 39

in early experiences, 129

in social experiences, 39

Culture: and society, 1

definition, 1

Cultural relativism, 77–78

Curiosity, 104–105